Slavery in New York

SLAVERY
IN
NEW YORK

EDITED BY

IRA BERLIN AND LESLIE M. HARRIS

PUBLISHED IN CONJUNCTION WITH
THE NEW-YORK HISTORICAL SOCIETY

THE NEW PRESS

NEW YORK
LONDON

Requests for permission to reproduce selections from this book should be
mailed to: Permissions Department, The New Press, 38 Greene Street,
New York, NY 10013

Published in the United States by The New Press, New York, 2005
Distributed by W. W. Norton & Company, Inc., New York

ISBN 1-56584-997-3
CIP data available.

The New Press was established in 1990 as a not-for-profit alternative to the
large, commercial publishing houses currently dominating the book publishing industry. The New Press operates in the public interest rather than
for private gain, and is committed to publishing, in innovative ways, works
of educational, cultural, and community value that are often deemed insuf-
ficiently profitable.

www.thenewpress.com

Book design and composition by Lovedog Studio
This book was set in Bodoni Book

Printed in Canada

2 4 6 8 10 9 7 5 3

CONTENTS

Slavery in New York

Introduction

UNCOVERING, DISCOVERING, AND RECOVERING: DIGGING IN NEW YORK'S SLAVE PAST BEYOND THE AFRICAN BURIAL GROUND

———◆———

IRA BERLIN AND LESLIE M. HARRIS

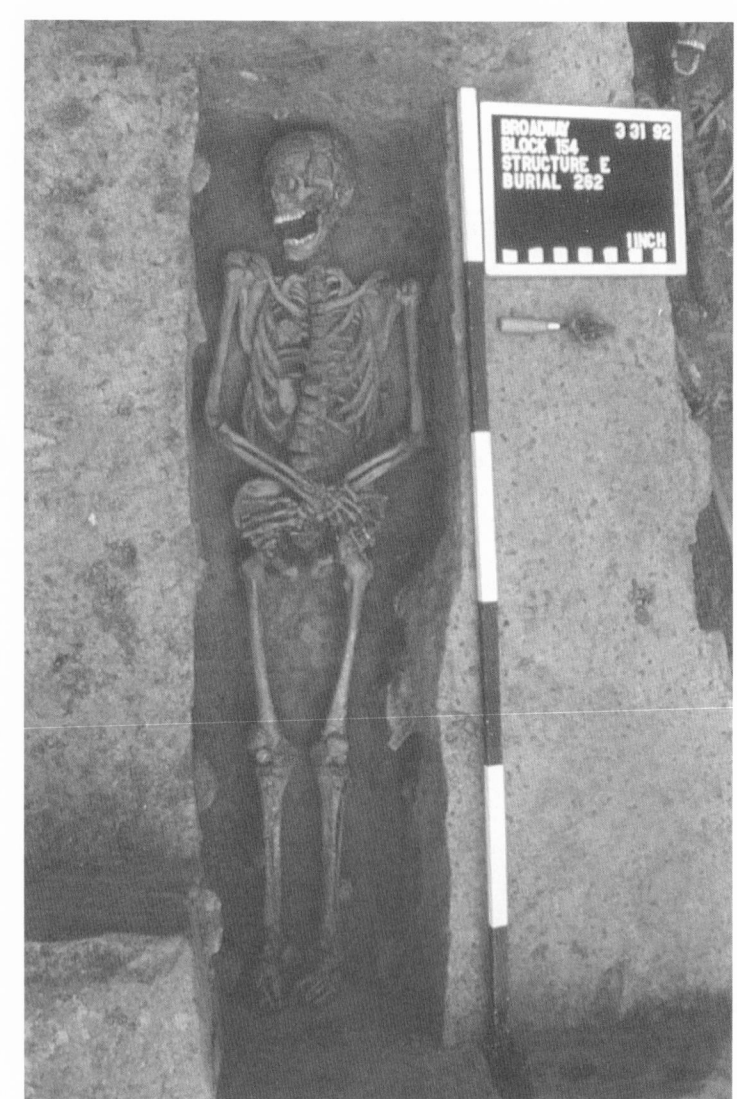

Intact adult male burial,
New York African Burial Ground.

IN 1991, WHILE EXCAVATING the foundation for yet another multistory behemoth in lower Manhattan, workers uncovered New York's "Negro Burial Ground." With that shovelful of dirt, New Yorkers began recovering their slave past. Amid the ensuing and continuing controversy over what soon became known as the African Burial Ground, New Yorkers learned that the cemetery for the city's seventeenth- and eighteenth-century slave population sprawled over several acres of the city, perhaps miles beyond the footprint of the future skyscraper.

Until that moment, most New Yorkers knew little of the city's deep association with slavery. Those who did considered the slave presence small and fleeting. From this perspective, slavery was a minor institution of little economic or political consequence and one that was immediately disposed of when New Yorkers recognized its heinous evil. The vast scope of the African Burial Ground challenged these notions.

The discovery of the slave cemetery began a process through which New Yorkers have begun to learn that slavery was central—not peripheral—to New York's history. Peeling back the layers of New York's slave past, like uncovering the remains in the African Burial Ground, is both a disheartening and an exhilarating task. If it reminds New Yorkers and all Americans of the suffering of thousands of Africans and African Americans, it also provides the opportunity to celebrate their lives and appreciate their contribution to the rise of New York City as the state's, the nation's, and the world's metropolis. In that spirit, the New-York Historical Society, under the direction of Louise Mirrer, organized two exhibits to recover the history of slavery in New York, from its inception in New Amsterdam at the beginning of the seventeenth century through the nineteenth century. The first, "Slavery in New York," opened in October 2005. The second, "Conscience and Commerce: Slavery and New York, 1815–1865," followed. This book accompanies both exhibits and encapsulates, in original works by leading scholars, the research that preceded the discovery of the burial ground and has continued since. "Slavery in New York" will neither right the wrongs of the past nor ease the pain suffered by so many. It will, however, help all who live in or visit New York appreciate the travail of those whose bones literally lie under our feet.

For nearly three hundred years, slavery was an intimate part of the lives of all New Yorkers, black and white, insinuating itself into every nook and cranny of New York's history. For portions of the seventeenth and eighteenth centuries, New York City housed the largest urban slave population in mainland North America, with more slaves than any other city on the continent. During those years, slaves composed more than one quarter of the labor force in the city and perhaps as much as one half of the workers in many of its outlying districts. Slavery died with glacial slowness; slaves could be found in New York into the fifth decade of the nineteenth century. As slavery atrophied, however, its place in New York's commerce, politics, and culture increased in tandem with the city's connections to the slave South. Although those ties were severed by the Civil War, slavery's presence gained new life with the arrival of black emigrants from the South, most of whom carried the experience as well as the memory of slavery.

The ubiquity of slavery in New York's history can be measured by the depth and persistence of the state's and city's leaders in matters respecting enslavement, emancipation, and allied structures of race. Involvement in slavery and race issues was a matter of course for black New Yorkers, as New York became the headquarters of leading antislavery associations and political parties, a main station on the Underground Railroad, and the locale of the black press, as well as home to dozens of black fraternal and benevolent organizations. But slavery also deeply affected white New Yorkers. Beginning with Pieter Minuit and Peter Stuyvesant through John Jay, Alexander Hamilton, Rufus King, and Martin Van Buren to William Seward and Samuel Tilden, every major political figure in New York's history from the seventeenth through the nineteenth centuries confronted slavery as opponent or apologist and as advocate of white supremacy or champion of racial equality. Even before Lincoln appropriated a biblical metaphor to describe the nation's great divisions on slavery, New York was a house divided.

What was true of politics was equally true of New York's economy, society, and culture. New York was divided over slavery and race. While New York businessmen like August Belmont grew rich on the cotton trade, Arthur and Lewis Tappan—the founders of what became Dow Jones—renounced the use of slave-produced commodities. The antislavery Reverend James Beecher opposed the Fugitive Slave Law, while the proslavery Archbishop John Hughes supported it. New York's African Grove Theater, the first African American theatrical company, performed *The Drama of King Shotaway*, depicting a slave rebellion, while Jim Rice's blackface minstrelsy ridiculed black men and women. Likewise, New York's journalistic history embraced both the proslavery editor of the *New York Journal of Commerce*, James Watson Webb, and the antislavery editor of the *New York Tribune*, Horace Greeley. Whatever the field of endeavor, leading men and women found themselves enmeshed in the question of slavery and the matter of race, making New York, in many ways, an enslaved city.

The rediscovery of the African Burial Ground also forced New Yorkers to come to terms with the diverse ways slavery affected life in New York. If slavery was ubiquitous in New York, it also changed over time. Enslaved people found their lives in constant flux, as the institution of slavery was continually made and remade. Depending on where they lived and how they worked, life in slavery differed for Africans and African Americans. Their putative owners claimed them as mere laborers—"hands," in the idiom of the day. But enslaved black men and women thought of themselves first as husbands and wives, parents and children, kin and friends. Slavery may have shaped the lives of black people, but it did not determine their beliefs or fix their aspirations. Depending on the place of their birth, they were Angolans or Kongos, and later Africans or African Americans. Depending upon their religious commitments, they were Muslims or Christians, and later Anglicans or Methodists. Depending on their employment, they were skilled or unskilled. As New York changed over time, so did they. The men and women whose bones were uncovered in 1991 represented but one moment in the history of slavery. There were many.

White New Yorkers also experienced slavery in different ways. Some earned their living as slave owners, others by transporting cotton, weaving "negro cloth," or entertaining visiting planters. Some white New Yorkers lived and worked alongside black men and women, while others entered associations to exclude black people from their workplaces and neighborhoods. Some laughed at the antics of white men who blacked their faces and danced in minstrel shows, others applauded African American musicians. Some participated in antislavery societies, others joined antiabolition mobs. Like the history of the African Burial Ground, the story of slavery in New York for blacks and whites is long, complicated, and just beginning to be unearthed.

AMONG THE men and women who may be buried in the African Burial Ground are those who were carried to New Amsterdam by the Dutch beginning in the 1620s. Historians have called these first arrivals Atlantic Creoles. They bore names like Paulo d'Angola, Anthony Portuguese, Simon Congo, Jan Guinea, Van St. Thomas, Francisco Cartagena, and—most tellingly—Jan Creoli and Christoffel Crioell. Although these were people of African descent, their names suggest that many of them had long experience in the Atlantic world and were familiar with the various systems of jurisprudence, religion, and trade etiquette of the nations that touched the Atlantic. They spoke a variety of languages, including a creole tongue that became the lingua franca of the sixteenth- and

AFRICAN BURIAL GROUND

Located in lower Manhattan within the seat of the present-day New York City government, the African Burial Ground provides material evidence of an African enslaved presence during the years of Dutch, British, and early American rule. The cemetery had its origins in the late seventeenth century, located on a five- to six-acre plot—about five city blocks—approximately 1.6 miles north of the original city limits, today's Wall Street. It is believed that during its more than one hundred years of operation (until its closing in 1794), both enslaved and free Africans and African Americans were buried in the cemetery. Evidence from the burial ground indicates that when possible, black people employed traditional practices in laying their deceased kin and loved ones to rest, although this elementary right was often denied them altogether. New York law forbade the presence of more than twelve persons in attendance at a funeral and also required that burials take place only during daylight hours, which was contrary to the customs of some African peoples.

A 1991–1992 archaeological excavation of the northern portion of the burial ground occurred as the site was being prepared for the construction of a federal office building. The remains of 419 men, women, and children were excavated; nearly half of the remains were of children under twelve years of age. Archeologists estimated that as many as ten thousand may be buried underneath nearby parks and buildings. Artifacts retrieved from the site included shroud pins, coffin nails, glass beads, metal tacks, coins, copper jewelry, clay pipes, cowrie shells, and a musket ball. More than a decade of public protest against the excavation of the site brought national and international attention to the historic African Burial Ground as a locus of past and contemporary human rights violations against Africans and their North American descendants. In 1993, the African Burial Ground was placed on the National Register of Historic Places and received official recognition as a national historic site. Between 1993 and 2003, an analysis of the human remains was conducted at Howard University. On October 4, 2003, some ten thousand participants in the "Rites of Ancestral Return" helped re-inter the ancestral remains on the preserved portion of the site in hand-carved wooden coffins made in Ghana, a final tribute to the men and women who lived and died in seventeenth- and eighteenth-century New York. Nearly 8,000 personal handwritten messages from living people to the African ancestors were also buried with the eighteenth-century remains. A permanent memorial will be built on the site, dedicated to the Africans, enslaved and free, who helped to build New York.   —*Sherrill D. Wilson*

seventeenth-century Atlantic world. When these men and women arrived in New Amsterdam, they entered a society in which people of many different nations—European, Native American, as well as African—were locked into a variety of forms of servitude. Slavery was one form of bondage among many.

Atlantic Creoles, most of whom were owned by the Dutch West India Company, soon made themselves at home in New Amsterdam. The Company worked them hard, clearing the land, splitting logs, milling lumber, and building wharves, roads, and fortifications, for slavery in New Amsterdam was first and foremost about work. Although weighed down by the burden of slavery, these first arrivals still found ways to use their knowledge of the Atlantic world to integrate themselves into New Amsterdam society, forming families, trading with residents, and communing in the Dutch Reformed Church, where they registered their marriages and baptized their children. They chose godparents for their offspring from among both the white and black population of the pioneer settlement. As historian Christopher Moore notes, theirs was still "a world of possibilities." Perhaps because of the ill-defined nature of slavery, many of these enslaved black men and women collected wages, and, in 1635, when their wages were not forthcoming, a small group petitioned the West India Company for redress.

By the middle of the seventeenth century, black men and women had become an integral part of New Amsterdam society, composing about one fifth of the population. While the Company continued to exploit them, their role had grown considerably, and some began to grope their way out of slavery. When the growing tension between the Dutch settlers and the increasingly hard-pressed Native Americans flared into open warfare, black people found the occasion to expand their freedom and move into the landowning class. Fearful of being overrun by the Indians, the Dutch officials freed black men and their wives, enlisting the men in the colony's militia. By giving these black families land between New Amsterdam on the southern tip of Manhattan and the Indians on the northern end, Dutch officials created a buffer zone that slowed Indian attacks. By mid-century, free blacks composed about one third of New Amsterdam's black population. Many had achieved the rank of freeholder, so that free black farmers owned some 130 acres around what is present-day Washington Square Park.

Like other free men and women, former slaves labored to integrate themselves into New Netherland society. They married in Dutch churches, sued in Dutch courts, celebrated Dutch festivals, and took Dutch names. The Atlantic Creole surname D'Angola, meaning *from* Angola, changed to the Dutch *Van Angola* and became briefly prominent among free people of color. The baptized son of Emmanuel Van Angola became Nicholas (Claus) Manuel, which followed Dutch patronymics of a child receiving the father's first name, and so within just two generations the Angola surname was gone.

As Moore observes, none of this reduced the Dutch commitment to African slavery. While some blacks gained their freedom, that freedom had been granted to assure the safety of a society committed to African slavery. Most black New Netherlanders remained enslaved, and the commitment to slave labor only grew over time. Moreover, the Dutch and other European settlers disparaged even those black people who were free, condemning them—in the words of a leading Dutch clergyman—as "trash." While promised "the same footing" as other free people, Dutch officials soon made it clear that black freedom was not quite the same as white freedom. The West India Company also required its former slaves to pay an annual tribute and, upon request, to labor in the Company's behalf. Perhaps nothing better represented the contempt with which the Dutch held black men and women than their refusal to extend freedom to the children of those who had been manumitted. Free black men and women struggled to extend their status to their children and others, petitioning and protesting—often all the way to The Hague—the generational anomaly of free parents and enslaved children, or accumulating the funds necessary to purchase their loved ones' liberty, although accumulating these funds remained beyond most. If unable to buy their way out of bondage, some fled the colony.

That ongoing struggle over half freedom spoke to the ambiguous place of black men and women in New Netherland. Exploited, enslaved, unequal to be sure, they were recognized as integral, if inferior, members of the Dutch colony on the Hudson. If they were deemed to be the lesser sort, that status was not theirs alone in a world that knew only hierarchy. Even in their lowly place, black people found ways to advance themselves as free men and women, property holders, communicants in the established church, and honored members of the militia.

If slavery was present at the founding of New Netherland, it was also there at the end. In 1664, at the very moment the British besieged the Dutch colony, a slave ship carrying nearly three hundred Africans docked in New Amsterdam. Its presence compromised Peter Stuyvesant's ability to defend the colony and assured the success of the British invasion. Stuyvesant's last official act and the British commander Richard Nicoll's first were their mutual assurances that the rights to slave property established under the old regime would be respected under the new one.

The British ousted the Dutch from the Hudson Valley and transformed New Netherland into New York and New Amsterdam into New York City. In the process, they threatened the position that black people had secured during the first forty years of European and African settlement. The black men and women who came of age under British rule—and who probably compose the majority of those interred in the African Burial Ground—worked harder and died earlier then their Atlantic Creole forbears. Whether understood in terms of status, work routine, ability to create families, or access to freedom, their experience was radically different.

From the first, the British exhibited a deep commitment to African slavery. Like James II, Duke of York—the proprietor of New York—many of those who invested in the colony were also stockholders in the Royal African Company, which enjoyed the exclusive privilege of supplying slaves to Britain's New World colonies. Not surprisingly, the number of slaves grew steadily, especially as New York became incorporated into the larger Atlantic economy. Between the beginning of the eighteenth century and the American Revolution, the British imported some seven thousand slaves into New York, with an ever-increasing proportion arriving directly from Africa. Africans—as opposed to African Americans—became ever more visible. As Jill Lepore notes in her wide-ranging survey of slavery in British New York, white New Yorkers learned to distinguish between Kongos and Angolans, Mandes and Mandingos, as they became familiar with the differences among African peoples. The traumatic passage of black men and women across the Atlantic left these new arrivals weak and susceptible to diseases against which they had limited resistance. Their towering mortality rate—well above that of white New Yorkers—bespoke the realities of slavery in eighteenth-century New York. While many of the first men and women put to rest in the African Burial Ground had been born on the west side of the Atlantic, most of those buried during the period of British rule had begun their lives in Africa.

As the number of slaves increased, so did their importance to New York's economy and society. Prominent merchants, farmers, and professionals—with hardly an exception—owned slaves, and much of the colonial council's time was spent regulating slavery. New York's streets became crowded with black, often African, workers. On the eve of the American Revolution, a visitor to New York City complained, "it rather hurts an Europian eye to see so many negro slaves upon the streets." What was true of New York may have been even more true of the countryside.

Slavery in the New York colony took two distinct forms, urban and rural, with each shaped by the nature of the slave trade, the character of labor, and the resultant sexual division of the slave population. By their numbers alone, women—cooking and cleaning for whites, suckling their infants, raising their children, and succoring their aged—were the face of slavery in New York City. Slave women were ubiquitous in the households of New York's elite and common among the white families of the middling sort. Men worked outside the house, laboring on the docks and in warehouses, loading and unloading ships and drays—performing the heavy, backbreaking work necessary to keep the New York economy moving. And as the urban slave population grew, slave men also moved into skilled occupations as carpenters, coopers, and the like—although not without protests from the city's white workers, who feared competition with slave labor. If New York's householders were dependent on slave women, its commercial economy rested equally firmly on the strong backs of black men. Probably nothing moved in and out of the port of New York without an enslaved worker handling it at one time or another, and few shops did not have a contingent of slaves.

While slavery was disproportionately urban in New York, most slaves—like most New Yorkers—lived outside the city and worked as agricultural laborers. Farmers in the richest agricultural regions of New York's hinterland—the Hudson Valley, Long Island, and northern New Jersey—were equally dependent on enslaved labor. There the face of slavery was male and often African, and women were in short supply.

The sexual imbalance in both city and countryside played havoc with black family life. The multigenerational families established by Atlantic Creoles during the seventeenth century withered under British rule. Men and women had difficulty finding mates. If they did, they rarely lived together as husband and wife in the same household. The cramped quarters in which urban whites resided gave slave owners little incentive to encourage family formation among their slaves. Many actively discouraged it, and slave masters regularly sold slave women at the first sign of pregnancy. The inability of New York slaves to reproduce themselves made New York increasingly dependent upon the slave trade, which, in turn, enlarged the proportion of New York slaves who had been born in Africa and increased the mortality rates of the slave population. The vicious cycle made New York into a death factory for black people. During the eighteenth century, the African Burial Ground filled quickly.

The death toll was only one indicator of the degradation of slave life in New York from the "world of possibilities" that had existed in the Dutch regime of the seventeenth century. As slave owners pressed their slaves—driving them hard, destabilizing their families, and threatening the society black people had created—slaves pushed back. The largest issues between masters and slaves were demanding work regimes and the right to move freely. New York law strictly controlled the movement of slaves, but slaves—living apart from their families and working outside their owners' homes—seemed to be constantly coming and going. The raw exploitation and attempts to restrain slave movement met with increased resistance and appeared to be the central issues in the deadly rebellion of 1712 and in a broad-ranging conspiracy in 1741.

Such resistance did little to improve the slaves' condition, which continued to deteriorate. Following the 1712 insurrection, the City Council passed a slave code so restrictive that it embarrassed the governor of New York, who urged British authorities to reject it. The new code required that slave owners receive the approval of the colonial legislature before freeing any slaves, making it all but impossible for black people to attain liberty. Free blacks found themselves on the defensive. Those freed after 1712 lost the right to own landed property. Black landowners who remained from the Dutch regime—now several generations American-born—fled the city to outlying districts, often after surrendering their property to swindlers or to the government for unpaid taxes, as whites were reluctant to hire them when white or slave labor was available. A century after the Dutch surrendered New Netherland to the British, the free black population had shriveled to a fraction of its former size.

Even as freedom ceased to be a possibility for black people in British New York, they nonetheless struggled to improve themselves. The school established by the Anglican Society for the Propagation of the Gospel (SPG) in 1703 under the direction of Elias Neau offered one such opportunity. Neau, a Huguenot refugee from France who had himself experienced slavery aboard a French galley, welcomed slaves, offering basic literacy along with access to Christianity. Despite the opposition of slaveholders who threatened to deport slaves who dared to attend his school, Neau's academy and its successors became something of a safe haven for upwardly striving black men and women. Still, there could be no doubt that under British rule the equation of blackness and slavery, familiar throughout the larger Atlantic, had come to New York.

By mid-century, slavery, which had been remade under British rule in New York City, was about to be remade again. In 1776, just as the simmering conflict between the American colonies and their British overlords broke into open warfare, the King's soldiers occupied New York City. While British commanders recognized and protected the rights of Loyalist masters to their slave property, they opportunistically offered freedom in return for military service to enslaved men who fled Patriot owners. Fugitives flocked to the city. Their numbers increased as British army and naval units rotated through the great port, which became the base for British operations in mainland North America. Patriot leaders showed less interest in playing the liberator, although a handful of slaves owned by Loyalist masters eventually gained their freedom in the rebel cause. Still other runaways avoided both Loyalists and Patriots and found freedom in the confusion and tumult of war. For the first time in more than a century, New York's free black population began to increase. As Graham Hodges reveals in his exploration of black life in wartime New York, the city became an island of freedom in a sea of slavery.

Wartime freedom allowed black people to begin to reconstruct their lives. They took new names, legitimated marriages, gathered family members who had been dispersed across the countryside, and began to create the institutional infrastructure of freedom. Waged labor allowed some former slaves to accumulate property, and the British presence permitted black men to enter the trades from which they had been barred under colonial law or by informal associations of white laborers.

As black Pioneer units and military laborers along with the personal servants of British officers funneled into New York, the city became a melting pot of the many diverse African American cultures that had evolved in mainland North America during the seventeenth and eighteenth centuries. Fugitives from South Carolina and Georgia joined with those from the Chesapeake region to mix with black New Yorkers and the occasional black New Englander. Following the British surrender at Yorktown, the number and diversity of black people increased yet again in New York, as the city became the staging ground for the final evacuation of British troops. Ships from Charleston, St. Augustine, and Yorktown added to the number of black refugees. Many of the men and women laid to rest in the African Burial Ground during these years began their lives elsewhere in North America. Some had labored in the rice swamps of the low country and others in the tobacco fields of Virginia and Maryland, as New York's black population was augmented by fugitive slaves from all over the continent. The changing character of the graveyard reflected the transformation of black life during the Revolutionary years.

With the American victory, New York became the site of a desperate confrontation between freedom and slavery. The British had promised their black allies freedom in return for military service, but the Treaty of Paris, which concluded the Revolution, guaranteed American slaveholders that they could reclaim their human property. In 1783, no less a personage than General George Washington, the victorious American commander, arrived in New York to see that the terms of the treaty were fulfilled, as well as to collect the runaways from his own Virginia plantation. Boston King, a fugitive slave from Virginia who had fought with the British, expressed the fears of many blacks that they would be retaken: "The dreadful rumor filled us all with inexpressible anguish and horror. . . . For some days we lost our appetite for food and sleep from our eyes." Much to the delight of King and thousands of other former slaves huddled in New York, Sir Guy Carleton, the British commander, respected the promise of freedom and ignored Washington's pleas for the return of runaways. When the British evacuated the city, thousands of former slaves sailed with them. Some 3,000 Black Loyalists migrated to Nova Scotia, their names carefully inscribed in the Book of Negroes, registering status, age, sex, occupation, and former owner. Others migrated to Europe, Africa, the Antilles, and even Australia, setting in motion an African American diaspora.

The war and the subsequent emergence of the American Republic reshaped the lives of the remaining black people—slave and free—and their relations with white New Yorkers. New York remained committed to slavery. The majority of New York's Founding Fathers—signators of the Declaration of Independence and the Constitution—held slaves. But spurred by emancipation in the New England states and Pennsylvania, antislavery New Yorkers began their own assault on what was becoming a peculiar institution in the North. Black New Yorkers began negotiating with individual owners for their freedom and that of their loved ones. Failing that, they also sued for freedom in court, and—when all else had failed—simply fled on their own. Some white New Yorkers also added their voices to the black chorus against slavery. As Patrick Rael observes, the "Long Death of Slavery" had begun.

At first, slavery hardly budged. New York's lawmakers took some small steps—loosening the rules for manumission, for example—but no act of emancipation emerged from the legislative deliberations immediately following the war. Instead slave holders, determined to maintain their valuable property, stiffened their resistance to abolition and articulated an ever more coherent defense of property-in-man. In some parts of New York, the number of slaves, and even the proportion of black people enslaved, increased.

Still the abolitionists pressed on, advertising the hypocrisy of the continued existence of slavery in the land of liberty. In 1785, leading merchants, politicians, and professionals added their weight to the antislavery cause by establishing the New York Manumission Society, although some members of the society continued to hold slaves. While the Manumission Society's genteel petitioning met stony opposition, the growing unrest among the slave population—evidenced by a veritable flood tide of fugitive slaves and a series of unexplained fires—frightened many white New Yorkers. With every Northern state except New Jersey committed to emancipation, New York's isolation became increasingly untenable. In 1799, New York lawmakers acted.

The Gradual Emancipation Law freed not a single New York slave. It promised to free their children, but not until after they had served a long apprenticeship, until age twenty-eight for men and twenty five for women—time enough for slaveholders to appropriate their most productive years. No slave needed to be freed under the law until well into the third decade of the nineteenth century, and slavery—in the person of those who were slaves in 1799—could conceivably survive until the brink of the twentieth century. Moreover, as the law went into effect, slaveholders developed new subterfuges to retain black men and women in bondage. At the last, when confronted with the possibility of losing their slaves, slaveholders were not above selling would-be freedpeople to the slave states to the south.

The 1799 law, in short, did not end slavery but rather initiated a new struggle for freedom. Under abolitionist pressure, antislavery lawmakers chipped away at the slaveholders' prerogatives and, in 1817, at the urging of Governor Daniel Tompkins, the legislature agreed that on July 4, 1827, all those promised freedom by the Gradual Emancipation Law would be free. Still, those black men and women not covered by the 1799 law remained in bondage, and slavery survived in New York for another two decades. Federal census enumerations continued to list black men and women as slaves until 1850, nearly three quarters of a century after the Declaration of Independence declared equality the common condition of mankind.

Piecemeal and partial, emancipation had two major effects, one on black New Yorkers, one on white New Yorkers. Most immediately, the onset of freedom initiated a massive transformation of black life. The changes that began during the war increased in velocity as more and more black people exited slavery. In quick succession and with enormous enthusiasm, black people married, reconstructed their families, established independent residences, secured waged employment, purchased property, joined churches, attended schools, and created a host of associations and organizations. As Craig Wilder details, a thick network of institutions soon blanketed African American society in New York, addressing the needs, promoting the interests, and articulating the aspirations of black people in freedom. Not the least of these was the burial of the dead. In 1794, New York officials declared the crowded African Burial Ground fully occupied and closed the ancient cemetery. Black people—anticipating its closure—had already begun organizing new institutions to meet the old need. The first of these was the New York African Society, founded that same year. Though the occasion for the society's formation was burying the dead, it soon concerned itself with the problems of the living, insuring members against illness and unemployment, assisting their widows and orphans, and providing a basis of good fellowship.

Like other such associations established in the wave of postemancipation institution building, New York's first black benevolent association took the name "African." That designation soon found its way to the placards on black churches, schools, fraternal orders, newspapers, and even a theater. The appellation gave weight to the moment, as the cultural transformation reinforced the change in status. Black New Yorkers, who had once been Atlantic Creoles in Dutch New Amsterdam and then been Angolans, Kongos, Mandes, and Minas in eighteenth-century New York had, by the beginning of the nineteenth century, become Africans. The dual change of both culture and status marked a revolution in black life.

But black people did not march into freedom as one. The staggered pace of emancipation—the long half-century from slavery to freedom—meant that some black men and women quickly secured their liberty, while others remained locked in bondage. As the first arrivals began to rebuild their lives anew, others remained fastened in the chains of lifetime servitude. Moreover, even those who escaped to freedom at the same moment exited with different resources. Some had long practiced skilled trades, accumulated property, gained a modicum of literacy, and established relations with white men and women—sometimes their former masters, fellow congregants, or wartime comrades—who assisted their transition to freedom.

Such differences immediately began to manifest themselves within New York's free black community. One line of distinction was that of class, as a small group of entrepreneurs and artisans had emerged with freedom. But, in general, distinctions within black society were measured not so much in material terms—since nearly all black New Yorkers worked, and usually with their hands, and few enjoyed substantial wealth—but by cultural aspirations and style. In addition, such class differences were given visibility by distinctions of color, as a light skin often reflected ties to white people—generally a white father—who might open avenues for economic and social advancement. Beginning in the 1790s, class and color distinctions were enlarged with the arrival of colored refugees from the Haitian revolution, many of whom had enjoyed the benefits of planter paternalism on the island of Hispaniola. Their attachment to French culture and even the French language added complexity to African American life in New York.

Atop black society was an elite which distinguished itself by its claim to respectability. Literate, churchgoing, and eager to demonstrate that they were the equal of any white person, many of these men and women had been connected with white institutions prior to the Revolution, most prominently the Anglican Church and the school founded by Elias Neau. After the war, these slaves and former slaves worked for emancipation with the members of the New York Manumission Society, with whom they shared notions of religious piety and social propriety. Eager for their children—the first generation of black New Yorkers to be born in freedom—to take their rightful place in the new Republic, they were quick to enroll them in the Manumission Society's African Free School on Mulberry Street. As Carla Peterson explains in her study of New York's African American elite, the alumni of the African Free School intermarried, formed business partnerships, worshipped together, and shared membership in the same organizations, creating a network of connections that served as the basis for their advancement as individuals and as a class. It also enabled them to establish and enforce standards of gentility and models of deportment by which they measured themselves and others.

Their world, however, was a fragile one. While they read Shakespeare and debated the issues of the day in book-lined drawing rooms, they found themselves increasingly excluded from the professions their aspirations demanded and for which their education had prepared them. Rather than recognize their achievements, white New Yorkers exhibited contempt, sometimes by the violent assault of white thugs and sometimes by the sneering condescension of white gentlemen. Still, the upper orders of black society refused to concede their inferiority, instead maintaining their lofty aspirations. They demanded their rights as citizens, certain that if accorded the equality that had been promised by the Declaration of Independence, they could compete with any. In the process, they became not only the bearers of the highest American ideal, but also what Peterson calls "cosmopolitan citizens of the world" and champions of equality wherever men and women were denied their humanity.

Although their example provided only one means of elevation for "their people," the black elite believed leadership to be their birthright. With the aid of their white benefactors, they founded African churches and schools, orphanages and reading rooms, offering every manner of assistance to the less fortunate. At every turn, they assaulted slavery and demanded full equality for all black people. They would, in the words of another generation, lift as they climbed. In the process, they did not hesitate to lecture those they deemed their social inferiors on the importance of hard work, temperance, frugality, and piety. Their words were not always warmly received.

Most black New Yorkers shared neither the skills nor the values of the black elite. Desperately poor and without the formal schooling or the connections that education provided, they had difficulty earning a living in a society that confined them to the most menial employment. Women—who made up an increasing proportion of the urban black population—could rarely find employment other than as domestics in white households. Black men held a broader range of jobs as chimney sweeps, privy cleaners, and waiters, among other occupations. Their confinement to a smaller and smaller range of demeaning, low-paid, and irregular manual labor forced many to take to the sea. The nature of casual and seafaring employment undermined family life and made it difficult for the vast majority of black families to meet the standards of domesticity set by the black elite. Low-paying jobs meant that both parents, as well as children, worked. Most working-class black people found themselves in small, dank apartments located in back allies and basements. As Shane White notes in his exploration of African American culture, black working people's lives overflowed to the streets, markets, taverns, back-alley groceries, gaming joints, and music halls, where the poor dressed the dandy, gambled, sang, and danced to the wee hours of the morning. It was a world of hard-working and often hard-drinking men and women, some of whom were not above hustling to make a few extra dollars as peddlers and hucksters, or as con artists, fortunetellers, and pickpockets. Within the bounds of motley bars and dance halls, the language, music, and art of Africa, the Atlantic, and New York's streets became one. It could not be a more different world than that of the upwardly striving respectables.

The two worlds often drifted apart. While the upper orders of black society debated the issues of the day and orchestrated their assaults against racial injustice, the poor joined together in smoke-filled gaming houses for noisy frolics. Their boisterous lifestyle, colorful dress, plaited hair, eel-skin queues, and swaggering gaits scandalized the respectables, who saw such behavior as a calumny upon the race and a special threat to their own efforts to secure full recognition. The working class, for its part, disdained the pretensions of elite black men and women. Such differences followed black people to the grave. With the closure of the African Burial Ground, the respectables were laid to rest in the well-manicured grounds behind St. Phillips Episcopal Church, while the less fortunate were often dumped in a potter's field.

But the two cultures of nineteenth-century black New York also came together in many places, if for no other reason than that both the respectables and the poor felt the tightening vice of racial exclusion. Distinctions that meant much to black people were routinely dismissed by white New Yorkers, who treated all blacks alike. Some white New Yorkers purposely took such a course to demonstrate that no black person—no matter how wealthy or accomplished—could rise above their vision of the lowly black slave. Thus, black people joined in the struggle for equality and the final liquidation of slavery, as well as the parades, balls, and dinners that marked such occasions. But the sources of black unity were not simply white opposition. Of necessity, most black people lived in both worlds, as the poor aspired to respectability and the respectables participated in the culture of the streets. Among even the poorest of the poor, there was an appreciation of the order and discipline—as well as numerous social services—provided by the African church and its subsidiary organizations. If the elite occupied the front pews, the backbenchers believed they shared ownership of these sacred places, for their labor and their pennies had contributed to the raising of the building and they well understood the parable about the rich man and the camel. While they recognized the elites' achievements, they had their own aspirations for improvement. The well-to-do appreciated their striving, just as they understood something of the genius emerging from the music halls and dance halls. If the elites' formal balls imitated the white upper crust while the dance halls of the poor parodied them, the music emanating from these socially distinctive sites was often remarkably similar.

The staggered emancipation set in motion in 1799 by the Gradual Emancipation Law also affected white New Yorkers. While Northern slavery was a diminishing presence, the presence of Southern slavery was strengthened and enlarged in the years that followed. During the nineteenth century, slavery was not so much abolished in New York as transformed. As David Quigley demonstrates, the new order deepened—not dissolved—the commitment of many white New Yorkers to chattel bondage.

Perhaps the most important element of this transformation was New York's increasing intimacy with the Southern economy. Following the War of 1812, New York City became the primary port for the shipment of raw cotton from the South to the textile mills of Europe. With the growth of the cotton trade, New York bankers, factors, and brokers became the chief financiers of slavery's expansion, which pushed the plantation westward from upcountry South Carolina into the black belt of Georgia, Alabama, and Mississippi and then across the Mississippi River. In bankrolling the cotton economy, New York businessmen assisted planters in purchasing the land slaves worked, the tools with which they labored, and—most importantly—the clothes they wore. New York's textile industry specialized in so-called "negro cloth." But the connections did not stop there. New Yorkers manufactured the whips that overseers wielded, the books that planters read, and the finery plantation mistresses prized. Money borrowed from New York lenders allowed planters to buy slaves, and insurance purchased from New York brokers protected the planters' investments. White New Yorkers lubricated the Southern economy and became rich in the process. Even as the number of slaves in New York shrank, New York's links to—even dependence upon—slavery grew.

From the economic ties to the slave South, others followed—political, cultural, intellectual, and familial. Led by Martin Van Buren, antebellum New York became the stronghold of the Democratic party. Van Buren built his career by assuring Southerners of New York's reliability on the question of slavery. In 1821, at the state constitutional convention, Van Buren's Democrats led the movement to disfranchise black men. Thereafter Van Buren rode his coalition of "Southern planters and Northern plain republicans" to the presidency. When that alliance broke, Van Buren, in an act of extraordinary political agility, deserted the Democratic party to join the antislavery Free Soil Party, demonstrating the continued importance of slavery to New York's politics. It remained so. While the Whig governor William Seward strengthened protections for fugitive slaves seeking freedom in the state, New York Democrats continued to look southward, so much so that in 1860, Fernando Wood, the Democratic mayor of New York City, proposed that the city follow the Southern states out of the Union. Wood's scheme came to nothing, but during the Civil War, New York became the copperhead capital of the North. No Northern governor evinced greater opposition to the Republican Party's wartime policies than New York's Horatio Seymour.

Economic and political ties drew Southern planters—often with their slaves—to New York to attend to business, seek the latest fashions, and marvel at the great metropolis. It was only natural that their business partners entertained them in their homes, sharing fine wines, sumptuous meals, and perhaps a good cigar. Together they attended New York's theater, took the waters at New York's spas, and cheered the horses at New York's tracks. From such intimacy, family ties sometimes emerged. Such connections literally made New York an outpost of Southern culture. Leading Southern writers took up residence in New York, and New York publishers not only issued their books but also published such voices of the plantocracy as *DeBow's Review*.

The slaveholders' growing presence in New York City encouraged the marginalization of black people, economically and politically. In fact, New York City became whiter during the nineteenth century as European immigrants—mostly Irish and German—flowed through its great port and country folk flocked from the farms. Proportionally, there were fewer black people in New York City in 1850 than there were in 1750 or 1650. As white immigrant men and women took their places as operatives in New York's factories and country boys entered the city's offices as clerks and bookkeepers, black people found themselves barred from the most dynamic sectors of the metropolitan economy. Measured by the wealth they accumulated or the trades they practiced, the economic standing of black people plummeted during the nineteenth century. The same process of racial exclusion prevented black men from full enfranchisement throughout the antebellum period, despite repeated attempts to remove the property requirement that kept the vast majority from the voting rolls.

Additional evidence of the marginalization of black people could be found in residential patterns. Increasingly, black people lived scattered on the fringes of the city. These neighborhoods were not yet ghettos, as they still contained many white residents, but they were generally defined as undesirable. More importantly, black men and women found their access to public places limited, as they were excluded from parks, libraries, and theaters and segregated on streetcars. Whereas once the black presence had been ubiquitous, by the time of the Civil War, black men and women had become increasingly invisible.

In pushing black people to the margins, New Yorkers pioneered in creating the institutions of racial domination. Disfranchisement, segregation, and economic proscription—institutions normally associated with the postbellum South—thus emerged in antebellum New York City (and other Northern cities). To support the structure of white supremacy, New York became home to a bevy of racial theorists who, drawing upon a strange mixture of biblical exegesis and pseudoscience and playing upon fears of racial amalgamation, created a new genre of racial discourse.

New York's connections to the South made it a primary battleground in the struggle over slavery. As they escaped bondage, black New Yorkers mobilized against their ancient enemy, helping to transform the antislavery movement from the gradualism that fostered the emancipation of 1799 into immediatism in the 1830s. Thereafter, as Manisha Sinha notes in her survey of antislavery activism, black New Yorkers could be found at the forefront of the abolitionist movement, whether in the attack on colonization, the embrace of moral reform, the advent of antislavery politics, or the call for direct action. A list of black New Yorkers involved in the antislavery movement, from Peter Williams and William Hamilton through John Russwurm, James McCune Smith, the Reason brothers, and David Ruggles to George Downing, James W. C. Pennington, and Henry Highland Garnet, reads like a who's who of black abolition, even without a mention of Frederick Douglass and Samuel Ringgold Ward. Likewise, New York–based black newspapers like *Freedom's Journal*, *Rights of All*, *The Colored American*, *Anglo African*, *The Ram's Horn*, and *Frederick Douglass' Paper* became the voices of antislavery. And New York's cities hosted a number of meetings of the National Black Conventions.

The struggle intensified as slave catchers and kidnappers roamed the streets of New York, along with gangs of thugs who disrupted antislavery meetings, smashed African churches and schools, and assaulted black men and women. Desperate times required desperate measures and, in the wake of both the 1850 Fugitive Slave Law (which gave slave owners greater rights to retrieve fugitives who had fled North), and the 1857 Dred Scott Supreme Court decision (which declared that black people had no constitutional rights), many black New Yorkers considered again whether it might be best to leave the city for rural areas, or leave the United States completely.

The outbreak of civil war in the spring of 1861, however, revived their hopes. Despite the disavowals of the Lincoln administration and the president himself, black New Yorkers understood the war as an assault on slavery. Eager to even scores with the master class, black men volunteered to take up arms against the Confederacy, and even after being rebuffed continued to assert their loyalty to the Union. By September 1862, when Lincoln announced the preliminary Emancipation Proclamation, it looked like their devotion was going to be rewarded. Congress had already abolished slavery in the District of Columbia and the Territories. Federal officials made it emphatically clear that the slave trade would no longer be tolerated, even hanging one New York merchant engaged in the trade. On January 1, 1863, Lincoln signed the Emancipation Proclamation, devoid of any mention of colonizing freed blacks in Africa, as he had considered previously, and inclusive of an invitation for black men to enlist in the Union army and navy. By the summer of 1863, several regiments of the United States Colored Troops had taken the field.

The possibility of black men in blue uniforms unnerved the friends of slavery in New York, and the divisions over race and slavery spilled violently into the streets. In July 1863, their fears—stoked by a threatened draft—exploded in New York's greatest race riot. For three days, a racist mob cheered Confederate president Jefferson Davis as it rampaged through the streets of New York, attacking black men, women, and children, leveling black institutions, and sending black people fleeing from the city. By the time federal troops fresh from the killing fields of Gettysburg restored order, at least one hundred people—mostly black—had died. Some 3,000 black people were homeless, as the rioters tried to drive black New Yorkers from the city.

Many black men and women left the city, but ironically, as Iver Bernstein reveals in a close examination of the Civil War years, the deadly assault identified black people more closely with the Union cause and tainted their enemies with the brush of treason. That summer, black New York regiments were mustered into federal service, and soon thereafter the Reverend Henry Highland Garnet celebrated the passage of the Thirteenth Amendment in an unprecedented address before the House of Representatives. The service of black New Yorkers in defense of the nation, along with more than 200,000 black soldiers and sailors from all parts of the Union, weakened the color line in New York, as it did elsewhere in the North. After the war, as the Radicals in Congress took charge of Reconstruction, black men gained the vote in New York, and segregation and racial exclusion eased.

But, as in the past, the upward trajectory of black life could not be sustained. The Civil War had put a stake into the heart of chattel bondage, but the memory of slavery survived in the minds of those black New Yorkers who had been slaves or whose parents or grandparents had been slaves. So too with those white New Yorkers who had known black people as slaves. The arrival of emigrants from the South in the decades following the war—most of whom were former slaves—refreshed those recollections.

In the post-Reconstruction rapprochement of North and South and the dewy-eyed celebration of the "Lost Cause"—as reflected in the darkeys and coons who came to inhabit New York's art, literature, music, and theater of the late nineteenth century—slavery's long shadow again appeared over New York. Black migrants from the former slave states sped the Southernization of New York's race relations. In the last decades of the nineteenth century, the wavering color line stiffened and the status of black New Yorkers deteriorated.

The new racism created new fissures within black society. Among the black people most affected were the "Old Knickerbockers," the name which scions of the black elite took to distinguish themselves from the new arrivals. Marcy

Sacks explicates their complex reactions both to the intensification of racial proscription and to the former slaves' presence in New York. New York's black elite, whose parents had battled for abolition before Southern Emancipation and had supported the Radical Reconstruction of the South, believing "the elevation of former slaves would provide a corresponding improvement in their own civic condition," suddenly objected to the presence of former slaves in their midst. For many Old Knickerbockers, the poverty of the new arrivals had caused the upsurge of racial animosity, threatening their position. Some criticized the immigrants' country ways, work ethic, and emotional religion, and hoped they would just go away. Others, drawing on their old tradition of uplift, tried to tutor the newcomers in the niceties of urban life. But neither the back of the hand nor the outstretched hand was well received by the new arrivals, who liked their lives the way they were. Differences among black New Yorkers would continue to fester in years to come, as the South continued to come North.

From the perspective of the twentieth century and the eve of the World War I–era Great Migration, the African Burial Ground had been long forgotten, paved over in the reconstruction of lower Manhattan. But the powerful effects of slavery remained, taking new forms as the lines between white and black and among black people were redrawn, hiding slavery's long shadow from the eyes of contemporaries, though not from the penetrating gaze of history.

UNCOVERING,

DISCOVERING,

AND

RECOVERING

Chapter 1

A WORLD OF POSSIBILITIES: SLAVERY AND FREEDOM IN DUTCH NEW AMSTERDAM

CHRISTOPHER MOORE

Nieu Amsterdam. Cum Privilegio Ordinum Hollandiae et West-Frisae, ca. 1640.

"CLEAR THE LAND!" was likely the command heard first and most often by the "Company slaves"—those black workers who were owned by the Dutch West India Company, or simply "the Company," in New Netherland. As the Dutch planted their settlement along the Hudson, enslaved blacks were hard at work. The orders issued by Company officers in May 1625 typified the labor assigned to black slaves during the first years: clear the land, lay out farms, and on each, "erect a barn for the cattle"; clear the shore at "a suitable place in which ships, sloops, or barges could be laid down or be repaired or caulked"; clear the land and construct a sawmill and a stone counting house. By July 1625, enough land had been cleared so that a Company boat "carrying sheep, hogs, wagons, ploughs and all other implements of husbandry" could deposit its cargo on the island of Manhattan. Given the Company's intense activity during these first years of settlement, slaves—numbering a dozen or more men and probably some women—were busy indeed.[1] By deploying slave labor to build farms, wharves, mills, roads, and fortifications, the Dutch West India Company quickly put in place the infrastructure required for a permanent settlement on the island, which the Dutch named New Netherland.[2]

Enslaved blacks, who did the bulk of this work, were drawn from all corners of the Atlantic world. Angolans—named Garcia, Big Manuel, Little Manuel,

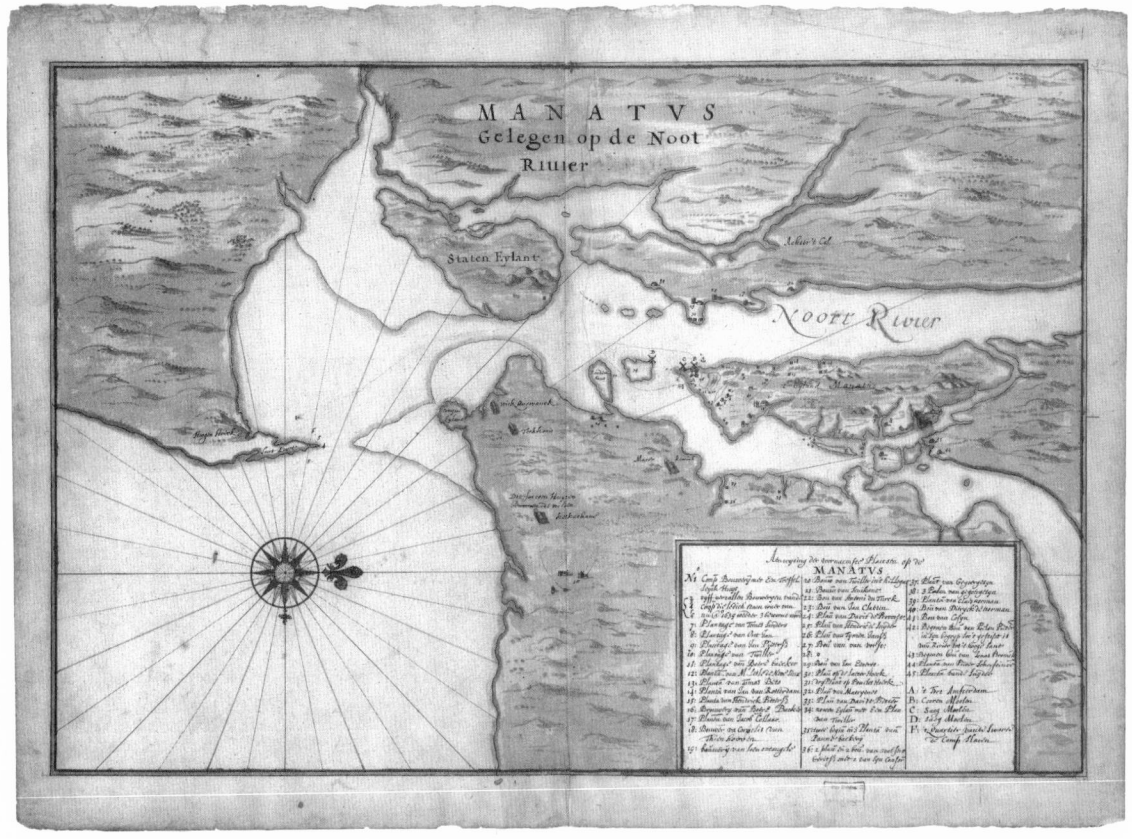

Johannes Vingboons, *Manatus gelegen op de Noot Rivier*, 1639.
Manuscript map on vellum in pen and ink and watercolor wash.

Little Anthony, and Paulo—were the largest African group among the first
Company-owned slaves. Like some of the others, Simon Congo and Pieter San
Tomé each had a surname that indicated his place of birth, ancestry, and per-
haps something about his physique. The rest of the first contingent included
Anthony Portuguese, Manuel de Gerrit de Reus, Jan Francisco, and Jan Fort
Orange, whose origin was more likely "Fort Orange" in Brazil or West Africa
than the Dutch outpost on the upper Hudson River. Many of these men had

Esteban Gómez and Mathieu Da Costa: Founding Fathers

In April 1525, Esteban Gómez, a veteran of Ferdinand Magellan's circumnavigation of the globe five years earlier, sailed a Spanish ship into the narrows that Giovanni da Verrazano had claimed for France a year before. After mapping the coast of present-day Maine as far south as Cape Cod, Gómez had continued southwest until, like Verrazano, he ventured into a deep bay and past the mesh of islands that secluded Manhattan from the Atlantic ocean. Gómez sailed upriver before satisfying himself that he had not discovered the fabled Northwest Passage to Asia.In his diary he called the waterway Deer River, noting the "abundance of trees, game, salmon, turbot and soles [types of flatfish], but no gold is found." Completing the voyage, he returned to Spain with thirty-seven Native Americans who were promptly sold as slaves.

Gómez was the first known person of African descent to explore the lower Hudson Valley around what is now New York.Of African and probably Portuguese descent, he was among the many black navigators, traders, pirates, and fishermen who traversed the sixteenth- and seventeenth-century Atlantic as free men. Like other such Atlantic Creoles, Gómez was knowledgeable of the many languages, laws, religions, and trading etiquettes of the larger Atlantic world. His presence suggests the porous character of racial lines in the sixteenth and seventeenth centuries, which allowed people of African descent to rise to positions of authority even in a world suffused with African slavery.

Farther north, in the St. Lawrence River and Lake Champlain region, another free black traveler, Mathieu Da Costa, arrived by 1607. Da Costa—a heroic figure in Canadian history but almost unknown to New Yorkers—probably came to know a good portion of what is now upstate New York, as he served as a translator of Native American languages for both French and Dutch traders in the early seventeenth century. The Dutch called him Matheus de Cost or Swart Matheu—Black Matthew—and so valued were his services that a suit between French and Dutch concerns over Da Costa's employment lasted in a French court from 1609 until 1619.

—Christopher Moore

Manhattan's First Merchant

Soon after Henry Hudson's 1609 exploration of the great river that now bears his name, Dutch ships began to frequent the region to trade with the indigenous peoples. In 1613, Dutch sea captain Thijs Volckertsz Mossel sailed the *Jonge Tobias* from the West Indies to Hudson's Bay, anchoring off Manhattan Island. There he left a black man named Jan Rodrigues to trade with Native Americans.

What happened thereafter is known only through a series of lawsuits between Mossell and Dutch traders, including captains Adrian Block and Hendrick Christiaensen, both of whom had encountered Rodrigues. When Block, who was mapping Long Island Sound and trading with Native Americans, returned to Holland, he found himself being sued by Mossel, who claimed Block violated his exclusive trading rights.

Block insisted that Mossel did not enjoy a trade monopoly on the island, pointing to the presence of Rodrigues, who lived alone and traded independently. Block's defense rested on the argument that Rodrigues was a "free man," who was acting on his own authority and not on behalf of Mossel's alleged monopoly.

Christiaensen supported Block. He declared that Rodrigues had boarded his vessel and presented himself as a free man. Rodrigues even offered to work for Christiaensen, who hired him as a translator to facilitate trade with the Natives.

In April 1614, Mossel returned to North America. Sailing his new ship, the *Nachtegael*, into the Hudson, the truth of the relationship between Mossel and Rodrigues became apparent, along with evidence that Rodrigues was Manhattan's first non–Native American merchant. Sighting the *Nachtegael*, Rodrigues fired his musket at the ship, and its crew returned fire. Brandishing torches, muskets, and swords, Mossel's crew chased the "black rascal" and briefly apprehended him. Though wounded, Rodrigues disarmed his pursuers and escaped. Later he found refuge with Christiaensen's crew, who took him aboard their boat and sheltered him.

The court ruled against Mossel, thus arguing implicitly that Rodrigues was free. But Jan Rodrigues disappeared from the written record thereafter. However, it is clear that Rodrigues, the "black rascal," was the sole nonnative resident of Manhattan Island for several months, and possibly for several years during the second decade of the seventeenth century. His trading post prospered, as his inventory—bolstered with axes, kettles, and beads from Christiaensen—was valued by local Native Americans, with whom Rodrigues apparently maintained good relations. Some accounts maintain that Rodrigues fathered children with one or more Native American women.

—*Christopher Moore*

spent some time in the Atlantic and its littoral, perhaps as slaves, perhaps as free men. They understood something about the languages, religions, legal codes, and trading protocols of the larger Atlantic world. Historians would call them "Atlantic Creoles," and the knowledge they carried to the Dutch settlement would shape their lives.[3]

For now, however, all they knew was work. The labor that engaged the enslaved men originally included the development of Notten (now Governors) Island in 1625. The land they cleared and the huts they built there soon accommodated some of the first free settlers on the small island just south of Manhattan. But by the end of 1625, the Company had chosen the southern tip of Manhattan for its headquarters. Slaves transported timber for the construction of Fort Amsterdam and the Company's farms and warehouses from Notten to the site where the present-day U.S. Custom House sits.

As construction of the fort progressed, the potential danger to the colony posed by the Mohawk Indians to the north made Notten Island appear increasingly vulnerable. The Company agreed to move the settlers to its Manhattan headquarters, and it set its slaves to constructing some thirty houses in the shadow of Fort Amsterdam. Slave laborers also widened the Indian trails between the fort and outlying farms, or boweries, and they built two new roads, later known as the Broad Way and the Bowery Road. In 1626, when Peter Minuit, the Company's director, arrived, he found a small community of whites and blacks huddled in a collection of rude buildings around the walls of Fort Amsterdam. The settlement soon became known as New Amsterdam.

That year Minuit also "purchased" Manhattan from the natives for $24. The letter that confirmed the bargain also noted that lush forests and a variety of woods—"Considerable Oak timber and Hickory"—were among the region's most valuable assets. Although the Company's chief interest in the settlement of New Amsterdam was as a center for trading furs, the magnificent forests of the island and the rest of New Netherland promised a limitless supply of timber, much needed by the growing Dutch maritime economy. The growing trade in gold, ivory, and slaves in Africa and the Americas also made New Netherland's timber a valuable resource for the shipbuilding industry. In 1626, Dutch shipyards built fifteen vessels for the Brazilian trade alone. Slaves, having helped build the first settlement on the Hudson, turned their attention to the forests. "They are also cutting wood and erecting another mill for the purpose of exporting to the Fatherland whole cargoes of timber fit for building houses and ships," reported Jonas Michaelius, a Dutch Reformed clergyman, in 1628.[4]

But there was yet other work to be done. The new mill to which Michaelius referred was a second wind-powered grain mill under construction north of Fort Amsterdam, west of the Broad Way; it would process wheat, corn, oats, and barley from the Company farms. A third water-powered sawmill was under construction on the Sawkill, or saw river, that drained into the East River at Seventy-fourth Street and Second Avenue—near the *Quartier van de swarten de Comp slaven*, or the Company's slave camp. By 1628, New Netherland had become a source of furs and timber for the Dutch empire, with ships traveling from Fort Orange, Esopus (Kingston), and Manhattan to Europe, the Caribbean, and Africa. Beaver pelts and deer skins were in great demand in Europe, and each month hundreds reached New Amsterdam to be traded at the new countinghouse, processed and tanned at the new horse-mill, and shipped across the Atlantic. At each stop, slaves provided essential labor. A 1628 report stated that the Company farms, which probably employed most of the enslaved men and women, were fully operational: "The six farms, four of which lie along the River Hellgate, stretching to the south side of the island, have at least 60 morgen [120 acres] of land ready."

Few Europeans could be found to work the land, operate the mills, and man the wharves of New Amsterdam. According to Michaelius, "Many among the common people would have like[d] to make a living and even to get rich, in idleness rather than by hard work, saying they had not come to work." As far as working is concerned, he added, "they might as well have stayed home." The fact was that no one appeared to want to do the work necessary to sustain the settlement on the Hudson without coercion. The Company's secretary, Isaack de Rasieres, seconded Michaelius's opinion, wondering aloud about the slothful character of the "rough lot who have to be kept at work by force." De Rasieres worried about the future of the colony: "I cannot sufficiently wonder at the lazy unconcern of many persons, both farmers and others, who are willing enough to draw their rations and pay in return for almost nothing."

Desperate for more and better workers, the Dutch West India Company proclaimed a new policy in 1629 designed to attract settlers—white and black—to the colony. To increase European immigration, the Company offered large incentives, establishing vast estates or manors in the Hudson Valley. In return for these manors, each grantee or patroon was expected to import some fifty white settlers. But the Company had small hope that these European migrants would work the land, so it redoubled its commitment to create a slave labor force. "The Company," asserted the new policy, "will use their endeavors to supply the colonists with as many Blacks as they conveniently can. . . . "5

The Company's plan attracted immediate attention. Kiliaen van Rensselaer, himself a founder of the Dutch West India Company, purchased a manor forty-eight miles long and twenty-four miles wide—a total of 700,000 acres lying in present-day Albany, Rensselaer, and Columbia counties. The tract was far larger than the Company envisioned, but Minuit approved the agreement. A year later, another would-be patroon, Michael Pauw, purchased land on the west shore of the Hudson River, at Hobocan Hacking (today's Hoboken) which he named Pavonia. Weeks later the yacht *Bruyrvisch* arrived at Pavonia "sending with it 20 men and 30 women, negroes, who were captured [in the Caribbean] in the last prize, and also a little barley, as much as was necessary to convey said blacks to Pavonia." With the creation of Pavonia, black people could be found on both sides of the Hudson. The first black people had arrived in what is now New Jersey.6

By 1630, about three hundred white settlers and some sixty black slaves lived in the lower Hudson River Valley, which included the area that later became the five boroughs of Manhattan, Staten Island, Brooklyn, Queens, and the Bronx. Among the black slaves, probably half were owned privately and the remainder were held by the Dutch West India Company. The Company's slaves acted as the colony's municipal workers, building and repairing fortifications, roads, warehouses, and other structures of the corporate state. They also quarried and transported stone for the St. Nicholas Church in the fort, the first permanent religious edifice in Manhattan.[7] Deployed "splitting palisades, clearing land, burning lime, and helping to bring in the grain in harvest time," Company slaves supplemented those held privately by merchants and farmers. It was doubtful the colony would have survived without its slaves, for they provided the labor that ultimately transformed the colony from a shaky commercial outpost into a permanent settlement. Slaves stood at the core of New Netherland's labor force.[8]

The slave trade remained open, and the enslaved population grew slowly but steadily in New Netherland during the seventeenth century. In general, the newly arriving slaves—some of them Africans—were sent upriver to the various patroonships and manors where they worked the fields along the Hudson River between Pavonia and Beverwijick (Albany). At mid-century, enslaved men, women, and children equaled about 25 percent of the population of New Netherland.

While the number of slaves grew, their legal status remained ambiguous. A minority within the Company who opposed the ownership of human beings refused to create a formal system for perpetual racial subjugation. The Dutch West India Company's policies establishing the great manors in the Hudson Valley and expanding the slave trade into New Netherland failed to define chattel bondage or identify it with people of African descent. While black men and women clearly were held as property in New Netherland, as they were throughout the larger Atlantic world, there was no statutory basis for their captivity.

Appreciating their legal limbo, black people struggled to expand their freedom. In 1635, black workers petitioned for wages in what certainly was one of the first organized job actions by workers in North America. Challenging the still undefined status of black people in New Netherland, five black men—slaves who had been receiving some payment for their labor—memorialized the Company's headquarters at The Hague for an increase of their wages, demanding the same pay as white laborers. The Company granted the request. Their victory not only signaled a considerable improvement in their standard of living but also confirmed their right to petition. Henceforth, slaves had standing in the eyes of Dutch authority, and the access of black people to the courts became

one of the defining characteristics of slavery in New Netherland.

Black men and women regularly used the courts, petitioning for relief, bringing suit, and testifying before the law. New Netherland courts treated them roughly at times, but black people just as often received a fair hearing. In 1641, Company slave Jan Primero was found murdered. The authorities had no trouble finding a suspect, as eight slave men each took credit for Primero's death. No reason was recorded for the group's animosity toward the victim. However, slaves named Primero were generally trusted and favored by slave owners and considered, quite literally, to be the owner's "number one" man. Not wanting to execute all eight, officials ordered the slaves to draw straws, with the shortest straw signifying guilt. The unlucky man was Manuel de Gerrit de Reus, but when the executioner pushed him off the execution ladder with "two good ropes" around his neck, both ropes broke. All who witnessed it were reportedly in awe and pleaded for mercy for the inexplicably saved man. Manuel was allowed to live.

The standing that black people enjoyed before the law extended to other spheres of New Netherland life. In 1636, Dominie Everardus Bogardus, who replaced Michaelius as the local Dutch clergyman,[9] included the colony's black children in his request for "a school master to teach and train the youth of both the Dutch and blacks." That school became today's Collegiate School for Boys. Bogardus, who had earlier served the Dutch West India Company in Africa, encouraged black men and

"Doop-Boeck"—register of baptisms of children and adults from 1639 to 1697 in the Reformed Protestant Dutch Church, New York City, containing the names of several black children. COLLEGIATE CHURCH, NEW YORK

women to attend religious services and observe religious holidays. In October 1639, Barent Jan Pieters, the son of enslaved workers Pieter and Susanna San Tomé, was baptized at the Dutch Reformed Church on Pearl Street—the church's first recorded baptism of a black child. Enslaved black men and women also formally married and had their marriages registered in the church's docket. The earliest recorded wedding of a black couple occurred in 1641, uniting Lucie D'Angola, widow of Laurens van Angola, with Anthony van Angola, widower of Catalina van Angola. During the next decade, black marriages composed more than one quarter of those recorded for New Amsterdam. Though some slaves may have been baptized or had some introduction to Roman Catholicism in Africa, and others may have been Muslim or practitioners of indigenous African religions, they found a warm acceptance or tolerance at Bogardus's church.[10]

While the lack of a strict legal definition of slavery allowed black people to expand their liberties, some white New Netherlanders condemned black people as so much "trash." If Dominie Bogardus welcomed black men and women to the Dutch Reformed Church, blessed their weddings, and baptized their children, his predecessor Michaelius left no doubt that he considered people of African descent to be devil worshippers who "speak so jeeringly and so scoffingly of the godlike and glorious nature of their Creator." By their public enactments and private actions, the Dutch and other Europeans in New Netherland equated blackness with slavery. The linkage manifested itself in numerous ways. In 1642, when a French privateer docked in New Amsterdam with a group of black men and women, the captives were sold despite their claims to freedom. Similarly, "Adulterous intercourse with Heathens, Blacks, or other persons" was deemed a crime for the colony's white residents. Disorderly conduct could land white men either in jail or working on a slave crew. A 1642 ordinance provided that "no one shall presume to draw a knife much less to wound any person, under penalty of fl. 50, to be paid immediately, or in default, to work three months with the Negroes in chains." Another man, who was caught deserting both his ship and his betrothed bride, was flogged and sentenced "to work two years with the Negroes."

Some people of color prospered in New Amsterdam. The pugnacious Anthony Jansen Van Salee was something of an oddity in Dutch Christian New

Amsterdam. Van Salee was a free-born man from Morocco. Although he lived and worked freely in the settlement, his feuds with neighbors were notorious and violent. A Muslim whom the settlers called the "black Turk" and "Mohammaden" or "Moslem," Van Salee repeatedly refused to contribute his assessed share of the salary of the Dutch minister. This, combined with gossip that his wife, Grietjen Reyniers, was a former prostitute, led to community outrage against him. Still, in 1639, the Company awarded Van Salee a 200-acre land grant "upon Long Island, opposite Coney Island" (in Brooklyn), where he later moved with his family. He sold his Manhattan farm to a Dutch baker. The sale included the land, house, and barn but excluded all fruit trees (twelve apple, forty peach, and seventy-three cherry trees, twenty-six sage plants, and fifteen vines), which Van Salee took with him to Brooklyn. [11]

Still, racial lines were not drawn so tautly as to prevent some black people from enjoying legal freedom. During the 1640s the number of free blacks increased rapidly amid the colony's growing struggle with its enemies. After almost two decades, the entirety of New Amsterdam extended less than 900 yards north from Fort Amsterdam to what is today Wall Street. In the shadow of the fort was a community of residences, shops, taverns, warehouses, and sleeping quarters for the Company slaves. Once envisioned as a grand gateway to the vast New Netherland territory, New Amsterdam remained a small village, still rugged and underdeveloped and with a hodgepodge of a population that spoke eighteen languages among some four hundred settlers, soldiers, fur traders, seamen, merchants, and enslaved laborers. With its attention drawn to protecting its more lucrative investments in Brazil, Curaçao, and West Africa, the Dutch West India Company had all but forgotten about New Netherland, leaving the colony to fend for itself against the Indians and the English. To defend the settlement, local officials turned to black people, and often rewarded them with grants of freedom and land.

Black men had long been called to the service of the colony. They were regularly armed, and they served in the militia. Earlier, when tenants near Beverwijick refused to pay quitrents to patroon Kiliaen Van Rensselaer, the schout (sheriff) of the manor used slaves "as brute forces against the malevolents." Between 1641 and 1644, when the Dutch were engaged in a series of wars with Native Americans, William Kieft, the Company's director, employed "the strongest and most active of the negroes as can conveniently [be] spare[d] and provide[d] them with a small ax and half-pike" to protect the Dutch enclave. The bloody warfare had driven Dutch settlers from the farms north of the fort, creating a desolate no man's land. The withdrawal left the town open to attack. Drawing from the experience of the Dutch in Brazil and elsewhere in the Americas, Kieft created a strategic buffer between New Amsterdam and the marauding Indians by replacing the white farmers with black ones.[12]

In the summer of 1643, Kieft began granting land to black soldiers and their widows in the area north of New Amsterdam. In August, as the conflict worsened, Domingo Anthony, a free black man, received some ten acres, one of the first of the grants from Kieft. It was soon followed by other land grants, including one to the widow Catelina Anthony, a free black woman, who was given "four morgens," or approximately eight acres, adjacent to Domingo's land.[13] Still others followed. In December, Manuel Trumpeter, a free black man, received eighteen acres. Trumpeter, who held the designation "Captain of the Blacks," was perhaps the leader of the black militia. His plot was situated at the northernmost frontier—a cut-off point for the Indian attacks at what is now Fifth Avenue and Washington Square North. Trumpeter's grant was followed by another six acres to one Marycke, a free black woman. The buffer zone seemed to have had an effect, as the attacks slowed in 1644.

As Kieft doled out land to free blacks, the Council of New Amsterdam, the town's governing body, met to consider a petition for freedom from eleven enslaved men. Commending the laudable character of the eleven as veteran employees of the Company—and perhaps considering the long-term savings that would accrue if these aging men were made responsibile for their own support—the council granted Paulo D'Angola, Gracia D'Angola, Simon Congo, Big Manuel, Little Manuel, Manuel De Gerrit de Reus, Anthony Portuguese, Pieter San Tomé, Jan Francisco, Little Anthony, and Jan Fort Orange their freedom. Many of the men were married, and, according to the council report, among their families there were "many children." The council extended freedom to the

Black Landowners in Manhattan's "Land of the Blacks," 1643–1664

During the 1640s, William Kieft, the director general of New Netherland, instituted a policy designed to protect New Amsterdam from the repeated incursions by Native Americans that had been plaguing the settlements. With the concurrence of the Council of New Amsterdam, Kieft freed slaves, particularly those slave men who had served as soldiers in the colony's defense, and then granted them and their families land north of the city with the understanding that their residences would create a buffer zone that would insulate the city from attack. Listed below are the grants issued between 1643 and 1664, when the Dutch were ousted from New Netherland and the policy ended. The "negroes land" or "land of the blacks"—legal terms used in later conveyances and descriptions of the property—was located about a mile from New Amsterdam, extending northward along the hilly and swamp-ridden region of Manhattan's rugged central wilderness and over 130 acres—100 square city blocks—of Manhattan.

—Christopher Moore

Landowner	Acreage	Farm Grant Received
Catalina Anthony (widow of Jochem)	8	July 13, 1643
Domingo Anthony	12	July 13, 1643
Cleyn (Little) Manuel	10	ca. December 1643
Manuel Gerrit de Reus	12	ca. December 1643
Manuel Trumpeter	18	December 12, 1643
Marycke (widow of Lawrence)	6	December 12, 1643
Gracia D'Angola	10	December 15, 1644
Simon Congo	8	December 15, 1644
Jan Francisco	8	December 15, 1644
Pieter San Tomé	6	December 15, 1644
Manuel Groot (Big Manuel)	8	December 21, 1644
Cleyn (Little) Anthony	6	December 30, 1644
Paulo D'Angola	6	December 30, 1644
Anthony Portuguese	12	September 5, 1645
Anna D'Angola (widow of Andries)	6	February 8, 1647
Francisco D'Angola	6	March 25, 1647
Anthony Congo	6	March 26, 1647
Bastiaen Negro	6	March 26, 1647
Jan Negro	6	March 26, 1647
Manuel the Spaniard	4	January 18, 1651
Mathias Anthony	2	December 1, 1655
Domingo Angola	4	December 2, 1658
Claes Negro	2	December 2, 1658
Assento Angola	2	December 2, 1658
Francisco Cartagena	2	December 2, 1658
Anthony of the Bowery	2	ca. 1658
Anthony the Blind Negro	2	ca. 1658
Manuel Sanders	4	ca. 1662

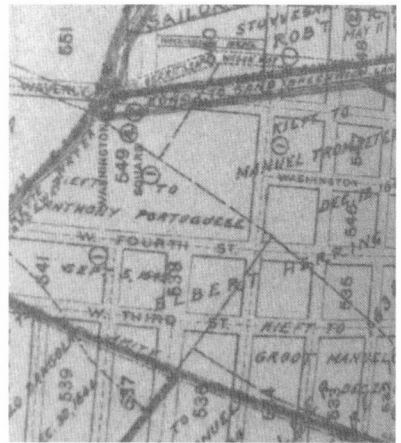

Detail of 1915 land map of original property owners of Greenwich Village, with overlay of streets with farms owned by free blacks.

Simon Congo
Land grant: 15 Dec. 1644
8 acres

Manuel Trumpeter
Land grant: 12 Dec. 1643
18 acres

Antony Portugies
Land grant: 5 Sept. 1645
12 acres

Paulo D'Angola
Land grant: 30 Dec. 1644
6 acres

Groot [Big] Manuel
Land grant: 19 Oct. 1645
8 acres

Washington Square Park in Greenwich Village, located on land once owned by slave Antony Portugies and his free black neighbors. PHOTOGRAPHED BY CHRISTOPHER MOORE

men's wives, releasing "the aforesaid Negros and their wives from their bondage for the term of their natural lives, hereby setting them free and at liberty on the same footing as other free people here in New Netherland, where they shall be permitted to earn their livelihood on the land shown and granted to them." As if to affirm the manumission and Kieft's wartime policy of creating a buffer zone, the council also granted each newly free man a small farm—all of them adjacent to Manuel Trumpeter's land.

Freedom for the eleven men and women, however, was not without conditions. The council ruling required each man to make an annual payment of a portion of his crops (twenty-two bushels of any two crops grown on his farm—corn, wheat, peas, or beans) and one fat hog, upon penalty of return to bondage. The requirement forced the newly freed slaves to toil as farmers and to remain indirectly in the service of the Company. Most important, the children of the newly freed men and women did not receive the full grants of freedom given their parents. Rather, the council intoned, "the express condition that their children, at present born and yet to be born, shall remain bound and obligated to serve the honorable West India Company as slaves."

The status of the newly freed black men, women, and their children (later described by historians as "half-free") was a continuing source of contention between blacks and the Company. But if the new status occupied by New Amsterdam's blacks was less than they desired, it was a considerable measure better than what they had endured, and whites, too, were required to work for the Company when called upon. Freedom, no matter how limited, would distinguish them from the enslavement they had suffered and that many other others would continue to bear.

By mid-century, free black farmsteads spread over 130 acres—100 square city blocks—of Manhattan. Commonly, the farms were thatched- or wooden-roof homes with some cattle, goats, and sheep, and a garden. The black-owned farms ranged in size from eight to twelve acres. The "negroes land" or "land of the blacks"—legal terms used in later conveyances and descriptions of the property—was located about a mile north of New Amsterdam, extending northward along the hilly and swamp-ridden region of Manhattan's rugged central wilderness. On this forbidding land emerged the first legally emancipated community of people of African descent in North America.[14]

Once free, blacks pressed for liberty for others—first petitioning the council to manumit their children who remained locked in slavery. When the council refused to free them, parents and guardians tried baptizing their children in the hopes that freedom would accompany Christianization. About one third of the baptisms performed in New Amsterdam churches during the 1640s were of free and enslaved blacks. But the church leaders saw through the scheme and tired of it, dismissing the baptisms as a cynical effort by slaves to achieve freedom. Dominie Selyns informed the Classis of Amsterdam (the board that governed the Dutch Protestant clergy) that he refrained from baptizing slave children because the parents "wanted nothing less than to deliver their children from bodily slavery, without striving for piety and Christian virtues."[15]

When the church failed as a source of freedom, blacks turned elsewhere. They received support from an unlikely source in 1649 when a local lawyer, Adriaen van der Donck, joined their cause. His "Remonstrance of New Netherland to the States General of the United Netherlands" (the Dutch government at The Hague) called for a democratization of New Netherland but also urged the emancipation of the children of New Netherland's ostensibly free black families: "There are various other negroes in this country, some of whom have been made free for their long service," he declared, "but their children remain slaves, though it is contrary to the laws of every people that any one born of a free Christian mother should be a slave and be compelled to remain in servitude."[16]

When that plea received no response, black people continued to petition the council, sometimes offering to buy their children out of slavery. In 1661, Emanuel Pietersen and Dorothy Angola went before the council with eighteen-year-old Anthony Angola, whom they had adopted as an infant and raised and educated. The parents urged Anthony's freedom, which the council granted. Two years later, freedman Domingo Angola petitioned for the freedom of Christina, the baptized daughter of the late Manuel Trumpeter and his wife, Antonya. The council ruled that the young woman could be freed if her owner was paid 300 guilders or a replacement fund. Christina's freedom was aided through a loan provided by mill owner Govert Loockermans. Adult slaves also tried to gain their freedom through petitioning and purchase. In April 1663, "old and sickly" Mayken, who had served the Company since 1628, petitioned for her freedom, which was also granted.

Buying freedom was costly, and even the most industrious free black could rarely accumulate enough to buy the freedom of a loved one or friend. But if money was not available, the will to freedom always was. Nearly two centuries before the Underground Railroad, black New Netherlanders harbored runaway slaves and aided their escape from bondage. Indeed, the free black farmsteads became so notorious for their assistance to the enslaved that the council set a fifty-guilder fine against any person who sheltered or fed a runaway. The council renewed the prohibition in 1648 and again in 1658, although neither imposition seemed to end the flight of black fugitives.[17] Escape from New Netherland was aided too by the refusal of the English colonies to return runaways. Regarding the Dutch as interlopers on English territory, New Haven and Maryland openly encouraged slaves in the Dutch territory to defect.[18] In 1650 Stuyvesant warned the governor of Maryland that asylum was a two-way street. Unless Maryland stopped harboring Dutch slaves, he would retaliate by "advertising free liberty, access and recess to all servants, fugitives, and runaways."[19]

Steadily—through natural increase, manumission, self-purchase, and flight—the free black population continued to grow. By the end of Dutch rule in 1664, about 75 out of a total some 375 blacks in New Amsterdam were free. The free black population also spread beyond the bounds of Manhattan. Two of the colony's free blacks, Jan DeVries II and Nicholas (Claus) Manuel, both baptized in the Dutch church, left Manhattan to become property owners in the Tappan Patent, a consortium of colonial pioneers in northern New Jersey.[20] In 1661, free black "Francisco the negro" was among the twenty-three founders of Boswijk [Bushwick] in Brooklyn.

The difficulties free people of color had in liberating their children, even as black men became more essential to the defense of the colony, pointed to an ever-deepening racism among the leadership of the New Netherland colony. Nothing illustrated this more clearly than the fate of Captain Jan DeVries, who arrived in New Amsterdam shortly after the freedom proclamation.[21]

In June 1644, amid the Dutch-Indian wars, Captain DeVries arrived from Curaçao with a battalion of 150 Dutch soldiers. A veteran of military campaigns in West Africa and the Antilles, DeVries deployed his troops into the still-dangerous frontier area, and he personally took up residence among the black farmers in the colony's buffer zone. As a military commander, DeVries was taken immediately into Kieft's inner circle and given a seat on the town council.

The Kieft-DeVries relationship soon soured. DeVries was not the Indian slayer Kieft had expected, but there were also other problems. DeVries befriended free blacks, slaves, Indians, and "Brazilian women," who regularly visited DeVries's estate. De Vries stood in church as a godfather and witness to the baptism of black freeman Paulo D'Angola's son in June 1646. DeVries also prevented the Dutch West India Company from taking "custody of a Negro woman, Elary, who belongs to the Company" from his compound. And finally and most egregiously in relation to Dutch New Amsterdam's emerging racial order, DeVries married a black woman. The Dutch Reformed Church official recorded her name simply as Swartinne—meaning dark lovely woman—in the church registry.[22]

DeVries's defense of black people and his marriage to a black woman was neither welcomed nor appreciated by Kieft, who sought to strip DeVries of his captaincy for allegedly stealing the enslaved woman Elary.[23] "Since his arrival here," Kieft informed the council in early 1646, DeVries "has cultivated the friendship and society of some dangerous persons, enemies of the Company's welfare and of this country and defamers of their authorities. . . . Furthermore, he is leading a scandalous life, highly dangerous in this infant republic; . . . he has also with unbearable arrogance called the director a liar in the presence of the entire council, taking hold of his Polish casse-tête with the intention of striking him, had he not been prevented." DeVries returned Kieft's contempt in kind. In June, DeVries, "in the presence of several persons" in a New Amsterdam tavern, made "many contemptuous remarks" about Kieft, publicly declaring, "I do not care a damn for the director's commission."[24]

Kieft eventually had his way. DeVries was cashiered and shipped back to Holland. But in Amsterdam, DeVries's superiors exonerated him, restored his captaincy, and returned him to New Amsterdam. In August 1647, Jan DeVries II, the child of Captain DeVries and Swartinne, was baptized at the Church-in-the-Fort. A month later, Kieft, who had been replaced as governor by Peter Stuyvesant, himself was returning to Holland aboard the *Princess*. The ship also carried Dominie Bogardus and DeVries, who was returning to settle personal business matters. When the *Princess* capsized and sank in a storm, black New Netherland lost some of its great friends and advocates. DeVries's Manhattan property, entrusted to Paulo D'Angola, who served as custodian for DeVries's surviving child, Jan II, was sold. His surname, and perhaps his lineage, survived too among the local Algonquian natives.

The Company's new director, Peter Stuyvesant, was no DeVries who befriended blacks, or a Bogardus who welcomed them into the Church, or even a Kieft who granted them land and freedom in return for protection from Native

Americans. Stuyvesant—also director general of the Dutch West India Company in Curaçao, Bonaire, and Aruba—was deeply committed to expanding slavery in New Netherland. In 1648, the Netherlands' States General had reproached the Dutch West India Company for the fact that "the Slave Trade has long lain dormant to the great damages of the Company," and argued that New Netherland would have been more extensively cultivated if the settlers had used more slaves. Stuyvesant sympathized with that perspective. Under his governance, the Dutch in the Antilles had profited mightily from trade with English and French planters in Barbados, St. Christopher, and other islands, whom he had helped convert from tobacco and cotton cultivation to more lucrative sugar production.[25] Stuyvesant had developed good relations with planters in Barbados, whose demand for slaves grew enormously in the mid-seventeenth century. Even through the Anglo-Dutch War, Stuyvesant continued to sell slaves to Barbadian sugar magnates, at great profit to the Dutch West India Company.

The Company shared Stuyvesant's appreciation for the profitability of slavery. It had long opposed allowing private investors to enter the slave trade, denying

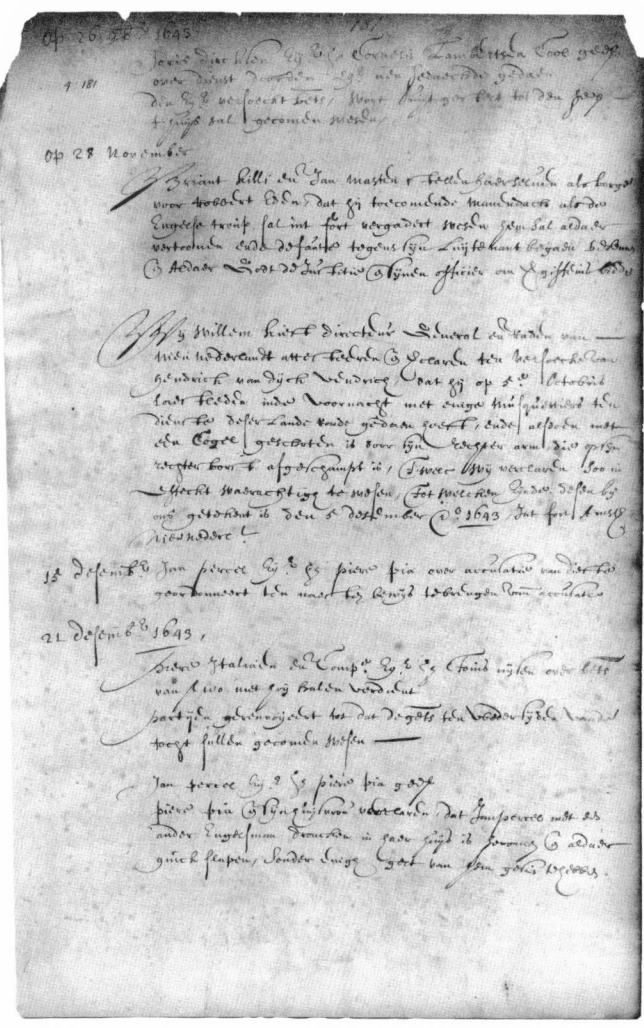

Detail of 1644 emancipation document of New Amsterdam.
NEW YORK STATE ARCHIVES

New Amsterdam's Poet Laureate

Jacob Steendam was a New Amsterdam merchant and an accomplished poet whose compositions included lyrical poems about whales frolicking in Hudson Bay and starfish on the beach of Manhattan.

Before coming to New Amsterdam, he had been a soldier and slave trader employed by the Dutch West India Company at Elmina, on the west coast of Africa, for more than a decade. In Elmina, Steendam lived with an African woman with whom he may have had children—an experience that touched him, and inspired a poem of unrequited love for an African woman, called *The Might of Chastity*.

> *Upon beholding her*
> *He could but ill restrain*
> *Himself from crying out,*
> *O! Blossom of my choice,*
> *What woman gave you birth*
> *In this barbaric land? . . .*
> *Had God united us*
> *In matrimonial bonds,*
> *How happy we could be*
> *We have discovered:*

> *Alas, it cannot*
> *(For reasons) come to pass . . .*

Another poem was written for the birthday of Jan Gelendonk, or John Darkyellow, a child of mixed racial origins who was probably Steendam's son.

> *Since two bloods course within your veins,*
> *Both Ham's and Japhet's intermingling;*
> *One race forever doomed to serve,*
> *The other bearing freedom's likeness . . .*

The poem concluded with a birthday wish:

> *I wish you (in this human form)*
> *Japhet's freedom, long foretold.*

In a perhaps telling insight about Steendam's understanding of the relationships between Europeans and Africans—most likely white men and black women—the slave-trader-turned-poet reveals his belief that the purported curse of Noah upon Ham was lifted when the Europeans and Africans joined together.　—*Christopher Moore*

requests by noting that "trade principally to Guinea and Angola, is the life of the Company; and the ruin of the latter would follow the deduction or diminution thereof." However, in 1652, amid the Anglo-Dutch War, the Company opened their market to all comers, and New Netherland merchants were quick to seize the possibilities of trading in slaves. Jacob Steendam and Cornelis Steenwyck, who later became the first Dutch mayor of New York, were the first of New Netherland's slave traders, but prominent local families, including the Philipses, Schuylers, Van Cortlandts, Van Hornes, and Van Zandts, soon joined them.

In 1654, the first of these private traders equipped the *Witte Paert* to transport slaves directly to New Netherland "in consideration of the promotion of population and agriculture." A year later, the *Witte Paert* arrived in New Amsterdam carrying 300 slaves. To deter the slaves from being sold out of the colony, Stuyvesant slapped an export duty of 10 percent on the slaves. Most remained in New Netherland.

Stuyvesant saw the influx of slaves as a way to greatly expand the New Netherland settlement as well as to protect the Dutch enclave from its enemies. In March 1653, he ordered Company slaves to build a barricade with logs "twelve feet long, eighteen inches in circumference, sharpened at the upper end" from river to river across Manhattan Island. "The wall"—Wall Street—was added to the slaves' workload.

Beyond providing protection, the newly arrived slaves enabled the Company to establish Manhattan's second Dutch settlement. In 1658, slaves began clearing the ground for New Haarlem, simultaneously building a nine-mile road from New Amsterdam to the new settlement, later known as the Boston Post Road, or Route 1. As the project moved forward, there never seemed to be enough slaves. In 1660 Stuyvesant sent word to Vice Director Beck in Curaçao demanding "clever and strong" blacks to work at the fort and to help in the war against the Indians. Beck sent a group of slaves, "all dry and well conditioned and marked with annexed mark," but Stuyvesant complained that most of them were old and sick. Angrily, he insisted that Beck give preference to "the Christians and those of the Honorable Company" before selling the good ones to "Spaniards and unbelieving Jews."[26]

Under Stuyvesant, black life was being re-Africanized, but much of the Dutch culture remained. The Afro-Portuguese surname D'Angola, meaning "from Angola," changed to the Dutch "Van Angola," was prominent in the free black community. The baptized son of Emmanuel Van Angola became Nicholas (Claus) Manuel, which followed Dutch patronymics of a child receiving the father's first name, and so within just two generations the Angola surname was gone. Other names that became common among free nonwhites in the colony included DeVries (DeFreese), Van der Donck (Van Dunk), DeGroot (DeGroat), and Manuel (later Mann). Freedom no doubt sped the creation of an Afro-Dutch culture as much as it aided in the assimilation of the newly free blacks as Americans. No longer facing a bleak future in bondage or the uncertainty of life as runaway slaves, the children of free blacks became craftsmen, tanners, carpenters, ship caulkers, sail weavers, surgeons, merchants, farmers, and property owners. Afro-Dutch culture thrived among the enslaved population. Advertisements for runaway slaves frequently listed fugitives as bilingual and trilingual, able to speak African dialects, English, and Dutch.

Black people also incorporated other aspects of Dutch culture into their lives. They celebrated the Protestant Dutch observance Pentecost, known as *Pinkster*. By the late eighteenth century, black New Netherlanders mixed Pentecostal fervor and African rites to create an annual Afro-Dutch festival in parts of the Hudson Valley and New Jersey. Observed too, though in Afro-Dutch fashion, was the Christmas custom of the annual visit of Saint Nicholas (Sinterklaas) and Pete the Moor (Piet de Moor, or Zwarte Piet).[27] Many Afro-Dutch kitchens in New York and New Jersey served *ollycakes* (donuts, derived from *oliekoeke*, or "oil cake"), *koolsla* (coleslaw), and *koeckjes* (cookies) even into the twenty-first century.

New Amsterdam's blacks also began to develop their own institutions, the first of which may have been a cemetery. Perhaps started by the free blacks who lived in the vicinity of the Negroes Burying Ground, as it was designated on colonial maps, permission for its continued use was probably largely due to the efforts of Sara Roloff Kierstede Van Borsum. A white woman who served the Company as an Indian translator, Van Borsum was the daughter of Anneke Jans and the stepdaughter of Dominie Bogardus. She was also frequently a sponsor of black baptisms during the era when few black baptisms were allowed. By 1673, Sara, who was then married to Cornelius Van Borsum, appears to have provided approval of the family's five-acre property (between Chambers Street and Duane Street) for use as a slave cemetery.[28]

But even as a distinctive Afro-Dutch culture emerged along the Hudson, the circumstances of black life were about to change. On Monday, August 25, 1664, word came of an approaching English fleet. To organize the city for its defense, the slaves were ordered to repair the city's wall. The slave ship *Gideon*, with 290 slaves aboard, had just arrived, and feeding the new slaves further diminished the colony's food supply. The new crop of grain was harvested but not threshed, and Stuyvesant had set his own slaves to threshing away at his bowery, but they still could not deliver enough food to supply New Amsterdam. Stuyvesant wanted to fight the soon-to-arrive English but was opposed by even his staunchest allies, who argued that food provisions were too low to sustain a war. A ship with a number of the city's slaves on board tried to get away, and some slaves were seen running into the woods.

On Monday morning, September 8, 1664, the Dutch surrendered New Netherland to the English. Stuyvesant then led his 150 Dutch soldiers from Fort Amsterdam to the now-empty slave ship, *Gideon*, lying in the East River. That afternoon the fort was rechristened Fort James in honor of its new proprietor, James II, the Duke of York—also a principal investor in the Company of Royal Adventurers Trading to Africa. The English would soon give port privileges and warehouse priority in the New York colony to ships engaged in the slave trade. With lenient terms of surrender, the English recognized the legality of all Dutch-claimed property, including slaves.[29]

Within months of the takeover, English authorities raised questions about the status of Manhattan's free blacks and their landed holdings. In 1665, an official certification from former governor Peter Stuyvesant was required to legitimize the "land of the blacks." Stuyvesant responded with a letter explaining the presence of homesteads owned by blacks along the "common highway" (Bowery Road). The land, as Stuyvesant wrote, that the blacks "have cleared and cultivated . . . and they have owned and possessed unmolested" was right-

Slavery and Servitude at the Pieter Claesen Wyckoff House

Slavery and servitude are a fundamental part of the history of New York City's oldest surviving structure, the Pieter Claesen Wyckoff House in East Flatbush, Brooklyn. Pieter and his wife, Grietje Van Ness, constructed the original portion of the house in 1652 after purchasing a small parcel of land in what was then an undeveloped but fertile marshland. Here they raised eleven children, all of whom survived childhood, remarkably, and their descendants continued to expand the house and farm for the next 250 years. For over a century of this time the Wyckoff farm relied on the labor of a small number of enslaved Africans, who lived alongside—or most likely, above—the family in the small farmhouse.

There is no evidence of Pieter Claesen Wyckoff having owned slaves during his lifetime (d. 1694); he himself had come to America in 1637 as an indentured laborer. However, by the time that his great-grandson Pieter Wyckoff added two living chambers to the original one-room structure in the 1740s and 1750s, there were slaves on the property. The slave census of 1755 for the village of Flatlands records two slaves on the farm. Pieter's son, Peter A. Wyckoff, inherited the farm in November 1776, soon after the British had marched up the nearby King's Highway to engage Washington's troops in the Battle of Long Island.

The most substantial documentary evidence of

Slave bill of sale for Sam, 1801.
COLLECTION OF THE WYCKOFF HOUSE & ASSOCIATION

the presence of slaves at the Wyckoff farm exists for the period during which it was held by Peter A. Wyckoff's son, Abraham, in the first two decades of the nineteenth century. At least four bills of sale or

Historic view of Wyckoff House and barn, ca. 1920.

Contemporary view of Wyckoff House and barn.

indentures for slaves on the farm survive and demonstrate Abraham Wyckoff actively seeking out slaves from his extensive network of familial and business connections in Kings County and elsewhere on Long Island. For instance, on May 30, 1801, Abraham purchased "one Negro boy Named Sam aged about Nine years" for forty pounds from his uncle, Nicholas Wyckoff, and his elder brother, Peter P. Wyckoff. Nicholas and Peter P. had farms in Bushwick and Flatbush, respectively. Nicholas's son and Abraham's cousin, Folkert Wyckoff, witnessed the transaction. Sam was one of the unfortunate many who, having been born before July 4, 1799, by the terms of New York's Gradual Emancipation Act, were condemned to live their lives in bondage, while their contemporaries born after that date were to be freed at the age of twenty-eight or no later than July 4, 1827.

Even as 1827 approached, however, Abraham Wyckoff continued to seek slave labor for the farm by adapting the language of bondage to imminent emancipation. On January 1, 1819, he entered into an "indenture" contract with Nicholas Schenk, also of Flatlands, to retain "a Black Child named Jack as a slave servant" for the next eight years in return for forty dollars. Unlike the earlier bills of sale, the indenture document specified that Abraham was to provide Jack with "sufficient meat, drink, apparel, lodging, washing and all other things necessary and fit for such a servant," to teach him to read and write, and to present him with a "New Bible at the expiration of his term of service." It was a small concession to freedom, grudgingly given. Like other New York farmers deeply committed to enslaved black labor, the Wyckoffs did not surrender their slaves easily.

—Sean Sawyer

fully theirs. "All of these parcels of land were given to the aforesaid Negroes in true and free ownership with such privileges as all tracts of land are bestowed on the inhabitants (of this) province." The thirty free black farmsteads—about 200 acres—were the most striking reminder of the presence of the free black population on Manhattan Island. Apart from the Dutch nod to the property rights of free blacks, the question of how blacks, both free and enslaved, would fare under English rule would be answered rapidly.

Chapter 2

THE TIGHTENING VISE: SLAVERY AND FREEDOM IN BRITISH NEW YORK

JILL LEPORE

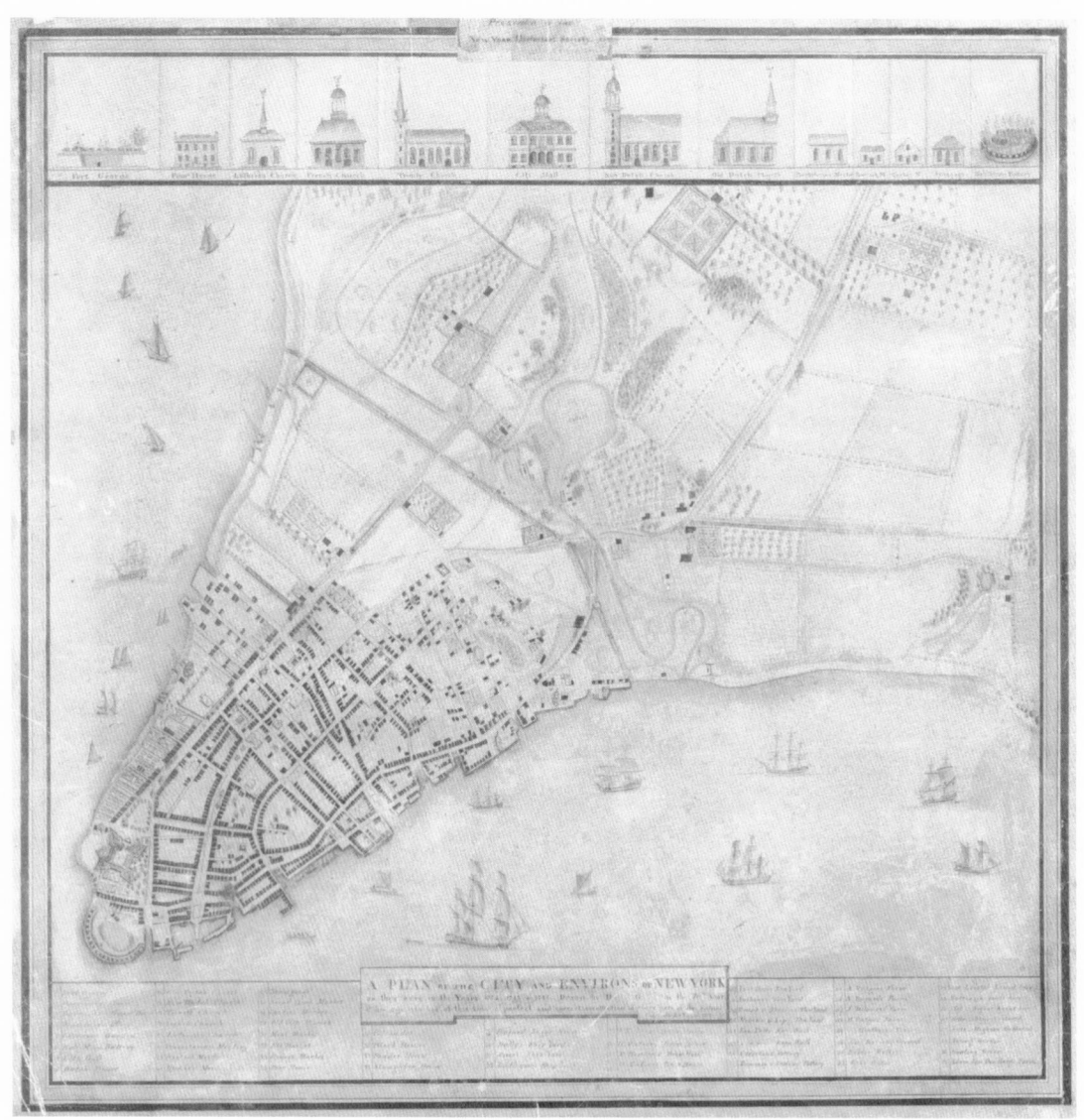

David Grim, *A Plan of the City and Environs of New York as they were in the Years 1742, 1743 or 1744*. Pen, ink, and watercolor drawing.

IN 1813, A SEVENTY-SIX-YEAR-OLD New Yorker named David Grim drew a map of the Manhattan of his childhood. He titled his pen, ink, and watercolor drawing "A Plan of the City and Environs of New York as they were in the Years 1742, 1743 or 1744." Although Grim had been a young boy during those years, he maintained that he had "a perfect and correct recollection" of the city. The map, Grim explained, "I made for my Amusement, with the intent that it be on a future day presented to the New-York Historical Society." Measuring a little less than two feet square, its once-vibrant colors faded by the decay of time, Grim's plan remains among the Society's more beautiful treasures. It is also chillingly illustrates the brutality of slavery in eighteenth-century New York City.

Depicting the city under British rule, Grim's map contains sixty numbered features. Grim highlighted monuments to imperial, cultural, provincial, and municipal authority: Fort George at the tip of the island of Manhattan, Trinity Church on Broadway, and City Hall on the corner of Broadway and Wall Streets. But the numbered places on Grim's map also trace the city's ethnic diversity: he listed not only the Anglican Trinity Church but also two Dutch churches, Presbyterian, French, Baptist, and Lutheran churches, a Quaker meetinghouse, and even a Jewish synagogue. On the top border of the map, Grim sketched the buildings themselves, in all their range of scale and elegance. But perhaps most poignant, Grim's map plots a city marked by slavery. A tiny icon that looks like a bonfire, just east of the Palisades, is landmark number 55: "Plot Negro's burnt here." And number 56, just to the north of it, shows a gallows from which dangles a silhouetted black figure: "Plot Negro Gibbeted."

In notes he scribbled on the back of his map, Grim related "a few of the most remarkable occurrences that happened in this City, to the extent of my memory." By far the most powerful recollection of his childhood was the execution in 1741, when Grim was just four years old, of slaves convicted of conspiring to burn New York City and murder its white inhabitants. Grim wrote, "I have a perfect idea of seeing the Negroes chained to a stake, and there burned to death."[1]

As much as Grim's memory was shaped by those executions, his map in many ways underestimates the black presence in New York: he neglected, for example, to mark or label the six-acre "Negroes Burial Ground," just south of the Collect Pond. But Grim's map also serves as a grisly testament to how slavery shaped every aspect of life in eighteenth-century New York.

W HEN THE English took possession of New Amsterdam and named it New York in 1664, about 1,500 people lived in Manhattan, roughly 10 percent of whom were of African origin. By 1737, the year David Grim was born, a door-by-door census counted 8,666 New Yorkers: 6,947 whites and 1,719 blacks. Put another way, by 1737, one in five New Yorkers was black, and nearly all of these men, women, and children were enslaved. For much of the eighteenth century, New York City was second only to Charleston, South Carolina, in its proportion of slaves in an urban population. It was a fact about New York that nearly always elicited comment from European visitors. "It rather hurts a Europian eye to see so many negro slaves upon the streets," one Scottish traveler complained.[2]

Under British rule, stricter slave codes were passed. British authorities both recognized the legitimacy of Dutch ownership of slaves and, in 1665, affirmed slavery's legality. The British also restricted white servitude and, in 1679, prohibited the enslavement of Indians, both of which contributed to an increased reliance on Africans as a source of cheap labor and made the status of black people increasingly anomalous. And whereas the Dutch had imported mainly from west-central Africa, men and women whom they called "Angolans," or sometimes "Congos," the British turned to a different region of Africa, the Upper Guinea Coast, where the Royal African Company traded. On average, the British imported about one hundred and fifty slaves each year. Many colonists were at best ambivalent about the province's reliance on slave labor, but, as Cadwallader Colden explained in 1726, many came to see it as an economic necessity. "It is true that it were beter for the Country, if there were no Negroes in it, and that all could be carried on by Freemen who have greater Interest in promoting the Good of a Country," Colden wrote, "But the want of hands and the Dearness of the Wages of hired Servants makes Slaves at this Time, necessary."

Between 1700 and 1774, the British imported between 6,800 and 7,400 Africans to the colony of New York. It was cheaper for New York slave traders to import directly from Africa; buyers in New York paid customs duties of only forty shillings "For every Negro and other Slave, of 4 years old, and upwards, imported directly from *Africa*," compared to four pounds (or eighty shillings) for those "From all other Places." Despite this deep discount, less than 30 percent of slaves imported to New York before 1741 came directly from Africa. Nearly all of the rest came the English sugar islands—"the hot Country," as one black New Yorker put it—of Barbados, Antigua, and most of all, Jamaica, from which 30 percent of all New York's slaves came. Another 35 percent came from elsewhere in the West Indies: Barbados, Antigua, St. Eustatia, St. Thomas, Curaçao, Bermuda, and St. Kitts. Less than 3 percent came from South Carolina. These were all places where New York merchants had long-established trading relations.[3]

Slaves arrived in New York in small numbers, just a handful on any given ship, and almost always on the return leg of voyages made by New York–based trading vessels. Of those slaves imported to New York, probably about a fifth to a quarter of them remained in the city. New York merchants exported grain and lumber to the Caribbean in exchange for sugar and sometimes slaves. Although the merchants desired to be paid in bills of exchange, their West Indian trading partners preferred to pay in goods, and were especially likely to use the opportunity to rid themselves of unwanted slaves.

Such slaves were either notoriously rebellious or too sick or too old to bear the backbreaking work of sugar cultivation. New York merchants, faced with slaves that were too expensive to re-export but having little use for their labor in the city, often sold them to farmers in the countryside. A 1732 law decreed that any New Yorker who imported more than one slave was required to pay the import duty, and many merchants, having paid the duty on additional slaves, decided to hire them out by the day to fellow New Yorkers needing workers on the docks or on building projects.[4]

Many of these slaves were themselves new to the Americas, often having merely stopped in the Caribbean en route to New York. Many came from the Akan-speaking regions of what is now Ghana. The British usually called these Akan speakers "Coromantees." They retained Akan "day names," given to mark the day of the week on which they were born: Quash (Kwesi, or Sunday), Cudjoe (Kwodwo, Monday), Quack (Kwedu, Wednesday), Cuffee (Kofi, Friday), and Quanimo (Kwame, Saturday). But just as often these names were anglicized: Cudjoe became Joe, Quack turned into Jack. And many other African names, having no easily pronounceable English equivalent, did not survive at all.[5]

Most of the West and Central Africans in early eighteenth-century New York had witnessed and endured extraordinary suffering. For every one hundred Africans seized in the African interior, only about sixty-four survived the journey to the coast and only about forty-eight or forty-nine made it across the Atlantic's Middle Passage. Of that forty-eight or forty-nine, only between twenty-eight and thirty were still alive after the three- to four-year period of "seasoning." In the New World, faced with catastrophic mortality and profoundly disorienting separation from family and community, enslaved Africans forged new bonds that drew on linguistic and cultural similarities, and even shared a variety of military experiences. Although the Africans who landed in New York came from dozens of independent states, "Coromantees" shared a common language, and "Angolans" shared a broadly similar cultural background. In the New World, these bonds could transcend political divisions that had mattered more in Africa. Meanwhile, their very endurance only increased their value: on the New York slave market, having survived smallpox was a particular selling point, frequently mentioned in advertisements of slaves for sale, as in that for "a Young Negro Woman, about 20 Year old" who "had the small Pox in *Barbados* when a Child."[6]

During the century of British rule, both the number and proportion of black people in New York City grew. On average, the annual growth of the black population slightly outpaced that for whites. While natural increase and immigration both contributed to white population growth, black population growth during the colonial period was almost entirely due to new arrivals.

TABLE 1.
THE BLACK AND WHITE POPULATION OF NEW YORK CITY,
1698–1756[7]

YEAR	WHITE	BLACK	TOTAL	BLACKS AS A PERCENTAGE OF TOTAL
1698	4,237	700	4,937	14
1703	3,745	630	4,375	14
1723	5,886	1,362	7,248	19
1731	7,045	1,577	8,622	18
1737	6,947	1,719	8,666	20
1746	9,273	2,444	11,717	21
1749	10,926	2,368	13,294	18
1756	10,768	2,278	13,046	21

Before 1711, traders generally auctioned slaves at the major wharves in the city. After 1711, slaves were sold and hired out at day rates at the "Meal Market," at the base of Wall Street. Young women, and especially "seasoned" adolescent girls, were highly sought after to meet the city's need for domestic labor, as revealed in a 1727 advertisement for a "Negro Woman, that has one child and can Spin, Knit, manage a Dary, and do all manner of House-work." In New York City, unlike in the rest of the colony, black women nearly always outnumbered black men. In 1703, for instance, women of childbearing age constituted 45 percent of the city's black population; in 1737, 35 percent. But they bore very few children. Most enslaved women were dead by age forty and their mortality rates peaked between ages thirty and thirty-four; they died of disease or complications of childbirth, exacerbated by poor nutrition and years of toil. Some were simply driven mad. In 1749, "a Negro Girl of about 15 Years of Age," who "had been for sometime disordered in her Sences," fell, or, more likely, jumped, "out of a Garret Window three Story, of which unhappy fall she was so Bruised, that she dyed in a few Hours."[8]

Slaves' low fertility failed to concern their owners. On the contrary, female sterility became a selling point in a city with limited housing. "To Be Sold, a young Wench about 29 years old, that drinks no strong Drink, and gets no Children, a very good Drudge," read one ad. Another placed in 1751 described "an excellent Negro Wench, about 20 Years old, with a male Child, about three Months old; the Wench has had the Small-Pox, can cook, wash, and iron, can be well recommended, and is sold for no other Fault than being too fruitful." One owner sold his female slave in 1756 "because she breeds too fast for her owner to put up with such inconvenience." Infant mortality was high, and infanticide not uncommon, although it is unclear who was committing infanticide—mothers or masters. In 1736, the *New-York Weekly Journal* printed this chilling news: "Yesterday Morning was found in the Negroes Burial-place, a small Infant in a Wigg Box, and partly buried underGround."[9]

Discouraged and even prevented from having children of their own, black women were employed in caring for their masters' children. Indeed, owners' desire to employ black women as nurses also contributed to their preference for barren slaves and their general discouragement of black childbearing.[10] That young black women nurtured white children did not mean that the women were necessarily beloved or even especially valued. Nowhere is this more brutally illustrated than in a short piece of local news printed in the *New-York Gazette* on September 12, 1737: "Saturday last a Boy about 14 or 15

Know all Men by thefe Prefents, That I *Abraham Quick of the City of New York Cooper*

For and in Confideration of the Sum of *Fifty Five Pound* Current Money of the Province of *New York* to me in Hand paid at and before the Enfealing and Delivery of thefe Prefents, by *James Beekman of the City aforefaid* the Receipt whereof I do hereby acknowledge, and myfelf to be therewith fully fatisfied, contented and paid: HAVE Granted, Bargained, Sold, Releafed, and by thefe Prefents do fully, clearly and abfolutely grant, bargain, fell and releafe unto the faid *James Beekman a Certain Negro Slave aged Fifteen Year or there abouts, Named York*

To HAVE and to HOLD the faid *Slave York* unto the faid *James Beekman his* Executors, Adminiftrators and Affigns for ever. And I the faid *Abraham Quick* for my Self, my Heirs, Executors and Adminiftrators, do covenant agree to and with the above-named *James Beekman His* Executors, Adminiftrators and Affigns, to warrant and defend the Sale of the above-named *Slave York* againft all Perfons whatfoever. *In Witnefs* whereof I have hereunto fet my Hand and Seal this *Fifth* Day of *May* Annoq; Dom. One Thoufand Seven Hundred and Fifty *Three*

Sealed and Delivered in
the Prefence of

Abraham Quick

Pieter Zabriskie

Abraham Beekman

Deed of sale for slave named York to James Beekman.

Advertisement for a slave, *New-York Weekly Post Boy*, May 17, 1756. NEW-YORK HISTORICAL SOCIETY LIBRARY

years old, in this City was handling a gun, a Negro Girl sitting in the yard, with a Child in her Arms, at the outside of the Window, the Boy, in a jesting manner said, *I'll shoot ye*, and the Gun went off and shot the Negro's Brains out." But, the newspaper hastened to add, "the Child in her Arms [was] not hurt." The boy went unpunished.[11]

For whites, leaving the care of a black nurse and the company of black children marked a transition out of childhood. Of his eleven-year-old son, Cadwallader Colden wrote his wife, "I hope he no longer looks on himself as a Child & that he'l be ashamed to play about the Doors with the Negro Children."[12] For enslaved people, childhood—a span of years that did not involve physical labor, and during which they lived with their mothers and kept company with their master's children—was short, ending by about age six, especially when some New York slave owners considered the separation of mothers and children as much a disciplinary as an economic necessity. Selling a thirty-three-year-old woman and one of her children to Barbados in 1717, Cadwallader Colden explained, "I could have sold her here to good advantage but I have several other of her Children which I value & I know if she should stay in this country she would spoil them." Colden regretted that he couldn't break this woman's will himself: "Were it not for her Alusive [or Abusive] Tongue her sullenness & the Custome of the Country that will not allow us to use our Negroes as you doe in Barbados when they Displeas you I would not have parted with her But I doubt not she'l make as good a slave as any in the Island after a litle of your Discipline." Young children, who were priced more cheaply than adolescents and adults, sold well in New York as sources of domestic labor, and as an investment in potential labor; one notice from 1760 advertised "a parcel of likely negro boys and girls from nine to twelve years of age."[13]

SLAVERY IN

NEW YORK

Most enslaved New Yorkers lived in households where there were only one or two other slaves. According to a detailed census taken in 1703, slave-owning households contained an average of only 2.4 slaves. Slaves could not legally marry until 1809, nor, in most cases, were slave unions recognized by the city's churches. As Reverend John Sharpe wrote in 1713, slave "marriages are performed by mutual consent without the blessing of the Church." Nevertheless, a lucky few men and women found mates in the same household, like "Robin, Mr. Chambers' Negro, and Cuba his Wife," both owned by attorney John Chambers. But even these fortunate men and women were likely to be separated, eventually, by sale. (Robin and Cuba were separated when Robin was burned at the stake in 1741, after being convicted for conspiracy.) Wealthy New Yorkers like James Alexander and Cadwallader Colden often congratulated themselves on their own happy marriages: "I agree with you in the Commendations of the married State & believe where it hits right it yields the greatest Satisfaction in this Life," Alexander wrote to Colden in 1730. Meanwhile, they attempted to sever romantic attachments among their slaves if the attachments threatened their authority and command of labor. Colden wrote to a North Carolina man who had purchased his slave, Gabriel, in 1726, "Since you went my Negro Wench tells me that Gabriel designs to return if he do not like the place but as one reason of my selling him was to keep him from that Wench that I value You must not allow him to return."[14]

In a world in which slave families most often lived apart, running away usually meant going to visit a spouse, child, or parent. Nearly two thirds of runaway slaves in colonial New York City were suspected of having fled to family members.[15] But running away was not always necessary. Since the city

RAN away from John Thorn at White-Stone-Ferry in Flushing, a new Negro Fellow named Prince, he can't scarce speak a Word of English; he is a short Fellow, about 20 Years of Age, had on when he went away nothing but an Ozenbrigs Shirt, and a Pair of Tow-Trowsers, and a striped worsted Cap; he also has taken with him a short Gun well mounted with Brass. Whosoever takes up the said Negro Fellow and Gun, and brings him to his said Master, shall have three Pounds Reward and all reasonable Charges paid by me,
JOHN THORN.

Advertisement for a runaway slave,
New York Evening Post, December 17, 1744.
NEW-YORK HISTORICAL SOCIETY LIBRARY

THE
TIGHTENING
VISE

was so small—a mile wide by a mile and a half long—a man might live just doors away from his wife, or a mother just blocks away from her growing children. Most family members must have lived less than a mile apart, others only a little farther away, in places like Westchester or New Jersey or Long Island. In these circumstances, some spouses belonging to different owners managed to come together after the workday ended. In the 1730s, one black New Yorker named Quack lived with his owner, the Dutch painter John Roosevelt, in the East Ward, but managed nearly every night to visit his wife, Barbara, who was the governor's cook. Will, a slave sold to New York from Antigua, walked across the city every evening to spend the night with his wife until the captain of the watch, Cornelius Van Horne, decided to stop him. "Mr. *Van Horn* would not allow him to come to his Wife," Will complained, and "would not allow a Candle." Undaunted, Will made a makeshift torch to find his way through the city at night, ducking behind buildings when the watch approached. On Sundays, while most whites went to church or stayed at home with their families, slaves spent their day of rest traversing the city to see family and friends. Especially in summer, black men and women went "frolicking in the Fields," a wide swath of land north of the Negroes Burial Ground. "Mate, we wanted you very much last Night at a Frolick out of Town," a black man named Curacoa Dick said to a friend when they met "at a Well by the New Dutch Church" on a Sunday in the summer of 1740. "They had a free Dance and were very merry."[16]

Such family and social ties among black New Yorkers depended on a common language. Many city slaves spoke more than one European language, having acquired over their lifetimes as many tongues as masters: English, Dutch, French, German, Welsh, and more. Sarah, a twenty-four-year-old "Mullatto Servant Woman" who ran away from English merchant Joseph Reade in 1732, spoke "good English and some Dutch." John Henricus, "a Lusty Young Negro Man" who ran away from Matthew Norris in 1727, spoke "very good English and Welch." Only the 30 percent of the newest arrivals who came directly from Africa could "scarce speak a Word of English," speaking, instead, one of their native tongues—Kikongo, Gã, Mandinga, Soninke, Temne, Fulbe, and Sere—

or any of the many other African languages heard on the streets of New York, and, most of all, Akan, a lingua franca in West Africa.[17]

Most black New Yorkers also spoke in ways that mixed Old World and New—creolized black dialects that, to whites, were worthy of ridicule. When the Annapolis physician Alexander Hamilton was on the road to New York City in 1744, his slave Dromo asked directions from a black woman on Coney Island. She spoke with such a strong Dutch inflection that Dromo, a Marylander who spoke an eighteenth-century black English, could barely understand her. Hamilton found their conversation so amusing that he recorded it in his journal:

> "Dis de way to York?" says Dromo. "Yaw, dat is Yarikee," said the wench, pointing to the steeples. "What devil you say?" replys Dromo. "Yaw, mynheer," said the wench. "Damme you, what you say?" said Dromo again. "Yaw, yaw," said the girl. "You a damn black bitch," said Dromo, and so rid on.[18]

A sizable number of black New Yorkers could read and write, a skill that was often mentioned in advertisements seeking the return of runaways, some of whom forged passes. Other runaways relied on other guises. One black New Yorker ran off in a soldier's clothing. Another wore a wig. But one eighteen-year-old runaway had no hope of disguising himself as a free man: he wore "an Iron Ring about his Neck and one about his Leg, with a Chain from one to the other."[19] However, few black New Yorkers were so shackled. To the contrary, compared to enslaved men and women in many other parts of the British colonies, they had an exceptional degree of mobility: most, especially men like Quack and Will and Curacoa Dick, were able to move throughout the city at will.

To a large degree, the daily life of slaves and free blacks in New York was determined by the geography of the city. Manhattan, when seized by the British in 1664, was a tiny settlement of two-story wooden houses on irregularly sized lots, barricaded at the tip of the island by the stone wall at Wall Street. A city charter adopted in 1683 divided the city into five wards: East, West, North, South, and Dock. A detailed census taken in 1703 reveals that one fourth of the city's black population lived in the East Ward, where over half of households contained at least one slave. And unlike the rest of the city, the East Ward's blacks were predominantly adult men—men who worked, undoubtedly, on the docks. In the city's South Ward, where householders were overwhelmingly Dutch in 1703, 60 percent of households contained at least one slave. Thirty percent of these slave-owning households contained only one slave, an adult woman employed as a domestic servant. In the Dock Ward, blacks comprised 25 percent of the population. Seventy percent of white households in the Dock Ward, generally wealthy French and English merchants, contained at least one slave. In the remote and less affluent North Ward, less than 20 percent of households contained at least one slave. In the West Ward, dominated by land owned by Trinity Church, thirty percent of households owned at least one slave,

TABLE 2.
THE POPULATION OF NEW YORK CITY IN 1737,
BY WARD, AGE, AND RACE

WARD	WHITE MALES		WHITE FEMALES		BLACK MALES		BLACK FEMALES		TOTAL WHITES	TOTAL BLACKS	TOTAL
	OVER 10	UNDER 10	OVER 10	UNDER 10	OVER 10	UNDER 10	OVER 10	UNDER 10			
East	558	246	610	229	213	76	203	69	1,643	561	2,204
West	298	144	396	136	65	7	48	8	974	128	1,102
South	305	221	414	111	66	20	96	21	1,051	203	1,254
North	357	111	312	168	88	47	43	38	948	216	1,164
Dock	274	161	292	167	117	36	126	35	894	314	1,208
Montg.	235	136	323	147	60	19	41	14	841	134	975
Bowery	150	47	134	54	44	15	30	10	385	99	484
Harlem	76	22	87	26	21	9	22	12	211	64	275
TOTALS	2,253	1,088	2,568	1,038	674	229	609	207	6,947	1,719	8,666

From E.B. O'Callaghan, *The Documentary History of the State of New-York* (Albany: Weed, Parsons, 1851), 4:186. Arithmetic errors from the original returns, left intact by O'Callaghan, have been corrected here.

but only 15 percent of the population was black. Separate from these five wards, the Outward, beyond the city limits, consisted of two separate neighborhoods of farm lots: Harlem and the Bowery. Here, blacks constituted 25 percent of the population, and the 60 percent of (largely Dutch) households that owned slaves owned on average nearly three slaves, the highest number in the city.[20]

Under the terms of a new city charter issued in 1731, the city's wards were redrawn. There were now seven wards, unevenly populated: the fashionable and densely settled Dock, South, and East Wards along the bustling East River waterfront; the less populated and less posh North and Montgomerie Wards; the remote and isolated West Ward along the Hudson River; and the quite rural Outward of rolling farmlands to the northeast. Tax lists and census records from the 1730s reveal the close correspondence between the wealth of the neighborhoods and the percentage of slaves living in them. In the well-heeled East Ward, where the average tax assessment was £26, blacks comprised 25 percent of the population; in the poorer Montgomerie Ward, where the average tax assessment was £10, blacks comprised just 13 percent of the population. The richest New Yorkers, in short, owned the most slaves.[21]

In the geography of the city, ward divisions mattered a great deal to whites, especially property-owning white men, who elected ward aldermen, paid taxes, and in general organized their political, economic, and social lives around ward divisions.[22] Slaves and free blacks, however, mapped the city differently. During an investigation into an alleged slave conspiracy in 1741, the Third Justice of the colony's supreme court, Daniel Horsmanden, concluded that "*the Conspirators had divided the City . . . into two Districts*": one at the east end of town, near the Fly Market, run by a gang called "the Fly-Boys"; and one at the west end, run by the "Long-Bridge Boys."[23] He may have been right. In any case, slaves' web of social connections stretched across the map, a pattern grimly, if persuasively, illustrated in the confessions of slaves accused of conspiracy: forced to name names, men jailed in the basement of City Hall almost never accused slaves from their own wards. Instead, the men they named came from across the city.

Unlike large rural slave plantations, where slaves lived with their families in

SLAVE HOUSING IN NEW YORK'S COUNTRYSIDE

While the slave plantation is commonly identified with the American South, similar agricultural units also dotted portions of New York's countryside, especially in areas originally settled by the Dutch. Among New York's largest slave masters was Lewis Morris who, at the time of his death in 1691, worked sixty slaves at his Bronx estate. Frederick Philipse—master of Philipsburg Manor in Westchester County—owned thirty slaves, and Robert Livingston operated his Rensselaer Manor near Albany with forty-four enslaved black men and women. In a memoir penned in 1808, Anne MacVikar Grant rendered an account of New York plantation life marked by the genteel tone of the "moonlight and magnolia" imagery most often associated with plantation life in antebellum Georgia and Mississippi. Recalling a period in the middle years of the eighteenth century when she frequently visited "The Flatts," the plantation of Colonel Philip Pieterse Schuyler outside of Albany, she wrote: "In summer negroes inhabited slight outer kitchens in which food was dressed for the family. Those who wrought in the fields often had their simple dinner cooked without and ate it under the shade of a great tree." Her passing reference to "slight outer kitchens" describes the slave cabins that Schuyler located along a roughly two-mile

expanse of the Hudson River shoreline. None of these structures stand today, but they doubtless resembled a surviving one-room kitchen that stood just behind the Schuyler house (Fig. 1). The slave cabin, essentially a small box fitted with a door, window, and fireplace meant to shelter captive workers, was as much a feature of New York's landscape as it was of the South's.

A fully intact example of New York slave quarters still overlooks the Mohawk River near the small town of Rotterdam Junction just a few miles to the west of Schenectady. Part of the homestead of the Mabee family, the building stands in front of a modest-sized farmhouse and slightly to one side so that the two structures have an L-shaped arrangement (Fig. 2). The house is rectangular in plan and oriented with its narrower side facing forward. Given that only a door pierces the front wall, the building has the austere, functional appearance of a toolshed—and slave quarters were exactly that: containers for human chattel.

A single diminutive slave house, often standing just to the side of an owner's residence, commonly marked slaveholding farms throughout the Hudson Valley. The Mabees located their slave quarter in a manner that suggested its inferiority as well as the inferiority of the black men and women who would reside in it. While it is unclear who Mabee housed in his quarter when he first acquired his estate, in 1755 his son Jacob owned five slaves. Jacob's son Cornelis, who inherited the farm, also held slaves. The pattern of slave ownership and the placement of the slave residence at the Mabee farm was typical of early Dutch settlements. Other representative examples in New York can seen at the Hendrick I. Lott House in Brooklyn and the Caleb Smith House in Commack, and in New Jersey, at the Captain John Huyler Homestead in Cresskill and the Nicolas Haring House in Rockleigh.

—*John Michael Vlach*

D.F. Schroeder, north elevation showing slave kitchen at "The Flatts," General Philip Schuyler House, Albany, New York, 1984.
HISTORIC AMERICAN BUILDINGS SURVEY, LIBRARY OF CONGRESS

Nelson E. Baldwin, view of the Mabee House, Rotterdam Junction, New York, 1936. Note that the slave quarter is the small structure on the left.
HISTORIC AMERICAN BUILDINGS SURVEY, LIBRARY OF CONGRESS

An Account of Trade on The Cost of Affricah For The
Livingston Esq.r And Sons Merchants In New York —
1748/9   gallons Rum

| Jan.ry 18 | To 13 gallons Rum | 13 | | 13 | | |

At D.o 19 — Bartered With William Addo black Man
To 5 Hhds Rum 98 gallons 4/8 . . . . ℔ 78:2   98
To 2 ℔ tobaco 1 . . . . ℔ 2
To ½ barrel of beef . . . . ℔ 6
To 18 ℔ of Shugar @ 6 . . . . ℔ 3
To 5 Chese 12 . . . . ℔ 2
To 2 hundred of bread . . . . ℔ 3
To 10 ℔ oynons . . . . ℔ 1
                                   Bars 95:2
                                                    5 15 2

At D.o 20 — Bartered With Robert Melvil
To 2 Cask bread 4:3:2 Neat @ 6 . . . . ℔ 28:0:7½
To 2 hhd tobaco 5½0 Neat @ 6 . . . . ℔ 33:1:8   211
To 2 Hhds Rum 213 gallons @ 3/9 . . . . ℔ 158:1
To 5 Firkin Butter . . . . ℔ 12
To 20 ℔ of oynons . . . . ℔ 2
                                   283:13:3½
                                                    17 11 3 3½

At D.o 20 — Bartered With Cap.t John Wade
To 5 Hhds Rum 112 gallons @ 3/9 . . . . ℔ 84   112
To 70 ℔ of oynons . . . . ℔ 7
To 18 ℔ of tobaco @ 6 . . . . ℔ 3
To 2 hundred bread . . . . ℔ 3
                                        97
                                                    6 1

At D.o 21 — Bartered With Clifford And Ourd
To 5 Hhds Rum 2½ gall @ 3/9 . . . . ℔ 83:2:6   110
To 2 hundred of bread . . . . ℔ 6
To 5 Firkin Butter . . . . ℔ 12
To 10 gall West India Rum . . . . ℔ 10   10
To 20 ℔ oynons . . . . ℔ 2
                                   112:2:6
                                                    6 14 2 6

| | Brought Forard gallons Rum | 554 | | | | |

Sloope Rhode Island Peter James Master & Philip
Commencing At Sortleon Jan.ry 18 1748/9

| Jan.ry 18 | By King Tom Custom for wood & warter | | | 13 | | |

D.o 19 — By 31 ℔ of brass Pans @ 2/4 . . . . ℔ 12:2
By 2 Cutlass . . . . ℔ 2
By 1 piece Nickenee . . . . ℔ 6
By 2 peices blew baft . . . . ℔ 12
By 2 Trading guns . . . . ℔ 8
By 2 muskets . . . . ℔ 10
By 2 Buckiear . . . . ℔ 12
By 3 Cags Powder @ 3/ . . . . ℔ 9
By 3 Cags of D.o 3/ . . . . ℔ 12:2:6
By 2 peices blew and white Calico . . . . ℔
                                        95:4:6   5 15 4 6

D.o 20 — By A Woman Slave N.o 1 @ ℔ 60
By 6 peices blew & white Calicos @ 6 . . . . ℔ 36
By 3 peices head & white D.o . . . . ℔ 18
By 2 peices Cotton N.s @ 12 . . . . ℔ 24
By 3 peices Patne Chinch @ 6 . . . . ℔ 18
By 1 peice of blew baft . . . . ℔ 6
By 24 ℔ of beads @ 3/4 . . . . ℔ 8
By 3 Kittels 28 ℔ @ 8 6/ . . . . ℔ 9:1:8
By 2 Iron bars . . . . ℔ 10
By 2 Dozen hatts @ 8/ . . . . ℔ 16
By 38½ Cures @ 2/4 . . . . ℔ 15:1:8
By 6 trading guns @ 4 . . . . ℔ 24
By 13 Cutlass . . . . ℔ 9
By 33 ℔ brass Pans @ 2/4 . . . . ℔ 12:1:8
By 1 Teeth 48 ℔ . . . . ℔
                                        283   17 11

D.o 20 — By 6 Peues of blew & white Calicos . . . . ℔ 36
By 1 Peice Patne Chinch . . . . ℔ 6
By 1 musdepot . . . . ℔ 8
By 1 musquespot . . . . ℔ 8
By 75 ℔ Pewter basons @ 3/6 . . . . ℔ 23
By 16 hatts @ 8/ D.o . . . . ℔ 10:0:4
By 20 ℔ of Screwlees at 6/ . . . . ℔ 3:1:8
                                        97   6 1

D.o 21 — By 2 Slaves one Boy one gearl N.o 2:3 @ ℔ 84
By 2 Cags Powder @ 7 . . . . ℔
By 6 Cutlass . . . . ℔ 4
By 50 ℔ brass pans @ 2/4 . . . . ℔ 4
By 1 Buckiear . . . . ℔ 6
                                        112   6 14

slave quarters well apart from whites, New York City slaves slept in the attics and cellars of their owners' houses, or in "Negro kitchens," and worked all day alongside whites as servants, skilled artisans, and day laborers. In New York, whites and blacks lived, literally, on top of one another. If slaves lacked separate quarters, they did have different hours: slaves woke up earlier than anyone else (servants woke up next), and stayed up later (servants went to bed just before them). And, since the very first and the very last chore slaves did every day was fetching water, which meant meeting friends and neighbors at water pumps scattered across the city, they heard the news first.[24]

While New York slaves were forced to live and work alongside whites, they sought out other black people for news, companionship, and love, which they found all over the city. In the small, crowded, bustling town that was colonial New York City, most people spent a good deal of time walking the streets, conducting errands, and picking up bits of news. But enslaved people, especially men, walked greater distances, conducted more errands, and picked up news earlier in the morning and later at night. Consider this walk described by a slave named Pedro in 1741: "last Fall he went out one Sunday Morning with Mrs. *Carpenter*'s Negro *Albany*; . . . as they went along the Broad-Way, they met with Mr. Slydall's *Jack*, who was going to *Comfort's* for Tea-Water; . . . at the Market near Mr. *DeLancey*'s House they met two other Negroes; and . . . *Albany* asked them all to go down to *Hughson's* and drink with them."[25] Pedro lived in the East Ward with his owner, the Dutch merchant Peter DePeyester. Albany probably lived near the Old Slip Market, a meat market at the bottom of Smith Street, because his owner, the butcher Elizabeth Carpenter, rented a stall there (the Old Slip was once known as the "Great Flesh Market"). The DeLancey house, home of supreme court Chief Justice James DeLancey, was on Broadway between Little Queen and Little Stone Streets, just south of the Broadway Market, a forty-two- by twenty-five-foot market in the middle of Broadway, at Crown Street. If Pedro began his trip in the East Ward, he would have had to walk south down Queen Street or Little Dock Street to meet Albany near Carpenter's house; north up Smith Street to Wall Street, which he would have followed for three blocks, past the sugar refinery, past City Hall to Broadway, and from there northeast to the Broadway Market, to meet "two other Negroes"; and west to the river, down Crown or Cortlandt Street, which would put him and his three friends at the water pump in front of the Dutch cooper Gerardus Comfort's house, on the North (now Hudson) River, next door to the tavern of a cobbler named John Hughson—and that's without accounting for where they picked up Jack (Sleydall), whose residence is unknown.

Pedro's walk was an ordinary one, the kind of walk he took every day. Yet, as ordinary as that walk was, it violated several laws, including a 1730 act stipulating that "it shall not hereafter be lawful for above three Slaves to meet together att any other time, nor att any other place, than when it shall happen they meet in some servile Imploym't for their Master's or Mistress's proffitt, and by their Master or Mistress consent, upon penalty of being whipt upon the naked back, at discretion of any Justice of the peace, not exceeding fforty Lashes." Of Pedro and his three companions, only Jack (Sleydall) was "in some servile Implym't": fetching water. If the sun was not yet up when Pedro left his house, and if he was not carrying "A Lanthorn and lighted Candle in itt so as the light thereof may be plainly seen," he was guilty of violating a municipal law prohibiting slaves from being in the streets in the dark without express permission. And if, along the way, Pedro and his friends laughed too loudly, or hollered, or gambled for money, they would have violated another municipal law, passed in 1731, charging that "No Negro, Mulatto or Indian slaves, above the Number of three, do Assemble or meet together on the Lords Day Called Sunday, and Sport, Play or make any Noise or Disturbance, or at any Other time at any place from their Masters service, within this City." If any of them was riding a horse, and rode it "Swiftly, Hastily, Precipately or disorderly, and Otherwise than softly Orderly Patiently without Pasing Swiftly, Trotting fast or Galloping," he would have been guilty of breaking a city law "for Punishing Slaves who Shall Ride Disorderly through the Streets." And if, at the Old Slip or Broadway Market, they had tried to buy or sell fruit, they would have broken a law, passed in August 1740, "to Prohibit Negroes and Other Slaves Vending Indian Corn Peaches or any other Fruit within this City."[26]

The body of legislation that constituted New York's "Negro Law" stands as a

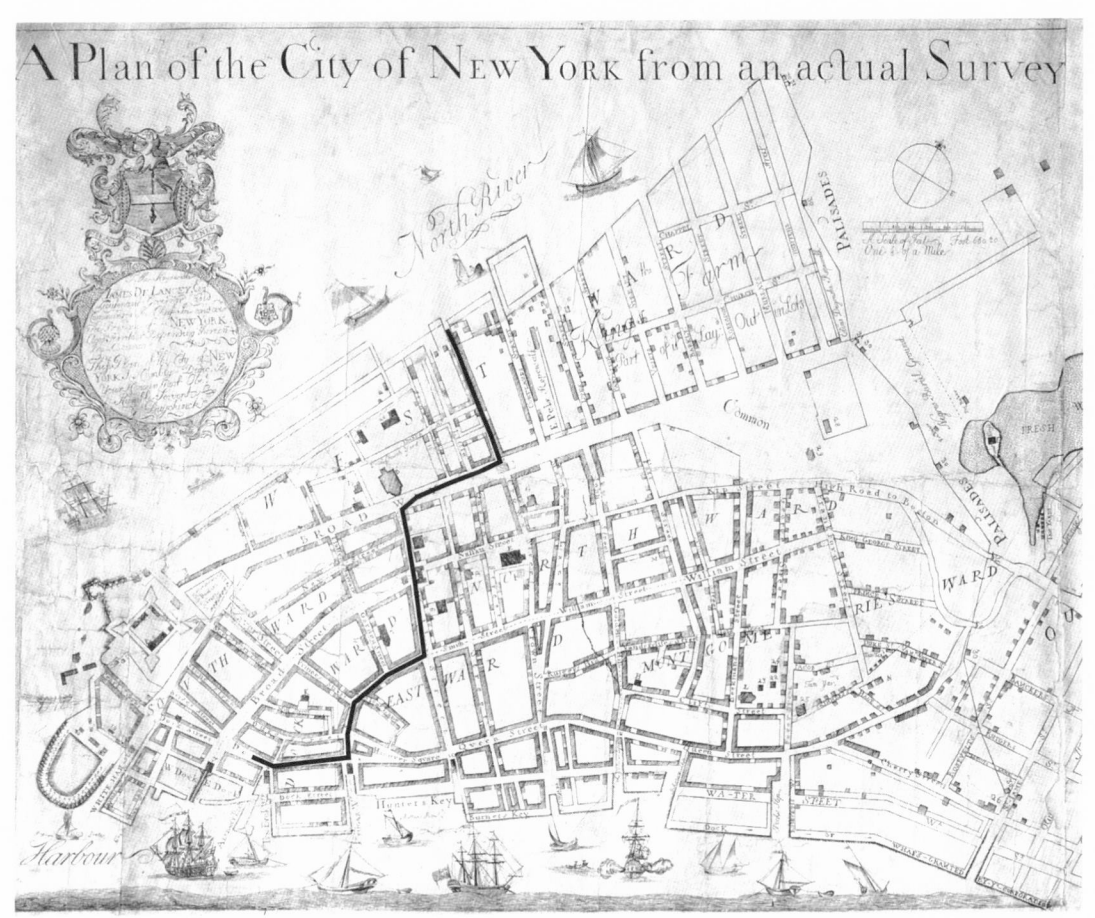

Map of Pedro's walk overlaid on Maerschlack
Plan of the City of New York, 1754.

brutal testament to the difficulty of enslaving human beings, especially in cities. All these laws were passed because slaves *did* walk through the city at night, even without lanterns or candles, just as they met together and gambled and sold fruit and galloped on horseback. New York's slave codes were almost entirely concerned with curtailing the ability of enslaved people to move at will and to gather, for fear, above all, that they might decide that slavery was not to be borne and one way to end it would be to burn the city down. So much anti-conspiracy legislation was passed during the first half-century of English rule that in 1730 Governor John Montgomerie recommended that all such acts be replaced with a simpler law, on the grounds that it would be better if magistrates had "a plain rule to walk by." Under the terms of Montgomerie's act, which consolidated provincial slave codes passed in 1702, 1708, and 1712, it was not only illegal for slaves to have or use "any gun Pistoll sword Club or any other Kind of Weapon"; it was also illegal for more than three slaves to meet anywhere, anytime, unless it was "in some servile imployment for their Master or Mistress." [27]

New York's slave code was not necessarily an overreaction to the possibility of violent revolt. On March 25, 1712, a group of New York slaves gathered at night to plan a rebellion. Sucking the blood of one another's hands, they pledged to a plot to destroy the city and murder every white person. On the night of April 6, 1712, between twenty-five and fifty black men and women, many of them Akan-speaking "Coromantees," met at midnight, carrying guns, swords, knives, and hatchets. Cuffee and John, owned by a baker named Peter Vantilborough, set fire to Vantilborough's outhouse in the East Ward. When whites raced to the scene, "the slaves fired and killed them." Adrian Hoghlandt's slave Robin stabbed him in the back. Nicholas Roosevelt's slave Tom shot Andries Beekman in the chest. Peter the Porter, owned by Andries Marschalck, killed young Joris Marschalck with a dagger blow to his breast. Before the night ended, nine whites had been killed and six more wounded. Governor Robert Hunter commanded the cannon at Fort George be fired to alarm the city and "order'd a detachment from the fort under a proper officer to march against them, but the slaves made their retreat into the woods, by the favour of the night." The next day, Hunter ordered the New York and Westchester militias to "drive the Island." Sweeping Manhattan, the troops captured nearly all of the rebels, although a handful, six men, had sufficient time and fortitude to kill themselves before the soldiers found them. "Had it not been for the Garrison there," most New Yorkers believed, the city "would have been reduced to ashes, and the greatest part of the inhabitants murdered."[28]

City magistrates prosecuted and punished slaves with ferocity. More than seventy enslaved men and women were eventually taken into custody, and forty-three were brought to trial by jury. Eighteen were acquitted and discharged. Twenty-five were convicted, of whom twenty were hanged and three burned at the stake, one roasted in slow torment for eight hours. Another man was broken on the wheel. One of the convicted, a pregnant woman, had her execution postponed. But after giving birth, she, too, met her death.

Governor Hunter was appalled by both the nature and the number of the executions in 1712. "I am informed that in the West Indies where their laws against their slaves are most severe, that in case of a conspiracy in which many are engaged a few only are executed for an example," he wrote to the Lords of Trade in London, complaining that "In this case 21 are executed." Hunter fought hard against the remaining prosecutions and was able to reprieve five men, including two "Spanish Negroes," whom he considered not only unjustly convicted but also unjustly enslaved. Yet, despite Hunter's objections, within months of the 1712 revolt, the New York Assembly passed "An Act for preventing Suppressing and punishing the Conspiracy and Insurrection of Negroes and other Slaves." It allowed slave owners "to punish their Slaves for their Crimes and Offences at Discretion, not extending to Life or Member," while mandating that any slave convicted of murder, rape, arson, or assault would "suffer the pains of Death in such manner and with such circum-stances as the aggravation or enormity of their Crimes . . . shall merit and

Portrait of William Walton.

SLAVES AND FREE BLACKS NAMED IN THE 1712 REVOLT

In 1712, New York slaves revolted, killing nine white men and wounding seven more. Reprisals were swift and fierce, as the militia rounded up hundreds of slaves. Eventually, the following men and women were implicated. Their fates are noted below. As was customary, slave owners were compensated for lost property.

—Jill Lepore

Name	Owner	Fate	Name	Owner	Fate
Abigail	Gysbert Vaninburgh	hanged*	Mingo	John Barberie	hanged
Amba	Adolphus Phillipse	discharged	Peter the Doctor	(free)	discharged
Ambrose	Isaac Gouverneur	discharged	Peter the Porter	(unknown)	not indicted
Aruba	Henry Courteen	discharged	Quacko	Joost Lynsen	not indicted
Ben	Cornelia Schuyler	discharged	Quacko	Abraham Provoost	burned
Bonny	Gilbert Ash	discharged	Quacko	Walter Thong	hanged
Caesar	Peter Morin	hanged	Quack	Rip Van Dam	hanged
Caesar	Cornelia Van Clyff Norwood	hanged	Quash	Joseph Latham	discharged
Claus	Allan Jarrett	broken on the wheel	Quash	Rip Van Dam	hanged
Cuffee	Peter Vantilborough	discharged	Robin	Adrian Hoghlandt	hung in chains alive
Cuffee	William Walton	reprieved by Hunter	Rodriguo	Robert Darkins	discharged
Dick	Harmanus Burger	discharged	Sam	Peter Fauconnier	hanged
Dick	Thomas Stoutenburgh	discharged	Sarah	Stophell Pels	hanged*
Furnis	Ruth Sheppard	burned	Titus	Richard Ray	hanged
George	Jacob Regnier	discharged	Toby	John Cure	hanged
Hannibal	Andrew Stuckey	hanged	Tom	John Dehonneur	hanged
Hosea	Mary Wenham	reprieved by Hunter	Tom	Helena Dekey	discharged
Jack	John Crooke	not indicted	Tom	David Lyell	hanged
Jarrett	Samuel Phillips	not indicted	Tom	Jacob Regnier	discharged
John	Peter Vantilborough	reprieved by Hunter	Tom	Nicholas Roosevelt	burned slowly
John Harris	(unknown)	discharged	Tom	Rip Van Dam	reprieved by Hunter
Jurorico	Rodrigo Pacheco	discharged	Tom	Jacobus Vaarck	not indicted
Kitto	Isaac Gouverneur	hanged			
Lilly	John Crooke	discharged			
Mars	Jacob Regnier	reprieved by Hunter			

*Either Sarah or Abigail was pregnant, and her sentence suspended until after giving birth.

require." The act also greatly restricted the city's tiny population of free blacks ("an Idle slothfull people") by prohibiting them from owning "any Houses, Lands, Tenements or Hereditaments," and requiring any owner manumitting a slave to pay two hundred pounds security to the government and a twenty-pound annuity to the freed slave.[29] Such a sizable financial penalty made manumission effectively impossible. Although the manumission decree was repealed in 1717, New York slave owners remained reluctant to free their slaves, and the free black community in the city—now over 10 percent of the black population—continued to decline through the period of English rule.[30]

Writing again to the Lords of Trade, Governor Hunter apologized for the brutality of the 1712 "Negro Act": even after the governor's council reduced its harshness, Hunter worried that "your Lordships will still think [it] too severe, but after the late barbarous attempt of some of their slaves nothing less could please the people." Hunter had cause to worry that his superiors would find the law "too severe." As early as 1686, authorities in London had been astonished at the viciousness of New York's slave codes. That year, the Duke of York instructed the governor to pass "a Law for the Restraining of Inhuman Severitys which by all masters or overseers may bee used toward their Christian servants, or slaves, wherein provision is to be made that ye wilful killing of Indians & Negros may bee punished with death, And that a fit penalty bee imposed for the maiming of them." No such law was ever passed. And Hunter, who served as the governor of both New York and New Jersey, was well aware that a 1704 New Jersey Act for Regulating Negro Indians and Mulato Slaves, modeled after New York's 1702 Act for Regulateing of Slaves, was so brutal (among other things, it mandated castrating black men convicted of raping or fornicating with white women) that the Queen overruled it five years later, on the grounds that "the Punishment to be inflicted on Negroes &c is such as never was allowed by or known in the Laws of this Kingdom."[31]

Those enslaved and free black New Yorkers who led the revolt of 1712 had two things in common: many were Akan, and many had complained about "hard usage" from their masters. But white New Yorkers failed to inquire into the sources of slave discontent. Instead, they blamed the revolt on a missionary

A JOURNAL

OF THE PROCEEDINGS

In the Detection of the

CONSPIRACY

Formed by some White People, in conjunction with Negro and other Slaves, for burning the City of NEW-YORK in AMERICA and murdering the Inhabitants.

Which conspiracy was partly put in execution, by burning his Majesty's house in fort George, within the said city, on Wednesday the 18th of *March*, 1741, and setting fire to several dwelling and other houses there, within a few days succeeding. And by another attempt made in prosecution of the same infernal scheme, by putting fire between two other dwelling-houses within the said city, on the 15th day of *February*, 1742; which was accidentally and timely discovered and extinguished.

CONTAINING,

I. A narrative of the trials, condemnations, executions, and behaviour of the several criminals, at the gallows and stake, with their speeches and confessions; with notes, observations and reflections occasionally interspersed throughout the whole.

II. An appendix, wherein is set forth some additional evidence concerning the said conspiracy and conspirators, which has come to light since their trials and executions.

III. Lists of the several persons (whites and blacks) committed on account of the conspiracy; and of the several criminals executed; and of those transported, with the places whereto.

By the Recorder of the City of NEW-YORK.

Quid facient Domini, audent cum talia Fures? Virg. Ecl.

Printed at NEW-YORK:

LONDON, Reprinted and Sold by JOHN CLARKE under the Royal Exchange, Cornhill. MDCCXLVII.

Title page of Daniel Horsmanden's *Journal of the Proceedings* of the slave revolt.

named Elias Neau, who had been attempting to convert the city's slaves to Christianity for nearly a decade. "Mr Neau durst hardly appear [in public]," one New Yorker wrote, for "his School was blaimed as the main Occasion" of the rebellion.[32]

In 1699, Neau began corresponding with Anglican evangelical societies, developing a plan to open "a Catechising School for the Slaves at *New-York.*" In 1703, the London-based Society for the Propagation of the Gospel offered Neau an annual salary of £50 to teach slaves if he would affiliate with the city's Anglican church, Trinity. Neau agreed and founded the school the following year.[33] In the beginning, a small group of slaves met at night in the attic of his house. "They were dull and sleepy, and remembered they must rise early the next Day, to their Labour." Yet Neau eventually boasted a handful of acolytes who had learned to read the Bible, recite catechisms from memory, and sing from psalm books. The number of students varied between fifteen and twenty-five a year, and some, Neau admitted, "came only for the books" and stayed away when his bookshelf was empty. Perhaps they simply could not afford to be absent from their owners' houses long enough to hear Neau's lessons. But they may have valued literacy more than Christianity, for writing a forged pass was one possible route to escape (10 percent of runaway slaves were literate).

Neau was virtually alone in his efforts to teach and convert slaves. New York slave owners believed that converting slaves to Christianity

ELIAS NEAU

Elias Neau, a Huguenot, settled in New York City in 1690 after fleeing violent persecution in Catholic France in 1679. On a business trip to London in 1692, he was captured by French privateers and sentenced to serve as a galley slave; later he was jailed on Iff, the infamous island off the coast of Marseilles. He was released in 1698, by which time he was a well-known Protestant martyr; in the 1690s, his letters from prison—mystical writings and hymns embracing the utility of despair—were published in Boston, New York, London, and Rotterdam. Neau knew bondage. When Neau returned to New York in 1699, he turned his attention to the spiritual condition of the city's slaves. Although a member of the city's French Huguenot church, Neau began corresponding with Anglican evangelical societies, developing a plan to convert New York's slaves. In 1703, the London-based Society for the Propagation of the Gospel offered Neau an annual salary of £50 to teach slaves, if he would affiliate with the city's Anglican church, Trinity. Neau agreed, and founded the school the following year.

—Jill Lepore

would liberate them. English laws stipulated that "No Christian shall be kept in Bondslavery villenage or Captivity." The possibility that conversion would mean freedom made slave owners nervous enough that in 1674 a clarification was added: "This law shall not set at liberty any Negro or Indian Slave, who shall have turned Christian after they had been bought by a person." However, most masters continued to fear that Christianity would lead to freedom, and kept their slaves away from Neau's school.[34]

As it turned out, only two of Neau's students were convicted of participating in the 1712 revolt, and Neau's school survived the scandal. Between 1704 and 1714, Neau instructed 134 blacks and baptized 54 of his pupils. In the year 1719 alone, he catechized 85, and baptized 31.[35] After Neau died in 1722, he was succeeded intermittently by a series of indifferent schoolmasters. Their work, however, was undoubtedly aided, in 1727, by the publication of the bishop of London's "Letter to the Masters and Mistresses of Families in the English Plantations abroad; Exhorting them to encourage and promote the Instruction of their Negroes in the Christian Faith." This pamphlet, widely distributed in New York and throughout the colonies, testified both to slave owners' considerable and continued unwillingness to convert their slaves and to "how small a Progress has been made . . . towards the delivering of those poor Creatures from the Pagan Darkness." The bishop sought to reassure jittery slave owners that baptism was no liberator: "Christianity and the embracing of the Gospel, does not make the least Alteration in Civil Property," he proclaimed.[36]

For a brief time in the 1730s, New Yorkers grudgingly agreed to send a handful of their slaves to be educated by Richard Charlton, minister of the Society for the Propagation of the Gospel. But by 1740, at the height of the Great Awakening, slave conversions had again become threatening to slave owners. In 1740 and 1741, the eighteenth century's most popular evangelical, Englishman George Whitefield, visited New York and preached to five or six thousand of "all sorts of People," both black and white.[37] Although Whitefield supported slavery, an essay he published in 1740 contained a more radical proposition—a statement that many slave owners read as a defense of slave rebellion: "Considering what Usage they commonly meet with, I have wondered, that we have not more Instances of Self-Murder among the Negroes, or that they have not more frequently rose up in Arms against their Owners . . . And tho' I heartily pray God they may never be permitted to get the upper Hand; yet should such a Thing be permitted by Providence, all good Men must acknowledge the Judgment would be just."[38] When an alleged slave conspiracy took place in New York in 1741, just months after Whitefield's visit to the city, Charlton and other New Yorkers came to blame Whitefield for inspiring it.[39]

The 1741 slave conspiracy for which Richard Charlton blamed George Whitefield was a central event in the history of slavery in New York City. After an unusually cold winter, ten fires blazed in the city over three short weeks in March and April. The first fire nearly destroyed Fort George. In early April, four fires erupted in a single day. A grand jury called by the supreme court quickly concluded that the fires were the work of black arsonists, acting as part of a vast conspiracy that seemed to involve just about every slave in the city. More than one hundred black men and a handful of black women and white people were soon arrested and thrown into jail in the basement of City Hall.

Convicted of conspiring to burn New York City and murder its inhabitants, thirteen Africans were burned at the stake in the spring and summer of 1741; seventeen more were hanged—two of their dead bodies chained to posts on a hill near the Negroes Burial Ground, as David Grim so powerfully remembered. Seventy others were sold into yet more miserable, bone-crushing slavery in the Caribbean. Four whites, the alleged ringleaders of the plot, were hanged, one in chains.

Even before the trials ended, critics accused New Yorkers of imagining a plot that had never existed. In July of that summer, an anonymous New Englander wrote a letter to Cadwallader Colden: "I am a stranger to you & to New York," he began, humbly. But he had heard of "the bloody Tragedy" afflicting the city. "I observe in one of the Boston News letters," the New Englander lamented, "that 5 Negros were executed in one day at the Gallows, a favour indeed, for one next day was burnt at the stake." This "puts me in mind of our New England Witchcraft in the year 1692," the New Englander wrote,

"Which if I don't mistake New York justly reproached us for, & mockt at our Credulity about."[40]

In truth, the 1741 New York conspiracy trials and the 1692 Salem witchcraft trials have much in common—except that what happened in New York was worse. Over one hundred and fifty accused witches were arrested in Salem, compared to nearly two hundred conspirators named in New York. But in Salem, only nineteen people were executed (four more died in jail), and, contrary to popular opinion, none were burned at the stake. "Excuse me & don't be offended," the man from Massachusetts wrote, blanched with horror, "if out of Friendship to my poor Countrymen & compassion to the Negros (who are flesh & blood as well as we & ought to be treated with Humanity) I intreat you not to go on to Massacre & destroy your own Estates by making Bonfires of the Negros."

What makes Salem and New York look so similar are not just the executions but the confessions. Crowded into a makeshift jail in the basement of City Hall, probably beaten, and interrogated before harassing, heckling New Yorkers, two whites and an astonishing eighty-one blacks confessed to conspiring to destroy the city. But such confessions, the opinionated New Englander told his New York correspondent, were no better than those so painfully extracted from Salem's witches, and "[were] not worth a Straw; for many times they are obtain'd by foul means, by force or torment, by Surprise, by flattery, by Distraction, by Discontent with their circumstances. . . or in hopes of a longer time to live, or to dy an easier death."[41] Dubious confessions, suspicious legal procedures, and bloodthirsty spectators: the events of 1741 reminded people in Massachusetts Bay of nothing so much as their own notorious trials. "Your present case, & ours heretofore," the New Englander reflected, "are much the same," and he hoped that the trials might swiftly end, "the sooner the better, lest all the poor People of the Government perish in the merciless flames of an Imaginary Plot."

Was the plot imaginary? This much, at least, seems clear: given the history of the city's slave codes, and the confessions of slaves themselves, much evidence points to a plot hatched on street corners and in markets, the forging of an Akan-influenced brotherhood—much like that formed in 1712—and a political order that encouraged individual acts of vengeance, of cursing whites and setting fires, skirmishes in the daily, unwinnable war of slavery. To the extent that men like Cato and Ben and Quash talked about freedom, this, perhaps, was the freedom they meant: the freedom to "take a Walk after Church-out," to dance at a frolic, to spend the night with one's wife, to play dice with one's mates. Dutch merchant Abraham Lefferts's slave Pompey said his fellow conspirators promised him that if they set their masters' houses on fire, "they would be all *Free*, and be free from Trouble."[42]

If Supreme Court Justice Daniel Horsmanden found this explanation compelling, he didn't find it sufficient. Instead, his *Journal* of the proceedings described a far more complicated plot, led by an alleged white priest named John Ury and a white tavern keeper named John Hughson. Horsmanden was unwilling to believe that blacks could have devised the plot themselves. But precious little evidence supports the Ury-Hughson story.[43] And what happened after 1741 supports the story told by the slaves themselves: they decided to set fires in an effort to seek vengeance for constraints on their mobility in the city, for the 1741 conspiracy trials led to the passage of new measures designed to hinder slaves' mobility in the city—the expansion of the night watch and a restriction on slaves fetching water from any but the nearest pump in their neighborhood. Nonetheless, slaves' "too great liberty" remained largely intact. Slaves continued to gather together and, occasionally, to be discovered doing so. In 1755, the New York Assembly found it necessary to pass a law stating, "It is well-known that . . . the negroes in this city of New York . . . have assembled . . . in Publick and Private . . . [and] have uttered very insolent Expressions and in other ways misbehaved themselves." But the following year, a New York newspaper reported that "nine of the Ethiopian Breed (to wit, Negroes), belonging to this city, have been apprehended, committed, try'd and whipt at the whipping post for assembling and meeting together in an Illegal manner, on Sunday."[44]

By far the most significant legacy of 1741 was New York slave merchants' decision to turn to Africa for the importation of slaves. Before 1741, fewer than one third of the city's slave imports came from Africa, and almost three quarters

1741

What happened in New York in 1741 is an extraordinarily complex story, one deserving at least as much scholarly attention—and as many competing interpretations—as the Salem witchcraft trials of 1692. While some historians have dismissed any possibility that slaves actually conspired to overthrow the system of chattel bondage or even to gain their freedom, others have argued that the events of 1741 were part of an Atlantic rebellion of a mixed-race proletariat.

Supreme Court Justice Daniel Horsmanden intended his 1744 *Journal of the Proceedings in the Detection of the Conspiracy formed by Some White People, in Conjunction with Negro and other Slaves, for Burning the City of New-York in America, and Murdering the Inhabitants* to be a definitive account of the conspiracy and the trials, and hoped that it would convince doubters that a conspiracy truly existed. But ironically, Horsmanden's own prejudices have convinced many historians that the confessions in his *Journal* are "not worth a straw"—and that the conspiracy was merely the product of hysteria. Horsmanden was unwilling to believe that black men and women could have devised the plot themsleves, and alleged that a white priest named John Ury and a white tavern keeper named John Hughson were the ringleaders of the plot. But precious little evidence supports this story.

Today, historians use Horsmanden's *Journal* for its rich evidence of the daily lives of slaves, while continuing to debate the extent—and even the existence—of the 1741 slave plot.   —*Jill Lepore*

from the Caribbean. After 1741, these numbers were exactly reversed. Evidently, New York merchants and slave owners hoped that African slaves would be more tractable, less able to communicate with one another and with city blacks, and less able to organize a revolt.

Meanwhile, as the anonymous letter from New England condemning the 1741 executions reveals, opposition to the institution of slavery was growing in both England and the colonies. In 1700, Samuel Sewall of Boston argued that "Ethiopians, as black as they are," are "brethren and sisters of the last Adam, and the offspring of God." Elsewhere, such views were expressed most often by Quakers as part of an emerging antislavery movement. The London Yearly Meeting of Quakers condemned slave trading as early as 1727. Two years later, Benjamin Franklin printed a tract by Quaker Ralph Sandiford titled *A Brief Examination of the Practice of the Times*, in which Sandiford called slavery "the most arbitrary and tyrannical oppression that hell has invented on this globe." In 1738, Franklin published a call by another Philadelphian, Benjamin Lay, addressed to "All

Slave-Keepers, That keep the Innocent in Bondage." Lay, an ascetic who lived in a cave, railed against slavery at Quaker meetings throughout the middle colonies. In addition, in 1741, Londoner John Bell warned Quaker slave owners in the colonies that the "Vials" of God's "Wrath shall be poured forth upon the Unmerciful, the cruel Oppressors, and all the Workers of Iniquity." Five years later, colonial Quaker John Woolman, in his essay "Some Considerations on the Keeping of Negroes," reminded readers "that all nations are of one blood (Gen. 3:20)." Like Bell and the revivalist George Whitefield, Woolman also warned of God's vengeance: "Many slaves on this continent are oppressed, and their cries have reached the ears of the Most High! Such is the purity and certainty of his judgments that he cannot be partial in our favour. . . . Should we now . . . neglect to do our duty . . . , it may be that terrible things in righteousness God may answer us."[45]

By the decade before the American Revolution, antislavery sentiment was beginning to be openly expressed in New York. In 1760, a writer in the *New York Weekly Post-Boy* described slaves as "poor pagans whom Christians have thought fit to consider cattle."[46] Meanwhile, as white colonists' growing resistance to English rule itself centered on cherished notions of political liberty, the "too great liberty" they believed they accorded their own slaves began to take on another cast.

Chapter 3

LIBERTY AND CONSTRAINT: THE LIMITS OF REVOLUTION

———————◆———————

GRAHAM RUSSELL GAO HODGES

Francois Xavier Habermann, *La Destruction de la Statue Royale a Nouvelle Yorck*, 1776. Engraving.

ON AUGUST 16, 1781, Murphy Stiel, a sergeant in the Black Pioneers, a British paramilitary group based in New York City, had a remarkable dream. Stiel was sleeping in the Pioneers' barracks on Water Street when he heard "a Voice like a Man's but saw no body." The voice commanded Stiel to deliver a message to Sir Henry Clinton, commander in chief of the British forces, that he should order General George Washington to surrender "himself and his Troops to the Kings Army." Failure to do so would mean God's wrath would fall upon the Americans. Stiel warned that all the "Blacks in America would rise up against Washington's forces. . . . For . . . the Lord would be on their side." Stiel had been fighting with the British since he had escaped from North Carolina in 1776 to join the Black Pioneers. His dream suggests the powerful impact of the American Revolution on African Americans in New York City. The war drew together the secular goals of African Americans in the revolutionary conflict with the Christian spirituality that was transforming black life at the end of the eighteenth century. In an intensely hierarchical world, a black soldier presumed to order the British commander in chief and his Patriot counterpart to lay down their arms or face an angry God. Stiel's dream and its larger message revealed a new assertiveness that African Americans gained as the Revolution transformed American society and black people with it.[1]

This new confidence emerged in a people weighed down by centuries-old servitude. African Americans had long constituted the core workforce in New York City and its hinterland. In 1771 there were roughly twenty-one thousand African Americans in the region around New York City, virtually all enslaved—and many of them were the children and grandchildren of slaves. Suddenly, their world changed. They found their home torn apart by intense partisanship and then open warfare, as New York became "the cockpit of the revolution."

The conflict also divided black New Yorkers politically. At the start of the war, some sympathized with the Patriots, although most sided with the king. Perhaps the greatest number, however, cared little about either cause and experienced the conflict on the sidelines as armies marched through the urban neighborhoods, villages, and farms where they lived. Yet, whatever their sympathies, the war touched all, for the conflict would propel thousands of black New Yorkers to freedom. The census of 1790 revealed that of 19,500 African Americans living in New York City and nine surrounding counties in New York State and New Jersey, some 3,700, or fully 17 percent, had gained their freedom. This surge of liberty came from a combination of white egalitarianism spawned by revolutionary ideology, changing religious perceptions of slavery, and—most important—the efforts of African Americans themselves. Amid the war and in its aftermath, black men and women secured freedom through military service, purchased themselves and their loved ones, and claimed freedom by running away. Although slavery remained deeply entrenched in New York and its environs, liberty gained ground. At war's end, black people in New York had profoundly reshaped their lives.[2]

Even before the war began, black New Yorkers—free and slave—had become deeply enmeshed in the growing crisis between the American colonies and their British overlords. Black New Yorkers lacked arms and political voice. They had no tradition of petitioning either legislatures or courts, as did their counterparts in Boston and Philadelphia. Eighteenth-century laws constrained New York masters' rights to manumit their slaves, which ultimately denied legal access to freedom to most black people. New York Quakers lagged behind their brethren elsewhere in the American colonies in shedding their commitment to slave ownership. Still, the scent of liberty was in the air, and black people caught its sweet aroma. In 1765 and again in 1768, when New Yorkers took to the streets to protest impositions on their liberties, black men were among them. As an intimate part of the "people out of doors," or mob, black sailors, day laborers, and occasionally house servants rioted against imperial policies. They were particularly visible in protesting the impressment of Americans into the British navy, as labor in the maritime trades was a prime occupation for free black men. Few revolutionary mobs did not include their fair share of black protesters. In 1775, when the Sons of Liberty tore down the statue of King George III, black men were prominent in the crowd.[3] Their participation alerted black New Yorkers to the onrushing struggle, tutored them in the language of liberty, and allowed them to take advantage of the changes that accompanied the Revolution.

The crisis expanded the freedom of black people. During the years before the Revolution, the number of advertisements for fugitives increased, as black people seemed to be walking away from slavery and hiding amid the forest of boardinghouses, taverns, and groceries that lined New York's waterfront. There they readily found employment in shipyards, ropewalks, and chandleries. Such self-emancipation appeared to be on the rise prior to the Revolution. William Livingston, a slaveholder with abolitionist sympathies who soon took his seat as governor of New Jersey, sought to sell an experienced house servant because the man "would be abroad at night after the Family was a bed and we never found by what avenue he went or returned." The mixture of slaves—owned, hired, and fugitive—and free blacks attracted runaways from the countryside into the city.[4]

The slaves' restlessness spurred repression. The city and a variety of outly-ing municipalities enacted laws constraining the movement of slaves and even free blacks. In 1773, New York City's Common Council revived an old act that mandated whippings for any black person found in the streets after dark. Once the war began, such repression intensified. In Queens County on Long Island, Patriots fretted over "enlisting Negroes," who they believed might defect to the British if the chance arose. Two years later their worst fears were realized. They hanged "two Tory Negroes" for "engaging to murder their masters who were supporters of Liberty."[5]

Such repression could not contain the growing contagion of liberty. In 1775, rumors that Lord Dunmore, the governor of Virginia (and former governor of New York), had offered liberty to "all indented servants, Negroes" who would defend the king, grabbed the attention of black New Yorkers. Long Island Patriots, who burned Dunmore in effigy, worried about their slaves being "too fond of British troops." But Loyalist slaveholders shared many of their fears as they too worried their slaves would flee to their enemy. In August 1776, when Dunmore's Ethiopian army, ravaged by disease and defeated in battle, retreated to Staten Island, dozens of blacks from New Jersey and New York joined them. Announcing they were ready to fight for their freedom, these black New Yorkers spoke for many black men and women who would do the same in the years to come.[6]

With the onset of the war, African Americans found new opportunities to gain their liberty. As British and Patriot armies stormed across New Jersey and New York in the late summer of 1775, large areas in and around New York City became a no man's land, devoid of constituted authority. With slaveholders stripped of the power of the state, slaves found it easy to leave their owners. When the British army occupied New York City in September 1776, many of these fugitives took refuge there. New York under British rule became an emporium for black freedom.

Patriots showed little interest in playing the liberator. Although they had long compared British impositions on their own liberty to servitude, Patriot demands for an end to enslavement did not extend to others actually held in captivity. In the summer of 1776, as Patriots grandly announced their commitment to universal equality, black men and women could only dismiss the Declaration of Independence as hollow rhetoric. In the years that followed, New York's Patriot leaders did little to contradict their standing as hypocrites in the eyes of black New Yorkers. They ignored the issue of slavery in the construction of the first state constitution in 1777. They offered no relaxation of the tight restrictions on manumission and, unlike the British, they promised no

exchange of military service for freedom. Although the Patriot army allowed slave masters to send slave substitutes to serve in their stead, such service did not guarantee freedom for the men who risked their lives for American independence.[7]

Still, a handful took the chance. In 1776, the slave Samuel Sutphin of Somerset County, New Jersey, replaced his master, Casper Berger, in the Patriot ranks. Sutphin fought in the battle of Long Island, where he was wounded and captured. He escaped with the help of "a colored man" who carried him back to New York City. When he regained his strength, Sutphin rejoined his regiment and fought in several battles in upstate New York. Still, at war's end, he remained a slave and the treacherous Berger rewarded the black veteran by selling him. Although Sutphin eventually gained his freedom, he had spent most of his life in bondage. Others fared better in Patriot service, but not by much. Peter Williams Sr. fled a Loyalist master and enlisted in the American army, but at war's end he too remained a slave. The parishoners of John Street Methodist Church, out of gratitude for his service as sexton, purchased Williams and then allowed him to buy his freedom from the church. Williams completed his self-purchase in 1785. [8]

The narrow routes that Sutphin and Williams had followed to freedom in Patriot service encouraged few others to try. Instead, black men and women moved steadily toward British lines. British commanders were pleased to welcome them. In 1777, General Henry Clinton reiterated Lord Dunmore's promise to exchange freedom for military service. The trickle became a flood, as the slaves of Patriot—and occasionally Loyalist—owners crowded into British-occupied New York.

The British were quick to employ former slaves in their efforts to discipline the rebellious Americans. In 1776 General Henry Clinton commissioned the Black Pioneers. Led by white officers, New York's Black Pioneers joined companies established in the Carolinas and Virginia. The New York Black Pioneers included three sergeants, three corporals, and thirty-two privates. The Pioneers served as guards, pilots, spies, and interpreters. They also proved to be capable horsemen, hunters, and drummers, and they performed a variety of fatigue

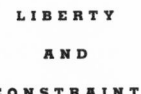

PETER WILLIAMS SR.

Perhaps the best-known black American in Revolutionary New York, Peter Williams Sr. was one of ten children born in New York City to George and Diana Williams, slaves of James Aymar, a prominent New York tobacconist. Reputedly born in an annex to Aymar's cowshed, Williams reveled in his humble origins, often proclaiming, "I was born in as humble a place as my Lord." Working in his owner's tobacco shop and worshipping in the galleries at the newly formed Wesley Chapel, which later became the John Street Methodist Church, Williams was a well-known figure in colonial New York. He married Mary "Molly" Durham, an indentured servant to Aymar's wife.

In the late 1770s, when Aymar, a staunch Loyalist, fled New York City, Peter Williams joined the Patriots, gaining fame for his refusal to reveal at the point of a British sword the hiding place of a noted Patriot cleric. Unlike most slaves in British-occupied New York, Williams maintained his loyalty to the American cause. At war's end, he did not leave with the Black Loyalists and, instead, remained Aymar's slave. But in 1783, when Aymar departed for England, Williams, his wife, Molly, and son, Peter Jr., were sold to the newly renamed John Street Methodist Church for £40.

Williams Sr. became the church's sexton and undertaker, and was allowed to purchase his

Alexander Hay Ritchie (1822–95), *Peter Williams, the Old Colored Sexton of the John St. Methodist Church*. Engraving.
NEW-YORK HISTORICAL SOCIETY LIBRARY

own freedom. Once free, he used his earnings to buy his family out of bondage and established himself as a tobacconist and cigar maker. Williams eventually led a secession of the black members of the John Street Church, becoming one of the charter members of the independent African Methodist Zion Church. His son, Peter Jr., later became New York's most famed black theologian and an important abolitionist.

—*Graham Russell Gao Hodges*

work. Within a few months of their muster, the New York unit assisted the carpenters in building fortifications to defend the city. General Clinton took a close interest in the Black Pioneers, and in 1777 requested that his commander, Sir William Howe, uniform them. He also saw that their pay was equal to that received by the white Loyalist infantry. But wages and clothing were not the only reasons black men entered the Pioneers. The unit provided a means of securing independence and an important avenue for advancement. Thomas Peters, later a leader of the Loyal Blacks of Nova Scotia and Sierra Leone, enlisted after he was promised that he and the other former slaves "would be at our own liberty & would provide for ourselves" when the war was over. [9]

Black Pioneers paid dearly for their liberty. Benjamin Whitecuff, born free on Long Island, joined the Pioneers on Staten Island in 1776 and became a valuable spy who worked for General Clinton, earning bonuses of fifteen guineas. But the Patriots captured Whitecuff near Cranbury, New Jersey, and hanged him. Left dangling, he was saved by the timely arrival of a British regiment. Sent to Virginia and then Boston, Whitecuff was nearly strung up a second time but again the British saved him. Having cheated death twice, Whitecuff traveled to safety in England. After the war, he remained in London, although he also served the king in the siege of Gibraltar in 1782.

In addition to the Pioneers, slaves and free black guerrilla rangers followed the "Army and Flag." Raiding enemy territory, they secured much-needed livestock and food for the British garrison in New York City and, upon occasion, returned with captured Patriot militiamen and politicos. Black rangers were also stationed as sentries and controlled blockhouses at key points along the Hudson River. They served as auxiliaries to British and Loyalist regiments. A handful of black pilots guided warships along the treacherous coasts and waterways that surrounded New York.

One black "follower" who played all of these roles was Colonel Tye. Originally named Titus Corlies, Tye fled his Shrewsbury, New Jersey, master in November 1775, aiming to join Lord Dunmore's black regiment. He returned to New Jersey sometime thereafter and in 1777 he became known first as Captain and then Colonel Tye, informal ranks bestowed upon him as marks of respect

Front page of the *Pennsylvania Gazette* including Colonel Tye's advertisement . NEW-YORK HISTORICAL SOCIETY LIBRARY

from the British authorities. Tye made his name first at the Battle of Monmouth when he captured several Jersey militiamen. Between 1777 and 1780, he led a series of raids into his old neighborhood, capturing local militia leaders and looting their homes of valuables and livestock. Operating out of Sandy Hook on the Jersey shore, Tye carried his captives and loot into New York City. By the summer of 1780, New Jersey Patriots had become so frightened that they beseeched Governor Livingston to install martial law and send emergency troops. Soon after, Tye led a daring raid in which he captured Josiah Huddy, one of the most prominent Patriots in eastern New Jersey. When Americans counterattacked, Huddy escaped and Tye was mortally wounded. He died in September 1780.

Other black Loyalists also found advantages behind British lines. Inchu Moore, a free black man, rented a cellar kitchen in New York City for £8 a year until a white soldier offered the landlord twice the amount. When he was unsuccessful, the prospective renter tried to oust Moore by threatening to return him to Virginia and slavery. Moore then lodged a successful complaint with the commander in chief.[10]

Even as the British rewarded Tye and protected Moore, the slaves of Loyalist masters did not fare nearly as well. Clinton's proclamation did not extend to them, and, indeed, the British saw no contradiction in welcoming runaways from Patriot slavery while buying and selling enslaved people or even indignantly advertising for the return of fugitives. Prices for slaves boomed as black men and women exited slavery and wartime closure of the transatlantic slave trade cut the supply, and Loyalist slaveholders were quick to use the market to their advantage. The *Royal Gazette*, published in New York, included some 1,600 notices of slave sales during the war years. Loyalists who left the city maintained their commitment to slavery by hiring their slaves to those Loyalists remaining in the city. Like most Patriots, Loyalist slaveholders showed little interest in advancing African American freedom. Other than the handful of manumissions, whatever liberty black New Yorkers gained during the war would be secured though their own efforts.[11]

Still, freedom in wartime New York allowed black men and women to begin to construct their lives anew. Laboring for British quartermasters or private employers, black men and women—many for the first time—worked independently and collected wages of their own. Black men built fortifications, drained ditches, and cleaned the streets, while black women labored at a variety of domestic tasks, cleaning houses, washing clothes, and nursing the sick and wounded. Such work was poorly paid, and sometimes hardly paid at all. The Royal Sweepmaster hired six black men to clean about twenty chimneys a day for nothing more than a dirty room and bad food.[12] But, as free men and women, black people aspired to something beyond these lowly jobs and paltry wages. Striving to better themselves, they demanded higher rates and sometimes gained them. Initially, the British quartermasters paid black laborers less than white ones, but as wartime labor shortages worsened, African Americans demanded—and received—the same wages as did whites. Others found good jobs for private businesses. "James, a Negroe boy," earned one pound eight shillings per week along with six other blacks who toiled for the Faulkner Brewery. Blacks also entered trades from which they had previously been excluded. Before the war, white carters had successfully petitioned the city government to ban black men from driving a wagon for hire. With the British in control, some fifty black men obtained carting licenses in the city. Privateering became another steady source of income. The British declared open season on American shipping by licensing piracy. Privateers—small coastal vessels that raided American ships and ports—were always looking for fresh hands and quickly employed refugee blacks.[13]

With money in their pockets, black people began to reconstruct other aspects of their lives. They took new names, abandoning the comic nomenclature that tied them to slavery by replacing Caesar, Cato, and Toby with full, anglicized names.[14] Likewise, they began to rebuild their families. Nothing was more emblematic of the remaking of African American New York than the wartme spiritual renewal of black life. Building upon religious ties established prior to the revolution, African American men and women in New York entered the city's churches in large numbers. The Anglican Church had long been a favorite of black New Yorkers. Missionaries from the Anglican Society for the Propagation of the Gospel in Foreign Parts had taught enslaved blacks their catechism, along with much else during the eighteenth century. Although a fire (perhaps set by retreating Patriots) had destroyed Trinity Church in 1776, Anglican Loyalists had quickly reconstructed the old building. When the new Trinity opened, it became the favored place for black men and women to worship, marry, and baptize their children.

The Anglican Church soon found competition for black worshippers, as black men and women joined Baptist, Methodist, and Moravian churches. While no separate African American churches emerged, each of these denominations seems to have spawned a cadre of black leaders.[15] Stephen Blucke stood out among the Anglicans, but others appeared from all over the continent, including the Methodist preachers John Marrant from South Carolina and Moses Wilkinson, David George, and Boston King from Virginia. Each of them became prominent in the postwar African American diaspora to the Caribbean, maritime Canada, and West Africa.[16]

The transformation of black life bred a new confidence. Murphy Stiel's injunction to the British and American commanders spoke to this new self-assertion. So too did Dinah Archey, a black Loyalist from Virginia who escaped to New York in 1778 "agreeable to his Excellency General How[e]'s Proclamation." At war's end, when her master tried to reclaim her, she appealed in a letter directly to Sir Guy Carleton, the British commander. As a loyal subject of the Crown, Archey expected Carleton to respect her petition and he did, protecting her from seizure and return to slavery.

Other evidence of the new standing for former slaves bolstered this new sense of self-esteem. The British officers arrested a white Loyalist, Micah Williams, for kicking Quamino, a black carriage driver, upon Quamino's complaint. Quamino dropped his charge only after Williams publicly apologized. Likewise, when the father of an American prisoner complained that black children "grossly insulted him" as he was marched through the streets, British officers simply ignored the charge. In the old days, the black children would have faced the whipping post. For black New Yorkers, the world had changed.[17]

Racial lines in New York became increasingly permeable. Public mixing that would have scandalized colonial New York became more common in the wartime city. Black Loyalists and British soldiers regularly competed in horse races. The city became the site of numerous "Ethiopian Balls," where black men and women and British officers and soldiers freely mingled to the music of black fiddlers and banjo players. So relaxed were racial attitudes that the Black Pioneers sent General Clinton a New Year's greeting on January 1, 1782, wishing him "the greatest success in all your Public and Private Undertakings." The British, in turn, demonstrated their familiarity by taking Prince William Henry, son of King George III and later to become King William IV, on a tour of the blockhouses manned by Black Pioneers along the lower Hudson River.[18]

Not everyone was pleased with the new state of affairs. The Patriot and Loyalist press derided such familiarity between blacks and whites. Patriot newspapers sneeringly described an evening when "his Excellency opened the balls with Colonel Quaco's Lady and danced very gracefully to the music of a full orchestra of banjoes and hurdy-gurdies. How far the superior beauty of Colonel Quaco's Lady may have contributed to his promotion is uncertain." Loyalist newspapers maintained the same tone, complaining that blacks had opened their own charade clubs or costume parties that only whites had previously enjoyed.[19] White New Yorkers were particularly disturbed by the airs taken by black women, who now acted the lady. While attending the races on Long Island, a Hessian chaplain observed that "even the lovely female Negroes were given time off by their mistresses, and appeared in such finery that, when seeing them from the rear, we were immediately prepared to pay our respects." Realizing his mistake, the Hessian was amused "to see a pitch-black person wearing a white summer dress with a white velvet sun hat and black velvet gloves."[20]

American victory threatened the new racial order. At war's end, slaveholders from all over the continent flooded into New York City to reclaim their property. In addition to those black men and women who had escaped to New York, the British—evacuating St. Augustine, Charleston, and Yorktown—had deposited thousands of former slaves in the city. As slave masters deluged British commanders for permission to retake their wayward property, blacks feared the loss of their new freedom. Boston King, a fugitive who had fought with the British, stated that "the dreadful rumor filled us all with inexpressible anguish and horror . . . for some days we lost our appetite for food and sleep from our eyes."[21]

But former slaves were not about to surrender their liberty. Some took matters into their own hands. When a slaveholder inquired "about some Negroes," he was "beset and murdered by about 12 or 15 of Ward's Blacks," who were described as "followers of the army." Though several were convicted, General Carleton, now British commander in chief, commuted their death sentences. He also protected black people from his own officers, many of whom saw easy money to be made in cooperation with slaveholders eager to retake their slaves. When Thomas Willis, a white policeman, threatened to return Caesar, "a Negro, who came into New York under a proclamation," to slavery, Carleton freed Caesar, fined Willis £50, and exiled him from the city.[22]

It would take more, however, to protect the thousands of black men and women who crowded into New York on the eve of its return to the victorious Americans. General George Washington, the American commander and a substantial slaveholder, regarded the black men and women under British protection as stolen

Representation du feu terrible à nouvelle Yorck, que les Américains ont allumé pendant la nuit du 19. septembre 1776. par lequel ont été brûlés tous les Bâtimens du côté de l'Ouest, à droite de Borse, dans la rue de Broock jusqu'au collège du Roi, et plus de 1600. maisons avec l'Eglise de la St. Trinité, la Chapelle Lutherienne, et l'école des pauvres.

A Paris chez J. Chereau rue St. Jacques au dessus de la Fontaine St. Severin aux 2 Colonnes N.º 267.

Francois Xavier Habermann, *Representation du Feu Terrible a Nouvelle Yorck*, ca. 1780. Hand-colored engraving.

105

property whose return was guaranteed by the Treaty of Paris. Carleton, however, believed that the black men and women who had entered the British lines before the end of the war were free according to the many proclamations offering liberty in exchange for military service. Washington was horrified at this news and further vexed when he heard that many black Loyalists had already departed New York for British territories. Carleton agreed to keep records of the blacks who had departed in case of any claims for compensation. Carleton's list, the Book of Negroes, identi-

THE BOOK OF NEGROES

With the British defeat in 1783, the black men and women who had gathered in New York from all over the continent feared for their freedom. Slaveholders from as far away as Georgia and South Carolina swarmed the city, identifying their fugitive property. General George Washington, the American commander in chief, would soon arrive and demand the return of "Negroes and other Property" in accordance with Article Seven of the Treaty of Paris, which had ended the war. Much to Washington's dismay, Sir Guy Carleton, the British commander, stubbornly refused to surrender the Black Loyalists who had fought for him, instead honoring the British wartime promise of freedom in exchange for military service. However, under pressure from Washington, Carleton did agree to organize a board of inquiry to identify the black men and women he had freed, so that American slaveholders might be indemnified at some future date.

The Book of Negroes is the resultant list. It names the 3,000 Black Loyalists—1,336 men, 914 women, and 750 children—who left New York City with the British in 1783, and notes their ages, former residences, owners (if applicable), and dates of enlistment in British service, along with general physical descriptions of each individual. In denoting how black people gained their liberty—by birth, manumission, or flight—the Book of Negroes documents the liberating force of the American Revolution.

—*Graham Russell Gao Hodges*

fied about 3,000 blacks—including 1,336 men, 914 women, and 750 children—by their name, origin, and sometimes occupation. Each received a precious certificate that guaranteed passage out of New York. The Patriots challenged some of the certificates and in some cases the board of inquiry set up on the docks by the British determined that bearers had to be returned to their alleged masters. Others were confirmed and left the country.[23]

The joy of the 3,000 or more former slaves at leaving was indescribable. Boston King noted with great understatement that Carleton's decision meant that "each of us received a certificate from the commanding officer at New-York, which dispelled our fears and filled us with gratitude."[24] Carleton also ordered that the Black Pioneers remain on the British payroll until the fall of 1783 and provided for continued payments after their arrival in Nova Scotia and Jamaica. He also recommended that upon arrival in Nova Scotia, each Pioneer should receive twenty acres of land. Carleton then ordered the Black Pioneers to remain in New York City until November 1783 to regulate the city during the interim period before the Americans took over. The Pioneers were among the last British soldiers to leave New York on Evacuation Day, November 25, 1783.

When they departed, they greased the flagpole on the Battery so thoroughly that it took some time for arriving American soldiers to remove the Union Jack and replace it with the Stars and Stripes. The African American militias watched from boats in the harbor until they sailed away to freedom on November 30.[25]

As 3,000 or more Black Loyalists sailed away from New York, they left behind a slaveholding society embittered by years of war and what many slave-holders believed to be the treason of their slaves. New York's republican government quickly reinstalled colonial laws that undergirded the institution of chattel bondage, putting slavery on a firm legal footing. The Americans had little enthusiasm for assisting those whom they regarded as traitors. Poet Philip Freneau lampooned Lord Dunmore and his black soldiers, portraying the erstwhile governor as wishing that "six years ago I had joined with your votes; Not aiding the Negroes in cutting your throats." Another author cursed African Americans who "in combination with their friends, the Quakers, would give every assistance to our enemies . . . in the late contest, when they fought against us by whole regiments and the Quakers at the same time supported every measure of Great Britain to enslave us."[26] Although many Northern states had begun the process of liquidating slavery, New York was slow to turn to the matter. Some leading New Yorkers—most notably Alexander Hamilton and John Jay—would join together in establishing the New York Manumission Society, but many more white New Yorkers took a firm stand against abolition. In fact, the number of slaves in New York was growing. African Americans who had secured their freedom under British rule and maintained it under American sovereignty found themselves increasingly frustrated, as the promise of American liberty was rarely extended to them. Many found themselves impoverished and subject to new demeaning racial restrictions. As the new republican government took power in New York, the end of slavery and the possibilities of equality seemed more distant than ever.

African Americans, having tasted and seen the fruits of liberty during the American Revolution, sought them as eagerly as did white artisans who looked to the nascent Jeffersonian Republican Party to push their political agenda. African Americans negotiated with masters, bargained years of work for free-

Black Loyalists in Nova Scotia and Sierra Leone

In 1783, with the American Revolutionary victory secure, the almost three thousand black men and women who had supported the British war effort—most of whom were fugitives from American slaveholders—left New York City for Nova Scotia. Organized in military units that were led by African American officers, the Black Loyalists soon faced the harsh realities of life in freedom. In Nova Scotia, British officials assigned them to rocky and barren lots in Birchtown and Shelburne, tiny ports miles down the coast from Halifax. During the winter of 1783–1784, they lived in tents, huts, and in the holds of transport ships, barely surviving the harsh Canadian winter. When spring arrived, colonial authorities procrastinated in distributing land, and though many Black Loyalists were skilled artisans, white merchants and craftsmen denied them employment, forcing the Black Loyalists to earn a meager subsistence as lumbermen, farmers, and fishermen.

Although the Black Loyalists began to form their own community, organizing churches, schools, and numerous associations, their dismal prospects in Nova Scotia encouraged many to look elsewhere. In desperation, many agreed to migrate to Sierra Leone, the fledgling British colony on the west coast of Africa founded by abolitionists Granville Sharp and John Clarkson. Led by Thomas Peters, David George, Moses Wilkinson, and Cato Perkins, over one thousand Black Loyalists sailed from Nova Scotia for Sierra Leone in an armada of fifteen ships in early 1792.

In Sierra Leone, the Black Loyalists suffered enormous hardships. Some two hundred of them died the first year. Conflicts with native Africans kept the Loyalists on the defensive, and, in 1794, an assault on the colony by the French navy nearly destroyed the settlement. But drawing upon their American experience, the Black Loyalists employed their understanding of republicanism and Christianity to create their own institutions. Although their struggle for independence had only just begun, within a decade of their arrival in Africa, the Black Loyalists had created a community that reflected their experience of two hundred years of American captivity.

—*Graham Russell Gao Hodges*

dom, probed religious aversion to slavery among Protestant denominations to secure freedom, and, failing those methods, voted with their feet by running away in growing numbers. Although manumissions were still few in the immediate postwar years, the demography of black freedom quickly changed drastically. Slavery still prevailed in New York County, but over a thousand free blacks appeared on the first census of 1790. Human bondage was entrenched in the agricultural counties, especially Dutch ones, around New York, but within another ten years, 3,333 free blacks lived in New York City. The city became the center of a thriving black community that would eventually produce a sturdy African American artisanship and some of the most important black political figures in American history.

Chapter 4

THE
LONG DEATH
OF
SLAVERY

❖

PATRICK RAEL

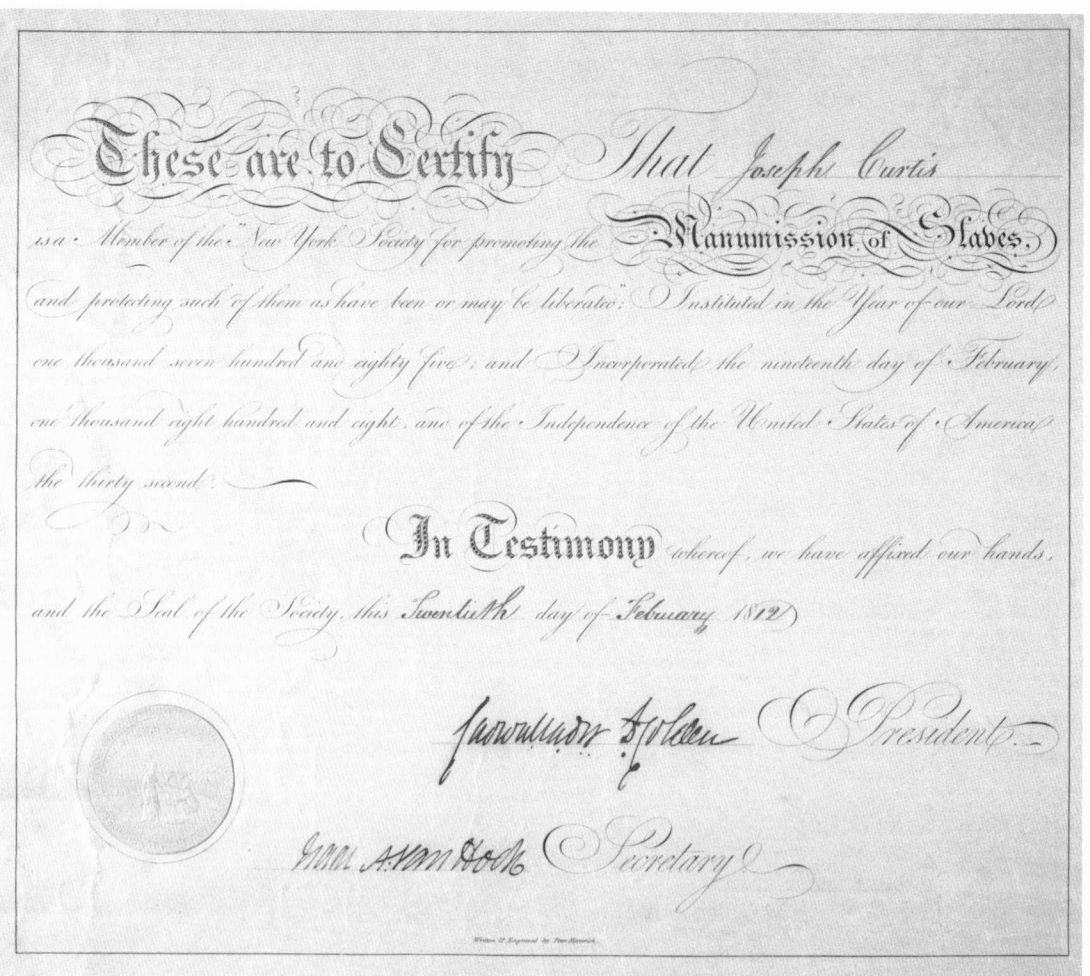

Membership certificate for New York Manumission
Society, signed by Cadwallader Colden.

THE WORD "EMANCIPATION" IS most often associated with the Civil War and the proclamation of President Abraham Lincoln that liberated hundreds of thousands of African Americans from bondage on January 1, 1863. So familiar has the idea of emancipation *as a moment* become that it is often forgotten that innumerable individual acts were required to abolish slavery in the nation, and that these began long before the Civil War. The "peculiar institution," after all, was not so peculiar: it thrived for almost two centuries in the Northern colonies until another great conflict—the American Revolution—helped destroy it. Slavery's demise throughout the North in the late eighteenth and early nineteenth century marked a critical starting point in the nation's arduous path toward complete abolition. Northern emancipation demonstrated that freedom for African Americans was not the inevitable product of a progressive movement toward liberty, but that it instead encapsulated a history fraught with irony and paradox—one which tested Americans' commitments to national founding principles and raised questions about the very meaning of words such as "freedom."

This was especially the case in New York City, which surrendered the institution with great reluctance. Emancipation required half a century and was accomplished only through a series of incremental measures, suggesting both the degree to which New York was beholden to slavery and the limitations of antislavery sentiment in the early national period. Even those white benefactors who worked most ardently for the abolition of slavery in New York harbored grave concerns about the qualities and characters of African Americans, and in the decades following the Revolution these attitudes blossomed into a vicious popular prejudice that placed entirely new constraints on the lives of African Americans. Emancipation in New York did not signal a fulfilled commitment to universal human liberty. Rather, it confronted black New Yorkers with a future of tightly circumscribed freedom.

NEW YORK, like several other Northern states, abolished slavery slowly, through a series of legal mechanisms that entailed hard-fought contests between proponents of slavery and of abolition. In New York the process took particularly long, proceeding incrementally from 1777, when New York law-makers first began proposing abolition measures, to 1827, when the state passed its last major piece of antislavery legislation. In contrast, Vermont out-lawed slavery entirely in its state constitution of 1777, while Massachusetts's Supreme Judicial Court abolished chattel bondage with the stroke of a pen in 1783. Even states such as Rhode Island and Pennsylvania, which, like New York, ended slavery through gradual measures, began and ended the process earlier. The only Northern state to outlast New York in preserving slavery was New Jersey; the last slaves were freed there in 1865.

New York's tenacious hold on bondage owed to benefits its farmers and arti-sans had long gained from slavery. Before the Revolution, the economy and society of New York were—of all Northern colonies—particularly beholden to slavery. On the eve of mass emancipation, the state's 319,000 slaves constituted over 6 percent of its total population; New York led the Northern states in both raw numbers of slaves and in slaves as a proportion of the entire population.[1] As the entrepôt for the region's rich agricultural hinterland, New York City depended as much on enslaved black labor as on free white labor. On the eve of the American Revolution, New York City's populace was over 14 percent African American.[2]

SLAVERY IN
NEW YORK

In the wake of the Revolution, white New Yorkers struggled over the future of servitude. By basing their armed resistance on appeals to universally held natural rights, rebellious slaveholders had raised troubling questions about black bondage. "How is it," quipped Samuel Johnson, the English writer and satirist, "that we hear the loudest yelps for liberty among the drivers of Negroes?"[3] The great paradox of the conflict was not lost on Empire State founders— none more than John Jay, the successful New York City attorney who was to become one of the most prominent political figures of early America. In 1774, he penned a list of grievances for the Continental Congress entitled "An Address to the People of Great Britain," which invoked the specter of servitude in the Patriots' defense. Jay believed that Britain had become an advocate for "slavery and oppression." The mother country was "forging chains for her friends and children" with an imperial policy that amounted to a "ministerial plan for enslaving us." He concluded by vowing that the colonials would "never submit to be hewers of wood or drawers of water for any ministry or nation in the world."[4]

After Alonzo Chappel (1828–87), *John Jay, First Chief Justice of the United States*, 1858. Engraving. NEW-YORK HISTORICAL SOCIETY LIBRARY

Jay equated the cause of the rebellious colonist with that of the yearning-for-liberty slave. In 1777, he urged that New York's new state constitution provide for eventual abolition,[5] and endorsed a resolution by the state constitutional convention calling for the end of slavery. "Till America comes into this measure," Jay wrote in private correspondence in 1780, "her prayers to Heaven for liberty will be impious."[6] Such phrases echoed the thoughts of Thomas Jefferson, whose ruminations on the injustice of bondage caused him to "tremble" when he reflected that "God was just." Unlike Jefferson, however, Jay suspected that blacks' natural capacities were "probably" equal to whites', which to him made American hypocrisy all the more damning. "To contend for our own liberty and to deny that blessing to others," he wrote in 1785, "involves an inconsistency not to be excused."[7]

Jay was not alone in these sentiments. Caught up in the fervor of the Revolution, a few New York slaveholders went farther than Jay, and manumitted their slaves. Those who saw themselves as particularly benevolent might provide for the care of freed people with promises of education, clothing, or money; others provided first for themselves, by making manumission conditional upon years of good service or extravagant payment. Across the Hudson, New Jerseyans debated emancipation measures similar to those that New Yorkers contemplated, suggesting the tenor of discussions throughout the region. John Cooper, a member of the Continental Congress from New Jersey, declared that consistency with republican principles dictated the emancipation of the slaves, lest the entire Revolution amount to nothing more than the statement "that we are resolved not to be slaves, because we ourselves mean to be tyrants." If these arguments were not enough, Cooper suggested—like Jay and Jefferson—that "the dread of divine retribution" might seal slavery's fate.[8]

Yet apart from passing minor measures to facilitate the process of manumitting individual slaves, the New York State legislature failed to take decisive steps to eradicate slavery in the wartime and immediate postwar years. Practical concerns tempered even the fierce ideological commitments of individual citizens who conditionally manumitted their slaves, and the conservatism of the new state's political elite doomed sweeping, state-sponsored efforts. Gouverneur Morris, the staunch Federalist congressman, tempered his call for the state "to dispense the blessings of freedom to all mankind" with the warning that "it would at present be productive of great dangers to liberate the slaves within this State."[9] The state constitutional convention proved still more hesitant; antiabolition forces managed to weaken and then table the resolution through adroit parliamentary maneuvering.

What hung in the balance against Revolutionary principle and divine favor was not the overt racism that so dogged later generations of abolitionists but a critical liberal ideal: the rights of property. To be sure, there was racism aplenty within the Revolutionary generation, but property concerns took precedence over racial concerns. Many argued that any act to deprive slave owners of their property in man would constitute "a solemn act of public ROBBERY."[10] Morris himself sought to postpone a general emancipation, calling delay "consistent with the public safety"[11]—a common euphemism for protecting the rights of the propertied. Surely there was self-interest at work in such arguments—some of the politicos who advanced the idea of abolition were themselves slaveholders. Jay held slaves even as he advocated abolition, though he claimed to "purchase slaves and manumit them at proper ages" after they had compensated him with years of "faithful services."[12]

Rather than hold up the Revolutionary ideals of New York abolitionists against the self-interest of their opponents, it would be more accurate to suggest that the paradox existed within Revolutionary ideology itself. Concerns over the rights of property, which fueled resistance to emancipation, drew from the same philosophical legacy that fired arguments for emancipation. After all, natural rights philosophy was first used to defend the colonists' property rights against the capricious taxation policies of the governing mother country. Indeed, Revolutionary rhetoric linked property rights and the idea of slavery. For Rhode Island Son of Liberty Silas Downer, nonconsensual taxation placed colonists "in the lowest bottom of slavery"; if their rulers could "take away one penny from us against our wills," he wrote, "they can take all."[13]

The application of natural rights philosophy to the enslaved logically extended the ideological justifications of the Revolution. But the problem with making citizens of slaves was that, in many Founders' eyes, black men lacked the qualities that made citizens capable of self-government—namely, the political independence thought to derive from holding property. "Equality of property," argued Noah Webster in 1787, "is the very soul of a republic"; property distributed with some equality to smallholders helped to destroy the powerful "combinations" that eroded democracy.[14] But, it was thought, slaves had neither the property nor the interest to take part in sound government. Wrote

After Alonzo Chappel, *A. Hamilton*, 1861.
Engraving. NEW-YORK HISTORICAL SOCIETY LIBRARY

Massachusetts Federalist Sidney Edwards Morse of the enslaved: "Have they liberty? It is sold to a despot. Have they property? They, themselves, are the property of another."[15]

It was at this point that racial stereotypes entered into play, fusing with Revolutionary notions of civic virtue rooted in independent property holding. In New Jersey, an anonymous editorialist made an argument that was repeated in all debates over abolition: the "deep wrought disposition to indolence and laziness" slavery had instilled in black men and women would make them dependent on private charity or public welfare in freedom. Furthermore, the "general looseness of passions," supposedly a "national" trait of Africans, would only be exacerbated once the restraints of enslavement were removed, making black people unfit to exercise the grave responsibilities required by the fragile experiment in self-government.[16] In the immediate postwar period, African Americans who yearned for freedom confronted the challenges not simply of slaveholder self-interest, but of tensions in Revolutionary ideology itself.

In the final fifteen years of the eighteenth century, the tide of Revolutionary-era thinking slowly turned in black New Yorkers' favor. One source of change was African Americans themselves, who in countless ways helped undermine slavery. As news spread that other states had enacted or were in the process of enacting antislavery legislation, African Americans in New York hastened their efforts to end their own servitude. Enslaved blacks from the countryside ran away to the city, where they hoped to meld in among the anonymous masses and live lives of tenuous liberty. Free blacks redoubled their efforts to purchase loved ones out of bondage. New arrivals of West Indian slaves—many brought with refugees from war-torn St. Domingue, where slavery had collapsed amid

THE NEW YORK MANUMISSION SOCIETY (1785–1849)

In January 1785, a small set of New York's elite founded the New York Society for Promoting the Manumission of Slaves and Protecting Such of Them as Have Been or May Be Liberated, which came to be known simply as the New York Manumission Society. These prominent merchants, professionals, and politicians included leading figures in city, state, and national politics, such as George Clinton, James Duane, Alexander Hamilton, and John Jay—as well as a goodly number of Quakers. Declaring slavery to be "the reproach of a free people," the Manumission Society's first purpose was to press the New York state legislature for abolition. The Society also lobbied slave owners to manumit their slaves voluntarily, offered legal representation to slaves seeking manumission, and protected free blacks and slaves against kidnappers. The passage of the Gradual Emancipation Law of 1799 culminated the Society's first fifteen years of effort. Thereafter the organization worked to tighten loopholes in other state laws: it sought to strengthen prohibitions on the import and export of slaves to the state, to prevent inhumane treatment of slaves, and to remove provisions of the slave code permitting courts to deport slaves deemed guilty of crimes.

In addition to spearheading legislative emancipation, the Society's most significant act was founding the African Free School in New York City. The first of what was to become a group of seven schools opened in November 1787 with a dozen students. Its purpose was to prepare newly freed New Yorkers for the responsibilities of freedom. By 1822, the African Free School enrolled some 800 students. Its alumni read as a who's who of antebellum black America: Ira Aldridge, Alexander Crummell, Henry Highland Garnet, James McCune Smith, Charles and Patrick Reason, and Samuel Ringgold Ward among others all passed through its corridors.

Following the passage of the 1817 Gradual Emancipation Law, which declared the official demise of New York slavery in 1827, the Manumission Society declined in significance. Ironically, its success in developing the talent of young African Americans undermined its purpose. As black New Yorkers increasingly assumed leadership of the black community, the Society's paternalistic style—which insisted that white men direct the struggle for freedom and equality—clashed with independent-minded free men and women of color. The society administered the African Free Schools until 1834, when all seven schools were incorporated into the New York public school system. The society slowly atrophied and, in 1849, dissolved.

—*Patrick Rael*

An Act for the gradual abolition of Slavery.

Be it enacted by the people of the State of New York represented in Senate and Assembly, That any Child born of a Slave within this State after the fourth day of July next, shall be deemed and adjudged to be born free. Provided nevertheless that such Child shall be the servant of the legal proprietor of his or her mother, until such servant if a male shall arrive at the age of twenty eight years, and if a female at the age of twenty five years.

And be it further enacted, That such proprietor his, her, or their heirs or assigns shall be entitled to the service of such Child until he or she shall arrive to the age aforesaid, in the same manner as if such Child had been bound to service by the Overseers of the Poor.

And be it further enacted, That every person being an Inhabitant of this State who shall be entitled to the service of a child born after the fourth day of July as aforesaid shall within nine months after the birth of such Child cause to be delivered to the Clerk of the City or Town where such person shall be an Inhabitant, a certificate in writing containing the name and addition of such master or mistress, and the name age, and sex, of every child so born, which certificate shall be, by the said Clerk recorded in a Book to be by him kept for that purpose provided, which record shall be good and sufficient evidence of the age of such child. And the clerk of such city or Town shall receive from said person twelve cents for every child so registered and if any such person neglects to make a return of every such child as aforesaid to said clerk within nine months after the Birth thereof, such person shall forfeit and pay five Dollars for every such offence; to be sued for and recovered by the Clerk of the city or Town in which such person resides,

the one half for his own use and the remainder for the use of the Poor of the said City or Town: Provided nevertheless that it shall be and is hereby made the duty of the Town clerk to register the certificate of any such child at any time after nine months from its birth, and every master or mistress masters or mistresses of every such child shall forfeit and pay the sum of One Dollar for every month, he, she, or they shall neglect to deliver such certificate to the Town Clerk.

And be it further enacted, That the person entitled to such service may nevertheless within one year after the Birth of such Child elect to abandon his or her right to such service by a Notification of the same from under his or her hand and lodged with the Clerk of the Town or city where the owner of the mother of any such child may reside; in which case every child abandoned as aforesaid shall be considered as a pauper of the respective Town or City where the proprietor or owner of the mother of such child may reside at the time of its birth, and liable to be bound out by the Overseers of the Poor on the same Terms and conditions that the children of paupers were subject to before the passing this act.

And be it further enacted, That every child abandoned as aforesaid shall be supported and maintained till bound out by the Overseers of the Poor as aforesaid at the expence of this State—provided however that the said support does not exceed three Dollars and fifty cents per Month for each Child. And the comptroller is hereby authorized and directed to draw his warrant on the Treasurer of this State for the amount of such account not exceeding the allowance above provided. And the accounts of the respective Towns or Cities being first signed by the Supervisor of the Town or the Mayor of the City as the case may be where such child may be maintained as aforesaid. And Provided also that the Person so abandoning as aforesaid shall at his own expence support and maintain every such child

civil war and servile rebellion—added "unruly" men and women to New York's enslaved population and exacerbated difficulties controlling the native-born. Many white New Yorkers suspected that disgruntled slaves instigated a rash of arson in the city in 1796.

The actions of slaves proved critical in helping to bring about the end of slavery in New York, providing the strongest possible testimony that blacks desired the thing for which white abolitionists worked. The steady chorus of resistance broadcast by the enslaved aided and abetted the efforts of the state politicians and antislavery advocates who now took center stage. These abolitionists hailed from two main sources: Quakers who had been active in New York since the 1760s, and elements of New York's political and economic elite. Joining forces in January 1785, these white men founded the New York Manumission Society in New York City.[17] Presided over by national luminaries like John Jay and Alexander Hamilton, the society worked on the principle that the well-placed New Yorkers who comprised it also numbered among the elite men who ran the city and state. In an age of hierarchical, highly personal politics, these men considered themselves natural leaders, capable of determining the best interests of the society at large. They pioneered a wide range of benevolent efforts, establishing institutions designed to aid the poor, succor juvenile delinquents, and educate the city's growing masses. The drive to manumit slaves and protect freed people from kidnapping was merely another arena for their benevolent intervention.

None of these enterprises should be confused with the far more radical reforms of the 1830s. The benevolent reformers of the turn of the century were social conservatives who sought not to alter existing hierarchies but to proclaim their place atop them. Nothing illustrated this better than the fact that about one fifth of the Manumission Society's members held slaves and continued to acquire them into the 1790s.[18] The society's tactics reflected its conservativism. Considering themselves above the petty squabbles of party politics, members chose instead to work through individual connections and local networks. "Gradual" was their motto. As Thomas Eddy, the wealthy New York merchant and philanthropist, reflected on abolition in New York: "The light with which Providence has been pleased to enlighten the minds of men, as it regards moral or religious truths, is gradual."[19] Such men's weapon of choice was the petition—the private solicitation for legislative action made to state elites by their own social peers.[20]

New York abolitionists began making such requests shortly after the Revolution. Following the quick defeat of a manumission proposal in 1784, the assembly, the lower house of the state legislature, considered a new manumission bill in 1785. The debate entailed no simple up or down vote on general emancipation but rather a web of interconnected questions, all suggesting that emancipation would be limited and gradual: Who exactly would be emancipated and who left enslaved? What responsibilities would the state assume for freed slaves incapable of caring for themselves? What intermediary periods of "apprenticeship" might be required of those freed? What responsibility would masters assume for the moral and civic training of those freed? How, if at all, would slave owners be compensated for the loss of their slave property? The assembly's final version followed the principle established by gradual emancipation edicts in other states: it would emancipate all slave children born after 1785 but indenture them to their former masters until they became adults (age twenty-two for women and twenty-five for men). The bill thus partially compensated owners by guaranteeing them many years of continued service and set forth a period during which black youth could receive the moral and civic education thought necessary to make them productive members of society. As a concession to the still-vigorous opponents of black freedom who feared the specter of former slaves participating equally with whites in civic life, the bill also restricted the rights of African Americans when freed. It denied them the right to vote or hold public office, established steep obstacles to racial inter-marriage, and forbade blacks' testimony against whites in court.

The bill foundered in the state senate, the domain of the states' elites. Unlike the more middling sort of the lower house, the senators held secure social and economic positions atop New York society, and found less to fear from free blacks' equal participation in civic life. These men opposed the assembly's restrictions on black political participation. Interhouse wrangling finally produced a bill that retained only the franchise restriction, thus permitting the peculiar circumstance that blacks in New York would be able to hold office but not vote. The final step was the Council of Revision, wherein the bill was reviewed by the governor, state chancellor, and one state supreme court justice. This body unceremoniously vetoed the measure, objecting solely to its franchise provision. Excluding black men from the vote would deny them consent in their own government, rendering them a "class of disfranchised and discontented citizens" who might in the future "become dangerous to the State." Furthermore, the bill deprived of the vote even those free black men who had formerly held it, thus "shocking those principles of equal liberty" upon which the state constitution rested. Finally, by defining blacks as an inferior caste, the bill was said to draw invidious distinctions among men on the basis of race, creating "an aristocracy of the most dangerous and malignant kind."[21]

The Council of Revision's veto of the bill offered a classic statement of Enlightenment-era racial egalitarianism. Since black men constituted a portion of the "all men" who had been created equal, they could not justly be denied the rights white men had secured for themselves. There were limitations to this thinking, not the least of which were the tacit assumptions that "all men" did in fact mean only men, and that the civilization of white Americans constituted a standard to which black Americans might hope to aspire. Additionally, in the social context of post–Revolutionary America, such racial egalitarianism seemed a luxury most affordable to the well-to-do. Many middling and poor whites argued against all forms of black civic equality, as did the assembly in the matter of black emancipation. The tenor of their thinking was evident in public debate over the bill. "It would be greatly injurious to this state if all the negroes should be allowed the privileges of white men," one New Yorker put it. Without some system to separate the races, the state would confront the "shame" of racial intermingling, and the specter of black faces—"General Quacco here, Col. Mingo there"—in the state legislature. The writer concluded by accusing the advocates of abolition of caring more for black freedom in the present than for white freedom during the Revolution. Their motives, he claimed, were obvious: once free, who else would black men vote for but those who had made them free?[22] White New Yorkers could grudgingly agree on ending slavery, but civic equality was another matter. The racialization of New York's class politics—indeed, of national party politics—was beginning.

In the wake of the manumission bill's demise, the state legislature took cautious steps toward black freedom. In 1785, the state rescinded a requirement that masters freeing slaves had to post a bond, a requirement intended to indemnify the state should freed slaves become incapable of providing for themselves and require the care of the state. The law also provided freedom for slaves sold out of the state, and guaranteed black people jury trials when charged with capital crimes. The next year, a new measure freed slaves who had become the property of the state—usually through the confiscation of Loyalist estates. New York took more small steps toward emancipation in 1788, prohibiting the sale of slaves with intent to remove them from the state and further loosening obstacles to private manumissions. But it did so at the cost of recodifying the state slave code for the first time since independence, thereby signaling that slavery was no mere vestige of colonial overlords, but the law of the newly independent state.

The tensions of 1785 heightened as the Manumission Society prepared for new campaigns in the 1790s. Between 1792 and 1799, supporters of abolition sought to enact abolition legislation each year. Early efforts were often killed before a bill made it to either house, but in 1795, the year the pro-abolition John Jay became governor, the full legislature finally considered an actual piece of legislation. For the next three years, lawmakers wrestled over the new measure, arguing particularly over compensation for slaveholders' losses. The abolitionists' successful attempts to guide the legislature polarized popular thinking on the question of slavery. The advocates of mass emancipation came under fire, charged with placing the welfare of black pariahs over that of white citizens. In the gubernatorial election of 1792, Jay's opponents sought to tar him with the brush of negrophilia, claiming that he sought to "rob every Dutchman of the property he possesses most dear to his heart, his slaves." Jay's response—that he supported blacks' freedom "in such a way as may be consistent with the justice due them"[23]—utterly missed the emerging logic of white supremacy. Antiabolition whites viewed the matter not in terms of

Revolutionary universalism but of Revolutionary liberalism and its concern for protecting property rights. A legislative committee considering a new abolition bill in 1796 reported that any attempt to deprive citizens of their slave property would be "unjust and unconstitutional" without compensation. Opponents of abolition argued in the press that legislated abolition would erode all property rights. Others argued that the rich could afford to emancipate their slaves, while the typical slave owner, the "poor man, whose only dependence is on domestics, must, with his numerous offspring, be reduced to penury and want."[24] Remarkably, slave owners had become victims.

Those propounding the alleged horrors of black freedom were confounded in 1799, the year New York's state legislature finally passed a sweeping emancipation measure. The act freed slave children born after July 4, 1799, indenturing women until the age of twenty-five and men until twenty-eight. The law freed no one immediately. Only the children of slaves would be liberated, and then only after serving for many of their productive laboring years. No explicit provision compensated masters for their losses, but the act permitted slave owners immediately to "free" slave children, the old, and the infirm, whose care would then become the responsibility of the state. Practically, the system amounted to a form of remuneration for lost slaves, since freed children were often bound back to their former masters, whom the state then paid to maintain. The act did nothing to liberate those born before 1799, but neither did it impose strictures on the civic and political participation of free blacks—the provisions that had doomed the 1785 effort. After fifteen years of wrangling, the state legislature had passed an emancipation act as rife with qualification and contradiction as was popular sentiment on race and slavery.

If the passage of the Gradual Emancipation Act tolled the death knell for slavery in New York City, few observers would have heard the bells in 1799. To the contrary, the manumission debates occurred at a time when slavery gained ground in New York City. Slaveholding in the region before the Revolution had been concentrated in the close-in counties of King's, Queen's, and Richmond. The city itself had been home to over 3,000 enslaved African Americans, but these constituted only about 14 percent of its total population. In contrast, over 30 percent of the prewar population of King's County (now Brooklyn) had been black, nearly all enslaved. The war, however, led to a general decline in the black population of the region, from well over 12,500 in New York City and its surrounding counties to not even 10,000 after the Revolution. New York County lost one-third of its prewar black population over the course of the war. The 3,000 who left the city when the British evacuated in 1783 had not all hailed from Manhattan, but enough had to radically diminish the black population there.

But the war did not disrupt things for long. Soon after the peace, slaveholders began moving from surrounding environs into the city with their human property. By 1790, New York County's black population had recovered, and was larger than that of any surrounding county. Ten years later, the black population in every county around New York except King's had declined, while in New York it had risen by 45 percent.

New York City became a haven for slavery. Of all the major northeastern cities, it alone remained committed to forced labor. In 1790, Philadelphia counted only 300 enslaved African Americans; even Baltimore, the rapidly expanding Southern port city, listed only 1,300. In contrast, over 2,300 resided in New York.[25] Paradoxically, as slavery entered its long decline in New York overall, the city rather than the countryside held fast to a system of unfree labor. In the wake of the Revolution, slavery started to wane in the surrounding counties, where free blacks began to make up an increasing proportion of the black population. By 1800, less than half of the African Americans of Suffolk County on the eastern half of Long Island remained enslaved. Only in New York itself did the slave population increase from the end of the Revolution to the turn of the century. Slave labor had never profited the city's urban economy as much as it had the rural counties, like the strongly Dutch, heavily agrarian King's County. But the very complexity of New York's thriving urban economy permitted a profitable sanctuary for slavery.

That economy was undergoing its own kind of revolution at the turn of the nineteenth century. Like other northeastern seacoast cities, New York was already an important hub of commerce, shipping, and manufacturing. In the last decade of the eighteenth century and into the nineteenth, its economy simply exploded. By 1799, the value of the city's exports had grown to almost seven and a half times its 1791 level.[26] People, though, were the most important indicators of New York's economic expansion. The population of most American seacoast cities boomed in the early nineteenth century: Philadelphia's expanded by 150 percent from 1800 to 1830, while Baltimore doubled its population. New York, however, outpaced even expanding British industrial centers like Glasgow and Manchester in this period, growing to two and a half times its size at the turn of the century.[27] On the eve of the industrial revolution in America, New York City became the nation's metropolis.

Throughout the eastern seacoast cities in the late eighteenth century, slavery and indentured servitude slowly gave way to wage labor. The latter, given a rich supply of immigrant workers, offered capital the benefits of a fluid and flexible workforce that could be hired in times of plenty and dismissed in times of want. Yet in New York, slavery retained a place in such a system, adapting to the new economy with remarkable ease. New York's slaves, once the primary source of menial labor in the warehouse and on the docks, became domestic workers— symbols of status and wealth for the entrepreneurs who successfully climbed the economic and social ladder. In the hands of merchants, professionals, and enterprising artisans, slavery found a home in the most profitable and progressive sectors of the urban economy.[28]

At the same time the city offered sanctuary for chattel bondage, it also employed free African Americans from the surrounding environs. In a time when slavery weakened throughout the region, it was remarkable that New York City's slave population increased by 20 percent in the last decade of the eighteenth century. It was even more remarkable that its free population increased as well—by over 200 percent. Far from enjoying the unfettered benefits of freedom, however, New York's free blacks often lived little differently than their enslaved brethren. In the last decade of the eighteenth century, free blacks worked alongside the enslaved in similar conditions. Those who resided with whites lived in households of merchants, retailers, and professionals—in roughly the same proportion as did enslaved blacks. Those who lived outside of white households exhibited the same patterns of work, further muting the distinction between slavery and freedom. These African Americans enjoyed greater independence, but economic straits forced them, with working-class whites, to create the storied slums of nineteenth-century New York: Five Points, Mulberry Bend, and the Bowery. At the same time, white elites began moving away from their downtown places of business to new abodes on Broadway and Park Way, creating and exacerbating economic divisions in Manhattan housing patterns. Modern New York—stratified by class and work, race and place—was being born.[29]

New York's continued dependence on black labor in the late eighteenth century demonstrates that slavery died in the city not suddenly and decisively but gradually and with ambivalence. The Gradual Emancipation Act of 1799 legally mandated the liberation of most slaves by 1827, specifying clear points at which slavery would end for black New Yorkers. Yet in a practical sense the law helped erode slavery by its very existence. Slave owners sought to wrest the greatest possible value from their slaves while the institution remained. The enslaved, meanwhile, used conditions of impending freedom to expand their liberties and secure some measure of economic security once manumitted. The result was an end to slavery characterized not by the lightning strokes of the American Civil War, but by a gradual, fitful movement toward liberty.

Nothing better illustrated the effects of the abolition law than the transformation in blacks' efforts to become free around the turn of the century—notably in patterns of slave flight. Running away had long served as an important indication of enslaved people's capacity to exploit fissures in the edifice of slavery. Escape attempts had skyrocketed during the chaos of the Revolution, only to subside in the years following the war. In the late 1790s, the number of runaways rose again, just as the Gradual Emancipation Act was being debated. The resurgence of escape indicated enslaved people's awareness of the abolition debates swirling around them and suggests their capacity to influence the formation of laws concerning them. The typical fugitive was a young man in his late teens or early twenties, born in America and likely to be lightly complected, who hoped to pass as free in New York City's dense urban environs. Most fugitives sought to use their knowledge and skills to live like free people: to reconstitute a semblance of family and community life and to control their own labor.

The passage of the Gradual Emancipation Law signaled an eventual end to slavery, and with it the possibility of attractive alternatives to flight.[30] While instances of slave flight did not stop, they declined in the new century, and negotiated manumissions became more frequent. Between 1783 and 1801, the Office of the Register in New York recorded 300 manumissions in New York City between 1783 and 1801; 260 of these occurred after the law's passage in 1799.[31] Masters and slaves negotiated nearly every facet of bondage and freedom: slaves' length of remaining service, the cost of self-purchase, slaves' capacity to purchase family and friends, conduct expected of slaves during the remainder of their service, possibilities for resale, and sometimes goods or funds to be furnished to slaves upon manumission. A typical example was the case of Yat, a male slave owned by John and Sarah Glen. In September 1805, the Glens agreed to free Yat if he served them faithfully for six years. The agreement included detailed stipulations of the behavior expected of Yat: it clearly spelled out his holidays, required him to attend church regularly, and even dictated limits on his leisure activities. Upon completing his required term of service, Yat had one full year in which to pay his former masters ninety dollars—no inconsiderable sum in 1805. Any breach of the agreement on Yat's part could result in perpetual servitude or resale.[32]

As the limits placed on Yat's behavior suggest, such negotiations were far from equal. Masters held the upper hand, and could renege on their promises with no legal penalty. Yet negotiating terms of service offered enslaved people important benefits. While escape held the possibility that slaves might gain tenuous control over their own lives, fugitives lived a perilous existence outside the law, and could expect little help from whites. Even the abolitionists who claimed to champion black rights urged slaves to await liberty rather than help themselves to it. Possessed of slaves themselves, they advocated the least disruptive possible end to the institution. By negotiating the remaining terms of their service with their owners, African Americans who were unwilling to risk flight could hope for a smoother, albeit far slower, transition to freedom.

For their part, slave owners gained much from negotiated manumissions. Masters found these agreements a means to secure reliable service from their slaves before the manumission law deprived them of their human property. Freedom thus happened not as a single moment in which slave owners were divested of their chattels, but as a process through which slave owners gained much of the labor value of their slaves even as those slaves became free. Furthermore, contracts for liberty such as Yat's offered a means for slave owners to regulate the behavior of black people, whom they believed to be inherently childlike and unruly. From the slaveholders' perspective, gradual manumission would prepare African Americans to exercise the responsibilities required of freedom.

For those African Americans fortunate enough to gain freedom through the Gradual Emancipation Law or through private negotiation, liberty entailed new opportunities rather than new expectations. In the early decades of the nineteenth century, New York City, already home to an emerging free black community, witnessed the flowering of African American social and cultural life. Freed people modestly expanded the range of occupations they filled, reconstituted family life as they were able, and sought to spend their precious leisure hours in enjoyments of their own crafting. In the same way that working-class whites were creating class-based cultural styles that distinguished them from a nascent white middle class, so too black workers used their speech, clothing, and behavior to distinguish themselves from whites and to nurture cultural pride and community cohesion.

Nonetheless, free black New Yorkers confronted strictures that sharply curtailed their personal and community lives. Families remained sundered by slavery, as some black men and women gained liberty while their spouses, parents, children, and kin remained in bondage. Freed into a fiercely competitive economy with few if any resources, African Americans changed their occupations as often as they changed their places of residence. Hard pressed, some black New Yorkers turned to petty crimes of opportunity to make ends meet, fencing stolen goods and clothing, running small-scale confidence schemes, or operating hidden gambling establishments.

Just as important to the opponents of abolitionism, working-class African Americans failed to measure up to the cultural norms of white society. White commentators' remarks about some blacks' styles of presentation—of their "broken" or "negro" English, their penchant for wearing "finery" suited for their social betters, and their "down look" and "swaggering walk"—formed the basis of destructive racial stereotypes.[33] By the early nineteenth century, growing numbers of New Yorkers—particularly the artisans, tradesmen, and small-holders who formed the core of the Republican Party's constituency—had come to view blacks' alleged deficiencies as innate and irredeemable. Problems created by slavery—such as African Americans' general lack of education, their relegation to low-paying unskilled labor when free, and their consequent over-representation in the jails and almshouses—all became the fault of blacks themselves. Rather than educate African Americans into equality, many New Yorkers came to be believe that the answer to the problem of black freedom was further to deny blacks the benefits of equal citizenship.

A running battle between Revolutionary-era abolitionists and opponents of black equality ensued. In the first decade of the nineteenth century the abolitionists contained slavery, successfully sponsoring legislation that legalized slave marriages, restricted importation and exportation of slaves, and favored fugitive slaves before the law. The second decade, though, belonged to the opponents of black rights. In 1811 the state legislature required black men to present a government-endorsed certificate of freedom in order to vote; in 1815, the law was strengthened with a comprehensive registration system for black voters that placed significant barriers between black men and the ballot. Ostensibly designed to help reduce the electoral fraud rampant in early national New York, these laws scapegoated African Americans as special threats to democracy while saying nothing of the far more widespread problem of white voter fraud.

Despite the growing success of forces arrayed against black equality, the tide of abolitionism did not entirely ebb. In 1812, the gradual abolitionists began the final assault on slavery in New York when Daniel D. Tompkins, the Republican state governor and longtime member of the Manumission Society,

The Abolition Laws of 1799 and 1817

Slavery in New York ended as the result of no single law, but the Gradual Emancipation Law of 1799 served as the central piece of legislation that doomed it. The law legally emancipated all people of African descent born into slavery after July 4, 1799, but liberated no one immediately. Rather, it mandated that women until the age of twenty-five and men until the age of twenty-eight would become the bound "servants" of those who had previously owned them. Excepting instances of individual manumission, 1824 was thus the earliest that blacks covered by the law could become legally free.

The law named no date at which slavery as an institution would end in New York, but it did mean that slavery would have a final endpoint. Slavery would survive only as long as the present generation of slaves lived. When the final enslaved New Yorker born before July 4, 1799 perished—perhaps as late as the 1880s or even 1890s—so would slavery. The apprenticeship of those emancipated under the 1799 law was likely to end more quickly than slavery. Enslaved mothers born before 1799 might continue to bear children well into the 1830s, who would be apprenticed under the 1799 law for twenty-five or twenty-eight years, depending on sex, thus permitting the persistence of bound black labor in New York as late as the 1860s.

Then, in 1817, New York enacted a second momentous piece of abolition legislation, stipulating that enslaved African Americans born before July 4, 1799—the portion of the slave population neglected by the 1799 law—would become free on July 4, 1827. By establishing a precise date on which the last slaves in New York would be freed, the law effectively abolished slavery in New York. It also accelerated the work of the 1799 law by shortening the period of apprenticeship required of African Americans emancipated under the 1799 law, to twenty-one years for both men and women. Since children born to slave mothers on the eve of July 4, 1827 could be apprenticed to the age of twenty-one, African Americans would remain unfree until 1848.

—*Patrick Rael*

urged the state legislature to liberate New York slaves unaffected by the Gradual Emancipation Law of 1799. Five years of legislative wrangling ensued before Tompkins's appeal became law, but in 1817, the state finally declared that those slaves born before July 5, 1799—that is, those not covered under the previous abolition law—would become free. Still, the law would not take effect until July 4, 1827, thus compensating slave owners for their future losses with many productive years of black labor.

While the law of 1799 had legally emancipated all born into slavery after July 4, 1799, it had provided no clear endpoint for slavery as an institution. The law of 1817 provided for the eventual end of slavery in New York. When the last enslaved New Yorker born before July 4, 1799, perished—perhaps as late as the 1880s or even 1890s—so would slavery. Enslaved mothers born before 1799 might continue to bear children well into the 1830s, who would be apprenticed under the 1799 law for twenty-five years if female, or twenty-eight years if male, thus permitting the persistence of some form of bound black labor in New York into the 1860s. The 1817 law accelerated the work of the 1799 law. It not only freed the portion of the population neglected by the 1799 law, it also shortened the period of apprenticeship required of African Americans emancipated under the 1799 law—to twenty-one years for both men and women. This shortened the potential life of slavery in New York, though for African Americans the end was still woefully distant. Since children born to slave mothers on the eve of July 4, 1827, could be apprenticed to the age of twenty-one, African Americans could remain bound until 1848.

Black and white abolitionists hailed the 1817 law in high-flown language, despite the fact that even this late gesture toward liberty was saturated with compromise, such as the last-moment stipulation releasing slaveholders of their responsibilities to aged and infirm slaves. The final nail in the coffin of slavery was not hammered in until 1841, when the state finally revoked the right of travelers to reside in New York for up to nine months with their slaves.

In the second decade of the nineteenth century, debates over black freedom and black voting rights signaled the coming of age of race as a central factor in formal party politics in New York. Differences between abolitionists and oppo-

THE
LONG DEATH
OF
SLAVERY

Loving cup, silver manumission item.

nents of black rights reflected long-standing social tensions among whites, and these came to be echoed in party strife. Wealthy elites who could afford to relinquish their slaves in favor of free labor tended to comprise the ranks of abolitionists, and these men had long been associated with the Federalist cause. Arrayed against them—often among the Republicans—were the more middling sort, who could only aspire to slaveholding, or for whom a few slaves might represent the bulk of their wealth. For whites even lower down the socioeconomic scale, freed slaves represented competitors for scarce jobs in an insecure economy. As party competition drove both Federalists and Republicans to court the popular vote, formal politics—once the preserve of Anglo-American social elites—slowly began to orbit around conflicted rhetorics of class, race, and ethnicity. Each party accused the other of using working-class dupes to stuff the ballot box: Federalists charged that Republicans had purchased the votes of noncitizen immigrants, while Republicans alleged that Federalists controlled black voters.

The reality was more complex. African Americans did nurture their ties to white philanthropists with Federalist leanings. For example, in a public address to black New Yorkers in 1809, Joseph Sidney argued that his fellow African Americans should support their "Federal friends" rather than the Republicans, whom he called "the enemies of our rights" and the puppets of Southern slaveholders.[34] But Sidney's anti-Republican diatribe was singular. While well-to-do blacks often sided with Federalists—hostile whites ridiculed the association at every opportunity—very few African Americans expressed anything close to Sidney's ardor. Far more important to leading black New Yorkers than political affiliation were larger questions of blacks' image in the eyes of an increasingly hostile public. Black leaders shared the concerns of conservative white moral reformers in Federalist ranks, but rather than rely exclusively on outsiders to effect black moral reform, African Americans in New York City created their own vision of racial uplift. All too cognizant of popular perceptions of the mass of black New Yorkers, the black leaders who emerged with freedom conceded that slavery had indeed degraded African Americans, but they worked tirelessly to demonstrate blacks' potential for equality. Sidney sounded these more typical themes best in his 1809 address. "Although the 'Ethiopian cannot change his skin,'" he said, "yet his heart may, nevertheless, become an habitation for all the virtues which ever adorn the human character." For black leaders, moral "elevation" promised to counteract the racial prejudice that black vice fed. Sidney continued, "A conduct, on our part, in all respects dignified and proper, will effectually put to silence every cavil which may be offered against African emancipation, and must eventually convert our enemies into friends."[35]

If such words seemed merely to repose the concerns of white gradual abolitionists, their practical consequences offered more concrete evidence of African Americans' independence. In the first two decades of the nineteenth century, black New Yorkers built a host of community institutions to foster concern with moral uplift. The first of these emerged from religious establishments, beginning with the African Society, established in 1795. The following year, black Methodists formed the African Methodist Episcopal Zion (AMEZ) Church. The next decade, following the passage of the Gradual Emancipation Law, witnessed an explosion of black institution building, as black Baptists and Episcopalians founded their own separate churches. Black churches often remained a part of their larger denominations, but the cloying intervention of white-led denominational establishments could lead to further independence, as when the Zion Church broke free and became its own Methodist denomination in 1820.

Black churches acted as far more than sources of spiritual solace. Sites of community solidarity and mutual support, they offered opportunities for African Americans to unite across lines of class and generated cadres of free black leaders. In these respects, black churches closely resembled other forms of black institutional activity, such as mutual aid organizations and literary societies, which enjoyed even greater independence from whites. Institutions such as the African Society for Mutual Relief, which began meeting formally in 1808, served as insurance agencies and educational charities, redistributing contributions of members to those in need. In 1809, New Yorker William Hamilton stated the African Society's goals: "To improve the mind, soften the couch of the sick, to administer an elixer to the afflicted, to befriend the widow, and become the orphan's guardian." Like the churches, mutual aid societies expressed considerable concern with the moral status of working-class black New Yorkers, as well as the public image of black institutions themselves. The societies required of their members "upright" deportment and a solid reputation, and their leaders insisted that they conduct their business with dignity. "Above all things," Hamilton advised the African Society, "let our meetings be conducted with order and propriety."[36]

Black New Yorkers' growing independence from white patrons was also evident in the changing course of black public celebrations over the turn of the nineteenth century. By the late eighteenth century, enslaved New Yorkers had transformed the Dutch celebration of Pentecost, or *Pinkster*, which fell in late spring, into a preserve of African American culture. In Pinkster, owners permitted their slaves several days of release, during which men and women of the black working class (and some whites) gathered to make music, dance, and play games. Widespread emancipation led black leaders in New York City to transform this master-sanctioned slave festival into something quite different: the parade. As they did throughout the North in the early nineteenth century, African Americans began proceeding publicly (often in martial regalia) in commemoration of key events in their recent past—notably, the abolition of the slave trade to the United States in 1807. Many whites found threatening these new expressions of African Americans' intent to participate equally in the civic life of the city—expressions in which blacks literally laid claim to the streets and central thoroughfares of Northern cities. In 1809, when New York blacks held such a parade, even their white "friends" cautioned them against the move. Black New Yorkers would not be denied, however, and proceeded nonetheless.[37]

Black parades demonstrated that the streets of New York City were every bit as important an arena for racial politics as were the statehouse and the court-

Portrait of Peter Stuyvesant, the last and greatest director-general of the Dutch New Netherland colony, probably by Henri Couturier, ca. 1660. One of the oldest and most important paintings produced in colonial America, it was given to the

Inquisition. Indented and taken at the City of New York the Ninth — day of April in the Eleventh year of the reign of our Sovereign Lady Anne &c. by the grace of God of Great Brittain France & Ireland Queen Defender of the Faith &c. before Henry Wileman Esqr Coroner of the s'd Queen upon view of the Body of one Augustus Grasset then and there lying dead by the oaths of Baron Bayard, Rutgert Waldron, Johannes Van Gisbert Van Imburgh, Stephen Richard, Francis Garrabrand, Johannes Van order, Daniel Goy, Bartholomew Roos, Isaac Brett, Johannes DeMarest, Martin Clok, William Waldron, Henry Vanderhule, Alexander Will, Andries Mayer, Francis Vincent, Doctor Welch, Jacob Brodie, sworn & Thomas Koorn, Johannes Vandoua, Doctor Beason Richard Abulaad, John Beason who being First and Foresd and Sworn to Enquire how when and after what manner the said Augustus Grasset came to his Death do say upon their Oath aforesaid that a certain Negro or Indian Man Slave (to witt) a certain Negro Man Slave called Caffee belonging to one Peter Van Elborough of s'd City aforesaid Boulter, a certain Mulatto Man Slave called John belonging to the said Peter Van Elborough a certain Negro Man Slave called Sam belonging to Peter Fauconier of s'd City aforesaid the a certain Negro Man Slave called Jack belonging to one John Cooks of the City aforesaid Merchant, a certain Negro Boy Slave called Dick — belonging to one Hermanus Burgher of s'd City aforesaid Baker, a certain Negro Man Slave called Maria belonging to one Forst Leyden of s'd City aforesaid Baker, a certain other Negro Man Slave called Frank belonging to Abraham Provost of s'd City aforesaid Boatman a certain Negro Man Slave called Jarret — belonging to Samuel Phillips of the City aforesaid Smith, a certain Negro Man Slave called Clauß belonging to Allan Jarret of s'd City aforesaid Marriner, a certain Negro Man Slave called Sam belonging to Jacobus Verish of the City aforesaid, a certain Negro Man Slave called Tom belonging to Nicholas Leyser of of the City aforesaid Baker — a certain Negro or Indian Man Slave called Hossey belonging to Mary — Wenham of s'd City aforesaid Widow, a certain Indian Man Slave called Ambrose belonging to Staat Governour of s'd City aforesaid Merch't, a certain Negro Man Slave to the Mars belonging to Jacob Reignier of this City aforesaid together with divers other Negro and Indian Slaves Offenders and disturbers of the peace of our s'd Lady the Queen aforesaid unknown to the Number of twenty Four or more with force and arms armed and Arrayed (to witt) with Guns Pistolls Clubbs Sword Staves then with Axes and Knives at the Break the day of April last past within the City of New York to witt the East Ward of the s'd City about the hours of Five of the Clock in the afternoon of the same day did Riotously, Routously and unlawfully Assembly and meet together to disturbe the peace of our s'd Lady the Queen that a own't And being soe assembled and met together they the aforesaid Negro and Indian Slaves or some of them and the said Augustus Grasset did then and there suddainly Dyed Ale &c of Jurors made an Assault upon him the said Augustus Grasset, and him the said Augustus Grasset did beate and wound Giving him four all wounds about this Brest and head and fingers of which said wounds hee the said Augustus Grasset then and there suddainly Dyed Ale &c of Jurors aforesaid upon their Oaths aforesaid doe say That the aforesaid Negro and Indian Slaves, or some of them the aforesaid Augustus Grasset to Die and Slay in manner and forme aforesaid against this publick peace of our s'd Lady the Queene. In Witness whereof as well the s'd Coroner aforesaid as the Jurors to this Inquisition have set their hands and Seals the day & year above written.

Johannis V: Water

Robert Benson

Thomas? of Rutland Roos

John Banker

Alex'r Mills

Andries Mayer

F: Vincent

Peter Welsh

Jacob Phœnix

Hernon Kerner

Dan'l Goy

Hendrick V: dous

Albert Hisbeck

Isaac Brett

Marten Clok

William Waldron

Henry Wileman Coron'r

B Cuyder

Rat'n Waldron

Johan Gisson

Stephen Richard

+

Silver pepper box made by Simeon Soumain, ca. 1730. In 1741, when the "Great Negro Plot" seemed to threaten the city with destruction, Soumain's slave Tom told the authorities that the conspirators asked him to get swords from his master's shop. Two years later, Soumain advertised that a pepper box much like this had been stolen. NEW-YORK HISTORICAL SOCIETY

Silver coffeepot, made by Peter van Dyck, ca. 1730, probably made for Susanna Phillipse, daughter of Frederick Phillipse, the master of Phillipsburg Manor in Yonkers and one of the colony's leading slave traders and owners. Van Dyck was also known to have purchased stolen silver from New York's slaves. NEW-YORK HISTORICAL SOCIETY

Three watercolor miniatures of Pierre Toussaint, his wife, and his niece, ca. 1825. Toussaint, a Haitian immigrant, was a successful hairdresser, emblematic both of the hardworking newcomer to New York and the free generation of black New Yorkers eager to establish themselves in business and the professions. NEW-YORK HISTORICAL SOCIETY

room. Public processions staged African Americans' demands for equality far more effectively than white abolitionists championed black rights. In fact, legislative developments in the period between 1799 and 1817 exposed the strange dualism of race relations in early national New York. Champions of black freedom hacked away at the vestiges of slavery, while fearful whites conceded black freedom only to sow new seeds of racial prejudice while many abolitionists sat idly by. Those seeds bore fruit in the final decade of slavery's long death in the Empire State.

The year 1817 was a significant one for black New Yorkers, not simply because it saw the legislature provide for the ultimate end of slavery in the state, but also because it inaugurated a new challenge to African Americans' rights and liberties. In that year, a group of leading national figures formally founded the American Colonization Society (ACS), an organization dedicated to settling manumitted slaves on the coast of West Africa. Prominent Americans lent their names, credibility, and fortunes to the enterprise, including Henry Clay, Andrew Jackson, Francis Scott Key, James Monroe, Daniel Webster, and Bushrod Washington. The movement found considerable support in the New York region. Among the most energetic members of the society was Robert Finley, a Presbyterian minister from New Jersey who served as a key point of communication between the society and African Americans. Important New Yorkers also counted themselves members: John Jay; Charles Andrews, director of the African Free School; William Leete Stone, editor of the *New York Commercial Advertiser*; and Rufus King, U.S. Senator from New York. Colonizationists across the Hudson captured the temper of these men when they warned that free blacks constituted a degraded class that "would provoke a civil and servile war" unless something were done to control them. They suggested the physical removal of black people, so that "the enormous mass of revolting wretchedness and deadly pollution" would be removed from the nation's shores.[38]

The American Colonization Society deftly captured the hardening logic of race in the age of emancipation. Many working-class and middling whites viewed blacks not as the victims of slavery but as the cause of whatever moral

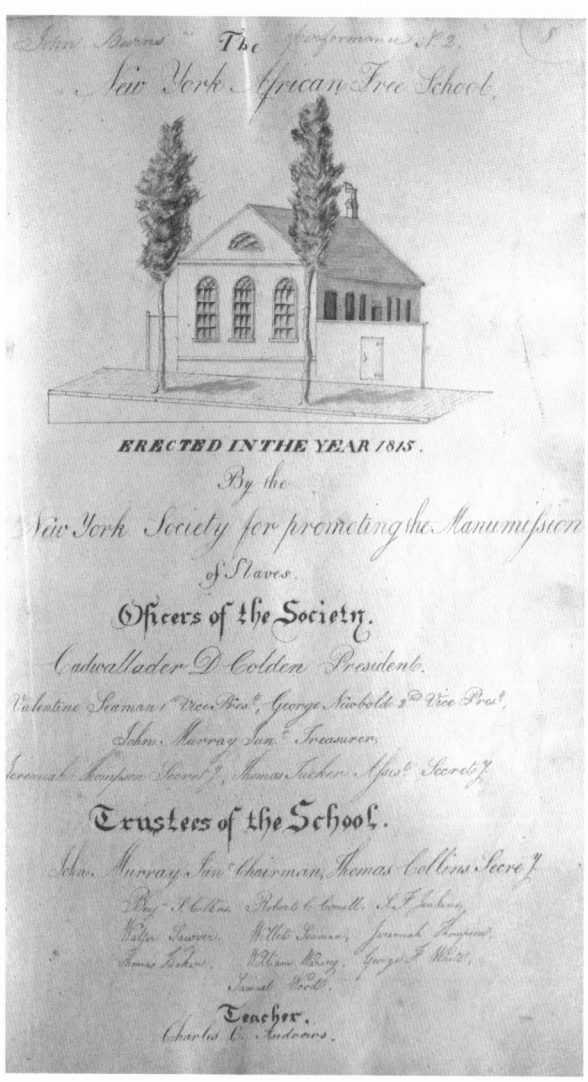

Drawing of the New York African Free School.

taint slavery had brought upon the nation. Until the society's founding, elite whites had tended to counter this "hard" racist impulse with a softer approach, conceding blacks' degradation but attributing it to the effects of slavery—to circumstances—rather than to any inherent racial deficiencies. Slaves could be redeemed, if only freed from the degrading influences of servitude and nurtured in the values of the expanding market economy. Expectations for blacks in freedom were thus quite high, regardless of the fact that the state had made no formal provision to ease the transition from forced labor to free. Even the minimal "charity" offered to freed people, such as the African Free School, came with troubling strings attached. Rather than atone for a century of enslavement, reforming whites sought instead to instill their own values in their charges without providing the material bases of those values, such as middle-class occupations. As the steady waning of slavery in New York heightened naive expectations, some of blacks' abolitionist champions called for retreat, claiming that their fight against slavery had already been won. A similar process happened among abolitionists' old opponents. They conceded the battle over slavery only to form new lines against black equality. On both the right and left, the old wings of popular sentiment coalesced around a new center, best represented by the American Colonization

Society's Janus-faced concern—with black redemption on the one hand, and black removal on the other.

By 1820, when the Colonization Society became a potent force in national politics, the abolition measures of 1799 and 1817 had badly eroded slavery in New York. The 10,000 remaining slaves in the state made up less than 1 percent of its total population. In the New York City region, Manhattan was atypically black and unusually free. While the African American population from 1810 to 1820 declined or remained steady in the counties surrounding New York City, the city itself welcomed over one thousand new black immigrants. The city's slave population declined considerably over the decade, but by 1820 it still numbered over five hundred, ranking it right behind Queen's and Richmond counties. New York's total black population was over three times that of Queen's, its closest rival. Still, even this growth could not keep pace with New York's exploding white population. While the number of whites in the city grew by over 30 percent from 1810 to 1820, the black population grew by not even 11 percent. For the first time since the seventeenth century, African Americans made up less than one-tenth of the residents in the city.

African Americans struggled in freedom. Contrary to contemporary popular opinion, innate deficiencies did not keep blacks poor, estranged, and disenfranchised, but the efforts of prejudiced whites did. Immigrant workers from Britain and Ireland supplanted blacks in the workplace, leaving African Americans the most miserable tasks the city had to offer, like sweeping chimneys and emptying privies. White workers generally denied black men and women places in the nascent white labor movement. Despite the external obstacles to blacks' economic mobility, many New Yorkers viewed African Americans as an ongoing source of moral decay and political corruption. In 1821, Mordecai Noah, editor of the popular *National Advocate*, declared that "high wages, high living, and the elective franchise" had filled city blacks with social pretense, causing them to ape their betters. For Noah, black freedom undermined white democracy. Blacks could not appreciate the right to vote; among them, the franchise was "a mere vendible article," available for sale to every corrupt political boss in the city.[39]

These sentiments came to a head during the New York State Constitutional Convention of 1821. Charged with revising the Constitution of 1777, most of the New Yorkers elected to meet during the summer of 1821 viewed their task as replacing an older, deferential style of politics with a more democratic order. The question of black rights stood in curious relationship to this democratizing impulse. The original state constitution had drawn no racial distinction in voting rights, requiring only that voters possess sufficient property to render them independent of the designing men who might corrupt the political process. Now, the very same political coalitions demanded the franchise be extended to all white men and argued for completely denying it to black men—all in the name of enhancing democracy.

Only the tortured logic of race could square this circle. The first premise of the argument to deny black New Yorkers the vote asserted that African Americans were by nature incapable of responsibly exercising this precious right of self-rule. "The minds of the blacks are not competent to vote," argued one convention member. "They are too ignorant to know whether their vote is given to elevate another to office, or to hang themselves upon the gallows," said another. Left to their own devices, the argument went, blacks would sell their votes to the highest bidder—who, these Republicans feared, would probably be Federalists. Suffrage restriction recapitulated and strengthened the thinking of the American Colonization Society, which asserted that freedom was one thing but political equality quite another. Republican convention delegate Peter Livingston was willing to grant blacks freedom, legal protection, and religious liberty. "But if they are dangerous to your political institutions," he warned his fellow delegates, "put not a weapon in their hands to destroy you."[40]

Such arguments did not go unanswered. Some in the convention stood against disfranchisement, noting that blacks were not the only source of political corruption in the state. These men argued that if New York was to deny black men the vote, it should also exclude "the many thousands of white fawning, cringing sycophants, who look up to their more wealthy and more ambitious neighbors for direction at the polls, as they look to them for bread." Blacks' defenders also pointed out that African Americans should not be blamed for their deficiencies,

Mordecai Manuel Noah (1785–1851)

Patriot, playwright, diplomat, and politician, Mordecai Noah was the most prominent Jewish American of his day. However, it was as editor and publisher of New York's *National Advocate* that he made his mark. Born of Sephardic ancestry in Philadelphia, Noah grew up in South Carolina, where, in 1811, he published editorials urging war with Great Britain. President James Madison rewarded him with the U.S. consulship to Tunis—a position Noah claimed was taken from him in 1815 on account of his religion.

When he returned from his post, Noah settled in New York City, where he began publishing the *National Advocate*, an organ of the Democratic Tammany political machine. He had a hand in editing several other newspapers, each of which—in the manner so typical of the antebellum press—united journalism and politics. His activities garnered him patronage positions in the city as sheriff, port surveyor, and judge. Noah was an energetic and multifaceted character, active in an amazing range of endeavors. He wrote popular patriotic plays and helped to establish New York University and Mount Sinai Hospital. Presaging twentieth-century Zionism, he sought always to connect Jewish and American interests. In the course of his career he embarked on a failed experiment to settle Jews on Grand Island near Buffalo, New York, and called for the United States to take the lead in securing Palestine as a Jewish homeland.

But as stridently as he promoted the rights and interests of New York's Jewish population, on the pages of the newspapers he edited, Noah offered incipient racial stereotypes of free African Americans. He posed black New Yorkers' alleged penchant for foppery and display as an effort to "ape" the "respectable" whites. His characterization of free blacks as "an evil and a blotch upon the face of American society" gave voice to the rising racism of Emancipation-era New York City. Despite this invective, Noah's racial attitudes also evinced an attraction to African American life. He often offered muted appreciation for the theatrical performances at the African Theater, and the African Company itself performed two of Noah's plays.

In 1851, at the time of his death, Noah had become an important public figure popularly associated, somewhat paradoxically, with both Jewish advocacy and racial intolerance.

—*Patrick Rael*

arguing that "it does not become those who have acted so unjustly towards them, to urge the result of that injustice as a reason for perpetuating their degradation." Finally, franchise exclusion removed potential inducements to black social mobility. Rather than fostering a "sober and industrious" African American population, franchise exclusion would establish "a large, a perpetual, a degraded, and a discontented *caste*, in the midst of our population."[41]

These appeals fell on deaf ears. Underlying Republicans' concern with political corruption lay a deep investment in maintaining a stratified racial order. Whites could not stay the course of emancipation, but they could still draw distinctions among the free. At some point in the proceedings, nearly all advocates of franchise exclusion feared the specter of what was commonly termed "social equality." Republican Erastus Root could not imagine poor black men standing at the polls, equal to "those who ride in their coaches, and whose shoes and boots they had so often blacked." White people would not countenance black men on the militia training ground, in the jury box, or in white churches, so why let them vote? Conjectured Republican Samuel Young, "If the time should ever arrive, when . . . the colours shall intermarry—when negroes shall be invited to your tables—to sit in your pew, or ride in your coach, it may then be proper to institute a new Convention, and remodel the constitution so as to conform to that state of society." Clearly, Young thought that would be a cold and terrible day, when the very distinctions that made whiteness of value would be erased.[42]

To such thinking there could be no reasoned response. "Do our prejudices against their colour destroy their rights as citizens?" asked Federalist Abraham Van Vechten.[43] White New Yorkers decided that they did. The convention removed all property restrictions on white men only to impose a $250 property requirement on black voters. By 1826, further limits on white voting were removed, yet by then only sixteen blacks in New York County could vote.[44] Still, popular race-baiters continued to harp on blacks' alleged affronts. When a band of free blacks attempted to liberate some fugitive slaves in 1826, an anonymous white writer asked, "Are we to be governed by a mob of Negroes[?]" Blacks were becoming "a privileged order—privileged to interfere with the administration of the laws."[45]

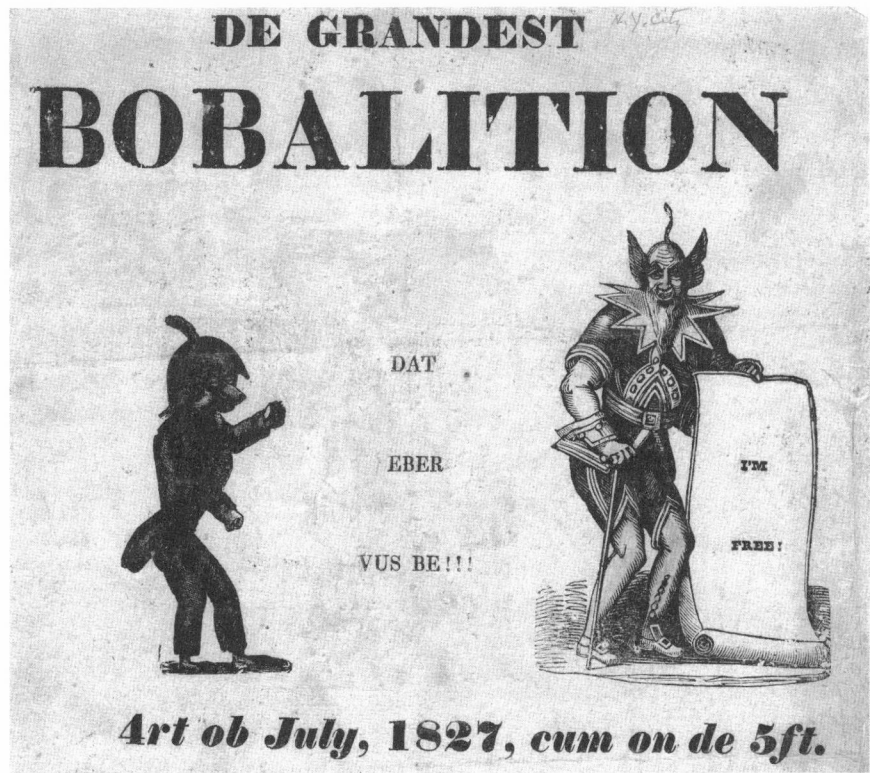

"De Grandest
Bobalition Dat
Eber Vus Be!!!"
NEW-YORK HISTORICAL
SOCIETY LIBRARY

The 1820s marked a dark age in New York's race relations as racialist think-ing spiraled downward to new lows, presaging the arduous decades to come. At the heart of the new racism of the antebellum years was the practice of collec-tively identifying all people of African descent—regardless of class, status, occupation, national origin, cultural practice, skin complexion, or degree of white heritage—as sharing a common, inherent degradation. "Black" became a monolithic category. Of course, whites had long tended to view all people of African descent as an undifferentiated whole, but the enactment of racially restrictive social policies like the franchise provisions of the Constitution of 1821 profoundly exacerbated the process. Law did not merely reflect popular attitudes, it also reinforced them, lending a new explanatory power to race. It was becoming unnecessary to argue why black people were inferior; blackness itself was becoming sufficient cause for assuming inferiority. The Constitution of 1821 has long been heralded as a victory of democracy over the forces of deference, but white New Yorkers had not erased hierarchy. They had merely downplayed old divisions of class and ethnicity among whites by asserting the new primacy of race. In the Age of the Common Man, African Americans paid the price for white democracy with their very rights.

By the census of 1830, only seventy-five slaves remained in New York State. Seventeen of these lived in New York County, either the property of Southern slave owners temporarily residing in the city, or the last remnant of those enslaved African Americans apprenticed under the provisions of the abolition laws of 1799 and 1817. The next census, of 1840, would list no slaves in the city. Two hundred years of slavery in New York had ended, but fifty years had been required to accomplish the task.

The long death of slavery in the Empire State illuminates a fundamental paradox in New York history: New Yorkers black and white owed their liberties to the principles of the American Revolution, but white New Yorkers did very little to ensure that freed slaves would enjoy the fruits of liberty equally with whites. To the contrary, law and popular opinion worked against black equality, relegating African American New Yorkers to second-class citizenship, and elevating race as the central division of the social order. This contradiction between principle and practice characterized not only New York, but every place in America where slavery died. Throughout the United States, liberty for African Americans did not easily translate into equality. This was no mere matter of economic interest conquering the ideological impulses of the American Revolution. Revolutionary ideology contained within it tensions that helped impose strict limitations on black freedom. Hanging in the balance against the Revolution's concern with universal human liberty was its commitment to liberal property rights, which argued against depriving any citizens of their property—even that held in humans.

For black New Yorkers in the age of emancipation, slavery remained a vital force long after law had eclipsed the institution. It did so not because slavery had actually damaged black people, but because a great many whites believed it had. Slavery impaired the post-emancipation black community in New York because of the ideological residue of slavery in white minds. For even the purported "friends" of blacks, slavery had imparted to black men and women a moral and perhaps even physical inferiority that could not be overcome through simple acts of manumission. Whites believed that coping with the aftereffects of slavery justified special restrictions on free black life. For whites of the middling sort and Republicans, these took the form of strictures on black political participation; for whites of the upper orders and Federalists, they took the guise of the paternalistic impulse behind the African Free School and moral reform efforts. Measures such as those limiting black men's access to the vote minimized opportunities for black "elevation," while those like moral education reinforced the all-too-common perception that blacks stood in need of special redemption before they could participate equally in city life.

Thus began a self-reinforcing cycle. Restrictive and paternalistic measures degraded black life, consigning African Americans to exploitative wage labor, unhealthful living conditions, and participation in the underground economy. The reality of black impoverishment then became the strongest argument for the further restricting blacks' participation in the social, civic, political, and economic life of New York, as blacks' detractors argued that such degraded beings could have no place in a civil polity. In turn, continued restrictions effectively worked to impair black elevation. And on and on the cycle went.

Black New Yorkers had had reason to greet their liberation with optimism. But the early years of black freedom in New York were not a tale of progressive betterment and expanding liberty. For African Americans, it must have seemed that history moved backward. Free blacks in the years after emancipation did not become more free over time but less free; as fundamental rights were stripped from black men, whiteness became the measure of civic inclusion, and the racial hostility of the mob grew beyond all bounds.

Nonetheless, the efforts of black New Yorkers in these bleak years bore fruit. In the streets of New York, African Americans had been the vital force that propelled abolition, and in the years following emancipation, black agency continued to serve as the most powerful counterbalance to white supremacy. As old white friends dwindled into insignificance or, like the colonizationists, actively turned against blacks, African New Yorkers strengthened their reliance upon themselves and forged new avenues to equality. They developed networks of institutions to nurture the fragile black community, and built a tradition of public protest that inspired generations of black activists and white abolitionists. Through their own uncompromising demand for liberty, African Americans transformed the legacy of slavery in New York from a tale of ignominy and defeat into a prophecy of liberation and deliverance.

Chapter 5

BLACK LIFE IN FREEDOM: CREATING A POPULAR CULTURE

SHANE WHITE

William Sidney Mount, *The Power of Music*,
1847. Oil on canvas. CLEVELAND MUSEUM OF ART,

LEONARD J. HANNA JR. FUND

ON A CRISP JANUARY DAY in 1838, Amos P. Fisher, a passenger on the *Providence* steamboat, gave up his seat and leaned against the ship's rail in order to admire the view as they covered the last few miles into New York City. One Henry Magrath ambled over to him and struck up a conversation. When it turned out that both men came from Providence, Magrath affably suggested that, when the steamboat docked, they should go for a stroll along the Battery. Not very far into their walk they came across a black man named Henry Childs, whom Magrath accosted, asking him if he were not the man who told fortunes. On being told he was, Magrath immediately offered to wager him $20 that he could not tell his fortune. Childs accepted the bet and, as the *Journal of Commerce*'s reporter would later write, "immediately took out a pack of cards to foretell the future destinies of Magrath." But, of course, at this point Magrath remembered that he did not have any cash with him and asked Fisher to lend him the money for half an hour until he could return to his boardinghouse and repay him. To quote his later testimony, Fisher, "thinking that Magrath was a Providence man, and of course honest," almost eagerly advanced him the $20. Childs then gave a splendid reading of Magrath's future; indeed "the colored man performed his part of the business so thoroughly to Magrath's satisfaction, that the latter like an honest Providence man, acknowledged that he had lost the wager, and most honorably handed Mr. Fisher's $20 to the fortune teller." As Childs pocketed the money, Fisher noticed out of the corner of his eye that the pair were signaling one another, "which foretold to him, without the aid of cards, that his destiny was to lose his $20, by them both running away, if he did not immediately lay hold of them." Fisher seized each of them by the collar and, with the aid of some passers-by, hauled them off to the police station.[1]

Henry Childs was but one of quite a few black men and women who, in the first half of the nineteenth century, lived by telling fortunes or hustling—at this distance who can tell the difference?—in New York. Contemporaries were anything but agreed as to how to deal with black soothsayers. On the one hand, writers in the newspapers wrote stories about them in prose that, as we have seen with the *Journal of Commerce*'s reporter, fairly dripped sarcasm. On the other hand, a stream of customers, both black and white, beat a path to their doors. In early 1826, the *National Advocate* reported that "a black prophet, who had let his wool grow for ten years so as to give himself a venerable appearance," had recently opened "a shop of fortune telling" near Canal Street and was doing a roaring trade. Young ladies flocked uptown to hear about sweethearts, "young widows to catch a word of husbands," and married ladies to learn the futures of their daughters and sons. The reporter ended his story by noting that "any occupation may turn the penny if it is shrewdly followed," but for all his cynicism, many white New Yorkers found solace or encouragement in the words of the black seer.[2] One can almost hear the drums of mysterious Africa that must have been reverberating in at least some white minds.

Black fortune tellers predicted the future, read cards, interpreted dreams, and offered advice on what numbers to take in policy, the forerunner of the well-known numbers racket so popular in Harlem in the 1920s.[3] The police sometimes called upon them to assist in the recovery of stolen property, exemplifying their role as cultural brokers. In 1826, a "queer looking black man" named Dr. White, "who had the reputation of a fortune teller and a conjurer," had his credibility called into question in a New York courtroom. "It was true," he stated, "that he had a 'planet book' in which he sometimes looked and gave advice"—but never for money, he hastened to add. White had also "been able to point out where stolen goods were likely to be found, as Mr. M'Lean, the High Constable, well knew." At this point, the conjurer's "very significant and imploring looks" across the courtroom were responded to by the policeman, who declared "that the *Doctor was no wizzard* and had, in his opinion, become *a useful citizen.*"[4]

If contemporaries' opinions were divided as to the benefits, or otherwise, of black fortune tellers, at least they noticed their existence. Later writers have not. The fact that Henry Childs, a black fortune teller, concocted an elaborate scheme with a white man to hustle some poor dupe is as good an indication as any of the way life had changed for black working people in New York in the few years since slavery had ended. The stories of Henry Childs and thousands of other black New Yorkers provide insight into how the city's African Americans shucked off the hated legacy of slavery and discovered for themselves what their newly won freedom meant.[5]

FREEDOM WAS a long time coming for slaves in New York City, but once it finally arrived, everything changed. In 1799 the New York Assembly legislated to end slavery, but the measure was a compromise that demonstrated both the power of the slaveholding interests and the respect accorded property rights, even if the property was human beings. It was now certain that slavery was going to end and that New York would align itself with the other Northern nonslave states. But the legislature had ensured that abolition would occur at a pace that could only be described as glacial. Unwilling to wait for slavery's demise, black men and women took things into their own hands and negotiated individually with their masters. Most of the advantages in such transactions still lay with the owners, but for once the deck was not stacked entirely against the slaves, and many played their cards skillfully. Not only was slavery in New York legislatively doomed, but the city's free black population was also rapidly increasing, making the successful pursuit of runaway slaves much more difficult. Moreover, implicit in every negotiation was the threat that, if some arrangement were not agreed upon, the owner would be left with either a sullen refractory slave, or, if

151

BLACK LIFE
IN FREEDOM:
CREATING A
POPULAR
CULTURE

SLAVE HOUSING IN MANHATTAN

In 1800, most of New York City's nearly 2,500 slave men and women worked as house servants and lived in two neighborhoods near the East River docks or along the lengthy promenade of Broadway near the southern tip of Manhattan Island. Because New York slaveholders generally owned only one or two slaves, they rarely lodged them in separate buildings. Instead, they lodged slaves in some marginal space—attic, basement, closet, or loft—where they might be out of sight but still readily available. The old urban dwellings of New Netherland were easily adapted to the desires of the city's slaveholders. Often standing three stories tall with a gabled end facing the street, the typical Dutch town house commonly included a kitchen in its basement and a storage space under its steeply pitched roof (Fig. 1). Either the loft above or the cellar kitchen below might serve as a place where a slave could sleep. The slaves' comfort, privacy, or solitude rarely mattered.

In placing their slaves at the literal margins of their households, Manhattan slave owners inadvertently encouraged the development of the black community. A cellar kitchen, usually located only partially below grade, often had a door leading directly to the street. This arrangement enabled slaves to communicate with neighboring blacks and other passersby.

Residential patterns also allowed slaves to claim the public sidewalks as their space—zones for various expressive performances in music, dance, sport, and festival celebration. There they also shared news of their fellow slaves and made plans for rendezvous beyond their masters' eyes. English-style row houses also utilized semi-subterranean basements (Fig. 2) and facilitated slaves' temporary escape from the burdens of bondage.

Because the northern end of Manhattan Island remained open farmland through the end of the nineteenth century, black men and women enslaved on estates located above what is now Washington Heights lived in buildings that typified those of the central Hudson Valley. The Dyckman House, a modest gambrel-roofed Dutch house overlooking the Harlem River, is the lone surviving farmhouse in Manhattan. Its slave quarters were located in the outkitchen attached to the southern end of the house (Fig. 3). The small loft floor (measuring only 11 feet by 13 feet), where both the domestics and field hands were quartered, was accessible only from the kitchen below. Even though the kitchen was positioned right next to the dining room, the building's configuration insured that Dyckman's visitors would always be appropriately separated from his slaves (Fig. 4).
—*John Michael Vlach*

Colonial-era Dutch row houses on Broad Street near Wall Street. From George Holland, *A View of the Federal Hall of the City of New York, as appeared in the year 1797, with adjacent buildings thereto.*
PRINTS AND PHOTOGRAPHS DIVISION, LIBRARY OF CONGRESS

Examples of British row houses, Grove Street, New York City, photographed by Arnold Moses, 1936.
HISTORIC AMERICAN BUILDINGS SURVEY, LIBRARY OF CONGRESS

View of the Dyckman House, Broadway at 204th Street, New York City, drawn by Edmund Volk, 1934. The outkitchen, built ca. 1725, is located to the left of the house. HISTORIC AMERICAN BUILDINGS SURVEY, LIBRARY OF CONGRESS

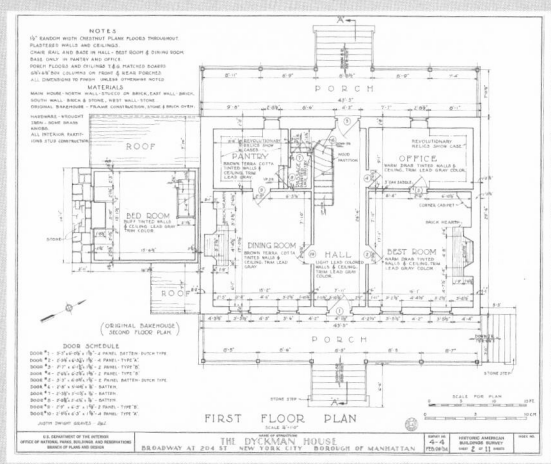

Plan of the first floor of the Dyckman House, drawn by Justin Dwight Graves, 1934. The small space to the left marked as "bed room" was the sleeping loft for the farm's slaves. HISTORIC AMERICAN BUILDINGS SURVEY, LIBRARY OF CONGRESS

the slave decamped, nothing at all. Strengthening the slaves' hand was the wave of slave violence, including arson and poisoning in the early years of nineteenth-century New York City, which gave an added impetus to these negotiations. In these circumstances, many owners took the path of least resistance, settling for whatever they could get from their human property.

New York slaves thus bore the costs of the tangled and often capricious process of emancipation, and for many, stuck in poorly paying jobs, those costs must have been huge. There were emotional costs, too, in this frequently demeaning process; having to behave like the perfect slave for a specified number of years must have been galling. To gain one's freedom depended, of course, on the slave's ability to negotiate, but also to a large extent on just plain luck. Moreover, because of the small size of slave holdings, families were dispersed among several owners, and while one member might secure freedom, his or her spouse or children, the property of more obdurate owners, might have to wait years longer.

Although bargaining for freedom caused slaves immense frustration and anguish, to be sure, by the time slavery ended in New York on July 4, 1827, there were virtually no slaves left in the city. Black men and women had by their own actions accelerated the legislature's lackadaisical timetable. Once free, the majority of black people became members of New York's nascent working class. Limited to low wages or street hustling, life in freedom was often difficult and precarious—but it was not slavery, a difference that black New Yorkers never forgot and were determined to remind whites at every opportunity.

With freedom, infuriated whites detected that black men and women carried themselves with a different demeanor, treating their former owners in new, unexpected ways, ranging from insouciance through to contempt and displays of outright aggression. Black New Yorkers saw little point in gaining freedom if they were to continue to be treated as if they were slaves. The workplace became the site of numerous confrontations. White New Yorkers found black employees particularly sensitive and quick to take umbrage and even legal action when employers snubbed them. On January 22, 1811, James Arden, a white merchant, hired Henry Lawson, a black man, as a servant. Lawson, however, did not meet Arden's expectations—the merchant complained of "improper conduct, and absenting himself," probably an indication that this free black man refused to behave like the slaves Arden had previously owned—and after twenty days Lawson was discharged. Arden tried to pay his former employee for the twenty days of his service, but Lawson indignantly refused to accept the proffered amount, demanding remuneration for the whole month. A heated argument ensued, during which, according to Arden, Lawson "was quite impudent and made considerable noise." Arden "then without any Violence raised his flat hand to the said Henry Lawson's mouth merely with a view of preventing a disturbance in his family and not to strike or injure the said Henry Lawson," a claim that stretches credulity now, as it did in 1811. The aggrieved servant promptly took Arden to court, suing to recover his wages. He lost his case but proceeded immediately to the police station, where he filed charges of assault and battery against his former employer. Impeached by his own unconvincing account of what had happened, Arden ultimately admitted his culpability; the cover of the district attorney's file bears the simple notation "submits."[6]

Myriad incidents—some minor, others more important—revealed that the old deference accorded whites was well and truly crumbling. Eliza Hazard, a young mulatto convicted of theft in 1822, "set the whole court to scorn" by shouting out that she wanted the judge "to go to hell along with her." On hearing that she was to spend the next fifteen months at hard labor in the penitentiary, she burst out, with "an audacious laugh: 'Oh, but that is but a little while.'"[7]

But it was on the city streets that white people found the worrisome forms of behavior most obvious. From a distance, whites' concern over the presence and demeanor of blacks in the city seems wildly out of proportion to their numbers. According to city censuses, the percentage of African Americans in the population in the early decades of the nineteenth century was not only low but was even diminishing: in the 1800s and 1810s the figure was about 10 percent, and in the 1820s and 1830s, as the city's total size soared to over two hundred thousand people, the black share hovered around only 7 percent. The most impor-

THE ROSE BUTLER CASE

Thomas DeVoe, nineteenth-century historian of New York City's markets, called the trial and execution of the young indentured servant Rose Butler "one of the most prominent transactions of my boyhood." Her case revealed how the fears generated among white New Yorkers by the prospect of emancipation created new dangers for black men and women. Born in 1799 in Westchester County to an enslaved mother, Butler owed twenty-five years of service to the Straing family, her mother's owners. When Butler was ten years old, the Straings sold her indenture to Abraham Child of New York City, and six years later, her indenture was sold again to William Morris. While with the Morris family, a fire of mysterious origins ravaged the Morris home. Butler was accused of arson with intent to commit murder. Despite the existence of evidence that the fire had been instigated by two white men of Butler's acquaintance, she never identified any accomplices. While she was in jail, the Morris house burned to the ground completely—an event that the *Evening Post* interpreted as an attempt to throw doubt on Butler's guilt. Butler was hanged several weeks later.

According to white New Yorkers, Butler's difficulties began with her move to New York City. Prison confidantes claimed that Butler, while owned by Abraham Child, fell into "the practice of stealing, and giving the articles to a coloured woman in the neighbourhood, who sold them" for her benefit. When Butler's indenture was sold to the Morris family, she "continued pilfering whatever she could lay her hands on," including three hundred dollars in silver. Butler bought gifts for family and friends and gallivanted around the city with the money: "I went a carriage riding with [my aunt] and several others, and paid all the expences. On the 4th of July I went with some girls, on board the steamboat, on a party of pleasure, and paid the charges; and $15 of it I spent at Mrs. Bundys, at Corlear's Hook, on a frolic!"

White New Yorkers focused on what they considered a world of immorality and criminality created by soon-to-be-free black men and women. If black people were uncontrolled as slaves and indentured servants, what would happen when the chains of bondage were removed? On the eve of Emancipation, the New York press dwelled endlessly on Rose Butler's alleged arson and other similar evidence of black people gone wild, with hardly a whisper of the aspirations of enslaved men and women for freedom, and never addressing the pain Butler's execution caused her family, friends, or the larger black community.

—*Leslie M. Harris*

tant explanation for the disparity between white perceptions of behavior and the demographic reality was black visibility and audibility: most black New Yorkers were forced to live not only a very public but also a very noisy existence.[8]

For many former slaves, the street became their place of employment. Here they helped feed the city's white inhabitants, cleared the snow from their paths, and cleaned up after them. Much of the work done by black people was of a casual nature. Thus, besides working on the streets, black men and women spent much time on the streets seeking employment, often to the inconvenience of whites. Black men jostled and crowded around as the steamboats docked near the Battery, importuning passengers to hire them to carry bags and undercutting the licensed porters. Sawyers, most of whom were black, hustled for custom on the street and then occupied the sidewalks to cut the wood.[9]

Black petty entrepreneurs, many of whom were women, were also an obvious and irritating presence. Among a long list of complaints arising from a walk he took in the Bancker Street

The Hot Corn Seller

Nicolino V. Calyo (1799–1884), *The Hot Corn Seller*, ca. 1840–44. Watercolor on paper.
MUSEUM OF THE CITY OF NEW YORK, GIFT OF MRS. FRANCIS P. GARVIN

area in 1820, "Humanitas" drew attention to the "oyster stands and numerous tables of eatables" that rendered passage along the sidewalks all but impossible. But most visible, and audible, were the street peddlers. From early in the morning until late at night—far too late by many accounts—their distinctive cries could be heard all over the city. Hollers such as "he-e-e-e-e-ere's your fine Rocka-a-way clams" and, most famously, in the autumn months, the ubiquitous "h-a-u-t corn," "h-a-urt ca-irr-ne," became a recurring and often disconcerting part of the city's soundscape. [10] It was the distinctiveness of the African American criers that made it clear that, even if a book such as *The Cries of New York* (1809) was inspired by a centuries-old English genre, its content was undoubtedly drawn from an American city. [11]

In the latter part of 1824, Samuel Jenks worked for several months as a newspaper editor in New York. Originally from Nantucket, he was, judging by the entries in his diary, particularly sensitive to the barrage of sound that constantly assailed his ears as he traversed the metropolis. At four o'clock on an August morning he was awoken by "incomprehensible and barbarous outcries" coming from the street below. On peering out of his window he discovered that the noise came from four black people "armed with besoms" (brooms made of twigs) and "iron instruments resembling a short hoe." The adult woman, "wrapped in an immense mahogany-coloured shawl," was urging on three children, garbed in "ragged cloaks of the same hue": "Come, wy de debble don't you hollar?" to which the answer came, "Yes, missee—Ek ho! Yaw, ak hikko yek! E oh! Yekko kik aw!" Jenks observed, "The long character in the shawl was a strapping, she-negro chimney sweep; and the smaller imps were her apprentices, thus compelled to proclaim their vocation in accents more dismal and appalling than those of Orpheus." [12]

Late at night, too, an army of black tubmen swarmed over the city. The job of emptying the privies—carrying the tubs down to the nearest dock and dumping the contents into the Hudson or East Rivers—was virtually a black monopoly. The work was hard, unpleasant, poorly paid, and nocturnal, and whites added to the burden by constantly complaining about the way in which it was done. In 1817, twenty-two inhabitants of the First Ward petitioned the city in an attempt to curb the "detestable cries" of the "vagabond negroes" vying for this business. Nor was excessive noise the whites' only complaint. As soon as they earned some money, the black sanitary workers bought rum, presumably to anesthetize themselves, and a few hours later were in such "a state of intoxication" that invariably tubs were dropped in the streets—leaving for hours the next morning pungent reminders of the workers' passage. Mostly, though, it was the din they made that irritated. Black tubmen usually worked in pairs, an arrangement that resulted in raucous duets cutting through the night air, and any request for quiet was greeted with "a torrent of clamarous abuse." Indeed, it was not just their "savage yells" that offended, but their "habit of bawling out such expressions as are most shockingly indecent." A person standing in Franklin Square could "often hear a dozen or twenty of them at once."[13]

Any unoccupied space in the city, but particularly the sidewalk, became a potential site on which black New Yorkers could spend their hours away from work; miserable housing conditions hardly induced them to stay inside. The years in which African Americans finally gained their freedom in New York were also those during which the sociability of the street, activities associated with what would later be called the "stroll," became established as a key element in an emerging and distinctive Northern urban black culture. As the *National Advocate* noted in August 1821, "Their modicum of pleasure was taken on Sunday evening, when black dandys and dandizettes, after attending meeting, occupied the sidewalks in Broadway, and slowly lounged towards their different homes." A year earlier, "A New-Yorker," writing to the *New-York Columbian*, had drawn attention to the same phenomenon. On an August Sunday afternoon, he revealed, two "gentlemen . . . had the curiosity to count the number of negroes, male and female, that passed a house in Broadway, near Washington-Hall." In just under two hours, no fewer than 1,480 black people had strolled past, and in the course of the evening several hundred more went by. This was an extraordinary number, somewhere between one in six and one in five of the black inhabitants of the city.

But it was more than just numbers that impressed this pair of white observers. These black men and women "were all well drest, and very many much better than whites." Almost without exception, the men wore "broadcloth coats, very many of them boots, fashionable Cossack pantaloons, and white hats; watches and canes," this last-mentioned accessory being "flourished with inimitable grace to the annoyance of all." The men walked "four or five a breast, arm and arm, with segars in their mouths, bid defiance to all opposition, and almost universally compel our most respectable citizens, returning from

159

BLACK LIFE
IN FREEDOM:
CREATING A
POPULAR
CULTURE

The Baker Cart

The Boot Cleaner

Nicolino V. Calyo, *The Baker Cart.*

NEW-YORK HISTORICAL SOCIETY, PURCHASE, THOMAS JEFFERSON
BRYAN FUND

Nicolino V. Calyo, *The Boot Cleaner.*

NEW-YORK HISTORICAL SOCIETY, PURCHASE, THOMAS JEFFERSON
BRYAN FUND

160

Baroness A.M.H.
Hyde de Neuvelle,
*Cook in Ordinary
Costume.*

NEW-YORK HISTORICAL
SOCIETY, PURCHASE

church with their families, to take the outside of the walk, and sometimes to leave the sidewalk altogether." Others were particularly taken with the appearance of black women on the streets. To Henry Fearon, a visitor from England, the "striking feature" of the New York of 1817 was "the number of blacks, many of whom are finely dressed, the females very ludicrously so, showing a partiality to white muslin dresses, artificial flowers, and pink shoes." Fifteen years later, Stephen Davis, another visitor to the city, "repeatedly saw coloured females in the height of fashion in Broadway.[14]

"A New-Yorker's" observations had a broader application, one that helps to explain the paradox of how the black minority maintained a disproportionate public profile. If the sheer number of African Americans on the city streets often seemed almost overwhelming, it was more than their apparently dominant physical presence that made them such a noticeable part of New York life. The larger-than-life style of black New Yorkers, the way they dressed, talked, and moved, often combining flamboyance and aggression, left a heavy imprint on observers' recollections. Any number of travelers' observations registered this transformation. In 1833, for example, E. T. Coke commented that on Sunday afternoons in New York, when the city streets "appeared entirely given up to the African world, it was a high treat to witness the switching of canes and important strut of the one sex. And the affected dangling of parasols and reticules of the other."[15]

White New Yorkers complained constantly about what they saw as the bumptious and often intimidating behavior of black people on the street. Newspapers constantly protested against the way in which African Americans

CHIMNEY SWEEP.

" Sweep, O—O—O—O. From the bottom to the top, Without a ladder or a rope, Sweep, O—O—O—O."

Chimney sweeps taken from *Cries of New York*, 1808. NEW-YORK HISTORICAL SOCIETY LIBRARY

BLACK LIFE IN FREEDOM: CREATING A POPULAR CULTURE

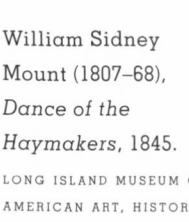

William Sidney
Mount (1807–68),
*Dance of the
Haymakers*, 1845.

shouldered "respectable citizens" off the sidewalk. In May 1815, there were
bitter complaints about black women in public using "obscene and infamous
language," particularly "profane oaths and vulgar epithets," and the aggressive
way they conducted themselves, "crowding and jostling" white citizens. A little
more than a decade later the *New-York Evening Post* reported a minor incident
in which a stout black man "was lately heard to exclaim, in a peevish tone, as
he elbowed a lady out of the way, '*Damn these white people, there's no getting
along for them.*'"[16] These were not mere violations of sidewalk etiquette.
Everywhere about white New Yorkers were signs that the old ways had crum-
bled under the sheer weight of an aggressive black volubility, and that the world
had truly been turned upside down.

And what nagged most at white New Yorkers was their awareness that free
blacks were behaving in this fashion deliberately. This was particularly evident

in the numerous parades in which African Americans criss-crossed the city in the early decades of the nineteenth century. Not all black parades met with white disapproval. When, in March 1827, the *New-York Enquirer*'s editor accidentally happened upon a parade of black masons on one of the streets branching off Broadway, he was pleasantly surprised. Not only had these marchers "conducted themselves with propriety, obedience and intelligence," but most important they were also "well dressed, silent and decorous."[17] But not many black New Yorkers were interested in marching silently along a back street. Most of the parades they organized were loud and lengthy affairs—the annual parades celebrating the end of slavery took at least three or four hours—traversing all the major and many of the minor streets of the city. Bands usually accompanied the marchers; in the case of the first parade to celebrate the end of New York slavery in 1827, there were, according to the *New York American*, as many as "four or five bands, comprising a great variety of instruments, played with much skill."[18] Anyone out and about on the city streets would have to have been stone deaf and blind to have missed these proud former slaves celebrating their freedom.

Prior to emancipation, blacks had been a visible but controlled part of New York life. Laws limited the number who could gather and, if the laws were enforced irregularly, they were a potent barrier to black congregations. With freedom, white authorities lost control over black life. As the number of free blacks increased, white people attempted to mark them off as a separate group and demonize them as undeserving of space in the city. If the look of a "dandified" black man or woman strolling on Broadway caused offense, so too did the touch of the black body that elbowed whites from the sidewalk, the "savage" sounds of black street cries, and, somewhat less frequently, the smell that black bodies were believed to emit. In large part, such unhappiness was caused by the deliberate actions of free blacks who declined any longer to remain quiet and unobtrusive. In 1823, a letter writer protested bitterly to the *National Advocate* about black behavior on the streets: "They are so rude, and talk so loud, and smell so bad, what are we to do—to whom shall we apply, Mr. Editor, to keep them more orderly?"[19] The assaults on their ears seemed to bother white

163

BLACK LIFE

IN FREEDOM:

CREATING A

POPULAR

CULTURE

people the most. Many whites considered the noise of everyday black urban life as an intimation of the chaos and lack of control that they saw as the almost inevitable accompaniment to the ending of slavery.

In these transitional years, as slavery ever so slowly died, the lives of working-class black men and women exhibited a kind of edgy vitality, a mood expressed not only in street life and parades, but also in music, dance, and, most surprisingly, theatrical endeavor. In the performance spaces available in the city, ordinary African Americans created a vibrant culture, one that not only reflected their new and exhilarating status as free people, but that also fascinated and not infrequently horrified white onlookers. The resulting conjunction between black creative activity and white voyeurism would not recur until the Harlem Renaissance of the 1920s.

The key figure in African American music in New York City—indeed in much of the rest of the mainland—was the fiddler. Black fiddlers were commonplace in colonial New York and in the early decades of the republic. They played at both all-white dances and all-black dances, and inevitably a good deal of cultural cross-fertilization occurred. The African American fiddler was ubiquitous in the region around New York, turning up in all manner of places. He made appearances in novels, short stories, and most notably in paintings. Here, the most interesting interpreter of the black fiddler is the white genre painter William Sidney Mount.

Mount was born in 1807 and raised in a slave-owning family near Stony Brook on Long Island. In 1853, he recounted a visit to the slave burial ground on his family farm. There, prominently displayed, was the tombstone of Anthony Hannibal Clap, a famed fiddler. Mount vividly remembered sitting "by Anthony when I was a child, to hear him play his jigs and hornpipes. He was," Mount continued, "a master in that way, and acted well his part." Mount's uncle, Micah Hawkins, a New York storekeeper and composer, had written an epitaph for Clap and had had the marker erected. Carved on the face of the stone was a violin with the bridge down and the bow and strings slack. The inscription under the caption, "Entirely tone . . . less," runs to over two hundred words and is a paean to the virtues of this "modest and polite" slave, and to his talent with the violin: "Nor old nor young, of either sex, stood on The Floor to Jig it, but he knew the gait, Peculiar of their Hobby, and unasked, Place'd best foot foremost for them, by his Fiddle." Mount's own sketch of the violin and description of the tombstone ends with the words "Tone has departed with Toney."[20]

Of course this language was sentimental and condescending, run through with racist assumptions about the "good, faithful slave." But the epitaph and the placement of the marker tell much more. However problematic it may appear, the tombstone was a genuine, indeed quite remarkable, attempt to acknowledge the brilliance of a black musician and suggests something of the way in which African Americans and their culture in New York could touch and influence even the most unlikely and obdurate of white men.

Mount was an antiabolitionist and certainly no champion of African Americans. He observed that "A Negro, is as good as a White man—as long as he behaves himself," exhibiting a condescension perhaps not unexpected from the scion of a former slaveholding family.[21] Later in life, as the institution of slavery rent the nation asunder in the Civil War, Mount penned numerous venomous racist aphorisms in his diaries.[22] But for all that, in the 1830s and 1840s Mount completed a number of canvases depicting African Americans with a degree of humanity that distinguishes him from virtually every other antebellum American artist. The most famous and enduring of these paintings depicted black men involved in some sort of musical activity. This was not coincidental. As well as being a painter, Mount was a musician, probably spending more time composing and playing music than he did painting, and in fact he patented his own design for a violin.[23] Mount's paintings of blacks drew on the idealized rural past of his youth, a past in which the black males who "behaved themselves" and thus attained the level of whites were musicians, the most notable example being the revered fiddler Toney.

Mount's *Dance of the Haymakers* (1845) and *The Power of Music* (1847) were apparently conceived of at the same time—there are working sketches of both images on one sheet among his papers—and in fact incorporate the same barn (see pages 148 and 162).[24] *The Power of Music* is probably the artist's best-

165

BLACK LIFE
IN FREEDOM:
CREATING A
POPULAR
CULTURE

known work. One's eye is drawn straight to the older African American man, the most sympathetically limned person in the painting. According to historians of nineteenth-century African American representations, this figure "is the most empathetic of all the antebellum images of the black male."[25] The African American man portrayed in *The Power of Music*—in fact modeled by Robin Mills, a local free black man—was not just passively listening to the music, but silently encouraging the young fiddle player. The "faint air of superiority in the smile and a sense of sure command in the curling grip of the fingers suggest that Robin has instructed the boy and is empathetically guiding his student's recital."[26]

Toney's influence on Mount lingered decades after his death. The titles of both the *Dance of the Haymakers*, which was first called *Music is Contagious*, and of *The Power of Music* suggest something of the way music joined blacks and whites in Mount's world. But the canvases, which have African Americans separated from the whites by the vertical lines of the barn door, and, in the case of *Dance of the Haymakers*, show a black man participating unequally with white men, also reveal the limitations of that intimacy.

But whatever may have been their influence on whites, African American fiddlers and their music were more important for black life in New York and doubtless elsewhere. Stories of legendary fiddlers abounded and some of this folklore found its way into the written record. George Schuyler, a black novelist and newspaper columnist writing in the twentieth century, heard from his grandmother, who had been born in New York City in 1831, stories of black "demon fiddlers" from New Jersey, "who caused people to dance all night until they fell exhausted."[27]

Similar accounts originated in Long Island. One sultry summer night, Pope's Joe, a slave from Flatbush, on his way to woo an enslaved woman on a neighboring farm, stopped to rest by the side of the road. As Joe began to play some riffs on his violin, there was a vivid flash of lightning and a huge clap of thunder, and a demon appeared in front of him. Having gestured to Joe to carry on playing, the devil began dancing to the music. Terror-struck, drawn along by the wildness of the spectacular dancing, and awed by the way the devil distilled the energy of the savage summer storm in his gyrating body, Joe played as he had never played before. His bow fairly flew across the strings and the music got faster and faster. But, after a while, the pace becoming too much, Joe's arm tired and he hit a false note. Jarred out of his trancelike state, the devil angrily stamped his foot on a rock and disappeared in a blinding flash. The locale of this haunting performance was memorialized after a fashion—it became Greenwood Cemetery—and for many years before it was finally lost, the stone with the imprint of the cloven foot of the evil one remained in a corner of the graveyard.[28]

Not only fiddlers achieved legendary status; the region surrounding New York City was also noted for its dancers. Proud of her own expertise, the former New Jersey slave Silvia Dubois lamented to her biographer in the 1880s that local blacks could no longer dance because "they had no step." Recalling her youth in the early years of the nineteenth century, Dubois explained that "I'd cross my feet ninety-nine times in a minute and never miss the time, strike heel or toe with equal ease, and go through the figures as nimble as a witch."[29]

Though such dancing occurred in the countryside, it was most obviously on display at Catharine Market in the city. According to Thomas DeVoe's oft-quoted account, after they had finished their master's business in the city, the Jersey blacks would "shin" it across town to vie with the Long Island blacks in dance competitions. Dancers brought their own shingles—wide, springy boards of about six feet in length—and on these confined spaces engaged in spectacular break-down contests to the beat of other black men "patting juba," or keeping time by stamping their heels and beating their hands against their legs or other parts of the body. The dancers who best pleased their racially mixed audience were rewarded with money, fish, and eels. DeVoe remembered that black men from Long Island—Ned, Jack, and Bobolink Bob were the best known—usually took the honors.[30] A drawing of blacks dancing for eels at Catharine Market in 1820 survives (see page 168). Unlike the vicious caricatures of black men and women created by better-known contemporaries such as Edward Clay, this image by an unknown artist appears to be a relatively straightforward attempt to represent an aspect of city life and culture. The emphasis in this set-

DANCING FOR EELS, 1820 CATHARINE MARKET.

ting was on the individual dancer and his virtuoso performance. The drawing also reveals the extent to which blacks were objects for the gaze of white spectators.[31]

DeVoe's account hints at the pull of urban life. Large numbers of blacks lived within a ten- or fifteen-mile radius of New York; in the 1790s, four out of every ten white households in this region owned at least one slave, a rate of involvement in the institution greater than that of whites in South Carolina or Virginia—but the small size of slave holdings and widely dispersed farms made life difficult for African Americans.[32] City life, by contrast, gave promise of greater communal activity. As told by DeVoe, the story of Jack, the dancer mentioned earlier, reveals much. A "smart and faithful man," Jack was the slave of Frederick De Voo, a Long Island farmer. When De Voo was forced by law to free his slave, he fitted him out in a new suit and then made him the following offer: "*Jack*, if you go home with me, you shall never want; but if you leave me now, my home shall never more know you." For Jack, and for most other New York slaves, the choice was not a difficult one: he decided on freedom and the city and became, in DeVoe's dismissive term, "a loafer." Jack died a few years later while at Catharine Market, the site of many of the spectacular dancing victories of his youth.[33]

There had, of course, been slave music and dancing in the city in the colonial period, but there had always been limits to these activities: no matter how successful black New Yorkers were at testing the limits of their bondage, they were still slaves, usually living under their owners' direct supervision. The exhilaration of recently won freedom, the shucking off of petty restrictions, the establishment of independent households, and the influx of blacks with diverse experiences in Africa, the Caribbean, or elsewhere in the United States was a potent mix that would influence the contours of black New York culture, particularly music and dance. As slavery gradually wound down, black music and dance found a new venue and, in the case of New York, that venue was literally underground.

From the turn of the nineteenth century, references to black dancing in New York City appear with increasing frequency. In 1799, an advertisement for Peter, a mulatto runaway slave, described him as a "great dancer and a very quarrelsome fellow, and is noted as such in the negro dancing cellars in the city."[34] In October 1810, James Johnson stabbed Lewis Robinson in one of these establishments, and testimony at Johnson's trial for murder affords a glimpse into the culture of the city's dancing cellars. The premises were Johnson's own residence, a rented cellar in Chapel Street. The way in led down a few steps, under the stairs leading up to the house, and through two doors which opened into a long hall. There was only one room off the hall and that was the Johnson abode. In the entryway, a table was set up, at which Mrs. Johnson sold spirits and oysters. The crowded room—jammed with somewhere

169

BLACK LIFE
IN FREEDOM:
CREATING A
POPULAR
CULTURE

near thirty black men and women—was hot, loud, and boisterous: people drifted in and out, alternating between dancing and seeking fresh air. Johnson's wife had arranged the dance as a money-raising venture, charging one shilling admission. Right from the start there was a decided commercial aspect to this burgeoning dance culture. The court testimony also revealed that men were the focus of attention. Black women danced, but they were either the foil for male brilliance on the floor or the prize for which the dancers vied. The performance style of these young black men and their general behavior in the dance cellars entailed an aggressive display of noisy working-class masculinity, and this contributed substantially to the scuffle that ultimately resulted in Robinson's death.

Yet for all the emphasis placed on the figure of the individual male dancer, it is important to remember that this dancing was a communal and not a solitary activity. Participants came to the dance cellars of New York in search of their own private pleasure, but the collective result of this shared and exhilarating experience of being part of a rollicking crowd of black men and women moving together on the dance floor was a crucially important part of the lives of many, mostly working-class, black New Yorkers in the first half of the nineteenth century.[35]

Over the ensuing decades the number of dance cellars mushroomed. Court records and brief fugitive items in the newspapers make it clear that these establishments were crowded, smoky (it takes little imagination to surmise the origins of the Tobacco Box's name), hot, sweaty, and, above all, noisy. They became an intimate part of the lives of black working people. In August 1824, the watch broke into a house on Crosby Street, interrupting well over a score of black men and women who were "shrieking, screaming and cutting antic capers." The *National Advocate* pointed out that the thermometer had been "near 85, and the atmosphere rather strong and smoky."[36] A few years later, the *Sun's* court reporter, describing a crowded dance in the well-known haunt called "Ogilvie's buildings," focused on the "contagion of licentiousness" that "soon made the house shake, the welkin to ring, and night to be terrible with their revelry and noise."[37]

Such clichéd descriptions, particularly if read against their grain, do suggest something of the milieu of the dance cellars, but mostly they point to whites' incomprehension of an African American culture that at once troubled and fascinated them. Fortunately, a few descriptions of blacks' dancing, penned by more gifted writers, survive. The most graphic account comes from the pen of Charles Dickens. In 1842, Dickens toured a stifling underground dancing hall in the Five Points, where he saw the "greatest dancer known" (who in fact was William Henry Lane, or "Juba") perform: "Single shuffle, double shuffle, cut and cross-cut; snapping his fingers, rolling his eyes, turning in his knees, presenting the backs of his legs in front, spinning about on his toes and heels like nothing but the man's fingers on the tambourine; dancing with two left legs, two right legs, two wooden legs, two wire legs, two spring legs—all sorts of legs and no legs—what is this to him?"[38]

A few years later the journalist and author George Foster visited a similar dance house in the Five Points. The three-piece band was playing the familiar enough instruments of the fiddle, the bass drum, and trumpet, but Foster believed his readers would have little chance of even beginning to conceive of how the music sounded: "You cannot see the red-hot knitting-needles spirted out by the red-faced trumpeter, who looks precisely as if he were blowing glass, which needles aforesaid penetrating the tympanum, pierce through and through your brain without remorse. Nor can you perceive the frightful mechanical contortions of the bass-drummer as he sweats and deals his blows on every side, in all violation of the laws of rhythm, like a man beating a baulky mule and showering his blows upon the unfortunate animal, now on this side, now on that."[39]

Dickens's and Foster's marvelous descriptions painted a picture of a music and dance that can be labeled, anachronistically, as "hot." While the fiddle was not an African instrument and the jig was not an African dance, the general vivacity of the players' and dancers' movements, the abrupt juxtaposition of different dancing steps and sequences, and the dense and complex rhythmic patterns evoked in these white observers an acute sense of cultural difference. American forms had been infused with African elements to create a musical and performance style that is properly and most accurately described as African

American. These musicians and dancers drew on their American circumstances and created something that was new. The result was also most certainly not a quaint relic preserved in amber, but a dynamic, unruly music and dance form constantly developing and responding innovatively to the changing environment.

The dance cellars and Catharine Market were not the only sites where black city-dwellers listened to music and danced. By the mid-1820s, several times during the winter "season," black New Yorkers held formal balls. As many as three or four hundred blacks, reportedly as many as six hundred on at least one occasion, dressed in their best outfits, often traveled by carriage to the hall hired for the night, and danced waltzes and cotillions until the early hours of the morning. These balls, too, intrigued and fascinated the press. In part, the balls opened a voyeuristic window into what the *National Advocate* labeled "High Life Among the Coloured Folks," providing racy glimpses of an urban milieu that confirmed all the prevailing stereotypes of black people. As a matter of course, and as if to imply that blacks who attended balls were behaving with ludicrous effrontery, newspapers reported disturbances associated with any of these balls.[40]

For all their sarcasm and crude humor, press stories revealed an underlying brittleness in the white reaction to them: there was something unnerving about the aggressive way black New Yorkers were refusing to fade quietly into the background and were asserting their rights as Americans. Partly it was African Americans' flamboyant clothing, and partly their use of the accoutrements of elite white life, such as carriages. But overall it was the clamorous way in which black people were occupying the public space that whites had unthinkingly assumed was theirs alone that disconcerted blacks' fellow citizens. At an event organized to raise money for Greek freedom, the *New-York Enquirer* pointedly drew attention to the fact that, at the start of the evening, there had been a queue of horses and carriages in Orange Street, waiting for their black passengers to alight; at another ball two years earlier, the bustle in Mulberry Street had been controlled, according to the *National Advocate*, by black managers "ordering the white drivers to turn 'de horses head to Pump street.'"[41] The supposed racial roles were being reversed and there can be little doubt that this was exactly the impression that black men and women were trying to plant in white minds.

Every now and then, when white authorities heavy-handedly interfered, black spokesmen asserted that a new order had been established and that black people would no longer behave as slaves. In 1828, in the early hours of the morning and after another of these functions, two women of mixed racial origins, interrupted by the watch while quarreling in the street, were hauled off to the police station. The magistrate, whom the *New-York Enquirer* described as "benevolence himself," proceeded to lecture them on the "consequences of dissipation," pointing out, among other things, that "the follies of the upper classes are too often imitated instead of their virtues." Cutting to the quick of the issue, one of the women retorted sharply: "If the big white folks dance why should not people of colour ?"[42]

African American balls were multifaceted and complex events that can be interpreted in several ways. A considerable element of "copying" or "imitating" white American practices was involved, as black people drew from the larger society in order to restructure their lives now that they were free. But the process was more intricate. Even if the origins of the black balls were to be found in American culture, that was just a starting point: black New Yorkers infused these events with their own cultural imperatives, creating something that was new. Participating in events that had cultural significance for themselves, they also, at least in part, parodied the behavior of whites. In its turn, too, the ways in which African Americans transformed the ball would have its own reverberations in the practices of whites: the distinctive "distortion" that black musicians gave to waltzes and cotillions at the white balls, where their playing was in much demand, is the most obvious example of this syncretic process.

At one and the same time, then, these black balls were part imitation, part parody, and part showy performance of African American culture. They must also have been something else that historians in their bookish dourness often omit from their renditions of human behavior: fun. Dressing up to the nines, and beyond; hiring a coach and a white driver to take oneself downtown; making a grand entrance; mingling and gossiping with friends and acquaintances;

173

BLACK LIFE
IN FREEDOM:
CREATING A
POPULAR
CULTURE

AFRICAN GROVE THEATER

On the evening of Monday, September 17, 1821, in New York City, a recently formed drama company staged its first public performance. The venue was a makeshift theater in a private dwelling on Thomas Street, but the house was full, and when Richard III limped onto the stage, the audience erupted into wild cheering. There was an air of self-congratulation about the production—and with good reason, for virtually all present had either been born into slavery or were children of former slaves. This was a bold black intrusion into the world of acting, an arena hitherto accepted without question as the exclusive and "natural" preserve of whites. The African Grove Theater, or simply African Theater, was the Mother Bethel of the African American stage.

The creative drive behind the black drama company's first production had come from a black impresario named William Brown. Over the next couple of years, the company would put on a variety of productions, including plays by Shakespeare; *The Fortress of Sorrento* by Mordecai Noah, a local author and newspaperman (see sidebar, page 141); *Tom and Jerry*, the international hit of the 1820s; and at least one play written by William Brown himself, *Shotaway; or, the Insurrection of the Caribs.* In its early months, the company performed in various venues, but in July 1822, their new theater, seating as many as three hundred patrons, opened on Mercer Street. Not only was this establishment the first theater built by and for blacks, but it also must have been one of the largest investments made up to that time by any African American entrepreneur. It was certainly the most conspicuous.

The quality of the performances was mixed. On the one hand, actors routinely forgot their lines, and props did not always materialize; but, on the other hand, James Hewlett, the troupe's star performer, was very good, and it is possible that Ira Aldridge, the greatest black actor of the nineteenth century, also got his start there. White New Yorkers were clearly intrigued, as were visitors to the city. It is most noteworthy that ordinary white New Yorkers continued to attend, pay their money, and applaud wildly.

Still, New York's press heaped derision on the African Theater. The theater's initial success and the troupe's aggressiveness irritated many white New Yorkers—not least of all Stephen Price, the city's main theatrical entrepreneur, who once used his influence to have the sheriff close down a performance. When the theater reopened, Price employed thugs to disrupt performances, assault actors, and destroy costumes. Although African American actors persisted for some three years or longer, Brown eventually went bankrupt. The company performed for the last time in late 1823 or early 1824.

—*Shane White*

eating supper and drinking—these were enjoyable things for newly free blacks to do. Then, of course, there was the music and the dancing—first the clipped precision of cotillions and the sweeping grace of waltzes, but as the evening wore on, and some of the formal clothing was shucked off or at least loosened, and the alcohol had taken its toll, there was the dimming of the lights, a slowing down of the music, and dancing of a rather different sort. This, as those who had started their lives as slaves must have particularly appreciated, was the way freedom was meant to be.

Almost certainly these balls appealed to a different African American social stratum than did the dance cellars. The expense—a ticket to the African Grecian Ball in New York in 1827 cost three dollars—does suggest that those attending were among the more comfortable class of black New Yorkers, those who were negotiating freedom in the city with at least some degree of success.[43] Nevertheless, and for all the differences between the balls and the dance cellars, these cultural sites were linked by what might be best labeled an African American aesthetic. Their freedom may have been precarious, the economic position dire, but that very precariousness gave a distinctive cast to the cultural convulsion that accompanied emancipation. These turbulent years saw a veritable explosion of black dance and music all over New York, in venues ranging from dance cellars through Catharine Market and formal balls. Dance and music were vital elements in a culture that, for all its flaws, was the creative and expressive response of ordinary black New Yorkers to their recently acquired and hard-won freedom. It was in this context, too, when anything seemed possible, that in 1821 a small group of African Americans in New York made their extraordinary decision to form a troupe of black actors.

On the evening of Monday, September 17, 1821, in New York City, a newly formed drama company staged its first public performance. The circumstances hardly seemed auspicious (the venue was a makeshift theater in a private dwelling in Thomas Street just behind the hospital, a less than salubrious part of town), but the house was full, and as the actor playing Richard III limped out onto the stage, the audience erupted into wild cheering. An even greater burst of applause greeted the conclusion of his first speech. In reviewing the com-

BLACK LIFE
IN FREEDOM:
CREATING A
POPULAR
CULTURE

JAMES HEWLETT, ACTOR

For about a dozen years in the 1820s and 1830s, James Hewlett may have been the best-known black New Yorker, an actor whose name gained instant recognition by most of the city's inhabitants, black or white.

Hewlett was probably born in Rockaway, Long Island, sometime in the 1790s. As a young man, he attached himself to New York's growing theatrical community, although it seems likely that, as with many other free black men, he survived by periodically shipping out as a sailor.

In 1821, when William Brown established the African Theater, Hewlett seized the moment. He missed opening night but soon established himself as the most important member of the black acting troupe, playing the major roles and singing almost all of the songs. When the company collapsed in 1824, Hewlett launched his solo career. For the next seven or eight years, he earned his living performing one-man shows in New York and elsewhere in the Northeast. On at least one occasion, he ventured into the slave states.

Hewlett specialized in imitations of famous actors in their best-known roles and by all accounts he was very good at his craft. One reviewer thought he had "a natural talent for theatrical performances"; another felt confident that those who saw his imitations of Edmund Kean, Charles Matthews, Thomas Philips and others "must have been convinced, by the accuracy and tact of his performance, that they were listening to no common individual." Hewlett also pioneered one-man shows in the United States. Turning the racial tables, he was an African American who imitated Anglo American actors at a time when white performers were putting on blackface in the minstrel shows, which would, ironically and cruelly, drive Hewlett from the New York stage. He gave his last performance in 1831.

As with many of his fellow actors, white and black, Hewlett's life was hardly beyond reproach. On at least one occasion in the 1820s, when touring in Pennsylvania, he reportedly slipped out of town without paying his hotel bill. In the 1830s, as the vogue for his act waned, his transgressions became more serious, and he served at least two terms in prison for larceny. Upon his release, he left the United States, appearing briefly in Trinidad in December 1839, where he gave a few performances in his own inimitable style.

Thereafter, Hewlett is lost to the historical record, although it seems likely that he returned to New York and died there sometime in the mid-1840s. Sadly, the curtain on Hewlett's career fell even before it fully opened.

—Shane White

Mr Hewlett
as Richard the third in imitation of
Mr Kean.
Off with his head so much for Buckingham. *Act 4. Sc 3.*
I am myself alone.

Engraved by I.Scoles, from an original Sketch by Bériveau, N.York

I. Scoles, *Mr.
Hewlett as Richard
the third in imita-
tion of Mr. Kean—
Off with his head so
much for
Buckingham.*
Engraving.

pany's performance, the *National Advocate*'s theater critic was unable to resist assaying a few obvious puns, but even his account (and it is the only one extant) could not obscure the enthusiasm and almost self-congratulation that surrounded the production. And with good reason: for virtually everyone present, whether members of the cast or of the audience, had either been born a slave or at the least was the child of a slave, and few among them could have been unaware that they were witnessing a bold intrusion of black people into the world of acting, an arena hitherto unthinkingly accepted as the exclusive and "natural" preserve of whites.[44]

If the very idea of blacks acting on stage was improbable to contemporaries, just as important was what they had in mind as they were doing it. Even well into the twentieth century there was something unusual and daring about so-called "colorblind" casting—that is, having African American actors performing roles assumed to be for whites only. In 1967, a sixteen-year-old Ricardo Khan, later to be a Tony Award winner, purchased a ticket for a matinee performance of *Hello, Dolly!* at the St. James Theater. Thirty years later, he remembered vividly the "awe" he had felt when the raising of the curtain revealed Cab Calloway and Pearl Bailey in the lead roles. "I wasn't inspired because it was on Broadway, but because it was an all-black cast. . . . It was a cast," Khan told a *New York Times* writer, "that looked like me." There is no surviving direct testimony from 1821, but the spectacle of a former slave performing as Richard III must have thrilled black members of the audience in much the same way.[45]

For a few years, the African Company presented various Shakespearean plays and at least one drama of their own creation before mixed audiences of blacks and whites. Indeed, they were successful enough to arouse the ire of Stephen Price, New York's major theatrical impresario, and the black actors were eventually shut down by a mixture of official action and thugs in Price's employ. Yet for all the brevity of its life, the African Company was important to black New Yorkers. It is likely that Ira Aldridge, the great black actor of the nineteenth century, got his start with the African Company before he migrated to England. The principal actor of the troupe, though, was a black New Yorker named James Hewlett, a talented man with an extraordinary stage presence. After the company closed, Hewlett made a living for the next seven or eight years by giving one-man performances all over the Northeast, and on at least one occasion in the South, in which he imitated famous white actors of the day in their signature roles. The vogue of whites for Hewlett ended in the early 1830s as audiences flocked to the new sensation of actors performing in black-face, and the black actor served several stints in prison. But at the height of his career in the 1820s, Hewlett repeatedly sold out halls of six or seven hundred people.

For this remarkable story of pioneering black effort, it is easy enough to identify a list of "firsts." The black New York actors involved constituted the first black theater company; built the first black theater; performed the first play written by an African American; and performed the first stage representation of slavery by blacks. Very few are today aware of the fact that the debut performance by an American-born singer of Italian opera in front of a paying American audience was given by James Hewlett. Hewlett was also, if not the first, one of the earliest American one-man performers, the progenitor of an enormous range of American entertainment from vaudeville through to the likes of Richard Pryor and Robin Williams. These theatrical endeavors reveal the rambunctious and unsettling response of New York's slaves, ex-slaves, and free blacks to slavery's protracted demise in New York, for the audacity and brashness of their attempt to open the stage to blacks was part and parcel of the exhilaration and exuberance that characterized African American life in New York in the early decades of the nineteenth century.

Throughout much of African American history, black cultural production has focused primarily on performance: on the development and expression of distinctive African American aesthetic principles at some remove from those prized by the dominant culture. In part, such efforts have been a response to oppression, but, importantly, they have also been the result of choice. It was this process on which black New Yorkers embarked as they sought to shrug off their slave past and test the limits of their recently won freedom. The pageantry of a black procession, over a thousand strong, striding out down Broadway, flourishing banners and slogans; the style of a black dandy, immaculately turned out, leaning against a post on the Battery and checking the time on his fob watch with a nonchalant flick of his wrist; the spectacle of strikingly dressed black men and women alighting from their carriages on Orange Street as they arrived for the African Ball for the benefit of Greek freedom; the theater of an insouciant black defendant ragging a pompous magistrate in the police station; the panache of a rollicking crowd of black men and women moving to the relentless beat in a sweaty, smoky dance cellar—all these and more bold public displays helped define the meaning of African American freedom in New York. And any consideration of African American culture must also leave room for the performances of Henry Childs and others of his ilk, who conjured up their stories of the future, living off their wits and fleecing white dupes whenever they came their way. To be sure, poverty imposed limits on black expressiveness, and the possibility of harassment by whites was ever-present, but whenever one probes beneath the surface in early nineteenth-century New York, it is difficult not to be impressed by the ever-restless vitality of urban black life.

Chapter 6

BLACK LIFE
IN FREEDOM:
CREATING AN
ELITE CULTURE

———————◆———————

CARLA L. PETERSON

NEW-YORK AFRICAN FREE-SCHOOL, No. 2.

Engraved from a drawing taken by P. Reason, a pupil, aged 13 years.

Engraving of African Free School, from a student's drawing.

Peter Guignon was born in 1813, in the city of New York. . . . At the early period of his boyhood he was sent to the old Mulberry St. school founded by the Quakers of New York City for colored children. He was the contemporary at that school from about 1822 of the most celebrated pupils which ever were enrolled upon its records. His schoolmates were George Allen, Thomas Sidney, the two Moores (Isaac and George), the three Reasons (Elwer, Patrick, and Charles L.), Isaiah Degrasse, J. McCune Smith, Samuel R. Ward, Henry Highland Garnet, George T. Downing. His standing and character in his school days can be seen that he was the friend and intimate companion of every one of these eminent boys, not only in their boyhood, but afterwards in their manhood and maturity.[1]

In his obituary of Peter Guignon, noted black Episcopalian clergyman Alexander Crummell portrayed the deceased as a fairly ordinary man fortuitously thrust from early childhood into the company of more "celebrated" and "eminent" black New Yorkers. As he reflected back on their school days together, however, Crummell might well have added that any black youngster fortunate enough to attend the Mulberry Street School, as the African Free School was sometimes known, was in some sense extraordinary. He might have mentioned how few black children received any schooling in nineteenth-century New York. He might have referred to the varied backgrounds from which he and his classmates came. Some boys had close ties to slavery. Crummell's mother was part of an old free black New York family, but his African father had been taken to New York as a slave and only later gained his freedom. Henry Highland Garnet was born into slavery in Virginia; his family escaped to New York but lived in fear of being reenslaved. James McCune Smith's mother was self-emancipated. Other students enjoyed origins with deeper roots in freedom. Both of Peter Guignon's free parents had emigrated from Haiti following the revolution on Saint Domingue. George Downing's father was a well-established restaurateur in New York. Georges Degrasse, father of Isaiah Degrasse, was reputed to be the Hindu foster son of Admiral Count Degrasse, commander of the French fleet that had been instrumental in George Washington's victory at Yorktown during the Revolutionary War.[2] Finally, Crummell could have placed other names on his list, adding his classmates Philip Bell and James Fields or reaching into the next generation and mentioning Philip White, who would marry Guignon's daughter in the late 1860s.

From humble origins, these young graduates of the African Free School rose to form the core of New York's antebellum black elite. Joined by recent arrivals to the city like Charles B. Ray, they built upon the efforts of earlier leaders who had come of age at the end of the eighteenth century. As a self-identified elite, the school's graduates formed a distinct class that created its own code of conduct and values, and gave itself the task of improving life for all African Americans. In the process, they created a multiplicity of organizations—some educational and literary, others religious and benevolent, and still others partisan and political. Through the work of these institutions, they sought to make their community economically viable, to insure its stability and security, protect its civil rights, and ultimately to acquire full citizenship for all. Members of this elite remained deeply rooted in the life of both the black community and the wider New York City community. But they also aspired to an identity that reached beyond the local and the national to a cosmopolitanism that would distinguish them both from the mass of impoverished black New Yorkers and also

"Five Points, 1827"
from *Valentine's
Manual*, 1885.

John F.E.
Prud'homme
(1800–1892),
engraver, after
William Bayley,
artist, *St. Philip's
Church*.
Engraving.

from the wealthy, educated—but racially estranged—white men and women with whom they otherwise shared much. Tracing the outlines of this elite through the careers of two of its more ordinary members—Peter Guignon and Philip White—provides insight into the class they represented.[3]

IMMEDIATELY FOLLOWING the American Revolution, New York's emerging black elite took leadership in establishing community institutions and, in the process, articulated two fundamental interrelated tenets that would bind black society together for the next century or more: religious faith and mutual aid. In the 1780s, a group of black men, among them William Hamilton, James Varick, and Peter Williams Sr., formed the New York African Society to oversee the spiritual and economic needs of their community. Many of the society's members were affiliated with Methodism and worshiped at the John Street Church. Dissatisfied with the treatment of black parishioners, however, in 1800, Hamilton, Varick, and others left to form Mother Zion. Some fifteen years later and under similar conditions, John Bees, Samuel Clause, John Marander, and other black Episcopalians petitioned Trinity Church for a separate place of worship that would eventually lead to the creation of St. Philip's Episcopal Church. Peter Williams Jr., became its first pastor in 1826. These men also established black New York's most important and long-lived voluntary association, the New York African Society for Mutual Relief, to provide aid to needy members and their families. They elected William Hamilton as the organization's first president in 1810.[4]

On the occasion of the society's second anniversary, Hamilton composed a hymn, the fourth stanza of which reads:

Bound by strong friendship's closest tie
In social union, we
Mutual relief and aid to give
Each other do agree;
So to fulfill a law divine

By God of nature writ
And meliorate the many ills
By which life is beset.[5]

To a much greater degree than the society's constitution or by-laws, this hymn nicely encapsulated the religious and communal ideals that Hamilton and his colleagues held so dearly, embracing "strong friendship" that would bind them together in "social union." Obedient to God's commandment, the society's members promised one another "mutual relief and aid" in times of distress. By couching his sentiments in the form of a hymn, Hamilton emphasized his homage to God's divine plan. But, just as significantly, Hamilton's use of the hymn underscored his deep belief in the bounties of education and most particularly in the value of literary expression.

Education would be essential to the formation of the new elite that emerged from the efforts of Hamilton and his fellow members in the African Society for Mutual Relief. Lacking sufficient resources, they supported white abolitionists who were building a school for black children. In 1785, several well-to-do New York merchants, ministers, and lawyers—among them Alexander Hamilton and John Jay—joined together to establish the New-York African Free School under the auspices of the New York Manumission Society. These philanthropic men acted from their belief that education would demonstrate the humanity of black people and their capacity to live and work as free men and women. Cultivation of their minds would lead to mental emancipation, and eventually to the eradication of all forms of racial prejudice. A school for boys and girls operated from 1787 until 1792, when a separate school for girls opened. In 1794, both African Free Schools were incorporated.[6]

In the 1820s, Peter Guignon and his classmates attended the African Free School for boys located on Mulberry Street. They followed a curriculum that was unusually comprehensive for a charity institution and reflected the trustee's purported goal of forming a class of "men of distinction."[7] Their studies not only provided practical knowledge but also alerted them to a world larger than the neighborhood or city they inhabited. It provided the seeds of a

187

BLACK LIFE

IN FREEDOM:

CREATING

AN ELITE

CULTURE

broader cosmopolitan outlook that would be central to the elite's understanding of themselves and the world. While the students learned the rudiments of reading, writing, and arithmetic and received lessons in Scripture, they also explored the physical sciences, natural history, and geography. Among their texts were *The Scientific Class-Book* and *Scientific Dialogues*, whose prefaces insisted that students needed to acquire "useful knowledge" of the physical sciences by first understanding its "technical language." These, in turn, were presented in a series of volumes that examined the principles of hydrostatics, mechanics, optics, and pneumatics. Endeavoring to substitute "interesting and instructive truths" in the place of "fictitious stories," Comstock's *Natural History* explained the characteristics and habits of birds and quadrupeds through both text and illustration.[8] Geography books offered a panoramic view of the world beyond the students' local New York neighborhoods, the city itself, and even the nation. *Travels at Home* transported them across the Atlantic on a grand tour of Europe not unlike that taken by Romantic poets Samuel Coleridge and William Wordsworth, while Cook's *Travels* promoted the virtues of exploration and seamanship by inviting the students to follow Captain Cook on his voyages to South America, the South Sea Islands, Australia, and New Zealand.

Such instruction endowed the brightest of the African Free School students with a strong sense of self. So too did their most influential teacher, Charles Andrews, an Englishman whose long tenure lasted from 1809 to 1832. In later years, James McCune Smith remembered him as a man who provided his students with a solid foundation: "Mr. Andrews held that his pupils had as much capacity to acquire knowledge as any other children, they were the object of his constant labors. . . . He taught his boys and girls to look upward; to believe themselves capable of accomplishing as much as any others could, and to regard the higher walks of life as within their reach."[9] But the school remained understaffed, and the trustees eventually resorted to the Lancastrian system of instruction under which the more advanced students—supervised by a master instructor—monitored and taught those less advanced. James McCune Smith served as monitor general and George Moore as monitor in 1827.[10] Although reliance upon student teachers had its limitations, the Lancastrian system gave the monitors authority and responsibility at a young age, creating a new cadre of leaders who would eventually replace William Hamilton and his colleagues.

Yet there were also aspects of the African Free School that its students found troubling. If the school's benevolent founders promoted the education of black children to hasten the abolition of slavery, their view of the role of free black people was constrained by a genteel racism. While they hoped to "rescue the minds of the descendants of Africa from that long and dark night of ignorance, in which by most unjust and cruel oppression, they have been compelled to grope," they also envisioned education as a mode of social control that transformed the children of Africa into "quiet and orderly citizens, and leads them to . . . insure not only their happiness in the present, but in the world to come."[11] Above all, they doubted these young black men and women could ever take their place as equals within the American republic.

To accomplish their goals, the school's trustees and teachers closely policed the students. They composed the oratorical exercises and literary essays students recited at public examinations. The students were nothing more than ventriloquists, mouthing the words of their benefactors. In their orations, the students humbly requested their audience's sympathy in order to garner donations for the school. In return for the public's patronage, they proffered statements of gratitude that fixed them in a dependent and passive position: "It behooves us to cherish feelings of the warmest gratitude and tenderness toward that community" of Christian philanthropy.[12] Student orators also repeatedly counseled their classmates that in their efforts to gain the public's sympathy they needed to acquiesce to the school's discipline, obey authority, observe punctuality, ensure cleanliness, and maintain proper order.

The students' written work followed much the same pattern as their speeches. In 1828, George Allen, Isaiah Degrasse, George Moore, and Elwer Reason composed short essays that they delivered to the American Convention for Promoting the Abolition of Slavery. Although the school's trustees insisted that the essays were "genuine, unaided productions," they were so formulaic that it would be difficult to call them original. In each essay, the student began by expressing gratitude to his benefactors, and contrasted his more fortunate

189

BLACK LIFE
IN FREEDOM:
CREATING
AN ELITE
CULTURE

situation to the plight of Southern slaves. He then extended his own sympathy to his enslaved brothers: "We often feel compassion for the thousands of our brethren in the South, who are groaning under the chains of bondage, while we are enjoying the benefits of freedom, and one of the most important of these, I conceive to be education." In repeatedly referring to themselves as "poor little descendants of Africa," however, the students collapsed the strict distinction between themselves and enslaved Africans in the South.[13] They found themselves ambiguously positioned as different from *and* similar to Southern slaves, as they simultaneously gave *and* demanded sympathy. These tensions would be carried into later life, and would continue to inform relations between the black elite and less fortunate black persons, slave and free.

As they contemplated life after school, the students recognized the very real and material power of the racial prejudice that plagued black New Yorkers, a power in which they might well have believed that the African Free School trustees were complicit. The trustees promised to produce "men of distinction," but the school trained its graduates for places that were hardly distinguished. Boys were taught to be mechanics and artisans, and in the African Free School for girls, the female students learned skills such as sewing and knitting. An employment service sought to place the graduates in trades by means of indenture.[14] The trustees boasted, often with a sense of "relief," that some of the students had been able to enter trades, "viz Sail Makers, Shoe Makers, Tin Workers, Tailors, Carpenters, Blacksmiths, etc.," and they encouraged others to cultivate the soil, suggesting that "a large tract of our country be settled by intelligent and industrious colored persons."[15] Charles Andrews himself was so frustrated that he went so far as to endorse the American Colonization Society's plan to send free blacks to Liberia—a suggestion that the black community vehemently rejected.

In 1819, James Fields delivered the school's valedictorian address at a public examination. Written by trustee Reuben Leggett, the speech underscored with painful candor the obstacles graduates faced when entering the world of work. It elucidates with perfect clarity the limits of benevolent activity and sentimental sympathy. Although Fields began his speech with the ritual solicitation of the audience's sympathy on his own behalf—"I still earnestly solicit your sympathy"—his supplications soon gave way to a more militant tone and demands for the opportunity to work: "What are my prospects? To what shall I turn my hand? Shall I be a mechanic? No one will employ me; white boys won't work with me. Shall I be a merchant? No one will have me in his office; white clerks won't associate with me. Drudgery and servitude, then, are my prospective portion." According to a correspondent for the *Commercial Advertiser*, "The finest feelings of the humane mind were awakened" by Fields' speech, but his plea for work remained unmet.[16]

The young graduates of the African Free School indeed wondered what fate awaited them in the harshly competitive and racially prejudiced world of antebellum New York. The older generation of New York's black elite had persevered on their own to establish themselves as tradesmen without the benefit of patronage. William Hamilton became a carpenter. William Powell ran a Colored Seaman's Home on Pearl Street, which eventually became a general boardinghouse. To supplement his income as editor of the *Colored American*, Charles Ray established himself as a boot maker as did Prince Loveridge, a recruiting agent for the African Free Schools. But the schools' new graduates started out with higher expectations. Proud of the cultural capital they had accrued, they hoped it would yield them substantial social and economic gains. Like their elders, however, many had to struggle on their own to find work as artisans or tradesmen. Fields established a shop on Thames Street as a "clothes dresser and tailor"; placing an advertisement in the *Colored American*, he added the motto: "Help those who strive to help themselves."[17] Philip Bell, also an editor of the *Colored American*, sold coal. John Zuille became a printer. Less successful, Peter Guignon floundered for many years after graduation. No record exists of his early activities, but in the 1840s he was still striving to establish himself in trade. He worked first as a porter and then went into the cigar business before turning to hairdressing, where he apparently also had little luck.

Some members of New York's striving black elite, however, did find windows of economic opportunity and took full advantage. In so doing, they came into daily contact not only with other blacks but also with whites who were variously

191

BLACK LIFE
IN FREEDOM:
CREATING
AN ELITE
CULTURE

Portrait of Pierre
Toussaint.

Portrait of Mrs. Pierre
Toussaint.

Portrait of Euphemia
Toussaint.

NEW-YORK HISTORICAL
SOCIETY, GIFT OF MISS
GEORGINA SCHUYLER

customers, competitors, or patrons. They participated in the life of the city as a whole, forging relationships with whites far more complicated than Fields's comments indicated.

Peter Guignon's struggles to establish himself without the help of patronage contrasted sharply with the rapid rise of Pierre Toussaint, who had been brought to the United States as a slave from Saint Domingue in 1787. Emancipated twenty years later, Toussaint remained in close touch with his former owners and benefited from their assistance as he took up the trade of hairdresser. His ties with his former master and mistress endowed his business with a substantial clientele among the exiled Haitian community and well-to-do white New Yorkers, and he was often called to their homes to dress the hair of as many as fifteen "demoiselles."[18] Another member of the black elite, Peter Ray, prospered as an employee of the Lorillard Tobacco Company, rising through the ranks from errand boy to supervisor.

To the extent that black patronage existed, it came largely through family ties that facilitated entrance into trade and made financial success possible— as eventually happened to Peter Guignon. Early in the 1850s, after the death of his first wife, Guignon married Peter Ray's daughter Cornelia Ray. Peter Ray's son, Peter Williams Ray, owned a drug store in Brooklyn and invited brother-in-law Guignon into his business as a partner where, at last, Guignon found his economic niche. Others also benefited from family ties. George Downing built on the business success of his father Thomas Downing, who owned an oyster bar on Broad Street that catered to both blacks and whites. After working with his father, Downing opened a hotel, the Sea-Girt House, in Newport, Rhode Island, a "first class fashionable" establishment that also brought together an interracial clientele.[19] Their network of shops suggests that the black elite was constituted in a manner similar to that of white merchants like John Jacob Astor, who, only a few decades earlier, had come together to create a "shop-keeping aristocracy."[20]

Connections with kin, classmates, and white patrons, which often had their origins at the African Free School, also allowed a few men to enter the liberal professions. After leaving school, Alexander Crummell, Henry Highland

BLACK LIFE
IN FREEDOM:
CREATING
AN ELITE
CULTURE

Garnet, and Thomas Sidney—all classmates of Guignon—applied to the Noyes Academy in Canaan, New Hampshire, to pursue higher education. Shortly after they enrolled, they were driven out by a hostile mob of neighboring farmers who attacked and destroyed the academy's buildings. They then entered the Oneida Institute in upstate New York, founded by a group of white abolitionists committed to an admissions policy of racial equality. From there Crummell, perhaps the most ambitious of the three, applied to the Protestant Episcopal Theological Seminary in New York City, but suffered the same fate as his former classmates, Charles Reason and Isaiah Degrasse: all three were denied admittance on account of their race. Degrasse was eventually ordained and became a minister at the Protestant Episcopal Free Church. After receiving a degree from Central College in McGrawville, a school established by the American Baptist Free Mission Society, Charles Reason was appointed professor, and taught literature, Greek, Latin, French, and mathematics at the college for many years.[21]

Crummell, as well as James McCune Smith, eventually received invaluable assistance from white patrons. After studying privately with several leading Episcopal clergymen in Boston and Providence, Crummell finally gained ordination as a minister. Then, with the aid of British friends, he spent five years in England, where he earned a degree from Queen's College, Cambridge. Still with all his degrees, it took Crummell many years and the help of numerous friends to raise funds to construct a church in New York. Much like Crummell's entrance to the clergy, McCune Smith struggled to secure a medical degree. Denied admission to medical schools in the United States, abolitionists underwrote his education at the University of Glasgow in Scotland and his clinical work in Paris. Upon his return to New York City, McCune Smith established a lucrative pharmaceutical and medical practice on West Broadway, offering his services to both black and white patients.[22]

The career of the younger Philip White, who would later become Peter Guignon's son-in-law, brought together black and white patronage, professionalization, and white racism in an unusually complex web of circumstances. Determined that the younger generation should not face the obstacles that he did, McCune Smith invited White into his drug store in 1840 for a four-year apprenticeship. That experience made White eligible to attend the city's College of Pharmacy. While no special training or diploma was required of druggists, in 1829 a group of progressive pharmacists founded the college to regulate and modernize their trade.[23] Perhaps because of the newness of the profession, White faced no racial barriers in entering the college, and he received his diploma in 1844.

White, however, faced obstacles in his efforts to establish himself in business. Fields's early lament that white benefactors all too often offered "sympathy" in lieu of material aid still held true at mid-century. At a meeting of the National Council of Colored People in 1855, Frederick Douglass complained bitterly that "since 1826 down to now, those who professed to be the strongest Abolitionists have refused to render the colored people anything else but sympathy; when an occasion offered and they might render them some practical service they shrunk back from the opportunity." And McCune Smith pointed specifically to White's difficulties after graduation when he spoke of "a smart young man who had been an apprentice in his drug store, and he got his diploma in colleges. He asked $500 from [white abolitionist] John Rankin to assist him. It was refused."[24] Yet White persevered and opened a drugstore in lower Manhattan in an area known as the Swamp, drawing customers from among his black and white neighbors. This time, he received assistance from local white merchants seeking to maintain the stability of the neighborhood. According to one account, "His industry and obliging disposition won for him . . . the favor of business men in the Swamp, many of whom took pains to put trade in his way until he was firmly established."[25] White later added a wholesale department to his retail business, advertising monthly from 1870 to 1886 in *The Druggists' Circular and Chemical Gazette*, the profession's most important trade magazine.

Businesses like those of the Downings, McCune Smith, and White became the economic cornerstone of the black elite, bringing material resources and offering models of successful entrepreneurship. In 1848, abolitionist William C. Nell wrote glowingly about visiting "the Apothecary's Hall of Dr. James McCune Smith in West Broadway, and also the establishment of Mr. Philip

195

BLACK LIFE
IN FREEDOM:
CREATING
AN ELITE
CULTURE

White in Frankfort Street, both of whom are practical men and conduct their business, preparing medicines, etc. etc., with as much readiness and skill as any other disciple of Galen and Hippocrates. . . ." Nell delighted in finding that McCune Smith and White were "proving their capacity . . . to their pecuniary benefit, and at the same time thus elevating the character of those with whom they are identified by complexion." Nell expected these successful black businessmen to transfer their business skills to the next generation, and McCune Smith and White were pleased to comply. In 1855, McCune Smith placed a series of advertisements in *Frederick Douglass' Paper* to hire "colored lads" willing to learn carpentry and cane-chair work.[26] Once established, White followed McCune Smith's lead and sought "an intelligent, well-educated colored boy to learn the drug business." Yet, despite their best efforts, New York's black businessmen failed to make their community economically self-sufficient and relied on connections with white entrepreneurs like the Lorillards. Moreover, black businesses, like the restaurants of Thomas and George Downing and the drugstores of White and McCune Smith, depended upon white customers. Such patronage sometimes caused trouble within the black community. In 1841, Alexander Crummell and Charles Reason publicly excoriated black restaurateur Thomas Van Rensellaer for refusing to seat blacks in his restaurant or "colonizing" them by placing them behind a screen for fear of offending white customers.[27]

Contributing to the insecurity of the black elite were their residential patterns—their dispersal throughout the city as well as their interurban migration over time—that left them vulnerable to intrusion from outsiders. Early in the nineteenth century, members of the nascent black upper class had resided in close contact with whites of all classes as well as poor blacks. Their homes could be found in every ward, and within the various wards, neighborhoods were rarely segregated by race or class.[28] The wealthiest among them established their businesses—and their homes—downtown in the heart of the city's commercial district near the exchange, courthouses, newspaper offices, and Trinity Church. These included Downing's oyster bar, Van Rensellaer's restaurant, and Henry Scott's pickle shop. Less prominent families were concentrated in the city's Fifth Ward near the Hudson River and in the Sixth Ward around Fresh Water Pond.[29] In the first decades of the nineteenth century, the Fifth Ward was home not only to some of New York's most fashionable residents but also to craft-based communities where artisans lived and worked.[30] Some of these were located on Church and Greenwich Streets, where Peter Guignon, Patrick Reason, and Peter Vogelsang resided for a time. These two streets were known as "Negro streets," but a contemporaneous account by an unnamed visitor from South Carolina gives a vivid picture of their interracial (and to him, lower-class) nature: "Did you ever see such a mixture of Negroes and whites all on an equality? Here are cobblers, drinking-holes, 'exchange' offices, cigar stores, etc., etc."[31] The Sixth Ward contained the notorious Five Points district. First settled by the Dutch, the district had formed around Fresh Water Pond, which had been filled in after the War of 1812, but remained a breeding ground for malaria and other infectious diseases. Its inhabitants—mainly Irish and black—were among the city's poorest residents and suffered from overcrowding, poor sanitation, malnutrition, and disease. Yet it was also home to some of the most important black institutions, such as the African Society for Mutual Relief and St. Philip's, as well as to some of their most prominent members like John Bees.

In their continued intraurban migration, some among the black elite eventually moved northward into the Eighth and Fourteenth Wards. By contrast, Philip White, William Powell, and Albro Lyons moved to the Swamp in the Fourth Ward near the East River. Many of New York's old merchant class had lived and worked there, making their fortunes tanning leather and storing hides in warehouses around Frankfort Street until the ill effects of the leather-making process led the city to close the yards down.[32] On the waterfront, white manufacturers ran shipbuilding industries where the Irish worked as longshoremen; the area also contained associated trades such as boardinghouses and outfitting stores for sailors.[33] William Powell and Albro Lyons both operated Seamen's Homes for Colored Sailors, and Lyons also owned an outfitting store. Although less notorious than Five Points, it suffered from many of the same social problems.

197

BLACK LIFE
IN FREEDOM:
CREATING
AN ELITE
CULTURE

Still other factors added to the uncertain lives of New York's black elite. Like the black poor, they too were vulnerable to tuberculosis, smallpox, and yellow fever epidemics that periodically ravaged the city. Kidnappers, hoping to snare unsuspecting blacks and sell them South, made no exception for wealthy, educated black men and women, especially after the passage of the Fugitive Slave Act in 1850. Rioting white mobs often sought out stores, residences, and churches of successful blacks, if only to demonstrate the vulnerability of black life in the city. In 1834, an antiabolitionist mob ransacked St. Philip's Episcopal Church and the home of its pastor, Peter Williams, as well as black businesses in the Five Points area.[34] A similar pattern would repeat itself in the draft riots of 1863.

Given their vulnerable existence, men and women of the black elite worried that the cultural, social, and economic capital they had so arduously built up would be for naught. They anxiously wondered whether they were in fact distinguishable from the mass of black men and women around them. Hence, they strove to nullify the kinds of equations drawn by the unnamed visitor from South Carolina, while at the same time engaging in racial uplift efforts that would eventually raise the masses to their level.

To accomplish their goals, the black elite self-consciously pronounced itself an aristocracy. A correspondent to *Frederick Douglass' Paper* proudly described "enterprising blacks" beginning "to take their places in every pursuit about town and country; and as their thoughts and sympathies partake of their varied and independent occupations, they naturally form an active and efficient business class. I call it," he grandly pronounced, "an ARISTOCRACY."[35] This aristocracy proceeded to close ranks. Its members married among themselves and socialized exclusively together, defining their own standard of behavior and system of values. Many of the elite's marriages resulted from connections initially made at the African Free School. Both Peter Guignon and Albro Lyons married sisters of a former classmate, Edward Marshall. Likewise, George Downing and Peter Vogelsang married into the Degrasse family.

Women took on the task of creating and maintaining the exclusive social circle through which the elite distinguished itself from the black masses. Albro

Lyons's daughter Maritcha nicely portrayed how the values and tastes of upper-class women shaped the elite's social life. "Among the friends of our family," she wrote in an autobiographical narrative, "were two circles founded on personal preference; these were led respectively by Mrs. Clorice Esteve Reason and Mrs. Elizabeth West Bowers. The former gathered about her the studious and conservative and kept open house for all visitors of note; the latter was surrounded by the mirth of loving folks, young and old. In this coterie, not to have a good time was impossible. No hard and fast lines were drawn, however, the same persons could be met, now in one circle, now in the other."[36] Maritcha emphasized that despite their different styles, the two matrons shared the same values and tastes—each above reproach. She also intimated that while members of the elite could readily move from one circle to another, both were closed to outsiders. Women like the formidable Mrs. Reason and Mrs. Bowers patrolled the new class boundaries with a vigilant eye.

In her disquisition on New York's black social elite, Maritcha Lyons also noted that "a main general distinction prevailed—persons attending the same church usually confined their intimate intercourse with members of that congregation." The congregation in question was St. Philip's Church. A large number of the African Free School graduates—George Downing, Peter Guignon, Albro Lyons, James McCune Smith, and others—worshiped at St. Philip's, as did the younger Philip White, thereby reinforcing the closeness and exclusivity of their social circle. St. Philip's had been founded earlier in the century by black parishioners of Trinity Church who, according to Maritcha Lyons, were the "colored servants" of New York's old families of the Anglican communion.[37] Much like William Hamilton and other black congregants of the John Street Church, they eventually sought a church of their own in which to carry out their spiritual practices as they sought fit.

Portrait of
Albro Lyons Snr.

FAMILY, SCHOOL, CHURCH AND THE MAKING OF A CLASS

James McCune Smith (1813–1865), Philip Augustus White (1824–1891), and Maritcha Lyons (1848–1929) shared much. McCune Smith and White each attended an African Free School—albeit under different circumstances—entered the same profession, joined the same associations, and prayed at the same church. They became neighbors, colleagues, and friends, and although not directly related, they shared various kin through marriage. Maritcha Lyons's career followed a different path, largely because she was a woman. But she was educated in the same tradition, also belonged to the same church and associations, and shared many kin ties. Not surprisingly, these three came to voice many of the same opinions. Their entwined lives reveal how in the century following Emancipation, the black elite molded itself into a distinct social class.

A scientist, reformer, and writer, *James McCune Smith* was a man of intellect and action. His influence during his lifetime was far-reaching, spreading well beyond New York's black community. His national and international connections gave him a significant presence within the city and shaped the development of black New York.

McCune Smith was born in New York City, the son of a white merchant and a self-emancipated black woman. In the late 1820s, he attended the

Patrick H. Reason, *James McCune Smith*. Engraving.
NEW-YORK HISTORICAL SOCIETY LIBRARY

African Free School, along with many of the future leaders of the city's African American community—among them Alexander Crummell, George Downing, Henry Highland Garnet, Charles L. Reason, and others. Although apprenticed to a blacksmith upon graduation, McCune Smith aspired to greater things. When he was denied entry to medical school in the United States, he sought out a white benefactor and enrolled in the University of Glasgow, finishing his clinical work in Paris. In 1838, he returned to New York, the first African American to receive a medical degree. Two years later, his medical practice and pharmacy well established, he married Malvina Barnet and moved to Brooklyn.

As a physician, McCune Smith enjoyed immediate success. His practice was large, including both white and black patients. He soon opened a drugstore, which enhanced both his reputation and his income. But McCune Smith's interests ranged beyond the medicine cabinet. The back room of his pharmacy became a place for New York's black leaders to debate the issues of the day, and McCune Smith—proprietor and convener—became the first among equals.

During the 1840s and 1850s, McCune Smith became one of the social, political, and intellectual leaders of black New York. He helped to found the New York Society for the Promotion of Education Among Colored Children, served as a vestryman at St. Philip's Episcopal Church, and was a member of the leading black literary associations and fraternal orders, including the prestigious Phoenixonian Society. McCune Smith organized many state and national Conventions of Colored People and was a leader in the struggle to enfranchise black men. He could count on the friendship of men of such diverse dispositions as Frederick Douglass, Gerrit Smith, and John Brown.

In all of his endeavors, McCune Smith complemented his activism with writing. He published technical pieces in the *New York Journal of Medicine*, wrote a history of the Haitian revolution, issued statistical reports on the condition of black people, and penned essays on citizenship and civilization. McCune Smith contributed regularly to *Frederick Douglass' Paper*, writing columns under the pseudonym "Communipaw," thereby reminding his fellow black New Yorkers that despite his national and international activities, his roots remained deeply local.

A full decade younger than McCune Smith, Philip Augustus White grew up in his shadow. He benefited from the older man's trailblazing successes, eventually drawing upon McCune Smith's civic ethos to become a model member of New York's black elite.

Born into a free but poor family, White's early years were weighed by difficulties, personal and professional. While he too attended the African Free School, the incorporation of the African Free Schools into New York's public school system in 1834 had resulted in their pedagogical deterioration, so the quality of education he received was much inferior to that which McCune Smith enjoyed. His apprenticeship from 1840 to 1844 at McCune Smith's pharmacy provided new opportunities, and marked the start of White's climb out of poverty. On the basis of this apprenticeship, White was admitted to the College of Pharmacy of the City of New York, from which he graduated in 1844, the first African American to do so. In 1847, he opened his own drugstore. Following McCune Smith's lead, he cultivated white as well as black customers, forging neighborhood and professional networks that would ensure his drugstore's growth. In time, he entered the wholesale drug trade, advertising his services in the profession's most important trade magazine, *The Druggists' Circular and Chemical Gazette*. In 1863, during the Draft Riots, his Irish neighbors, whom he had assisted through illness and hard economic times, protected his store, which survived unscathed.

White followed McCune Smith's lead in other ways as well. He joined St. Philip's and became a vestryman. He also sat on the board of the Society for the Promotion of Education Among Colored Children, serving as its secretary from 1851 until at least 1865, perhaps even longer. Although White remained focused on local affairs and never participated in state or national conventions, he supported McCune Smith's campaign to secure suffrage for black men.

In 1867, two years after McCune Smith's death, White married Elizabeth Guignon. When the construction of the Brooklyn Bridge disrupted his neighborhood near the East River, White joined the exodus of black New Yorkers to Brooklyn, where he settled in Communipaw Flats, his mentor's old neighborhood, taking McCune Smith's place as an important leader of an increasingly exclusive black elite. White also moved in wider social circles as a founding member of the Metropolitan Museum of Art. In 1883 Mayor Seth Low appointed White to the Brooklyn Board of Education. During his tenure, White ensured the integration of Brooklyn's public schools while maintaining separate "colored schools," both advancing the cause of racial equality and protecting the jobs of black teachers. In 1957, White's service would be recognized when the city named a school after him.

Toward the end of her life, *Maritcha Lyons* wrote a short autobiographical narrative that provided insight into her own family, the lives of James McCune Smith and Philip Augustus White, and the class to which they all belonged. Her parents, Albro and Mary Lyons, were close friends of both men. Albro Lyons and McCune Smith had been classmates at the African Free School. McCune Smith was best man at the Lyons' wedding, later became the family's physician, and served as godfather to the Lyons's children. Like McCune Smith and White, Lyons belonged to St. Philip's Episcopal Church and to many of the same organizations, so it was inevitable that Lyons and White should soon become acquainted. During the 1850s, before White's move to Brooklyn, the two men were also neighbors in Manhattan's Fourth Ward, where Lyons operated a Seaman's Home for Colored Sailors out of his home. Elizabeth Guignon, White's wife, was Lyons's niece and had been raised in the Lyons's household after her mother's death.

Maritcha's narrative provides a harrowing account of the attack on the Lyons home during the Draft Riots that contrasts sharply with Philip

White's experience. Catering to transient blacks, Albro Lyons had few contacts with the white community, particularly within the ward's growing Irish population. Moreover, he had not been shy about displaying the trappings of his financial success. The members of the mob, perhaps jealous of the black man's material comforts, took aim at the Lyons home, assaulting it repeatedly and finally demolishing it on a third attempt. The Lyons took refuge in White's drugstore until the police transported them to safety.

In the aftermath of the Draft Riots, the Lyons family moved to Providence, Rhode Island. There, Mary Lyons focused on her daughter Maritcha's education. While in New York, Maritcha had suffered from a debilitating illness that had prevented her from attending school. Her education at home had been enriched by the constant presence of her tutor, James McCune Smith.

Maritcha returned to New York as a young woman. She found employment as a teacher in the Brooklyn Colored Schools of the New York school system, doubtless assisted by her godfather, Philip White. When the Colored Schools were merged into the public school system, she became an assistant principal of one of them. Within the gender norms of the time, Maritcha followed McCune Smith and White's tradition of community activism. She belonged to all the appropriate literary societies and was fully conversant in the political issues of the day. Maritcha debated Ida B. Wells on the topic of

Portrait of Maritcha Lyons.

lynching at a meeting of the Brooklyn Literary Union. At the St. Philip's centennial, Maritcha Lyons was one of two women to address the congregation. Finally, in 1901, she was the only woman to speak to an interracial meeting of the Constitutional League held at Carnegie Hall. In so doing, Maritcha was carrying on the tradition set by the earlier generation of leading men.

—*Carla L. Peterson*

Although St. Philip's parishioners were a socially and economically diverse group, the church was home to New York's black elite. Some congregants were unskilled laborers, working as porters and washers; others were engaged in skilled trades as barbers, shoemakers, and tailors. Vestrymen, however, were drawn exclusively from the elite. In the 1840s and 1850s, they included the older Thomas Downing, William Powell, Peter Ray, and Henry Scott, as well as younger men like James McCune Smith and Philip White. To a large extent, these vestrymen modeled themselves after their former white patrons and employers. Relying on their business skills to direct the financial affairs of the church, they exuded a confident sense of middle-class manliness. In overseeing the spiritual aspects of St. Philip's, they made sure that it hewed closely to Episcopalian practices and beliefs.

St. Philip's parishioners gloried in their Episcopal affiliation. According to Anglican belief, Episcopal bishops could trace their lineage in an unbroken chain of succession back to the early Christian church and hence to the Apostles themselves.[38] Black Episcopalians deliberately placed themselves within the ancient and universal traditions of the Anglican Church, which they believed superseded the more recent histories of enslavement and Americanization. In linking them to broader manifestations of Western culture, Episcopalianism provided blacks, and particularly the black elite, with an expansive cosmopolitan identity.

St. Philip's parishioners expressed their denominational commitment in concrete and immediate ways. During the nineteenth century, New York's Episcopal churches were heavily influenced by the spread of High Church ideology, which sought to reassert ideas of tradition and order, reviving the rituals lost under liberalizing tendencies within Anglicanism. High Church practice insisted that Anglican beliefs be expressed through a return to more formalistic ritual and sparked a renewed interest in Gothic architecture. Every Sunday, the prayers, hymns, service rituals, and adornment of the church sanctuary reminded St. Philip's parishioners of their affiliation to Anglican tradition.

For just this reason, St. Philip's vestrymen insisted their church be admitted to the New York State diocesan convention from which it had been pointedly excluded. Admission was of the utmost importance because the convention itself was a reflection of church unity; not to be part of the convention meant not to be part of the denomination. Their demands thus represented a bold attempt on the part of a black institution to claim a legitimate place within a white institutional structure. The vestry waged a bitter ten-year battle to become a member. Year after year, and with the vocal assistance of prominent white Episcopalian John Jay, St. Philip's sent a delegation to the convention only to be denied admission. It was only in 1853 that St. Philip's three delegates—Philip White among them—would be seated.[39]

Whatever particular social circle or church they belonged to, members of New York's black elite shared a common set of values, which became the moral touchstone of their class identity. They gave special weight to what they called character and respectability. Character turned away from the external—the trappings of wealth and physical attributes of complexion and hair—to focus on the internal, the moral, and even the spiritual. Elite men and women exemplified their character by their piety, temperance, industry, and economy. Respectability related the internal to the external: proper conduct manifested good character. This was especially important to the black elite because it both defined status within the black community (thus distinguishing it from the masses) and provided protection from those outside it (white racists). A resolution passed at a public meeting in 1837 affirmed that "at all times, but especially in the present crisis it behooves us to place the most careful watch over our own demeanor, living down, by consistent and virtuous conduct, every charge which may be brought against us."[40] These values appeared to replicate those of their white benefactors at the African Free School, in fact they did not. To the black elite, respectability was an avenue to equality, but not social subordination. Moreover, the elite insisted that character and respectability were active rather than passive traits to be acquired through education and perseverance.

In addition, although rooted in local communities, the graduates of the African Free School and their friends remained deeply influenced by the cosmopolitan values acquired from their school curriculum. Cosmopolitanism—

being a citizen of the world—encouraged these young black men and women to create an expansive identity for themselves that embraced a multiplicity of cultural and social factors, including yet also transcending blackness. They envisioned cosmopolitanism as the means to negotiate the double consciousness of being simultaneously elite and "poor descendants of Africa," and ultimately to wrest national citizenship from the United States.

Cultural and moral values such as these guided men and women of the elite as they moved beyond their own narrow social circle to broader public activism. Many entered into leadership positions within established organizations, even as they created new institutions—schools, literary societies, political associations, and the press. Through their overlapping membership in these diverse organizations, they further consolidated their elevated status. Yet, the elite's activism further emphasized the ambiguities of their social position; and their struggles underscored the tremendous challenges facing them.

In asserting their leadership, the graduates of the African Free School and their colleagues both rejected and built upon the principles upon which the school had been founded. On the one hand, they threw off the mantle of passivity and dependence in which the school's trustees desired to cloak them, insisting on their own capacity to fight slavery, eradicate racial discrimination, and work for full national citizenship. Even in joining white-led abolitionist organizations like the American Anti-Slavery Society or, later, the American and Foreign Anti-Slavery Society, they maintained their own voice and articulated their own interests. Black leaders did not hesitate to turn against mentors when their views countered their own. Their near-universal opposition to colonization placed them on a collision course with Charles Andrews, who championed the movement to transport black Americans back to Africa. As James McCune Smith reported, the confrontation was "something of a struggle in which the old heads of the people ultimately triumphed," as Thomas Downing, William Hamilton, and Henry Sipkins forced Andrews's dismissal.[41]

Through actions such as these, the black elite expressed a deep sense of racial solidarity with Southern slaves and Northern poor blacks. Nevertheless, the elite's position within the black community remained highly ambiguous. For one, as in the larger society, black women working in the public sphere struggled to have their voices heard. Moreover, the elites' own words and actions often replicated ideas of hierarchy reminiscent of the white trustees' benevolent agenda. They too positioned themselves as members of a favored class extending sympathy, largesse, knowledge, and moral values to the less fortunate members of the black community. Condescending attitudes and paternalistic benevolence replaced William Hamilton's earlier egalitarian ethos of "social union" and "mutual aid," just as social control substituted for "strong friendship's closest ties." In the language of the period, the elite sought to uplift and elevate the race.

Education was key to the black elite's racial uplift efforts. It had offered the African Free School students mental emancipation, and it would do the same for the mass of black New Yorkers. Members of the elite focused their attention on improving their schools. Following the end of slavery in 1827, the Manumission Society concluded that it had completed its mission and transferred control of all its schools (renamed Colored Schools) to the Public School Society. The quality of the Colored Schools declined precipitously as the Public School Society made a series of deleterious decisions: the demotion of all Colored Schools but one to the level of primary schools; the discharge of black teachers who had been responsible for the more advanced grades; and the abandonment of spelling books and other texts.[42]

In the face of such blatant discriminatory actions, the black elite established its own community schools under the leadership of graduates of the African Free School. Thomas Sidney was made supervisor of the New York Select Academy, while James Fields took charge of an evening school for adults. Shaped by his education at the African Free School, Sidney sought to teach more than just basic literacy and computation. The Select Academy offered a broad array of courses, undoubtedly modeled after the African Free School's curriculum, that included geography and natural philosphy.[43] In addition, throughout the black community individual teachers provided private instruction in specialized fields, notably Patrick Reason in drawing and William Webster in sacred music. In 1847, black leaders formed the Society for the

207

BLACK LIFE
IN FREEDOM:
CREATING
AN ELITE
CULTURE

Promotion of Education Among Colored Children to bring together all of these efforts. Charles Ray, James McCune Smith, and Philip White were among its most active members. White's interest in black education and his close association with the society derived from his unsatisfactory experience at the African Free School in the 1830s, after it had been taken over by the Public School Society. He served as the society's secretary from 1851 until 1865, perhaps longer.[44] In anticipation of W.E.B. Du Bois's later call for the Talented Tenth, one of the society's most ambitious goals was to establish normal schools that would train a professional cadre of African American schoolteachers. These goals never materialized, however, and the education offered at the schools remained at a basic level.[45]

At the same time, the black elite continued its efforts to improve the public colored schools, seeking to place its members in leadership positions. Significantly, it encouraged black women's participation in education, seeing it as an extension of their work in the domestic sphere as nurturers of black children. John Peterson, Charles Reason, and Ransom Wake were named principals of the boys' schools, and Sarah Ennalls, Eliza Richards, and Fanny Tompkins took command of the girls' schools.[46] In 1853, all of New York's public schools were absorbed into the Board of Education, yet even then the Society for the Promotion of Colored Children continued to monitor the progress of the colored schools. For example, for many years Charles Ray and Philip White awarded Ridgway prizes to the best scholars in "Writing and Spelling, Geography and Grammar, and Arithmetic and Astronomy."[47]

The black elite was all too often frustrated in its attempts to improve educational standards for the mass of black New Yorkers, but it remained determined to cultivate cosmopolitan forms of knowledge for itself, thereby reaffirming its elevated status. Some did so by traveling abroad. McCune Smith and Crummell studied in Scotland and England, while other African Free School graduates like Henry Highland Garnet and Samuel Ward toured Britain on behalf of the antislavery cause. Black cosmopolitanism, however, was not only predicated on travel; it was also absorbed while at home through schooling, reading, and other cultural activities. As inadequate as it might have been, the African Free

School had encouraged its most "eminent boys" to cultivate a sympathetic imagination that expanded their horizons far beyond local and national boundaries. As they matured and attained leadership positions within the community, these young men formulated a set of cosmopolitan ideas that situated black Americans within broader Western traditions—those of Anglicanism, the European literary canon, and Enlightenment humanistic thought.

To articulate these cosmopolitan ideals, the black elite created a series of literary and political associations beginning in the late 1820s. Their members included many African Free School graduates—Crummell, Degrasse, Downing, Fields, Garnet, Patrick and Charles Reason, Sidney, and McCune Smith. Most notable among the literary societies were the Philomathean Literary Society, established in 1826, whose membership included Peter Guignon; the Phoenix Society founded in 1833; and the Phoenixonian Society begun in 1837. The Phoenix Society had as its major goal the dissemination of basic literacy to both adults and children in the black community. In contrast, building on the academic curriculum of the African Free School, the Philomathean Society promoted the acquisition of a highbrow literary cosmopolitanism.

The content and style of an essay published in the *Colored American* emphasized the Philomathean Society's elevated cultural aspirations. Written by a Philomathean Society Committee that included Guignon, it quoted from the preamble of the society's constitution: "We turn in vain to find among the aspirants of wisdom a proportionate number of our own race, sharing the toils of ascension with their more ambitious neighbors, or contributing their mite to the offering of nations. This want of energy and spirit (too degrading to be endured by rational beings), having at length engaged the attention of a few associates, determined to erase the inglorious record of the past by an active future, they hereby solemnly engage to support." Guignon and his friends then proceeded to invite New York's young men of color to join the society, noting that the only prerequisites were the possession of good character and an agreement to donate half a dozen volumes to its library. They proposed to fulfill the society's goal of elevating "the colored man to the level of high moral and mental attainments" through the expansion of the library, the establishment of discussion groups,

209

BLACK LIFE
IN FREEDOM:
CREATING
AN ELITE
CULTURE

and the creation of a lecture series.[48] African Free School graduates were the main speakers. Many of their lectures reflected the broad culture gained through their years at the school. While James McCune Smith spoke primarily on scientific (and pseudoscientific) topics such as "Organs of the Senses," "Circulation of the Blood," and "Phrenology," Isaiah Degrasse gave a course on "Evidences of Christianity" and James Fields spoke on "Decision of Character." Charles Reason delivered an address in which he compared Wordsworth to Milton and argued that the Romantic poet "was possessed of as creative a fancy, and of as sublime conceptions, as the illustrious author of Paradise Lost."[49]

Women of the elite did their part in the work of cultural advancement, forming the New York Female Literary Society, whose first president was Henrietta Ray. Similar to the activities of the men's societies, the women read and discussed books, composed essays, performed music, and recited dramatic dialogues. In September 1837, on the third anniversary of its founding, the Female Literary Society held a public exhibition to showcase the talents of its members. The occasion allowed women to take the radical step of performing before a "promiscuous" audience composed of both men and women. But it also served as a reminder of women's secondary status within the black community. The need to demonstrate female cultural proficiency in public harked back to the public examinations conducted by the African Free School's trustees.[50] Moreover, downplaying its own importance, the society chose to give the benefit's proceeds not to their own organization but to the male-dominated New York Vigilance Committee and *Colored American* newspaper.

Importantly, black cosmopolitans refused to abandon their ties to home and country. Rather, men like McCune Smith operated on a cultural continuum that reaffirmed their multiple affiliations to local community, nation, and world; their ties were overlapping rather than distinct, and resulted in attachment rather than detachment. New York's black elite insisted that the cosmopolitan must lay claim to national belonging. In an essay titled "This Country Our Only Home," a contributor to the *Colored American* pointed to the incongruity that would ensue if African Americans were denied both American citizenship (because their ancestors were not born in the United States) and African citizenship (since they were not born in Africa): "If this principle were carried out, it would be seen that we could not be even a *cosmopolite*, but must be of nowhere, of no section of the globe."[51]

Thus, New York's black elite grounded its cosmopolitan thinking in allegiance to nation. To fulfill their claims to nationhood, they founded a series of political associations beginning in the early 1830s and agitated for the restitution of suffrage to black men who had been all but disfranchised by the revised state constitution of 1821. Once again, it was primarily the African Free School graduates who were responsible for creating black New Yorkers' first political associations. In calling for the right to vote, these young men reinforced their elite status by excluding women as well as those too poor to pay taxes, own land, or even rent property. Among the earliest organizations was the *Société des amis réunis*, founded in 1833 and in existence until about 1841. Its members included George Downing, Guignon, and Elwer Reason. Little is known about this society, but its name betrayed an elite self-consciousness. It echoed the *Société des amis des noirs* of revolutionary France that had brought Saint Domingue's "*gens de couleur*" together with French radicals to agitate for the full political rights for property-owning mulattoes.

In early 1837, George Downing, Peter Guignon, Thomas Sidney, Charles and Elwer Reason, and others participated in a series of meetings held by "colored young men" of the city to continue lobbying for black manhood suffrage.[52] By September, they had formed a Standing Corresponding Committee of Ten and drafted and circulated a petition for signatures that they planned to submit to the state legislature at its next session.[53] A year later, this committee was re-formed as the New York Association for the Political Elevation and Improvement of the People of Color, and Guignon was named a member of the Fifth Ward's committee. Joined by Alexander Crummell, Charles Ray, Thomas Van Rensellaer, James McCune Smith, and many others, these young men broadened their fight for the right of suffrage beyond the city to a series of county and state conventions. Given that suffrage was ultimately a national issue, in the 1840s they joined with similar associations in other cities to launch a concerted drive for black manhood suffrage in annual national conventions.

The leaders of these political associations were also the founders of the literary societies, and increasingly approached the issue of political rights from a cosmopolitan perspective. In calling for the restitution of the franchise for black men, Charles Reason couched his argument in the language of British Romantic poetry. In a poem titled "The Spirit Voice; or, Liberty Call to the Disfranchised (State of New York)," Reason imagined that this voice,

'Tis calling you, who new too long have been
Sore victims suffering under legal sin,
To vow, no more to sleep, till raised and freed
From partial bondage, to a life indeed.[54]

By the 1850s, these men were interpreting their own experiences as an oppressed minority in light of the numerous national revolutions sweeping through Europe. In a trip to America in the early 1850s, the Hungarian patriot Louis Kossuth came to New York and met with a black delegation that included Philip Bell, George Downing, James McCune Smith, and John Zuille. Downing delivered a speech in which he extolled the "great principle . . . that a man has the right to the full exercise of his faculties and powers in the land which gave him birth; and that it is his first duty to devote all the energies of his being to maintain that right for himself and his compatriots."[55] Downing used the Enlightenment ideals of universal humanism to link black New Yorkers' concerns about citizenship to those of Kossuth and his fellow Hungarians.

Ever attentive to the importance of the printed word, New York's black elite well understood how the newspaper could become the primary vehicle for expressing the links between local, national, and global concerns. New York was the birthplace of the black press. In 1828, John Russwurm and Samuel Cornish co-founded and co-edited *Freedom's Journal*. After its demise, Philip Bell started the *Colored American* in 1837; at different times, its editors were Bell, Cornish, Stephen Gloucester, Charles Ray, and McCune Smith. Neither paper survived for long, and by the late 1840s Frederick Douglass's *North Star* (later renamed *Frederick Douglass' Paper*) had become the central organ for African Americans in New York and elsewhere in the North.

Contributors to the black press, many of whom were African Free School graduates, believed that the newspaper could be a teaching tool with which to instruct a broader audience. They envisioned the reading of newspapers as a community activity in which the literate could read and communicate the information garnered from them to the nonliterate masses in the community. From a local and national perspective, they kept readers informed about meetings of organizations, published their minutes and proceedings, and voiced their opinions about current issues. But they also thought globally. From their local base in the United States, some writers reported on events taking place around the world in Europe, Africa, and the Caribbean, often relating these to their condition at home. Others, traveling for their own education or as emissaries for abolition, wrote from abroad to relay their cosmopolitan experiences back to those in the United States. Between December 1837 and July 1838, the *Colored American* reprinted extracts from McCune Smith's "Glasgow journals" in its pages. Some years later, *Frederick Douglass' Paper* published a letter from William G. Allen, who was traveling through England on behalf of the antislavery cause. Allen listed the many black New Yorkers he had met and proceeded to express his enthusiasm for British values and style: "'Old England' is a wonderful country—there is grandeur in the looks of it. There is poetry too. . . . The English people, too—I am in love with them. There is nobility in their hearts and dignity in their bearing."[56]

At the same time, many among New York's black elite asserted that cosmopolitanism existed right here at home. In newspaper columns, writers expressed their emerging cosmopolitan sensibility in new literary styles. As they wrote, they sought both to distinguish themselves from the black masses and to cast off the sentimental forms that the African Free School trustees and teachers had imposed on them. In contrast to the "Negro streets" drawn by the unnamed visitor from South Carolina, a correspondent to *Frederick Douglass' Paper* painted a vivid portrait of "black Broadway's" display of fashion, emphasizing in particular its cosmopolitan flair: "If you would know the height of fashion, you can as well learn it there. . . . Patent leather boots and claret coats, tight pants and painted collars, French wrappers, and Scotch shawls, diamond rings and studded breast-pins, gold watches and California chains, all are exhibited." Finally, little predicting the life of black New Yorkers a century later, Philip Bell writing as "Cosmopolite" contrasted out-of-style Harlem to cosmopolitan New York: "A suburban village about ten miles from New York," Harlem is "a dwarfish elder brother of New York, with high heel boots on to disguise his pigmy height, and paint, powder, wig, etc., to hide the wrinkles and decrepitude of age." In contrast, as the mark of a truly cosmopolitan city, New York offered cultural opportunities of all kinds to its white and black citizens alike, for "Art knows no distinction of color, science recognizes no prejudice, education and wealth are the ladders by which we must rise, the weapons with which we can assail and conquer the demons, slavery and prejudice."[57]

Chapter 7

BLACK LIFE IN FREEDOM: CREATING A CIVIC CULTURE

CRAIG STEVEN WILDER

CONSTITUTION AND BY-LAWS

OF THE

Abyssinian Benevolent Daughters

OF

ESTHER ASSOCIATION,

OF THE

CITY OF NEW-YORK.

ADOPTED APRIL 19TH, 1839.

New-York:

PRINTED BY ZUILLE & LEONARD.

At the Junction of West Broadway & Hudson Street.

1852.

Document of the
Abyssinian Benevolent
Daughters of Esther
Association.

BETWEEN THE PASSAGE OF New York State's Gradual Emancipation Law in 1799 and the beginning of the Civil War, black New Yorkers established a complex institutional network to address their social, political, and spiritual aims. As communities of free black people formed, they faced the daunting challenge of securing their liberty and enriching their lives and life chances by founding churches, schools, meeting halls, and newspapers—institutions that asserted their presence in civic affairs. Voluntary associations—including benevolent societies, fraternities, literary clubs, and self-defense organizations—had overlapping charitable, mutual aid, and political functions and could be distinguished more by emphasis than kind. These associations proved the most flexible and muscular of the institutions that sat at the center of civic life in antebellum black New York. They allowed black people to organize across class, ethnic, and religious lines and adjust the emphasis of their activism to the changing social and political landscape. They were the mechanism through which black Manhattanites united with other free black communities. In little more than a generation, black people erected an institutional and intellectual public culture with international reach.

A pantheon of institutions worked to craft a black public sphere: a political and social network that facilitated the movement of ideas and the creation of political

217

BLACK LIFE

IN FREEDOM:

CREATING

A CIVIC

CULTURE

consensus within black communities while articulating black people's political will to the broader urban community. The origins of that institutional crucible drew on traditions that enslaved Africans brought to New Amsterdam and later New York, their adjustments to enslavement in the Americas, and the creolization of black life in a city that combined African people of varied religious, ethnic, linguistic, and cultural backgrounds. These institutions protected free black people in a hostile city, preserved the community's ethical and religious values, fulfilled the community's moral and social obligations, and fought to overthrow slavery.

Short-lived and informal committees and clubs were the most common of these associations. For instance, black men and women routinely organized and participated in reading groups to expand their literacy and facilitate the sharing of books, pamphlets, and newspapers. When the powerful orator Maria Stewart arrived in New York City from Boston, she joined a black women's literary club. In Boston, Stewart had used the language of evangelical Christianity to challenge the city's black men, the "sons of Africa," to throw off every vestige of slavery and subordination until the black community "consumed the fruit of the vines that they planted." Although Stewart withdrew from public life in New York, she still had an impact through the reading group. When young Alexander Crummell returned to Manhattan in 1840 from school at Oneida Institute in Whitesboro, New York, he was emboldened by Stewart, "a young woman of my own people full of literary aspiration and ambitious authorship."[1] Literary clubs provided spaces for black New Yorkers across class and gender lines to debate the major issues of the day.

More formal mutual aid societies were the first associations to bring black voices into the civic life of the city. These private insurance cooperatives protected members against unemployment and illnesses, and provided for their burials. To meet these obligations, mutual aid organizations collected dues, held property, and distributed benefits; therefore, they evolved complex hierarchies with elected officers, by-laws, and constitutions. The largest societies became major forces in the daily life of the black community, using their networks, resources, and personnel to expand into social work by adding benevolent and charitable functions to their missions.

For example, in 1784 the New York African Society sponsored a lecture by the enslaved poet Jupiter Hammon. The event announced black New York's intent to establish an independent voice in the civic culture of the city. Hammon's historic "Address to the Negroes of the State of New-York" remains the subject of debate among historians because of its modest critique of bondage. But that controversy should not cloud the fact that the city's first black society arranged for an enslaved person to engage a public audience fifteen years before New York State enacted its gradual emancipation law.[2]

Hammon's "Address" marked the beginning of a permanent black presence in the city's civic life. In the following decades, benevolent societies continued to bring black people together for speeches and debates on issues impacting the community. More significantly, by the nineteenth century, black associations had assumed responsibility for organizing black New York for political action, facilitating public discussion, raising funds to build and support independent black schools, determining the calendar of holidays and celebrations, and creating consensus for concerted action. These organizations were the preferred mechanism for responding to community crises and unanticipated needs.[3]

The unstable economic and political lives of free and freed black people gave a moral gravity to the New York African Society's mission to bury the dead, insure members against economic downfalls, and provide assistance to the widows and orphans of members. John and Elizabeth Maranda's struggle to free and reunite their family reveals the challenges that black New Yorkers faced. Active in the black associations of early national New York, the couple negotiated their family's freedom with remarkable skill and determination. In October 1795, John Maranda purchased his own freedom for $200 from John De Baan

Portrait of Alexander Crummell.

JUPITER HAMMON

Jupiter Hammon was born in 1711, enslaved to Henry Lloyd, a prosperous Long Island merchant. Because of the nature of his owner's business, young Jupiter was trained and employed as a clerk and bookkeeper, achieving a level of literacy that was rare for enslaved black men and women. Swept up in the religious awakening of the eighteenth century, his life was defined by evangelical Christianity. "Dear Jesus let the Nations cry / And all the People say / Salvation comes from Christ on high / Haste on Tribunal Day," wrote Hammon in his 1760 Christmas poem, the first published verse of an African American. Black evangelicalism merged with black verse in Hammon's writing, and the two remained wed in Hammon's later literary efforts. Among his more famous poems was his 1778 tribute to Phillis Wheatley, the enslaved African girl who in 1767, at only thirteen years of age, published her first poem and who, in 1773, became the first black person to publish a book of poetry in the United States. In 1784, Jupiter Hammon formally entered the debate over slavery, penning an "Address to the Negroes of the State of New-York." While not directly attacking slavery, Hammon's verse and prose exploited the evangelical belief in the equality of all human beings in the eyes of God. Hammon, like

AN

ADDRESS

TO THE

NEGROES

In the STATE of NEW-YORK,

BY JUPITER HAMMON,

Servant of John Lloyd, jun, Esq; of the Manor of Queen's Village, Long-Island.

" Of a truth I perceive that God is no respecter of
" persons :
" But in every Nation, he that feareth him and
" worketh righteousness, is accepted with him."—
Acts x. 34, 35.

NEW-YORK:

Printed by CARROLL and PATTERSON
No. 32, Maiden-Lane,

M,DCC,LXXXVII.

Jupiter Hammon (1711–ca. 1800), *An Address to Negroes in the State of New-York*. NEW-YORK HISTORICAL SOCIETY LIBRARY

Wheatley and other early African American writers, drew upon the egalitarian impulses of Christianity to press the case for freedom. He died at about the age of eighty, still enslaved to the Lloyd family. — *Craig Steven Wilder*

through an intermediary. John and Elizabeth immediately bought their daughter from her New Jersey owner for $50. Three years later, they secured Elizabeth's freedom from one Dr. Gardner Jones for $150, and for an additional $10 bought their son from Jones.[4] The family fully understood the precarious place of free black people in the racial order of the city, and John Maranda became a founding member of the New York African Society for Mutual Relief, black New York's most prominent mutual aid association, as part of his commitment to protecting their freedom.

That same determination fueled black New Yorkers' movement for an independent black church. In 1796, several black members of the classes at New York's first Methodist house of worship, the John Street Church, secured permission from Bishop Francis Asbury to open an African Chapel. By establishing a separate place of worship, the black community broke free of the increasingly racist culture of American Methodism while preserving the uniqueness of black spirituality and egalitarian Christianity. Their work in the African Society provided the founders with the institutional expertise to organize a separate chapel, and the black church later provided the spiritual enthusiasm that sustained black benevolent associations. The historical records list several prominent black men as the leaders of the movement. They included older men like Peter Williams Sr., who had gained his freedom while serving as the sexton of the John Street Church, and William Hamilton, a young freeborn activist. However, two thirds of the black people attending Methodist classes were women, who demonstrated an equal commitment to establishing a house of worship under their own ministers. By 1799 the chapel was successful enough for its directors to plan a separate black church. A year later, they opened the African Methodist Episcopal Zion Church, or Mother Zion, under the regular Methodist government. Fund-raisers in the black community paid for a building and a cemetery. In 1820 the ministers, trustees, and congregation completely separated Mother Zion from the white Methodists by establishing their own denomination.[5]

In the summer of 1808, the Reverend Thomas Paul of Boston organized the Abyssinian Baptist Church in New York City. As in the Methodist Church, women dominated the membership while men controlled its administration.

221

BLACK LIFE
IN FREEDOM:
CREATING
A CIVIC
CULTURE

Henrietta Ray, a teenager when she joined in the 1820s, was drawn to the church because it was governed by black people and thus was free of the abuses that black New Yorkers suffered in predominantly white churches, and more dedicated to the moral and social elevation of the black community. By 1830, women accounted for 75 percent of Abyssinian's 245 congregants and they were the cornerstone of its social outreach programs.[6]

Although black people achieved significant independence over their spiritual affairs, they remained marginalized and vulnerable in the urban economy. "In the early part of the year 1808, a few mechanics of the people of colour in this city, taking into consideration the importance of providing for a sick day, and of devising means to administer assistance to those of their friends, whom the vicissitudes of time or the freaks of fortune might reduce to want, held several consultations for that purpose," recalled Peter Vogelsang, secretary of the New York African Society for Mutual Relief, during an 1815 anniversary celebration.[7]

As originally designed, the African Society united skilled craftsmen in a mutual aid program, a focus that likely responded to white workers' campaign to remove black men from the skilled trades and reduce them to the status of freed servants. The assault on skilled black workers was especially intense. In 1816, William Hamilton and James Latham almost lost their Stone Street carpentry shop when white neighbors objected that the business devalued and endangered their property. Latham and Hamilton were founders of the African Society for Mutual Relief, and Hamilton served as its first president. Black businessmen were also at risk. White restaurant owners and shopkeepers attacked entrepreneur George Downing, also a member of the Mutual Relief Society, because they could not compete with his upscale oyster house. They blasted Downing in the press and demanded that white customers and businesses boycott his establishment.[8]

In fact, a third of all free black people lived and worked in white households and those who did not labored to support themselves in a tightly restricted job market. Four out of ten black men were in the unskilled ranks and their proportion in the skilled trades sharply declined during the first decade of the nineteenth century. White workers employed their numerical advantage and

The New York African Society for Mutual Relief

Founded in 1808, the New York African Society for Mutual Relief was the first black association to incorporate and among the longest-lived of the early African benevolent societies. Established as a mutual aid association to provide health insurance, death benefits, and relief from other tribulations that newly emancipated people faced, the Society quickly captured the social imagination of New York's black community. To the surprise of its founders, nearly one hundred black men joined in its first year, bringing the Society the capital and visibility that catapulted it to the center of social and political life in antebellum black Manhattan. In 1820, with financial assistance from Juliet Toussaint, a member of the city's expanding black Haitian community, the Society purchased land and constructed a meetinghouse. Thereafter, the Society continued to invest its money in New York real estate. As its members would later boast, the careful governance of the Society's finances allowed it to fulfill its obligations without interruption and to support a variety of charitable and political work in the city's black communities. After the Civil War, the New York African Society for Mutual Relief faced a series of challenges that eventually brought about its

Seal of the New York African Society for Mutual Relief. LONG ISLAND UNIVERSITY, BROOKLYN CAMPUS, LIBRARY ARCHIVES

demise, as the spread of black insurance companies and the rise of black politicians reduced the traditional role of African benevolent societies. However, the Society's lucrative investments and careful management allowed it to continue functioning as a black men's benevolent and "secret" society into the twentieth century. It was only in 1945, at the close of World War II, that an aging membership agreed to disband the venerable institute for lack of suitable applicants.

—*Craig Steven Wilder*

political power to push black laborers from occupations like street carting, in which black people gained a foothold during the labor shortages of the Revolutionary era, beginning an exclusion from the city's transportation industries that lasted well into the twentieth century. Black women operated in a more restricted labor market, limited to domestic and service trades like household servants, seamstresses, and laundresses.[9]

Despite their own unsteady economic position, the black mechanics who founded the African Society for Mutual Relief opened the association to all men of color regardless of their occupations. They explained that the "most efficient method of securing ourselves from the extreme exigencies to which we are liable to be reduced is by uniting ourselves in a body for the purpose of raising a fund for the relief of its members." The decision reflected a growing awareness that the plight of black artisans was tied to the fate of all free black people. In hindsight, Secretary Vogelsang praised their decision "to open the door for the admission of all moral characters of colour . . . [and] to lay a good foundation for the improvement of morals among us."[10]

The range of membership also allowed the African Society to speak for a broad cross-section of the black community, a responsibility that it used to move itself to the center of public life in the black metropolis. In 1810, the officers and members incorporated in order to secure their members' bonds and to provide the black community with a symbol of their changing social and legal status. New York City mayor DeWitt Clinton's personal appeal convinced the state legislators, and an act of incorporation passed in March 1810. Black New Yorkers celebrated this occasion a few weeks later. More than a hundred members of the African Society took to the streets of Manhattan in a formal parade, carrying painted silk banners and the emerging icons of the antislavery movement: a sign with the figure of a black man and the motto, "Am I Not a Man and a Brother." Before a large crowd, the brothers of the African Society read their act of incorporation, sang the organization's song, and delivered addresses that recorded the meaning of this accomplishment for the community.[11]

Black voluntary associations infiltrated the city's deeply racialized and tightly policed public sphere in order to agitate for equal citizenship and the abolition of slavery. By parading, black people transformed their earlier attempts to establish a separate public sphere of lectures, debates, and discussions in the confines of their own institutions into a bold demand upon the city's public spaces. Parading declared black people's claims upon citizenship and the common culture in aggressive political terms.[12]

Yet it was in these very public spaces that white New Yorkers expressed themselves most violently in defense of the racial order. In 1807, a committee planning black New York's celebration of the impending end of United States participation in the slave trade had to petition the city council for a "sufficient number of peace officers" to protect the celebrants. An 1809 parade honoring the African Society for Mutual Relief's first anniversary and an 1810 celebration of its incorporation were met with threats of violence and warnings from city officials, who refused to guarantee the safety of the participants. "Secure in the their manhood and will," wrote an antebellum member, "they did parade." Similarly, on July 5,

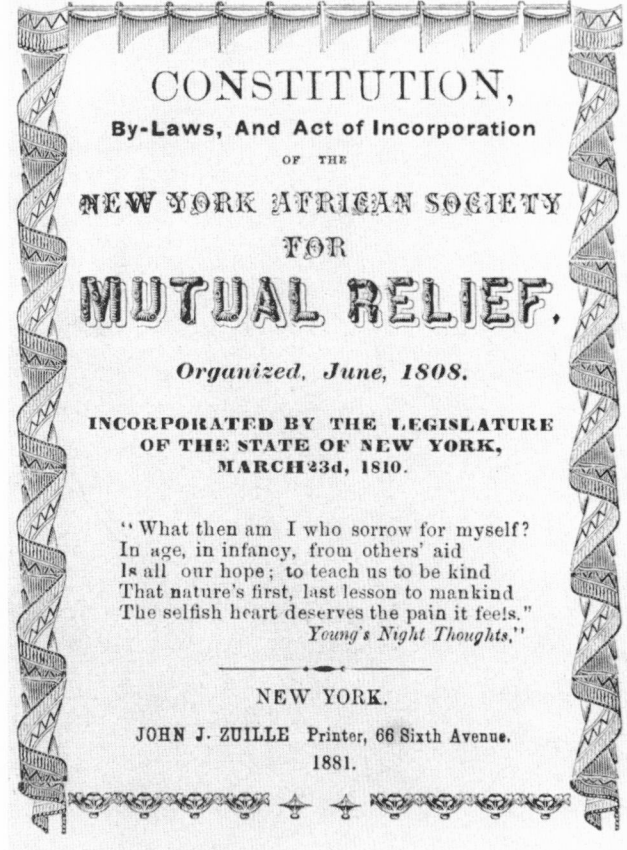

Front page of the *African Society Constitution*.
NEW-YORK HISTORICAL SOCIETY LIBRARY

1827, the black benevolent societies swarmed New York's streets to commemorate the legal end of slavery in the state. A long procession of black men and boys in rows five and six wide marched behind the major men's associations. African Society members flew brightly colored silk banners and were "splendidly dressed in scarfs of silk with gold-edgings, and with colored bands of music, and their banners appropriately lettered and painted." The main orator was on horseback with a scroll tightly clasped in his right hand. The grand marshal, Samuel Hardenburgh, sat atop a white horse trotting beside the procession. Hardenburgh drew his sword as he led the marchers to City Hall to meet the mayor. "The sidewalks were crowded with the wives, daughters, sisters, and mothers of the celebrants," recalled a young participant.[13]

Such brash intrusions into the public sphere amplified the prestige of black associations, but their social influence derived from their ability to address the day-to-day needs of the black community. Renowned for its extravagant costumes and pageantry at parades, the Wilberforce Philanthropic Association, founded in 1812, was primarily a mutual relief association that existed "to aid such of the members as shall, by sickness or infirmity, be incapable of following their usual employments, to assist the widows and orphans of deceased members, and for improvements in literature." Significantly, Wilberforce was one of the only organizations to include a librarian among its officers. The New York African Marine Fund for the Relief of Distressed Orphans, founded in 1810 and one of a few associations open to both sexes, dedicated its efforts and resources to public charity rather than to the support of its members—in fact, women's and open associations tended to have broader charitable functions. Under the guidance of leading black ministers, the Marine Fund's constitution required that all members donate monthly to "schooling the poor African children" and that the managing officers use any additional money to provide poor school children with clothing. African Marine Fund initiates formed visiting committees to identify economically distressed black people and report their needs to the governing elders. Additionally, the fund held special collections whenever the treasury was insufficient to meet legitimate community needs.[14]

Black associations built schools, defended teachers, and took responsibility for educating and training poorer and orphaned children. These commitments reflected the community's faith in education as a tool of uplift and black parents' dissatisfaction with the schools available to their children. John Teasman, one of the early principals in the African Free School, used his position to expand the black community's authority over their children's education and to turn the school into a site for training black youths as leaders and activists. In 1809, the trustees of the New York Manumission Society, which governed the African Free Schools, fired Teasman for his involvement in public parades. The African Society for Mutual Relief then hired Teasman to run schools that it was establishing to broaden the educational opportunities for both black children and adults.[15]

Regardless of which schools children attended, many black families could not afford to properly clothe them. "Several benevolent *colored females*, have recently formed themselves into a society, under the name of 'The African Dorcas Association,' for the purpose of procuring and of making up garments for . . . destitute [students]," wrote Charles C. Andrews, the boys' teacher at African Free School No. 2. While the New York Manumission Society sponsored the association and black men governed its work, the women conducted their own meetings, collected dues, and planned their charitable efforts. Henrietta Ray, a nineteen-year-old member of Abyssinian Baptist Church, became assistant secretary of the new benevolent society and gained organizational experience that she later used to establish more political and activist black women's societies. Influenced by the success of the Dorcas Association, a small group of black men and women established the Phoenix Society in 1833. In one of its initial outreach efforts, the society sent its members to each neighborhood in the city to help black women establish local Dorcas societies. The Phoenix Society encouraged the "old and young, and of both sexes, to become members." Its broad uplift agenda included persuading black parents to improve their church attendance and utilize the night schools, send their children regularly to Sunday schools and the local colored schools, and, if their income allowed, subscribe to abolitionist newspapers.[16]

Creating a community able to fight for its economic and political rights required expanding and protecting black people's access to education. Black associations opened educational opportunities for black youths, and that community involvement in education empowered black teachers in the colored schools. Concerned about the quality of their daughter Maritcha's education, Albro and Mary Lyons, both activists in the black community, entrusted her to

PATRICK AND CHARLES REASON

Elizabeth Melville, a native of Haiti, and Michel Rison (later Reason), born in Guadeloupe, had four children in New York City. Policarpe, a four-year-old girl, died in 1818 and was survived by three younger brothers: Patrick, Charles, and Elwer. Patrick and Charles Reason both became prominent anti-slavery leaders, conductors in the "Underground Railroad," assisting fugitives from slavery who passed through New York; and key community activists who helped guide the black community's struggle for educational opportunity, civil rights, and the abolition of slavery throughout the nation.

Patrick Henry Reason (1816–1898), already a talented illustrator at only thirteen years old, drew the image of New York African Free School No. 2 that appeared on the cover of Charles Andrew's 1830 history of the academies run by the New York Manumission Society for colored children. After graduation, he apprenticed as an engraver for four years. His drawings and engravings appeared in books, magazines, and virtually every print media, and he also created plates for paper notes, coins, and other government and private currency. His work was seen throughout the Americas and Europe. In 1852, Patrick Reason was selected to engrave a piece that adorned the coffin of former United States congressman, senator, and presidential candidate Daniel Webster.

Charles Lewis Reason (1818–1893) also attended the African School in Manhattan, where he began teaching when he was only fourteen years old. He studied mathematics and foreign languages at Union Academy in McGrawville, New York. Upon graduating, he was hired as an instructor at MacGrawville, although he was then only seventeen years old. The following year, Charles began teaching in New York City's African Free Schools. For nearly sixty years, he served as a teacher and principal in the New York schools, retiring in the spring of 1893.

—Craig Steven Wilder

"a life long friend, Prof. Charles L. Reason, principal of Colored School, No. 3, then located at Broadway and Thirty-seventh Street, New York City." Maritcha Lyons's journey to school required a rather long trip, especially for a child, and she was often forced to walk because the stage drivers typically refused black passengers. Still, in the years before the Civil War, young Maritcha had the extraordinary experience of learning with one of the city's master teachers. Charles Reason, the son of Caribbean refugees to New York, became a teacher in the Colored Schools in 1835, when he was only eighteen years old. Reason taught in the New York City schools for fifty-seven years, training some of the leading black figures of nineteenth-century America, including Maritcha Lyons, who became one of the first black women to serve as assistant principal of a New York public school.[17]

The success of voluntary associations required that they meet their members' needs while addressing the concerns of the larger black community. Their entrance into the public life and civic affairs of antebellum New York City meant a careful balance of collective action and individual uplift. Thus, benevolent societies incorporated mutual assistance for their members, thereby freeing them to engage in political work. Black women structured the New York Female Literary Society, founded in 1834, to balance their need for mutual support and their dedication to community uplift and political action. Although established as an academic and mutual aid association, the Literary Society, under the leadership of Henrietta Ray, broadened its work by raising money to assist fugitive slaves and, later, venturing into abolitionism.[18]

Black women's determination to control their own fates defined the Abyssinian Benevolent Daughters of Esther Association, founded in 1839. The association was one of the only women's organizations to publish a constitution and by-laws, and the sole women's society to hold considerable property. Although the association had male advisors, the Benevolent Daughters' structure was intended to solve crises that were likely to impact a black woman's life. For a three-dollar initiation fee and seventy-five cents in quarterly dues, women of good moral character could become members, entitled to a plot in the Daughters' burial ground and other services. Each Daughter was eligible for

229

BLACK LIFE
IN FREEDOM:
CREATING
A CIVIC
CULTURE

weekly salary supplements if illness prevented her from working so long as her injury or sickness did not result from "immoral conduct." When spouses were ill, Daughters were also entitled to support, and the society's burial policy allotted twenty dollars for a member who died and ten dollars for the death of a member's husband.[19]

Antebellum black New Yorkers also organized youth associations. Black men and women used these youth societies to apprentice the rising generations in community organizing and political action. The Philomathean Literary Society (1829) created opportunities for boys and young men to improve their academic skills through debates, essay contests, and lectures. An observer at one of their gatherings praised the "spirit which has animated the young Philomatheans of this city." In the following years, Philomathean societies were established in other cities, including Boston, and the New York Philomatheans were successful enough to open their own hall.[20]

The struggle for equality needed new generations of skilled community organizers and leaders, and youth associations introduced teens and children to the major political and social issues of the day. "We have the honor to inform you that there has been formed in this city a Society for literary and benevolent purposes, composed of boys from 4 to 20 years of age," wrote the officers of the Garrison Literary and Benevolent Association to the editor of the *Liberator*, informing him that, as "a small token of our respect for your person," they had given the organization his name. The Garrison Association trained several future leaders of the black community, including Henry Highland Garnet, a fugitive from slavery who rose to a career in the ministry and became one of the nation's militant opponents of slavery. "Whereas we believe the downfal[l] of prejudice, slavery, and oppression, and the moral and intellectual improvement of the rising generation of our race, depend on early improvement," wrote the boys, this association was formed "to see the youth of color distinguish themselves by their good conduct and intellectual attainments." One of the boys' first actions was to pass resolutions declaring certain white people's objections to the name of the association "an uncalled for usurpation of authority," and announcing their intent to pass the name Garrison down through history.[21]

Supporting community endeavors was not easy for those forced to the margins of society, and the young men in the Garrison Association had to develop a commitment to working in community organizations while bearing the heavy demands and burdens on free black people. Mutual aid, benevolent, and literary associations routinely used secret initiation ceremonies, rituals, and oaths to cultivate social bonds among members and preserve unity. Initiations and rites also grayed the distinctions between benevolent and secret societies—associations organized around esoteric rituals and contrived secrets used to create social bonds—allowing members to experience their organizations as sisterhoods and brotherhoods. Such fraternal and sororal ties helped sustain charitable work. The remnants of a secret ritual from around 1841 for an African Dorcas Society demonstrate the self-conscious use of secret rites to create and sustain unity. An official in "solemn fantastic canonicals" conducted the Dorcas service by taking an oath of loyalty from kneeling candidates. At one point a piece of bread was brought toward the initiate's open mouth and then pulled away to emphasize the organization's commitment to sacrifice. Such fraternal and sororal cultures provided cohesion even when organizations underwent transitions in their functions and dramatic restructurings of their missions. For instance, during the Civil War, the Ladies Benevolent Dorcas Society of St. Mark's Church changed its mission to sewing uniforms and undergarments for soldiers in the Union Army.[22]

It is not surprising that the constitution of the Abyssinian Benevolent Daughters of Esther swore members to secrecy and directly tied that oath to the organization's ability "to increase its members and extend its influence." In fact, such rituals were common in even the most ordinary associations. The young men's Philomathean Literary Society awarded a collar of distinction— "made of velvet, having two silver stars attached to it, and a silver medal with the inscription, 'Annual Chief'"—to the best essayist, and rituals allowed members to regularly rehearse their obligations and duties as they provided a mechanism for refining and transforming the functions of the group.[23]

Black fraternal and sororal organizations shared leadership and personnel with the mutual aid and benevolent societies. As a consequence, black secret

231

BLACK LIFE
IN FREEDOM:
CREATING
A CIVIC
CULTURE

societies were drawn into social and political work, while black benevolent societies borrowed rituals to enhance their internal unity. The Philomathean Society took this cross-fertilization to its logical conclusion by transforming from a benevolent academic society to an Odd Fellows lodge. The literary association expanded its fraternal features, and, on March 1, 1843, a Liverpool lodge of the Grand United Order of Odd Fellows chartered the black Philomatheans of New York City.[24]

The grandfather of New York City's black fraternal organizations, the Boyer Masonic Lodge No. 1, founded in 1812, included some of black Manhattan's most active abolitionists, ministers, and political leaders. The Boyer Lodge frequently hosted the black community's conventions and political gatherings. For instance, in February 1831 black Manhattanites gathered in the Boyer Lodge rooms to discuss and respond to the increased activities of the American Colonization Society, formed by prominent white men across the nation for the purpose of creating and enacting a plan to remove free black people from the United States to the Caribbean or West Africa. The community declared the United States "the place of their birth" and condemned any attempt to remove them.[25]

Shared personnel was not the only reason that fraternities joined mutual aid organizations, literary societies, and benevolent associations in shaping the public sphere. The prominence and broad social responsibilities of these voluntary organizations protected the community's churches and schools and individual private property from destruction by white mobs seeking to disrupt and punish political meetings of the black community. Society halls hosted the most contentious gatherings of antebellum black New Yorkers. "From the conventions of that date, the memory naturally glides to another 'institution,' hardly less remarkable, or of less influence in the city of New York—Union Hall, the great meeting room, the *agora*, the *forum* of the people and their leaders,—a Tammany Hall, except that it was not the property of a party, nor the minion of slavery, nor the tippling room of the 'great unwashed,'" wrote James McCune Smith of the meeting space in the basement of the Broadway Tabernacle. Here, generations of black New Yorkers gathered in a room that occupied "nearly one-half its basement story, a space of fifty feet by one hundred, broken into by huge round brick columns, which supported the floor above; dimly lighted by a half dozen camphene lamps badly rimmed, the floor nearly covered by movable benches, a dilapidated platform with a slightly elevated seat for the Chairman—such was the appearance of Union Hall."[26]

In the halls of their own benevolent associations, black New Yorkers pressed their political campaigns for the abolition of slavery and for equal rights into the statewide arenas. In 1837, the Phoenix Society held a community meeting at its hall that brought petitions to the state legislature demanding that persons arrested as fugitives from slavery be guaranteed a trial by jury, that the state constitution be amended to allow all adult men to vote "without distinction of color," and that the state repeal the laws allowing persons to be held in bondage. The petition for a trial by jury was signed by the "fathers and mothers, and men and women of color" on behalf of the city's fifteen thousand colored people. In 1841, the black community held a convention at Union Hall to erase the "last vestige of oppression" from the state constitution and to achieve political equality for all New Yorkers. They forwarded resolutions demanding equal voting rights, civil rights, and legal protections to the state legislature.[27]

The rise of an independent press solidified black New Yorkers' capacity to engage in public debates and discussions at the state and national levels. The black press dramatically extended the impact of local community conventions and meetings by opening their proceedings and resolutions to a mass audience. Black families proved an important and reliable source of funding for abolitionist newspapers, and black community organizations often reminded households of the importance of subscribing to such organs.

New York was the "birthplace of black journalism." In 1827, the Reverend Samuel B. Cornish and John B. Russwurm launched *Freedom's Journal*, the nation's first black-owned newspaper. Many of the board members and editors were trained in black associations, and those organizations provided the paper with its first offices. The editors declared their intent to use the paper in defense of the nation's half-million free people of color: "Daily slandered, we think that there ought to be some channel of communication between us and the public."[28]

FREEDOM'S  JOURNAL.

"RIGHTEOUSNESS EXALTETH A NATION."

BY JNO. B. RUSSWURM.　　　NEW-YORK, FRIDAY, MARCH 14, 1828.　　　VOL. I.—NO. LI.

THE COLORED AMERICAN.

SAMUEL E. CORNISH,
EDITOR.　　　*New-York, Saturday, May 13, 1837.*　　　PHILIP A. BELL,
PROPRIETOR.

Combined image of John B. Russwurm, Samuel E. Cornish, and *Freedom's Journal* masthead.

The black press coordinated the community's political work, facilitated the movement of information among black communities, and made black folk's ideas, values, and politics accessible to a broader national audience. In 1829, Cornish founded the *Rights of All* specifically to target colonization. Through the *Weekly Advocate*, later renamed the *Colored American*, Philip Bell sought to promote the central themes of the black community's struggle, including the abolition of slavery, the broadening of educational opportunity, securing the right to vote, and opposing colonization. Antebellum black New Yorkers established more than a dozen newspapers.[29]

As an agent for the *Emancipator*, young David Ruggles learned the power of the press as a tool for unifying and informing black communities. Ruggles's early experience in organizing came while he was a member of the boys' Garrison Literary and Benevolent Association. In November 1835, Ruggles became a founding member of the New York Vigilance Committee, formed to protect free black people from intimidation and kidnapping by slave hunters and to assist fugitives from slavery. Ruggles called a mass community meeting to respond to the kidnapping of George Jones, who had been arrested on false assault charges in the summer of 1836, secretly brought before the city recorder, and "pronounced to be a slave!" Ruggles demanded that black people organize and respond to this assault on their most basic rights to life and liberty. "Unknown except to the initiated, a committee of thirteen was formed in our city," wrote Maritcha Lyons of this moment. "Without officers, headquarters, passwords or treasury, this band was liberally supported. Aid was given to escaping slaves, financially or otherwise, by those who required no other details save that such help was needed." This committee also worked to use the "grape vine telegraph" to spread the news among the enslaved that black New York was prepared to help them escape. As Lyons recalled, "Every thinking man and woman was a volunteer in the famous 'underground railroad.'" Ruggles agreed, noting that the efforts of "the Ladies, who collect from their friends one penny a week," provided the committee with the wherewithal to assist more than three hundred black fugitives from bondage. Beginning in 1837, Ruggles edited the *Mirror of Liberty*, the newspaper of the New York Vigilance Committee.[30]

235

BLACK LIFE
IN FREEDOM:
CREATING
A CIVIC
CULTURE

A sign of the community's willingness to use its institutions to fight injustice came in the aftermath of the federal Fugitive Slave Act (1850). That fall bounty hunters seized James Hamlet in New York City under the new federal law. Led by William Powell, a local black businessman and a veteran of the local political conventions and meetings, a delegation of black seamen marched on City Hall and convinced the mayor to end police involvement in capturing suspected or claimed runaways. The leading societies gathered the black community in Old Zion Church, and black community meetings were also held in Williamsburg and Brooklyn. Black assemblies raised more than eight hundred dollars to purchase Hamlet's freedom. "Many families, who had lived in the city for twenty years, fled from it now. Many a poor washerwoman, who, by hard labor, had made herself a comfortable home, was obliged to sacrifice her furniture, bid a hurried farewell to friends, and seek her fortune among strangers in Canada," wrote Harriet Jacobs of the terror that the fugitive law created in New York. Many a husband had to confess to his wife that he had escaped slavery years earlier, Jacobs continued, and "worse still, many a husband discovered that his wife had fled from slavery years ago, and as 'the child follows the condition of its mother,' the children of his love were liable to be seized and carried into slavery." Not limiting itself to responding to kidnappings and arrests, the black community moved for more aggressive defense. In a spring 1851 meeting, the community resolved "that this Convention impress on the minds of the young men of this city and the city of Brooklyn and Williamsburg, to organize military companies."[31]

Black New Yorkers' determination and capacity to confront slavery directly had crystalized much earlier. In the 1830s, black churches, benevolent and aid societies, schools, and newspapers extended the community's political voice and vision into the state and national discourse about slavery and inequality. The free black communities of Baltimore, Philadelphia, and New York had debated the practicality of a national convention for years, but violent proslavery attacks on free black communities and a growing assault on their political liberties provided the incentive to move forward. When the first Annual National Convention of the People of Color began on June 6, 1831, the representatives from New York were all members of the African Society for Mutual Relief. Members of the city's leading associations continued to represent New York City at the subsequent National Colored Conventions, including the fourth convention held there. In control of the proceedings, New Yorkers pushed their own ideas. They issued strong statements against colonization, organized committees to explore attacks on the civil rights of free black people, launched studies of trades that were closed to colored workers, advocated the support of abolitionist newspapers, investigated legislation that undermined black people's rights, and coordinated responses. The New Yorkers' imprint is perhaps best seen in the use of the term "revolution" to describe their vision of the thrust and purpose of convening.[32]

And something quite revolutionary was under way. In 1831 James McCune Smith boarded a ship leaving New York City for Europe. A product of the African schools of Manhattan and one of the "graduates," to employ his own term, of its benevolent societies and religious institutions, he was going to Scotland to enroll at the University of Glasgow, where, during the next five years, he earned three degrees, including a doctor of medicine. He also joined the Glasgow Emancipation Society, bringing to it a set of antislavery values and ideas that were cultivated in black New York, and launching a process that placed black Americans at the center of the Atlantic abolitionist movement.[33]

In little more than a generation, free and freed black New Yorkers constructed a community of institutions and ideas with transatlantic reach. The humble organizations that they formed while making the transition from slavery to freedom matured into institutions capable of guiding the international debate about slavery. McCune Smith's impact began with generations of men and women who courageously sought to unify local black communities in the struggle against slavery and inequality. And the societies, churches, schools, and halls that they left to their descendants are a lasting reminder of their confidence that black New York, and black America, had the personnel and talent to realize universal emancipation and universal equality.

237

BLACK LIFE
IN FREEDOM:
CREATING
A CIVIC
CULTURE

Chapter 8

BLACK ABOLITIONISM: THE ASSAULT ON SOUTHERN SLAVERY AND THE STRUGGLE FOR RACIAL EQUALITY

———— ◆ ————

MANISHA SINHA

Peter S. Duval, *Rev. Christopher Rush*. Lithograph.

IN 1827, AS BLACK New Yorkers celebrated the liquidation of the last remnants of chattel bondage in their state, they began an assault on Southern slavery and racism in the United States and the larger Atlantic world. Black New Yorkers had long been at the forefront of the movement against slavery—sometimes in silent protest, sometimes in open revolt, sometimes petitioning for their own freedom, and sometimes contesting the institution itself. As the chains of slavery loosened in New York with the passage of the Gradual Emancipation Law in 1799, black abolitionists had expanded their assault, attacking the transatlantic slave trade even as they pushed for a final end to slavery in New York. In 1808, when Congress finally outlawed the importation of slaves into the United States, black New Yorkers found little time to celebrate. The decline of slavery was accompanied by new constraints placed on black liberty. Indeed, as white New Yorkers—including many of the most reliable opponents of slavery—confronted the realities of African American freedom, they thought it best if black people were physically removed, urging colonization to Africa or some other distant place, as if the United States was not their country.

In the face of indifference and opposition, New York's black abolitionists kept alive the antislavery impulse even as it atrophied among white Americans. Their ideas became crucial in the transformation of the gradualism of

Revolutionary antislavery into the unconditional abolitionism of the nineteenth century. The movement against slavery reached a new stage in the 1820s and 1830s as black New Yorkers, joined by others throughout the North, began to reshape of the tenets of antislavery, taking the movement against slavery in new directions that included immediatism, political action, urging of slave insurrections, and emigration from the United States. As home to the North's largest free black urban population, New York City's black abolitionists shaped the struggle against racism, demanding an end to racial exclusion and segregation and leading attempts to expand suffrage for black men. Throughout the period, African American New Yorkers played a critical role in developing the intellectual, political, and social critiques of slavery that came to characterize abolition. Their war against slavery was not just based on personal experience but was profoundly ideological, as their principled opposition to chattel bondage and second-class citizenship ran deep.[1]

IN THE late 1820s, most white opponents of slavery in New York, like their counterparts throughout the nation, were committed to gradualism, and many joined the American Colonization Society (ACS) and supported its program to remove black people to the west coast of Africa where the society had established the colony of Liberia. In 1823, at its annual meeting in New York City, leaders of the ACS—which included some of the nation's most prominent white politicians—reasserted their determination to colonize "the free people of colour of the United States" in Africa, calculating that the annual removal of 30,000 African Americans could rid the United States of its black population in fifty years. While some Northern reformers continued to support colonization as a means of ending slavery, the scheme was increasingly aimed at the deportation of free blacks. In fact, if the colonizationists were successful, the only African Americans left in the United States would be slaves, an eventuality which attracted many slaveholders, particularly in the Upper South, to the colonizationists' standard. Even in the North, the colonizationists' antiblack animus became increasingly apparent. In 1829, the New York branch of the American

Colonization Society recommended removal as a way to get rid of a "degraded population."[2]

Most black New Yorkers understood colonization more as an attack on them than as a means to end Southern slavery. The racial thermidor of colonization and the simultaneous expansion of "the white man's democracy" and restriction of black rights reinvigorated rather than stifled black resistance. An anticolonization meeting in New York City, organized by leading black abolitionists, confronted those who would remove black Americans, declaring, "Here we were born, and here we will die." Opposition to colonization asserted the determination of black Northerners not to abandon their "brethren in slavery" and to fight for their rights in the United States. In New York, as in cities throughout the North, protests against colonization by African Americans gave birth to a new, radical abolition movement. They crystallized the agenda of radical abolition: the immediate end of slavery and equal rights for all. The founding of New York's *Freedom's Journal* in 1827 marks this change. Its editors—Samuel Cornish, a black Presbyterian minister, and John Russwurm, one of the first black college graduates in the United States—stated the dictum of the radicalism that surged through the black community and captured the spirit of black abolition in New York: "We wish to plead our own cause." The founding editorial elaborated the essential components of black abolitionism, the education of the people of color, their civil rights and political unity, the rights of "our brethren who are still in the iron fetters of bondage," and the correction of "misrepresentations" and prejudice against African Americans.[3]

In later decades, antislavery black New Yorkers continued to struggle against what they perceived as the false philanthropy of colonizationists. In 1830, in a brilliant and powerful anticolonization Fourth of July speech, Peter Williams Jr., pastor of St. Philip's Episcopal Church, observed that "the freedom to which we have attained is defective. . . . We are oppressed by an unreasonable, unrighteous, and cruel prejudice. . . . NATIVES of this country, we ask only to be treated as well as FOREIGNERS." In 1840, Cornish and Theodore Wright, the minister of the Colored Presbyterian Church, publicly addressed prominent New York colonizationists Theodore Frelinghuysen and Benjamin

Butler. Cornish and Wright called their attention to the historic opposition of black New Yorkers to colonization and the recent gathering that "deliberately and unanimously" protested *against the whole scheme.*" According to them, colonization was the slaveholders' plot to get rid of "so feeble an adversary as the free colored people" and was based on racial prejudice. They urged Frelinghuysen and Butler to attack racism in America rather than deport black people from their native land. Embarking on a lengthy critique of the history of colonization, Cornish and Wright summarized more than two decades of opposition by black New Yorkers. New York's black abolitionists helped make anticolonization an essential component of Garrisonian abolitionism.[4]

As the new abolition movement emerged from the assault on colonization, black New Yorkers—Peter Williams Jr., William Hamilton, Samuel Cornish, and Theodore Wright—found themselves in the forefront, devising new antislavery strategies, tactics, and ideologies. In 1827, celebrating the final liquidation of slavery, William Hamilton, a New York carpenter, launched the first full-scale attack on Jeffersonian racism. Hamilton's oration was one of the first attempts by African American abolitionists to refute the tenets of the emerging pseudoscientific racism, even if it meant taking on the revered Jefferson. Beginning cautiously—"I know that I ought to speak with caution"—Hamilton nevertheless directly criticized the racialist arguments of the "ambidexter philosopher" who kept "around him a number of slaves" and who "first tells you 'that all men are created equal, and that they are endowed with unalienable rights of life, liberty, and the pursuit of happiness,'" and "next proves that one class of men are not equal to another, which by the bye, does not agree with axioms of geometry, that deny that things can be equal, and at the same time unequal to one another." For William Hamilton, Jefferson was not only illogical, but also immoral, and his immorality infected the very foundations of the American nation: "Does he reason like a man of true moral principles? Does he set a good example? . . . What jargon does the law of the United States form with the principles here laid down, that gives to one class of men, the right to arrest, wherever they may find within its jurisdiction, another class of men, and retain them as their lawful property?" Turning the table on white Americans,

Hamilton asked them sarcastically to justify their "superior" reasoning and laws.[5]

Led by Hamilton, New York's cadre of black abolitionists thus became among the first to employ the unsparing and scathing rhetoric that became the hallmark of the new assault on slavery. Placing aside the sentimental "appeals to the heart" to make their case, they developed a distinct abolitionist style of uncompromising condemnation of slavery and racism that prefigured the rise of Garrisonian abolitionism. And black New Yorkers, joined by African American abolitionists throughout the North, did not just restrict their attacks to Southern slavery but condemned racism throughout the republic. They helped make antiracism as well as antislavery the twin goals of the abolitionist movement. In renouncing gradualism and colonization, William Lloyd Garrison would adopt the ideas and style of these pioneering black abolitionists. David Walker's famous 1829 *Appeal* was not an aberration but a continuation of this black abolitionist tradition. In his less-known *Ethiopian Manifesto*, published the same year, New Yorker Robert Alexander warned "the fiendish cast of men" who dare hold others in slavery of divine retribution and predicted the arrival of a messiah who would lead black people out of the house of bondage.[6]

The fusing of militant black abolitionism with a predominantly white religious and moral reform impulse of the Second Great Awakening initiated interracial abolitionism in the early 1830s. William Lloyd Garrison, who enjoyed close ties with black opponents of slavery, became the voice of immediatism, but Garrisonian abolitionism drew upon the uncompromising stance and rhetoric of early black abolitionists. As he began his crusade against slavery, Garrison was especially dependent upon black support. Blacks composed two thirds of the subscribers to Garrison's journal, *The Liberator*, established in

W.L. Garrison.
Lithograph.
NEW-YORK HISTORICAL
SOCIETY LIBRARY

245

**BLACK
ABOLITIONISM**

1831, and supported the formation of the Garrisonian New England Anti-Slavery Society organized a year later. In 1833, when Garrison established the American Anti-Slavery Society (AASS) in Philadelphia, African Americans emerged as the backbone of the new movement. Despite the ongoing tensions between white and black opponents of slavery, African Americans participated as equals in the antebellum abolitionist movement and imbued its agenda with their radicalism. During the 1830s, New York's black abolitionists such as Cornish, Hamilton, Thomas Van Rensellaer, Christopher Rush, and Wright served as officers of the AASS.[7]

Black New Yorkers secured the cooperation of two prominent white merchant abolitionists, Arthur and Lewis Tappan, converts to Garrisonianism (actually, Garrison converted the Tappans) in the early 1830s. Evangelical Christians and more conservative than Garrison, the Tappans were nevertheless committed to the twin abolitionist goals of immediatism and black rights. In 1832, Arthur Tappan wrote to Garrison, "We have reason to fear as a people the vengeance of Heaven for the sins [we are] guilty of . . . to the [people] of Africa." The Tappan brothers bankrolled the activities of the American Anti-Slavery Society and helped found the New York Anti-Slavery Society and the antislavery newspaper, *The Emancipator*. Unlike most of the city's merchants who had close business ties with the slave South, the Tappan brothers put their wealth to the service of antislavery and a host of other reforms. And, like Garrison, the Tappans maintained their connections with New York's black abolitionists.[8]

The rise of a radical, interracial abolitionism infuriated some white New Yorkers. In the summer of 1834, fear of racial amalgamation or intermixture incited in part by the New York press sparked one of the most violent attacks on African Americans and their white abolitionist allies. On the Fourth of July, hundreds of white toughs attacked an abolitionist meeting at the Chatham Street Church. Three days later, an altercation at the same church between African Americans celebrating emancipation and the white members of the Sacred Music Society set off four days of rioting. White mobs rampaged through the city and destroyed the African Society for Mutual Relief Hall along with churches—black and white—associated with abolition. The homes of prominent blacks as well as those of the Tappan brothers were also leveled, as local authorities stood by, unable and unwilling to put a stop to the violence. Like antiabolitionist riots elsewhere in the North, "gentlemen of property and standing" encouraged the New York street mobs.

The riot transformed the nature of antislavery in New York. In the short run, it dampened antislavery activities, but in the long run the riot drew converts to the cause from among those disgusted with the violation of what they deemed basic American liberties. Even Peter Williams Jr., forced to distance himself from the antislavery cause after a reprimand from his clerical superior, Bishop Benjamin Onderdonk, spoke of the growth of sympathy for the abolitionists in the wake of the riots. "I doubt not that good will come out of evil," wrote Williams, "and that when the present excitement is over, it will appear that we have been so cruelly & wickedly oppressed, that all who have fear of God before their eyes, will be stirred up to make greater efforts than ever to elevate us to the enjoyment of those rights, which the Constitution of the United States guarantees to all its citizens."[9] Prominent white New Yorkers like William Jay, himself a distinguished jurist and the son of John Jay, a founder of the New York Manumission Society, joined the movement as much because they feared mob violence and the destruction of civil liberties as for the cause of black freedom. During the 1830s and 1840s, membership in abolitionist organizations grew steadily, particularly in the "burned over" districts of upstate New York.

Lewis Tappan.

David Ruggles, editor of *The Mirror of Liberty*.

Even as antislavery gained white adherents, grassroots activism and a critique of white racism defined black abolitionism in New York. No issue weighed heavier on black New Yorkers than the threat of kidnapping as slave catchers from the South flooded into the city. David Ruggles, who had migrated from Connecticut and opened a grocery store in Manhattan, inaugurated a new activist phase in black abolitionism, which spoke directly to those concerns. In 1835, Ruggles founded the New York Committee of Vigilance to protect free blacks and fugitive slaves from catchers and kidnappers. The committee became the center of the Underground Railroad in New York City. The Committee of Vigilance's activities were publicized through the *Mirror of Liberty*, a newspaper Ruggles published in New York between 1835 and 1841.[10]

Ruggles argued that "self-defence is the first law of nature," and black New Yorkers rallied to his radical call. Only through "ACTION! ACTION! ACTION!" argued Peter Paul Simons before New York's African Clarkson Society, "we will be in truth an independent people." According to one estimate, Ruggles's committee protected hundreds of free blacks and saved over one thousand fugitive slaves, including Frederick Douglass, from recapture. The committee also worked through the courts to protect fugitives. In 1840, Ruggles's committee, assisted by antislavery lawyers, won the right to trial by jury for fugitives. Under the antislavery Whig governor William H. Seward, New York also barred Southern slaveholders from bringing their slaves into the state. Ruggles advocated direct action if legal means failed. His bold-

MIRROR OF LIBERTY.

"LIBERTY IS THE WORD FOR ME—ABOVE ALL, LIBERTY."

Vol. I.   NEW-YORK, AUGUST, 1838.   No. 1.

The MIRROR OF LIBERTY is published quarterly by DAVID RUGGLES, Editor, corner of Lispenard and Church Streets, New-York City. Terms—*One Dollar*, per annum, payable in advance. Any person sending *Five Dollars*, shall be entitled to one copy gratis. All letters and communications must be *post paid*.   ☞ S. V. BERRY, *Traveling Agent.*

INTRODUCTORY REMARKS.

This journal enters the arena in behalf of the dumb—for the restoration of Equal Liberty, and the full enfranchisement of my down-trodden countrymen in this,

"Our own
Our native land."

But there are circumstances connected with the outset of this enterprize, which will necessarily diminish the merits of the present number.

We confidently hope, however, that all future numbers (which shall be filled and decked with a greater variety of subjects, many of which are excluded from this number for want of room,) shall maintain at least equal claims with the present one. The character of this periodical is expressed in the title chosen for its name. It will go for Truth and Equal Liberty. It will vindicate outraged human nature at all times, in season and out of season. It will never attempt to treat questions of public interest in a manner to avoid giving offence to men, when principle is involved; even if we possessed that art, we question the propriety of describing errors without showing the actors with them. Unless we stab slavery through the conscience of the slaveholder, hope of its removal would be chimerical.

The reader need not examine the MIRROR for long and theoretical disquisitions on abstract questions, though it will present a retrospective view of the past, and contain a large amount of important intelligence connected with the history of my proscribed race, which has been for ages suffered to pass unnoticed.

It will contain facts and arguments, strictures and animadversions upon things as they are; strictures and disquisitions shall be applicable to existing persons and events.

The greedy appetite of scandal and abuse shall never be satisfied in the columns of this journal, though Truth shall be decked in her natural habiliments of plainness, which will require no sacrifice.

The MIRROR will endeavor to show, by its example, that there is nothing unusual in plain truth to the dignity of any good cause, and that Equal Liberty cannot exist without it. The MIRROR is consecrated to the genius of liberty. It is trammelled by no sect, association, or company of men; but is, in a word, a free and independent journal. It will endeavor to avoid the fatal error of flattery at all times and on all occasions; but will vindicate right and expose error and the existing evils, which evidently obstruct the pathway to that consummation so long desired by a scattered, pealed and down-trodden people. It will never pay that fealty to men that is due to truth. It will fearlessly attack vice and immorality, in high places and in low places. We wish our readers to understand distinctly that we claim and shall maintain it too. come what will, the right to discuss and animadvert freely and frankly upon all subjects connected with the present well being and future destinies of my emaciated countrymen.

Because there is no subject connected with the interest of mankind that is so delicate, that it can, with conduciveness to our elevation, exist beyond the reach of investigation and comment before the open view of the world.

Therefore, we shall never hesitate to remark freely and frankly upon the many blighting evils which are nurtured and cherished in the bosom of society.

It will be one of the primary objects of this periodical to point out the errors which have evidently proved snares to our feet, in the pathway to Equal Liberty. To show by every rational mode of reason and argument the perniciousness of the indifference, apathy and neutrality which exists upon all subjects connected with the present and future salvation of outraged Human Nature.

We have published no long and swelling prospectus to solicit subscribers for this paper; for them we depend, under God, upon its merits and the goodness of the cause we advocate.

The MIRROR will be published quarterly, on fine paper, in a quarto form, and shall contain 16 pages neatly covered; at the end of the volume, the subscriber may possess 64 pages of valuable and interesting matter in a style for binding, which can be preserved.

Terms of subscription, ONE DOLLAR per annum, payable in advance.

Any person sending FIVE DOLLARS, shall receive one copy gratis. All letters and communications must be *post paid* and addressed to the Editor, 36 Lispenard street, New-York City.

DAVID RUGGLES, Editor.

NEW-YORK, August 1st, 1838.

EDITORIAL NOTICES OF OUR ENTERPRISE.*

"MIRROR OF LIBERTY.—Such is the title of a new publication which has been commenced in New-York by our indefatigable colored brother, DAVID RUGGLES, the enterprising and efficient Secretary of the N. Y. Committee of Vigilance. It is in the quarto form, and will be issued quarterly at $1 per annum—each number to contain sixteen pages. For his untiring exertions in the cause of his oppressed brethren, Mr. Ruggles deserves their warmest gratitude; and we hope he will be encouraged to proceed in his noble efforts. The Mirror of Liberty will contain the proceedings of the New-York Committee of Vigilance, and on that account alone, even if it had nothing else to recommend it, would be worthy of a liberal support.—*Boston Liberator, of July 20th,* 1838.

"MIRROR OF LIBERTY.—We call attention to the advertisement of a new quarterly, of 16 pages quarto, by the New-York Committee of Vigilance. The great efforts now making by the kidnappers and man-hyænas in the free states, to carry off those who are free *de facto,* affords good reason why the Committee of Vigilance should be supported with adequate funds to see the laws executed, and that due means should be employed to enlighten the public mind as to the atrocious system of piracy that is going on in the midst of us."—*Emancipator of July 19,* 1838.

If friend Leavitt will lay our "Introductory Remarks" before his readers, they will see that the Committee of Vigilance do not publish the "Mirror of Liberty." It is an independent journal, established by individual enterprise.

"MIRROR OF LIBERTY.—This is the title of a new quarterly

* These notices refer to the number published in July.

David Ruggles

David Ruggles served as the chief conductor on the main line of the New York branch of the Underground Railroad. Born of free black parents in Connecticut in 1810, Ruggles attended the Sabbath School for the Poor in the town of Norwich, which unlike most such schools admitted black students. He then studied in the Connecticut Manumission Society's academies for colored youth. In later years, he wrote fondly of his childhood in the schools and churches of New England. But his education did little to help him find regular, lucrative employment, so he took to the sea. Then, at the age of seventeen, Ruggles moved to New York City, where he became a "butter merchant." By the 1830s, Ruggles's dairy had become a grocery and one of the most successful black businesses in New York.

A grocer's life could not contain Ruggles's entrepreneurial energies, political ambitions, and wide-ranging intellect. Soon after his move to New York, he became enmeshed in the antislavery movement. He opened a bookshop from which he circulated antislavery literature, and he established a reading room that became the library of the abolitionist movement. His printing press served the entire black community. By the mid-1830s, *The Emancipator* listed him as its traveling agent, and Ruggles was lecturing before white and black audiences throughout the state.

Ruggles vigorously advocated abolition and equal rights and opposed the plan of the American Colonization Society to resettle black Americans in Africa. But he had little patience for mere advocacy. In 1835, he founded the New York Committee of Vigilance to prevent the kidnapping of Northern free blacks and to aid fugitive slaves from the South. Ruggles himself assisted as many as six hundred runaway slaves, among them Frederick Douglass, whom he sheltered in his own home. The Committee of Vigilance was a testimony to Ruggles's activism and organizational skills. His own newspaper, *The Mirror of Liberty*, published from 1835 to 1839, publicized the work of the Committee.

Ruggles's militancy brought him into conflict with some of New York's leading black abolitionists, many of whom embraced Garrisonian nonresistance principles. In 1838, a black man accused of participating in the slave trade sued the Vigilance Committee for libel. The suit bankrupted Ruggles and the Committee, from which he resigned in 1839. Impoverished and going blind, Ruggles accepted an invitation to establish an hydropathic (or water cure) center in Northampton, Massachusetts, where he died in 1849.

—Manisha Sinha

ness eventually compromised the committee, and a libel lawsuit forced Ruggles to leave the state. But the Committee of Vigilance left important marks on the development of antislavery in New York. In the 1850s, black and white abolitionists adopted Ruggles's tactics with spectacular success.[11]

Along with direct action, New York's black abolitionists continued their ideological assault on the structures of white supremacy that supported slavery. Theodore Wright developed strong arguments against the prevalence of racism that denied black people citizenship and equality. Tracing the rise of the abolition movement, Wright argued that antislavery societies should not only point out the "vileness of slavery at the South," but also make whites "call the dark man a brother" and "burn out" racial prejudice. The colored man, according to Wright, was still enslaved by racism, which was "like the atmosphere, everywhere felt by him" and proscribed him from trades, learning, churches, and even public transportation. For black abolitionists such as Wright, the struggle for equal rights for African Americans constituted an important part of the abolitionist program.

Like African American abolitionists and their white allies elsewhere in the North, black New Yorkers mounted a concerted challenge to racially discriminatory laws and practices. The fight against New York's segregated streetcars was central to the struggle for equality. Black passengers demanding equal access to public transportation found themselves regularly harassed by white conductors and drivers. In 1854, an officer of the Third Avenue Railway Company demanded that Elizabeth Jennings, daughter of black abolitionist Thomas Jennings, leave the streetcar. Jennings stood her ground, stating, "I [am] a respectable person born and raised in New York. . . ." The conductor, observing that he was born in Ireland, forcibly ejected her and her companion, Sarah Adams, from the car. Jennings sued the railway and won damages. But the victory was short-lived. In 1855, the black abolitionist James W.C. Pennington lost a similar case following his ouster from a streetcar. By 1860, some of New York City's streetcar companies voluntarily integrated their cars, but the Sixth Avenue Railway Company, which Pennington had sued, continued to operate Jim Crow cars.[12]

Perhaps no aspect of the struggle for racial equality attracted greater attention from New York's black abolitionists than the demand for suffrage. Charles Ray, writing in New York's *Colored American*, initiated the campaign, arguing that black men must "Take a stand for our rights . . . more firm and decisive, than that by Patrick Henry, and the fathers of the revolution." Beginning in 1840 and continuing intermittently until 1858, New York State conventions of "Colored Inhabitants" conducted a long fight for "equal suffrage." Led by black abolitionists such as Ray, Wright, James McCune Smith (a Glasgow-trained physician) and Henry Highland Garnet (a Presbyterian minister) the conventions made the $250 property-holding qualification for black male voters in New York an issue in state politics. In their resolutions, petitions, and reports to the state legislature, they regularly demanded "an end to complexional difference in the State of New York" and access to "the elective franchise as a mighty lever for elevation in the scale of society." In 1840, their address to the people of New York complained that since 1821, black New Yorkers had only "the partial enjoyment and limited possession of freedom." As "*descendants of some of the earliest settlers of the State*" and recalling their military service in the Revolutionary and 1812 wars, they demanded their "republican birth-right." In 1846, the constitutional convention of New York submitted to the voters an equal suffrage amendment to the state constitution. It was defeated by an overwhelming 224,336 to 85,406 votes. But the fact that the amendment was put forward at all was an important moment in New York State history and the result of the unstinting efforts of black and white abolitionists.[13]

The same year, Gerrit Smith, the wealthy upstate abolitionist, sought to circumvent the property-holding qualification for voting imposed on black men by a spectacular gesture. In a letter to Wright, Ray, and McCune Smith, he announced his plans to deed one hundred and forty thousand acres of his land to black men who would then be able to meet the property qualification to vote. It was, as the three black abolitionists put it, a "great experiment" for the race. A Liberty Party man and founder of the Radical Political Abolitionist Party, Smith enjoyed close relationships with McCune Smith and Frederick Douglass, whose Rochester newspaper he supported generously. With McCune Smith, he shared a vision of "Good Government" and "Bible politics" that would purify politics. Smith's gift of land to black New Yorkers capped years of generosity to abolitionists, African Americans, and social reform. As a philanthropist, politician, and abolitionist, he was also closely allied with black abolitionists' quest for political equality in New York. For McCune Smith, Gerrit Smith's "generous Deeds" shone through the "sad memories of crushed hope" excited by the "terrible majority" against black suffrage in New York.[14]

Into the 1850s, the right to vote continued to be an important part of the state black conventions' agenda even as other issues came to dominate its meetings. In 1858, the last statewide suffrage convention resolved to "never cease our efforts to procure the repeal of the property qualification in our State Constitution, until success shall crown our efforts." Under the auspices of the newly formed Republican Party, the voters of New York once again considered a referendum to remove the property-holding qualifi-

Gerritt Smith. Albumen photograph.
NEW-YORK HISTORICAL SOCIETY LIBRARY

cation for black voters in 1860. William Cooper Nell, a black Garrisonian from Boston who nevertheless was active in New York antislavery politics, wrote the influential pamphlet *Property Qualification or No Property Qualification* on the issue. Quoting extensively from the speeches of black abolitionists in New York and from the resolutions presented by William J. Wilson, a Brooklyn schoolteacher, and passed by a suffrage convention in New York City, Nell asked for "the last shackle, the last emblem of degradation" to be "removed from the man of color!" In a presidential election year when many Republicans were distancing themselves from abolitionism and charges of advocating racial equality, the referendum went down to defeat by a vote of 345,791 to 197,889, even as Abraham Lincoln won New York's electoral votes. African American men in New York would enjoy equal suffrage rights with white men only with the passage of the Fifteenth Amendment after the Civil War.[15]

The demand for political rights and the turn to political abolition among New York's black abolitionists came after the schism in the abolition movement between Garrison and those who supported political action and opposed women's rights. As the division between the moral and political abolitionists widened during the 1840s and 1850s, most African Americans in New York turned from Garrison's philosophical radicalism to political abolitionism. Many black abolitionists such as Cornish, Rush, and Wright were also clergymen and therefore wary of Garrison's assault on the established churches. In addition, they did not share Garrison's commitment to women's rights. But ultimately it was Garrison's opposition to abolitionists entering politics that drove New York's black abolitionists into alternative antislavery organizations such as the Tappans' American and Foreign Anti-Slavery Society and the antislavery Liberty Party. In New York, most black abolitionists sought to use politics to secure slavery's demise.

The break between New York's black political abolitionists and Garrison, it should be emphasized, was ideological rather than personal. Indeed, Ray and others continued to support Garrison: "If the colored people of this City, or any section of this country do manifest less warmth of feeling than formerly towards *Mr. Garrison*," declared Ray, "it is in part owing, to our *Friends* having multiplied who are equally active & equally efficient with *Mr. Garrison*, & as a necessary consequence our good feeling is scattered upon all, instead of being concentrated on one, as when Mr. Garrison stood alone."[16]

Still, political abolitionism came to dominate the movement against slavery as a whole in New York. While Garrison condemned the proslavery constitution and advocated disunion, New York's abolitionists, black and white, hoped to use the constitution and the electoral system to their benefit. Though the Liberty Party garnered few votes in the presidential election of 1840, it estab-

WEEKSVILLE

In the 1830s, African American land investors organized the community of Weeksville to promote economic, social, and political rights for African Americans. Located four miles east of downtown Brooklyn, Weeksville grew rapidly. In 1855, with a black population of 521, Weeksville had become the second largest independent African American community in the United States, and the only one with urban rather than rural roots. Its residents originated in various parts of the United States and the Caribbean. Two came from Africa.

With a high rate of property ownership, Weeksville became a highly politicized black community, with two newspapers—*Freedom's Torchlight* and the *National Monitor*—and a host of African American institutions, including several churches, an orphan asylum, and a home for the aged. Its residents participated in movements against slavery and for equal rights. Weeksville became a major station on the Underground Railroad, and following the Draft Riots, it became a shelter for refugees from the vicious pogrom in Manhattan. Weeksville's was also the first New York City public school to fully integrate its teaching staff.

As the thicket of community institutions grew, so did Weeksville's national importance. Weeksville became the national headquarters for the African Civilization Society. Junius C. Morel, who settled in Weeksville following his escape from slavery in South Carolina, became a nationally known convention organizer, journalist, and educator. Susan McKinney Steward, another Weeksville resident, was one of America's first African American women doctors. T. McCants Stewart—lawyer, school board member, and African Methodist Episcopal pastor in Weeksville—promoted the integration of Weeksville's school system and later emigrated to Liberia.

Today, four frame houses on Hunterfly Road, maintained by the Society for the Preservation of Weeksville and Bedford Stuyvesant History, represent the historic Weeksville community.

—*Judith Wellman*

Portrait of Henry
Highland Garnet.

lished important precedents. With the rise of the sectional controversy over the expansion of slavery in the aftermath of the Mexican War, political abolitionism came into its own. Most black abolitionists not only fought alongside those seeking to prevent the westward expansion of slavery into newly acquired territories, they also continued to wage a less popular battle in the North: the fight for black rights, especially the right to vote.

On the eve of the Civil War, a new generation of black abolitionists—many of whom like Frederick Douglass, Henry Highland Garnet, James W.C. Pennington, and Samuel Ringgold Ward were former slaves—propelled the radicalization of the struggle against slavery in New York and the nation. They were joined by others of like mind—such as Alexander Crummell and James McCune Smith—who had been born in freedom. Together they devised new means to bring the struggle against slavery to a swift end. But perhaps no one better represented the new militancy of the rising generation of black abolitionists than the Reverend Henry Highland Garnet, minister of the Shiloh Presbyterian Church in New York City. Brandishing the revolutionary slogan "Liberty or Death," Garnet demanded "RESISTANCE! RESISTANCE! RESISTANCE!" by the slaves. Urging the revolutionary destruction of chattel bondage, Garnet invoked a pantheon of revolutionary heroes, including Toussaint L'Ouverture of Haiti; slave rebels Denmark Vesey and Nat Turner; Cinque, leader of the *Amistad* revolt; and Madison Washington, leader of the *Creole* revolt. Published in 1848 in tandem with David Walker's 1829 *Appeal*, Garnet's *An Address to the Slaves of the United States of America* gave evidence of the black abolitionist reinvention of the revolutionary tradition to demand an immediate and even violent end to racial slavery. Slave resistance and radical black abolitionism complemented each other in the "great tradition of black protest."[17] Though the National Black Convention rejected

Garnet's address in 1843 by a single vote, it soon became one of the most influential documents written by a black abolitionist. From New York City, Charles Ray and James Gloucester opposed Garnet, while Theodore Wright supported him. Douglass had led the opposition to Garnet's address and the convention under his leadership condemned advocacy of slave rebellion as "folly" and "suicidal." But even Douglass began printing the news and rumor of any slave revolt as the start of a "revolution that would probably be associated with the emancipation of the slaves."[18] The issue of the use of violence to end slavery was thus fully debated in the national black conventions that were revived under the leadership of New York's black abolitionists.

The invocation of slave resistance motivated black abolitionists to take a stand against the 1850 Fugitive Slave Law. The new federal law nullified New York's personal liberty laws, which had prevented state officials from assisting slaveholders in recovering their runaway slaves and ensured a modicum of fairness in the trial of alleged fugitive slaves. The new law denied suspected fugitives a trial by jury, mandated the participation of ordinary citizens in the recovery of runaway slaves, and doubled the fee of the federal commissioner who decided against the apprehended slave. Several cities in New York State established vigilance committees composed of black and white abolitionists, modeled on Ruggles's original New York Committee. In New York City, a Committee of Thirteen, composed of prominent black abolitionists—among them Philip Bell, a founder of the *Colored American*; caterers Thomas and George Downing; Robert Hamilton, the editor of the *Weekly Anglo-African*; McCune Smith; and William Powell, owner of Manhattan's Colored Seamen's Home—vowed opposition to the law. John J. Zuille, black abolitionist and printer, chaired the committee. Powell and the committee had their greatest success in the case of a suspected fugitive, James Hamlet (also known as James Hamilton Williams). Powell not only marched to City Hall to inquire whether the mayor would protect the colored citizens of the city from slave catchers, but also organized a meeting at Mother Zion Church where he delivered a fiery speech urging black New Yorkers to "resist oppression" and "defend liberty." No "bloodthirsty slaveholder" should invade their "domiciles, or workshops, or the places where we labor, and carry off our wives and children, our fathers and mothers, and ourselves, without a struggle," asserted Powell. Within two days, mass meetings of African Americans in Manhattan and Brooklyn had raised $800 to purchase Hamlet. [19]

The Fugitive Slave Law marked another decisive turning point in the history of resistance to slavery in New York. Black abolitionists again reconsidered the use of force against slavery. For many, the new law broke their remaining faith in nonviolence and the possibilities of a peaceful end to slavery. As Douglass wrote, "It has become the business of a powerful government to perpetuate 'the abomination that maketh desolate.' Fidelity to our 'glorious Union' requires it!" Sarcastically, he noted that the law was a monument to liberty in "the Model Republic in the year 1850." The "true remedy" for the fugitive slave law was "*a good revolver, a steady hand and a determination to shoot down any man attempting to kidnap.*" In "A letter to the American Slaves from those who have fled from American Slavery," Douglass asserted, "When the insurrection of the Southern slaves shall take place, as take place it will, unless speedily prevented by voluntary emancipation, the great mass of the colored men of the North, however much to the grief of any of us, will be found by your side, with deep-stored and long-accumulated revenge in their hearts, and with death-dealing weapons in their hands. . . . We tell you these things not to encourage, or justify your resort to physical force; but simply, that you may know, be it your joy or sorrow to know it, what your Northern colored brethren are, in these important respects." Comparing the cause of the slave with that of the American Revolution, he pointed out, "If the American revolutionists had excuse for shedding but one drop of blood, then have the American slaves excuse for making blood flow 'even unto the horse bridles.'" Samuel Ringgold Ward reiterated, "Such crises as these leave us the right to Revolution, and if need be, that right we will, at whatever cost, most sacredly maintain."

Both Douglass and Martin Delany, who grew in prominence as an advocate of emigration during the 1850s, penned works of fiction featuring slave rebels. Douglass wrote of the fortuitously named Madison Washington and his *Creole* slave rebellion; Delany in his novel *Blake*, first published serially in New

York's *Weekly Anglo-African,* had a slave lead a hemisphere-wide revolt against slavery in the American South and Cuba. A majority of black abolitionists openly advocated a violent overthrow of slavery. As the *Weekly Anglo-African* later put it, "We want Nat Turner—not speeches; Denmark Vesey—not resolutions; John Brown—not meetings."[20]

The vast majority of black New Yorkers supported John Brown's raid on Harper's Ferry. In New York, leading black abolitionists such as Douglass, Garnet, and McCune Smith had been informed of Brown's plan. Their growing militancy no doubt influenced Brown, who had helped to fund the publication of Garnet's *Address to the Slaves.* After the raid, black abolitionists published some of the most thoughtful justifications of the right to rebellion against Southern slaveholders. Douglass argued eloquently, "They have by the single act of slave-holding, voluntarily placed themselves beyond the laws of justice and honor, and have become only fitted for companionship with thieves and pirates—the common enemies of God and all mankind. While it shall be considered right to protect one's self against thieves, burglars, robbers, and assassins, and to slay a wild beast in the act of devouring his human prey, it can never be wrong for the imbruted and whip-scarred slaves, or their friends, to hunt, harass, and even strike down the traffickers in human flesh."

A group of black women in New York City expressed their "deep, undying gratitude to him who has given his life so freely to obtain for us our defrauded rights," and promised Brown's widow to support her and her family even though "We are a poor and despised people—almost forbidden, by the oppressive restrictions of the Free States, to rise to the higher walks of lucrative employments, toiling early and late for our daily bread. . . . " Thomas Hamilton, editor of the *Weekly Anglo-African,* republished the "Confessions of Nat Turner" in 1859 and in his headnote comparing Brown and Turner predicted boldly, "Emancipation must take place, and soon. There can be no long delay in the choice of methods. If John Brown's be not adopted by the free North, then Nat Turner's will be by the enslaved South." Douglass reiterated that slavery would be abolished "the John Brown way."[21]

Even though the National Black Conventions that often met in New York

National Black Conventions

Between 1830 and 1864, a wide-ranging "Convention Movement" came to epitomize autonomous black politics, representing an attempt to create a national racial organization that would address the problems of slavery and racism in antebellum America. African Americans held twelve national conventions in thirty years, many of which were held in New York.

In 1843, at the National Black Convention in Buffalo, Henry Highland Garnet issued his famous call for a slave insurrection. Garnet's proposal threw the meeting into an uproar, and the convention voted against making Garnet's proposal official convention policy, although it lost by only a single vote. Four years later, the convention met in Troy, where forty-six of the sixty-six delegates were New Yorkers. The New York–dominated meeting divided between those who eschewed political action and those who favored it.

In 1852, at the Rochester convention, a very different division emerged. Frederick Douglass dominated the meeting that came out against emigration and established a National Council to coordinate black activism. Two years later, the convention again reversed course. The meeting under the leadership of Martin Delany explored the possibility of black emigration to Africa, Haiti, and Central America. The participation of black New Yorkers in the various conventions bespoke consistent engagement in the problems of slavery and race, and their changing opinions on how to address these deeply felt concerns.   —*Manisha Sinha*

never formally endorsed the violent overthrow of slavery, they evinced a growing radicalization of black New Yorkers. In 1843, when the convention reconvened in Buffalo after a lapse of eight years, Samuel David laid out its purpose in his opening address; "It is our right, our duty, and I hope I may say, our fixed determination, to make known our wrongs to the world, and to our oppressors; to cease not day nor night to 'Tell, in burning words, our tale of woe.'" Four years later, the report of the convention's Committee on Abolition argued that "the power of the government, and the sanctity of religion, church and state, are joined with the guilty oppressor against the oppressed—and the voice of this great nation is thundering in the ear of our enslaved fellow countrymen the terrible fiat, *you shall be slaves or die!*" In 1853, in its address to the people of the United States, the National Black Convention in Rochester contended, "As a people, we feel ourselves to be not only deeply injured, but grossly misunderstood. Our white fellow-countrymen do not know us. They are strangers to our character, ignorant of our capacity, oblivious of our history and progress, and are misinformed as to the principles and ideas that control and guide us, as a people. The great mass of American citizens estimate us, as being a characterless and purpose-less people; and hence we hold up our heads, if at all, against the withering influence of a nation's scorn and contempt."[22]

The events of the 1850s, particularly the 1857 *Dred Scott* decision, pushed New York's black abolitionists toward greater and greater radicalism. Increasingly, they embraced the Haitian revolution, the only successful slave rebellion in world history, as an inspiration in their struggle against American slavery. James McCune Smith set out to write a full and objective history of the Haitian rebellion, anticipating the efforts of twentieth-century black intellectu-als such as C.L.R. James. Noting that five thousand African slaves died each year in Haiti prior to the revolution, Smith compared this holocaust in black lives to the casualties of the *"wars, insurrections* and *massacres"* of the revolu-tion, and he praised Toussaint L'Ouverture for abolishing slavery and caste in the new black republic. On the eve of the American Civil War, black abolition-ists repeatedly turned to this example of violent revolution against slavery. [23]

The same changes that pushed black abolitionists toward the revolutionary destruction of slavery drove others to contemplate emigration from the United States. Many black New Yorkers, fearful for their freedom, abandoned the coun-try of their birth. New York City's black population fell by 15 percent in the five years after the passage of the Fugitive Slave Act. Many went to Canada, but it was African emigration that attracted the largest attention. Many black New Yorkers reconsidered their position on migrating to Africa, a possibility that once smacked of support of colonization. In 1829, when John Russwurm migrated to Liberia, the city's black abolitionists had condemned him as a trai-tor to the cause. Now, some, like Alexander Crummell, became staunch advo-cates of emigration to Liberia, to which he eventually migrated.[24]

Taking his cue from Crummell and Martin Delany, Henry Highland Garnet's Africa Civilization Society also recommended emigration to Africa as the appropriate destination of people of African descent. At its 1861 annual meeting, attended by Delany, the society announced the civilization and Christianization of Africa and the "welfare of her children" everywhere in the world as its goals. Reversing decades long black opposition to the American Colonization Society, it also promised to cooperate with other organizations with similar aims. The constitution of the African Civilization Society announced its black nationalist and pan-African ideology, which was clearly inspired by Delany: "The basis of the society, and ulterior objects in encouraging emigration, shall be—Self-Reliance and Self-Government, on the principle of an African Nationality, the African race being the ruling element of the nation, controlling and directing their own affairs." A special meeting was called on November 4, 1861, "to hold a Conference with Dr. Martin R. Delany, as the representative and exponent of the African movement, as understood by the emigrationists and others, among the colored people of America, to effect and complete a oneness and harmony of sentiment and action, that their white friends, as aiders and assistants, may have a true and definite point as a datum before them." Supported by Robert Hamilton and Tunis Campbell, Garnet faced the ire of Douglass, George T. Downing, and McCune Smith, all of whom remained opposed to emigration. The Reverend J.W.C. Pennington, who initially supported Garnet, spoke against emigration in 1860. Some like Douglass momentarily considered Haiti as a possible site for black emigration but rejected the notion that Africa was the true homeland of black Americans. These men remained convinced for the most part that emigration would damage the fight against slavery and for equal political rights in the United States.[25]

With the coming of the Civil War, African American abolitionists in New York put aside their differences over the best methods to achieve black liberation in antebellum America. Years of honing their ideological attacks against slavery prepared them right at the outset to fight a revolutionary, remorseless war against slavery and to convert the war for the Union into a war against slavery. They greeted the Civil War as an American apocalypse and looked forward to emancipation—what the slaves called the Day of Jubilo—with millennial expectations.[26] Little did they realize that their battle, unlike the war they supported, would have no end. It would be the first chapter in the long fight for racial equality in New York and the nation.

Chapter 9

SOUTHERN SLAVERY IN A FREE CITY: ECONOMY, POLITICS, AND CULTURE

———————◆———————

DAVID QUIGLEY

William J. Bennett, *South Street from Maiden Lane*, drawn 1828, published 1834. Aquatint.

On July 4, 1827, William Hamilton, the longtime leader of New York's black community, addressed the congregation of the city's African Methodist Episcopal Zion Church. Slavery, the state legislature had decreed in 1817, would forever end in New York State on that date. Across the state, African American New Yorkers and their white allies celebrated the long-anticipated moment of emancipation. Black churches and local meeting halls filled as communities gathered to herald slavery's end. Three decades after the state had first enacted gradual emancipation, Hamilton proclaimed, "This day has the state of New-York regenerated herself—this day has she been cleansed of a most foul, poisonous and damnable stain."[1]

And yet, the coming decades revealed a far more complicated fate for New York's black community. The final arrival of emancipation by no means put an end to slavery's place in metropolitan life. In politics, economics, culture, and social life, New Yorkers—black and white—remained implicated in the slave system down to the onset of the Civil War a full generation later. The free city which William Hamilton celebrated on that summer day in 1827 maintained strong ties to the Southern slave states until the outbreak of the Civil War and after. Local politicians helped lead the ascendant Democratic Party as it advanced a national proslavery politics. Manhattan's merchants made great fortunes from cotton; this slave-produced commodity helped drive the city's emergence as the financial capital of the nation in the generation before the firing on Fort Sumter. New York was a receptive home for various Southerners in the antebellum era: writers and intellectuals, plantation owners and politicians all flocked north across the Mason-Dixon Line to Manhattan. Slavery was also present in less tangible form in the memories—individual and collective—of thousands of black men and women who had been born into bondage and had only recently gained their freedom. By far the most troubling manifestation of slavery's continued hold on New York life was the regular presence on the city's streets of Southern slave catchers—"kidnappers" in the vernacular of antebellum black New Yorkers—whose assaults on the freedom of local African Americans were generally supported by the city's police and political leadership.[2]

In the generation before the Civil War, New York City's long-standing ties to the economy, politics, and culture of the slave South at once deepened and grew more tenuous. Slavery and slave-produced goods helped propel the city's prosperity throughout the early nineteenth century. The records of the city's cotton exchange and individual trading houses illuminate the centrality of Southern trade to New York's booming antebellum economy. Alongside the opening of the Erie Canal in the 1820s, local merchants' success in establishing and maintaining long-term business ties to the Southern planter class fueled New York's financial ascendancy. The city's merchants came to dominate the export market for cotton and served as critical middlemen for the domestic cotton trade, and metropolitan tradesmen disproportionately benefited from Southerners' consumerism by mid-century.

The decade after the War of 1812 was a decisive moment in New York City's history, initiating a decades-long period of growth that set the city apart from its competitors and secured for New York its still unrivaled place as the nation's economic capital. In the seventeenth and eighteenth centuries, New York merchants often lagged behind rivals in Philadelphia, Boston, and even Charleston. As late as the first years of the nineteenth century, it was not at all obvious that New York would come to dominate national trade and culture. Between 1815 and 1825, a series of developments would transform forever the city's place in the nation's political, economic, and social life. In that crucial decade, white New Yorkers would take decisive steps to set the dimensions of the impending reality of black freedom. The state legislature's 1817 vote—setting July 4, 1827, as the date for final emancipation—meant that the second quarter of the nineteenth century would bring freedom to all New Yorkers. Politically, an 1821 state constitutional convention designated free African Americans as a lower caste in the state's emerging "democracy." The new political order born out of the 1820s ushered in a new age of partisan politics, with black men disfranchised and the majority of New York City voters committed to a pro-Southern, proslavery ideology.

Economically, New York merchants and traders consolidated the city's growing dominance in the transatlantic cotton trade to Great Britain and France. This consolidation, in turn, drove the city's financial ascent. Since the new nation's founding, New York merchants had done business amid profound instability. But the second decade of the nineteenth century concluded a long period of political and economic instability in the Atlantic world, with the defeat of Napoleon's forces in 1812 and the end of the War of 1812 three years later. New York merchants now had an enormous opportunity but also a considerable dilemma. Their ships' westward voyages from Europe to North America were growing ever more profitable as American consumers eagerly devoured European manufactured goods that had been unavailable in recent years. But the merchants' eastward voyages back to Europe were far less lucrative. There were few European markets for American finished goods, and British postwar policy had blocked British imports of American corn and flour. Manhattan merchants struggled to rationalize the imbalanced Atlantic trade.[3]

New Yorkers quickly seized upon exports of raw cotton to the British market as the solution to their problem.[4] Decades of industrial development in England, driven by the growth of textile manufacture, had created an escalating demand for raw cotton. Simultaneously, cotton production in the American South skyrocketed in the last decade of the eighteenth century and the first decades of the nineteenth century. By the 1820s, New York investors and their

SENECA VILLAGE, 1825–1857

Even before the legal end of slavery, free black New Yorkers began to forge independent communities throughout the city. One of the most important of these was Seneca Village.

Seneca Village began rather modestly. In 1825, John Whitehead, who owned a good portion of the land between present-day 85th and 88th Streets near Seventh Avenue in Manhattan, divided his estate and began to sell small parcels. To Whitehead's surprise, black New Yorkers purchased the land, attracted by the opportunity to create a community, and perhaps regain the political standing which had recently been taken from them. The 1821 New York State Constitution had limited black men's suffrage to those who owned two hundred dollars in real estate. Land ownership became the key to black electoral power, and thus a farm or garden in Seneca Village offered the opportunity for both community-building and enfranchisement. Over the next fifteen years, black men and their families constructed homes and barns, and began cultivating the land. African institutions—churches, schools, and associations—followed. By the early 1850s, Seneca Village had blossomed into a flourishing community.

White New Yorkers—many of whom had sponsored the disfranchisement of 1821—noted the success of Seneca Village. That the Village occupied land that was increasingly valuable as the settlement of Manhattan marched north was not lost on them. Led by Mayor Fernando Wood, a prominent Democrat whose political ties reached deep into the slave-holding South, they determined to oust Seneca's black residents. In 1855, Mayor Wood invoked the power of eminent domain, and the Village officially became city property, the land cleared for a great new park in the center of Manhattan Island.

For two years, the residents of Seneca Village ignored Wood's edicts and battled the police sent to evict them. Neither government proclamations nor police actions could convince the residents to abandon their homes, churches, schools, and cemeteries. "The policemen find it difficult to persuade them out of the idea which has possessed their simple minds, that the sole object of the authorities in making the Park is to procure their expulsion from the homes which they occupy," reported the *New York Daily Times.* In August 1857, another order was issued, and the remaining black landowners were forcibly and violently scattered throughout the city. Nearly a decade later the *New York Tribune* observed that the raid upon Seneca Village would "not be forgotten . . . [as] many a brilliant and stirring fight was had during the campaign. But the supremacy of the law was upheld by the policeman's bludgeons."

—*Leslie M. Alexander*

firms secured leading roles in regularizing the movement of capital and supplies between the plantations of the black belt and the mill towns of Britain. In the process, New York's merchant houses created a network of Northern agents who spread across the South, developing lasting business and personal connections. New York emerged as the dominant entrepôt in the Atlantic cotton trade.

New York's turn to cotton initiated the most important era of economic growth and capital accumulation in the city's history. Through metropolitan investment and innovation in the transatlantic cotton trade, the city secured its position at the center of American banking and finance by the middle of the nineteenth century. As early as 1822, over half of the exports out of the Port of New York were goods produced in the South. Cotton, more than any other single commodity, dominated New York's businesses, accounting for more than 40 percent of the city's exports.[5] Even as Southern merchants began to voice concerns over competition from the Northern metropolis, New York City positioned itself as the primary mediator between the leading Southern ports of New Orleans, Mobile, Savannah, and Charleston, as well as the two most important European destinations for American cotton, Liverpool and Havre.[6]

Throughout the early nineteenth century, New York ships were substantially involved in the Atlantic slave trade, with metropolitan engagement in the trade actually increasing in the years before the Civil War.[7] Even though the British and American governments had outlawed the transatlantic slave trade in the first decade of the nineteenth century, New Yorkers remained involved in the now-illegitimate endeavor for the next half century. While United States courts in antebellum Manhattan heard a number of cases brought against local companies for "engaging in the slave trade,"[8] participation, though a risky undertaking for nineteenth-century New Yorkers, remained lucrative; ship owners could net nearly $200,000 in profits from a single voyage.[9] New York City investors were involved in the Atlantic slave trade as late as 1860; in that final antebellum year, nearly fifty New York ships engaged in the market in enslaved Africans.[10] The last known New York ship involved in the trade was the *Erie*, seized by the U.S. Navy in 1860 off the coast of Africa with 800 slaves aboard. The enslaved Africans were returned to freedom in Liberia while the ship's captain was returned to

Major, *The Colored Stevedore—A Reminiscence.*
Wood engraving. NEW-YORK HISTORICAL SOCIETY LIBRARY

Manhattan for trial. Captain Nathaniel Gordon was eventually found guilty of "engaging in the slave trade" and hanged in 1862.[11]

The years after the War of 1812 marked the opening of an era in which metropolitan merchants grew ever more reliant on the Atlantic cotton market. The wealth produced by the trade drove New York businessmen to focus increasingly on the commodity. By 1835, 119 of 120 New York ships arriving at Liverpool carried cotton. That same year, Manhattan-based packets averaged nearly 700 bales of cotton per voyage. The rise of cotton coincided with a dramatic decline in New Yorkers' brokering of other commodities to European markets. The 1830s witnessed a historic expansion of New York investment in shipping lines—both transatlantic lines involved in international shipping as well as coastal lines that shipped between Southern ports and New York. Profits from cotton allowed for a thorough reorganization and modernization of the New York–based shipping industry.[12] This restructuring, in turn, rendered New York businesses even more profitable compared to those headquartered in other American ports, furthering the competitive advantages enjoyed by metropolitan investors and financiers.

As cotton propelled New York's economic ascendancy in the second quarter of the nineteenth century, New York merchants also profited from the sale of products to Southern consumers. The "Southern trade," so important to the profit margins—and the imaginations—of antebellum New York merchants, signified the lucrative market among slaveholders. Southerners relied upon New York merchants for supplies drawn from around the American interior and larger Atlantic: Midwestern wheat, New England textiles, and British luxury goods. Davy Crockett, writing in 1835, deemed New York "the London of America, the Big Prairie of the North, the Mississippi of Commerce."[13] This "Southern trade" was largely paid for with the fruits of slave labor and often involved items necessary for the survival of the plantation economy. "Negro cloth"—cheap, coarse fabric produced in New England textile mills and worn by the enslaved masses at the South—was one such necessity marketed by New York merchants.

The power and wealth that New Yorkers accumulated through their control of the Atlantic cotton trade inspired numerous jealousies. White Southerners, in particular, voiced frustration and at times outright rage over their dependence on New York bankers and factors for credit. The Panic of 1837 inspired a series of Southern commercial conventions to address these concerns. Delegates spoke to a deepening regional sense of "enslavement" to Northern—and specifically New York—capital.[14] Voicing hostility to the growing power of New York, one delegate noted that "the South thus stands in the attitude of feeding from her own bosom a vast population of merchants, ship-owners, capitalists and others, who, without the claim of her progeny, drink up the life-blood of her trade."[15] Antebellum Southern resentments over New Yorkers' parasitical role in the cotton trade would reverberate in late-nineteenth-century Populist attacks on Wall Street and on New York more generally.

In spite of Southern hostility, New York's merchants continued their leading position in the cotton trade for most of the antebellum period. The years in which New Orleans led New York in cotton exports were exceptions that affirmed New York's dominance, as New Orleans traders employed New York ships and relied upon New York banks for credit.[16] New York City's economy became the "hinge of union," for as sectional tensions deepened, New York's merchants provided the most regular form of interregional connection in the years leading to the Civil War.[17] New York investment houses employed "factors" across the South. These men—many from across the rural Northeast—established and maintained relationships between Southern slaveholders and New York firms.[18]

Even as these agents of Northern capital brought New York understanding and values into the South, far greater numbers of white Southerners, many of

COTTON EXPORTS FROM THE PORT OF NEW YORK

In the years following the War of 1812, New York's economy—and then its politics— became tied to the slave South. These figures give some sense of the linkage.

YEAR	TOTAL VALUE OF COTTON BALES EXPORTED
1822	$3,925,000
1860	$12,439,983
1870	$46,331,278

—David Quigley

them substantial planters, traveled north to the nation's metropolis. Some slave owning planters made regular visits to New York City, tending business while enjoying the sights. Summers brought the greatest numbers of such visitors, as slaveholders scheduled their annual visits north to avoid the worst heat at home and to benefit from the milder climate of the metropolis. The city's leading hotels filled with Southern guests, often accompanied by enslaved servants, and local merchants worked long hours filling a year's worth of orders for many slave plantations.[19] J.C. Myers, a Southern visitor in 1849, provided one of the most vivid descriptions of a Southerner's encounter with city life, noting "the eager shopmen, who from every door will beseech him with bows and gentle violence, and will promise to sell cheaper than his neighbors." Myers marveled at New York "ladies and gentlemen who are bred in the lap of luxury, who employ and practice all the accomplishments and seductive arts that most enchant society." Always eager to contrast the agrarian South with New York's metropolitan culture, Myers admired New York women for their "vivacity of mind, grace of manner, and . . . most exquisite taste in all appertaining to dress." In contrast, Myers characterized the city's men in extremes of cultivation and immorality—either dangerously overrefined or appallingly unrefined.[20] Myers's competing depictions of New York's men and women reflected Southerners' conflicting attitudes toward the city—a mixture of awe and envy at the culture that capitalism wrought and fear at the potential for immorality.

White Southerners who visited New York and wrote about their experiences articulated a range of ideas and judgments not just about the city but about freedom, slavery, and contemporary American life. Many were impressed by the city's unrivaled growth and the wealth evident along lower Broadway. Others were troubled by the extremes of poverty found throughout the city. The intensity of urban life—its hectic pace and disorienting diversity, its endless noises and smells—overwhelmed many visitors. Again and again, Southerners noted the centrality of the marketplace in New York life. From Wall Street to the city's street vendors, the act of sale dominated outsiders' accounts. For some, New Yorkers' work ethic merited celebration; others lamented the dehumanizing impact of the daily urban grind.[21]

A visitor's time in New York often led to decidedly un-Southern pursuits. Some slaveholders attended sermons and lectures delivered by leading antislavery orators; Henry Ward Beecher's Sunday sermons in Brooklyn Heights were especially popular for Southerners looking to be horrified and outraged.[22] An entire genre of Southern literature arose in these years devoted to accounts of travel northward, quite often featuring extended remarks on New York City. William Carruthers's 1834 *The Kentuckian in New York* and William Bobo's 1852 *Glimpses of New-York City* feature descriptions of big-city life alongside melodramatic accounts of Southern character encountering brash Manhattanites.

The flow northward of sometimes horrified, sometimes enthralled visitors continued unabated into the 1850s. In the decade before the outbreak of war, contemporaries estimated that 100,000 Southerners descended upon the hotels of New York each summer.[23] At other times of the year, the city greeted the annual arrival of distinct groups of white Southerners. Sons of leading planter families studying at Northern colleges—especially Princeton—often spent their holiday breaks in New York.[24] White Southerners descended upon the city in various configurations—families with young children, newlyweds, single businessmen. There was a ritualized quality to visitors' itineraries, as many Southerners, upon arrival in Manhattan, flocked to the same few sites: City Hall, the Stock Exchange, a day trip by ferry to Brooklyn to take in Greenwood Cemetery.[25]

Visiting white Southerners, especially the wealthiest planters, generally brought a retinue of domestic slaves. As these enslaved blacks moved in and out of Manhattan, they highlighted the continuing barriers to full freedom and equality for black New Yorkers. The presence of enslaved black servants was a profound challenge to metropolitan race relations. A visit to New York City with one's owner presented many Southern blacks their best opportunity to race to freedom. Numerous enslaved blacks took advantage of the city's vast size and overwhelming crowds; New York's African American neighborhoods offered at least temporary anonymity for escaping black men and women on their way to other, safer havens.

But some Southern blacks also realized the limits of freedom and equality in New York City. James P. Thomas, an enslaved black barber in Nashville, was more independent than most enslaved black Southerners. Thomas operated his own business, returning a set portion of his earnings to his owner. When a white patron in Tennessee offered a generous payment if Thomas would accompany him and his family on a Northern sojourn in the 1840s, Thomas agreed, hoping to save sufficient funds to secure freedom for himself and for several other family members. In his post-Reconstruction autobiography, Thomas conveys a sharp sense of the awkward position in which black Southerners found themselves in free New York. He wrote of New York with a mixture of admiration for the vitality of city life and an unexpected sense of anger over the status and treatment of black Northerners. In particular, Thomas was enraged at being ousted from a theater, remembering, "I felt as though I would like to meet another man who would have the affrontry to advise me to run away to live in New York."[26] Yet the visit was a crucial moment in Thomas's life, serving to accelerate his struggle for liberty. Intimately acquainted with a kind of "quasi-freedom" at home in Tennessee, Thomas recognized a similar state of not-quite-liberty for New York City blacks. [27]

In fact, even as the city held out the possibility of escape to many Southern blacks, local elites conspired to prevent any such attainment of black freedom. In local courts and in the halls of Congress, New Yorkers worked to close off any prospects of liberation on the city's streets. New York's political leaders supported the rights of slaveholders in the antebellum era and demanded that runaway blacks be returned to enslavement. Such pro-Southern political commitments, which dominated antebellum New York, had their beginnings in the first years of the nineteenth century. Just as the origins of the state's rise to economic power can be traced to developments in the aftermath of the War of 1812, so too did that war shape the city's political culture for the next half century. Beginning in 1815, veterans mounted first local, then statewide campaigns for expanded suffrage in New York, grounding their argument upon the special contributions propertyless soldiers had made fighting the British. Strict property-holding qualifications—in place since New York's first constitution was drawn up in 1777—continued to restrict voting rights in the state, and veterans argued for immediate liberalization of the suffrage statutes. The 1821 state constitutional convention in Albany marked the culmination of such political organizing and the realization of the hopes of many disenfranchised white New Yorkers. A new state constitution cleared the way for the removal of property qualifications by 1826. Thus, just as New York was emerging as the nation's financial center, the state also led a national movement toward democratization in the 1820s.[28]

The state's 1821 constitutional convention—which enfranchised all New York's adult white men while simultaneously maintaining the property requirement for African American men—racialized New York politics. The new political landscape, which would soon lead to the ascendancy and then dominance of the Democratic Party in New York and nationally, rested upon the bedrock of racial exclusion. Convention delegates, led by future president of the United States Martin Van Buren, justified their removal of property qualifications for most of New York's propertyless men by enacting a $250 property-holding requirement that applied exclusively to New York's African American men. Van Buren, in particular, argued that "democracy" only made sense with racial exclusion. Thus, the coming of mass democracy in New York—and the simultaneous emergence of the Democratic Party—coincided with the designation of African Americans as a politically subordinate caste. In the four decades that followed, New York Democrats forged a series of alliances with proslavery politicians in the South.

Williams, *August Belmont*. Engraving.

Mathew Brady, *Fernando Wood*. Albumen photograph.

The ascendancy of the Democratic Party with its powerful Southern base shaped New York politics in the half century prior to the Civil War. Leading New York Democrats, ranging from Fernando Wood and John O'Sullivan to August Belmont and Samuel Tilden, were unapologetic in their support of the Southern Democracy and its increasingly extreme defenses of slavery. New York Democrats regularly denounced abolitionists while embracing white supremacist policies. Fernando Wood, a rising Democratic politician from the nineteenth ward in upper Manhattan, attacked antislavery activists in the

1840s while celebrating the South, "where true freedom, chivalry and honour characterizes the people."[29] August Belmont, a New York financier and the Democratic Party's key fund-raiser, maintained close relations with various Southern politicians. His wife's uncle was John Slidell, a Louisiana congressman before the Civil War and then a diplomat for the Confederate States of America; Slidell linked Belmont to the political elite of the slaveholding South.[30] Belmont, Tilden, and other party leaders organized the Democratic Vigilance Committee in late 1859 in hopes of convincing proslavery politicians that New York remained reliably pro-Southern.[31] Tilden, Wall Street lawyer, state party chair, and governor in the 1870s, sympathized with the plight of white Southerners throughout his career. His failed presidential campaign in 1876 attracted its most passionate support in South Carolina and elsewhere in the former Confederacy.

John L. O'Sullivan, editor of the *United States Magazine and Democratic Review* and originator of the phrase "Manifest Destiny," was the city's leading Democratic publicist in the 1840s. His *Review* advanced a forceful urban nationalist ideology founded upon New York City's alliance with the South. O'Sullivan sympathized with the South even as he privately expressed misgivings about slavery. By 1860, disillusioned with his fellow Northerners, O'Sullivan set sail for England, where he ruminated on the crisis of the Union and voiced support for the Confederacy: "I am frankly and decidedly with the South now in their stand of resistance against subjugation and for independence."[32] O'Sullivan's long-held admiration for the slave South was part of a broader pro-Southern mindset shared by both Democratic politicians and by party journalists and writers around Manhattan.

The Democrats' Southern commitments shaped both the city's politics and its mainstream culture in the antebellum era, through journals such as the *Democratic Review* and daily papers such as William Cullen Bryant's *Evening Post*, as well as through bestsellers and pamphlets put out by many of the leading publishing houses. Daily editorials regularly promoted Southern politicians and their causes. Metropolitan critics celebrated Southern writers and artists, crediting the virtues of the plantation culture. An urban, populist culture took

The Honorable and Mrs. John Louis O'Sullivan,
Count and Countess of Bearhaven.

root, advancing expansionist politics deeply sympathetic to the interests of the planter class. New York's publishing industry grew to national importance in the decades before the Civil War, with only Boston as a rival. The city's publishing houses extended the reach of the city's economic and political elite to a broader metropolitan and national public.

The strange publishing history of James D.B. DeBow's *Review*, the leading Southern monthly of the antebellum era, illuminates the intersections of Southern economic, political, and cultural connections with the urban world of New York City. In the 1840s, after struggling for years with local New Orleans printers and their unreliable equipment, DeBow eventually purchased an expensive Adams printing press on one of his visits to Manhattan. Even that investment in technology did not end DeBow's dissatisfactions with Southern workmanship. Beginning in 1848, DeBow edited his *Review* in New Orleans but printed it in New York.[33] Advertisements placed by New York firms also supplied DeBow with most of the revenue which supported his journal. Thus the leading fire-eating, anti-Northern, and eventually prosecessionist journal in the South traveled the same New Orleans–New York circuit followed by Southern cotton.

William Gilmore Simms, the most celebrated Southern novelist of the antebellum era, shared with DeBow a decades-long relationship with New York's great metropolis. As a young man in the early Jacksonian era, the South Carolina native had lived in Manhattan. Like O'Sullivan, Simms supported the Young

America movement and its dedication to cultural nationalism. His intellectual commitments nurtured and sustained long-lasting friendships with many of New York's most powerful antebellum intellectuals; among his Manhattan friends he counted William Cullen Bryant at the *Post* and Evert and George Duyckinck of Scribner's. These friendships, in turn, helped Simms cultivate a national audience for his work. In the early 1850s, Simms wrote a friend from New York, "I am here, according to my wont, of a summer."[34] Like many of his fellow Southerners, he was making his annual warm-weather sojourn in New York. In Simms's case, the important business to be conducted was a series of meetings with editors at his publisher, Harper and Brothers, with whom he worked for a quarter century. Simms contributed essays and stories regularly to leading metropolitan magazines and reviews.

Simms's personal history in New York City came to a dramatic end in November 1856, as the city's public culture erupted over the place of Southerners in the Northern metropolis. Bryant, Evert Duyckinck, and the historian

After Alonzo Chappel (1828–87), *W. Gilmore Simms*, 1867. Engraving. NEW-YORK HISTORICAL SOCIETY LIBRARY

George Bancroft had invited Simms to deliver a series of three lectures in the city. On November 18, Simms delivered "The South in the Revolution," to be followed three nights and seven nights later by "The Appalachians, A Southern Idyll, Descriptive of Southern Scenery, Life, Manufactures, etc." His first lecture, delivered at the Universalist Church of the Divine Unity before an audience of one hundred, was a sustained defense of the patriotism of South Carolinians in the American Revolution. Less than six months earlier Senator Charles Sumner of Massachusetts had been caned on the floor of the Senate

Horace
Greeley.
Engraving.

chamber by Representative Preston Brooks of South Carolina, who claimed to be defending the honor of South Carolinians from recent attacks by Sumner. Simms linked his remarks on the American Revolution to a blistering denunciation of Sumner. This first lecture came under withering attack in the local press, with Horace Greeley's Republican *Tribune* in the lead, and Simms delivered his second lecture to only a small handful of listeners. Canceling his third lecture, Simms returned home to the South, where he wrote, "I had been so defeated, so disappointed of my expectation, that I was in no mood for society, even that of friends; and I hastened home to my forest cover, with the feeling of a wounded hare flying to the thicket."[35] The controversy surrounding Simms's lectures revealed that metropolitan political culture had become divided between established Democratic voices and emboldened dissenters like the Republican Greeley. By the 1850s, political struggles had intensified the clash of conflicting metropolitan ideas about slavery and the South.

At mid-century, New Yorkers occupied a strange space apart from America's deepening sectional divisions. As North and South grew further apart, New Yorkers tried to carve out an economic and political middle ground. Yet the aftermath of the Mexican-American War and the impact of the Compromise of 1850 rendered the city's position more and more untenable. In particular, the enactment of the federal Fugitive Slave Law of 1850 forced issues of slavery, race, liberty, and home rule to the surface in the metropolis. In struggles over fugitive slaves, new voices came forward in the city, further complicating metropolitan public culture and suggesting that some New Yorkers would question the persistence of the city's special relationship with the slaveholding South. These activists, editors, and intellectuals struggled to redefine the city's relationship with the South and with the rest of the nation. Late-antebellum New

Yorkers—like men and women across the nation—found themselves unable to reconcile the fundamental contradictions of slavery in a free city.

Black New Yorkers had lived for decades with the fear of being captured by Southern slave catchers—"kidnappers," as they were known in the black community. Even as visiting enslaved blacks sought to find freedom in New York, local blacks faced increasing obstacles in the quarter century before the Civil War. Democratic politicians and their allies worked to return runaway slaves to captivity, offering considerable assistance to the kidnappers, who hunted down runaways in the city's black neighborhoods. Slave catchers, for their part, rarely distinguished between runaways from the South and black people who were free by birth. And whereas the overwhelming majority of those captured by slave catchers were adults, recurring statements of concern for the safety of the young revealed a more general sense of vulnerability among African American New Yorkers. Black parents warned their "children as much as possible out of the streets especially after nightfall."[36] One particularly troubling case in the 1830s saw Henry Scott, a seven-year-old boy, dragged from school on suspicion of being a runaway.[37] For many runaway slaves as well as for many legally free African Americans, antebellum New York City was dangerous ground, especially when compared to communities upstate and in New England, not to mention farther north in Canada. Numerous cases of kidnapping filled the black press and abolitionist journals throughout the 1830s and 1840s, signaling to African Americans around the nation that the metropolis provided no safe haven.[38]

Recurring fears of reenslavement shaped the city's black community and propelled black political mobilization in the decades before the Civil War. Formed by leading black Manhattanites in 1835, the New York Committee of Vigilance—dedicated to the collective defense of black freedom—emerged as a significant new organization within the city's antislavery movement. As its name suggests, the group committed itself to protecting African Americans on the streets of New York from the ever-present threat of lurking slave catchers.[39] Some committee members organized to file suits against Southern slave catchers; others documented the comings and goings of slave ships in the mid-Atlantic region, some in New York harbor itself. In the aftermath of the antiabolitionist riots of 1834, the Committee of Vigilance targeted the collusion between city police and slave catchers.[40] By 1842, the committee reported knowledge of 1,373 Manhattan cases of "kidnapping" in its seven-year existence.[41] David Ruggles, one of the leaders of the committee, spent two days in a city jail in 1838 on charges that he had housed Thomas Hughes, a fugitive slave who himself was accused of a felony.[42]

The fear of slave catchers shaped not only life in the city's neighborhoods but also helped to define emerging patterns of antislavery activism around the Empire State. The New York State Vigilance Committee, founded in 1847 and headquartered in New York City, assisted hundreds of runaways in its few years in operation. The organization pursued cases in federal courts under the leadership of upstate abolitionist Gerrit Smith.[43] In 1850, the implementation of the federal Fugitive Slave Law produced statewide mobilization among African Americans, modeled along the lines of the vigilance committees. With growing threats to black freedom across the Hudson River, Manhattan and Brooklyn blacks joined together to organize across city lines more regularly in the early 1850s.[44] The federal census of 1850 reported 13,815 blacks in Manhattan; five years later, the New York State census recorded fewer than 12,000 African Americans in the city. The federal Fugitive Slave Law likely inspired hundreds of the city's African American residents to leave for safety elsewhere.[45]

Even as black New Yorkers mobilized and formed statewide coalitions, antiabolitionist New Yorkers rallied around the Compromise of 1850 and its fugitive slave provision. One hundred leading metropolitan merchants formed the Union Safety Committee; the organization's primary objective was the defense of the Compromise of 1850. Committee leaders, including wealthy New Yorkers like William B. Astor and Moses Taylor, devoted considerable effort to supporting the Fugitive Slave Law. Members issued public statements and delivered lectures advocating for the law. The Union Safety Committee became involved in several cases, arguing for the return of individual fugitives to slavery in the South.[46]

Both antislavery and proslavery New Yorkers intensified their political work in response to the Fugitive Slave Law. With federal power deployed on the city's streets in support of the interests of slaveholders and in opposition to the interests of black New Yorkers, the stage was set for a decade in which metropolitan politics became divided ever more deeply on the issue of slavery. While a majority of New York City voters continued to support the Democratic Party in the era of Franklin Pierce and James Buchanan, a rising chorus of antislavery New Yorkers forced their way into the city's public life. The controversy surrounding the Simms lectures in 1856 and the confrontation between vigilance committees and the Union Safety Committee marked the onset of the final stage of the politics of slavery in a free city, one which would culminate in the outbreak of Civil War in April 1861.

As the rest of the nation hurtled toward catastrophe, New Yorkers' economic and political relationship to slavery underwent a dramatic transformation right before war broke out. The economic dislocation sparked by the Panic of 1857, much of which centered on the Atlantic cotton trade, hit the city especially hard. New York merchants noted the decline in Southern visitors beginning in 1857, and a substantial dropoff in the "Southern trade" and business in the last years of the 1850s.[47] Divisions which had slowly arisen a few years earlier exploded by decade's end; the city's merchant elite, in particular, split over sectional questions in the aftermath of guerrilla warfare in Kansas in 1856, the Supreme Court's *Dred Scott* decision the following year, and finally John Brown's ill-fated raid on the federal armory at Harper's Ferry in October 1859.[48]

With new patterns of thought about slavery taking shape in the city, certain enduring habits remained in place. James DeBow, writing in 1860 as secession neared, viewed New York "almost as dependent upon Southern slavery as Charleston itself."[49] In that year's political campaign, leading politicians in the city and across the North and South engaged in a striking argument over the exact nature of the metropolis's relationship to the slave states. Many Americans' struggles over questions of Union and slavery forced them to confront New York City's dialectical position—at once powerful and powerless, central and marginal—in the nation's economic and political life.

The various political arguments about New York City's loyalties, developing since at least the Southern commercial conventions of the late 1830s, intensified amid the economic crash of 1857. Southern writers voiced deepening concerns about their region's unequal relationship with the nation's metropolis. J.A. Turner, author of the widely read *Cotton Planter's Manual*, published a lengthy brief for severing the special relationship between the planter class and New York's businessmen in *DeBow's Review.* Turner complained that "we have the snug little sum of a half million dollars expended by Southerners, in that city alone, each day during their stay in it." The Southerner denounced "the whole host of street blood-suckers who can scent a Southern man from afar."[50] Turner and other Southern writers in the late 1850s used a sharpened critique of New York capitalists as a critical way station on the road to secession.

Northern voices responded to the Southern critique, struggling to make sense of the exact role that Southern slavery had played in New York City's recent ascendancy. The Philadelphia Republican Stephen Colwell felt it necessary to rebut the Southern argument that traumatic consequences for the North would follow from secession. Colwell dismissed "the idea, now pretty extensively entertained in the South, that New York is fattening on Southern trade and business."[51] The prime beneficiary of New York's mastery of the cotton trade was the slaveholding South; "If New York capital should be suddenly diverted from this channel of employment," he stated, "it would have disastrous effects upon the interests of the Cotton States"[52] But even as Colwell engaged fire-eaters Turner and DeBow, he was also responding to New Yorker Thomas Prentice Kettell, former editor of the *United States Magazine and Democratic Review.* Kettell, a comrade of John L. O'Sullivan in the Young America movement and a longtime Southern sympathizer, published a pamphlet in late 1860 arguing that secession would result in "lower wages and diminished work" for New York's workingmen.[53] Kettel's anger was not directed at Southern secessionists but rather at New York Republicans and abolitionists. As with proslavery ideologues in the South, Northerners like Colwell and Kettell came to their differing understandings of nationalism and secession by rethinking the relationship between New York merchants and workers and the slave South.

The ongoing debate over Southern slavery in the free metropolis came to a conclusive end in April 1861. The outbreak of Civil War reordered metropolitan pub-

EXECUTION OF GORDON THE SLAVE-TRADER, NEW YORK, FEBRUARY 21, 1862.—[SEE PAGE 130.]

Execution of Gordon the Slave Trader, February 21, 1862, from *Leslie's Illustrated News.*

lic opinion; merchants and politicians, cut off from the cotton-producing and Democrat-voting South, struggled to remake their economy and politics. As New Yorkers adjusted to the new wartime realities, Southerners voiced a series of extreme denunciations of New York City for having betrayed its longtime partners in the South. The editors of the Richmond *Dispatch* denounced "Execrable New York." Two weeks after the events at Fort Sumter and just days after Virginia had decided to secede, the secessionist editors gave voice to the region's sense of betrayal and anger. Comparing New York to Sodom, the editors credited the latter for "having in it at least one man who stood by his principles amid an unclean and accursed generation. If New York has one, he has not the courage to let his voice be heard." The *Dispatch* editorial's tone was one of shock, professing, "We could not have believed, nothing could have persuaded us, that the city of New York, which has been enriched by Southern trade, and had ever professed to be

NEW YORK'S SECESSION FROM THE UNION

The election of Abraham Lincoln in November 1860 and the subsequent movement toward secession in the South pushed many proslavery New Yorkers to contemplate a future for their city apart from the United States. Leading merchants and politicians discussed the possibility of secession for New York all through the winter of 1860–1861. New York would not join the still emerging Confederacy; instead, the city would establish itself as an independent republic. Mayor Fernando Wood's address to the Common Council in early January 1861 was the boldest public statement of such an idea. Equal parts a rejection of Lincoln's election, a statement of sympathy for white Southerners, and a defense of the city against recent incursions by state Republicans, Wood's address raised the matter of New York's secession from private whispers into an open, public debate.

White New Yorkers—many of whom had long enjoyed profitable business and political ties to Southern slaveholders—struggled in the face of the Southern secession conventions of early 1861. Even as the Democratic financier August Belmont viewed the possibility of a separate secession for the city as an opportunity for New York to "open her port to the commerce of the world," he eventually rejected the idea of breaking from the Union on patriotic grounds. Other prominent New Yorkers like Moses Taylor and John A. Dix similarly wrestled with questions of nationalism, ideology, and material interest, and for a time imagined a nonviolent disintegration of the federal union.

New York's secessionist debate echoed across the crumbling nation. Southern observers took heart in the words of Mayor Wood and other New York secessionists. George Fitzhugh, one of the South's leading defenders of slavery, remarked that "the proposition to make the city of New-York, with a few adjoining counties, a free port and an independent nation, is the most brilliant that these eventful times have given birth to."

Initial public discussion of secession quickly provoked a firestorm of controversy among New Yorkers. State Democratic Party leaders, fearing a nationalist backlash, disciplined Wood and publicly rejected the idea of a separate republic of New York. Early Confederate tariff policies further alienated New York businessmen and helped consolidate a growing Unionist movement in the city. And yet substantial damage had already been done. The city's flirtation with secession remained in the minds of other Northerners, resulting in persistent attacks from Republican leaders and nationalist journalists on New York's lack of patriotism. Such criticisms would only deepen with the draft riots of July 1863.

—David Quigley

true to the Constitution and the South, would in one day be converted into our bitterest enemy, panting for our blood, fitting out fleets and armies, and raising millions for our destruction." New York's sudden anti-Southern consensus seemed "impossible—incredible," with an entire metropolis transformed from "men to devils."[54] Journalists, slaveholders, and politicians across the new Confederacy held New York in particular contempt in the early days of the Civil War.

While April 1861 marked one end to the history of slavery in the free city, New York business interests and political leaders were reluctant to abandon fully their enduring connections to the South. In 1861, Mayor Fernando Wood denounced the Lincoln administration and contemplated a New York secession, proposing a separate republic on Manhattan island. Two years later, amid the horrific racial violence of the draft riots, Governor Horatio Seymour openly sympathized with white rioters, voicing an unrepentant Copperhead vision of the war. In 1864, New York Democrats led the campaign against Abraham Lincoln, rallying behind his Democratic opponent, General George McClellan. After the war, New York merchants reestablished their position in the international cotton market, consolidating dominance over postbellum Southern production while investing in newly important areas like Egypt and India.[55] New Yorkers advanced their interests across the South and around the world in the early Reconstruction years, establishing patterns of New York–based investment in agrarian regions overseas that would shape the Gilded Age and beyond. A key institutional innovation in this new era was the 1870 creation of the New York Cotton Board.

Politically, Reconstruction also brought renewed ties between New York City and Southern Democrats. The 1868 Democratic National Convention, the first since the war's end, was held at Manhattan's Tammany Hall. Local ward politicians mingled with Confederate veterans. White New Yorkers resisted the federal enactment of equal manhood suffrage, voting as late as 1869 to maintain the racially discriminatory property qualifications for suffrage. Even as the federal government directed a series of Enforcement Acts at securing the rights of freedmen in the South, over 25 percent of all expenditures were directed at the wards of New York City. The 1876 presidential campaign—between Republican

Rutherford B. Hayes and New York Democrat Samuel J. Tilden—cemented political ties between New Yorkers and Southerners in the Democratic Party. Tilden's anti-Reconstruction rhetoric of "retrenchment and reform" attracted its greatest support among white elites in South Carolina and elsewhere in the states of the former Confederacy.[56]

By the end of the nineteenth century, New York's business and cultural leaders had consolidated their positions of dominance nationally even as they sought to expand their influence internationally. The city's exceptionally close relationship with the slave South had proved instrumental in the critical era of metropolitan development. Profits from slave-produced cotton propelled New York's financial rise, while political and literary ties to Southern elites expanded the city's influence. The paradox of slavery in a free city turned out to have been essential to the making of the modern metropolis.

Chapter 10

SECURING FREEDOM: THE CHALLENGES OF BLACK LIFE IN CIVIL WAR NEW YORK

————◆————

IVER BERNSTEIN

J.W.C. Pennington

(FAC-SIMILE OF THE ORIGINAL AUTOGRAPH)

THE ODOR OF CHAR had likely dissipated when James W. C. Pennington returned to his New York City neighborhood on Saturday, July 18, 1863, expecting to find his home and family. But a thickly ominous mood still hung in the air.

By that Saturday morning New York's titanic draft riots had been over for at least a day, suppressed by regiments rushed north from Gettysburg and kept down by the six thousand soldiers stationed around the city. The riots were at once a four-day insurrection against President Abraham Lincoln's Republican government and its discriminatory draft and a pogrom of the desperate against the more desperate in which the Irish poor aimed their murderous fury at their black neighbors. By the time quiet was restored, at least 119 were dead, many of them rioters killed by the military in its battle to retake the city but at least twelve of them African Americans slaughtered by the white rioters. Pennington's neighborhood was an epicenter of the racial violence: on Wednesday, July 15, mobs looted and burned black residences and, in separate incidents, lynched two black men, James Costello and Abraham Franklin. Costello had died trying to defend himself with a revolver, but Franklin was utterly defenseless. An invalid and confined consumptive, the twenty-three-year-old Franklin was yanked out of bed, beaten and kicked through the street, and hanged from a lamppost on the corner of West Twenty-eighth Street and Seventh Avenue. The city's black newspaper underscored the savagery of the rioters, who cut off Franklin's pants at the knees while he still dangled from the lamppost and "[sliced] bits of flesh out of his legs, and afterwards set fire to him! All this was done beneath the eyes of his widowed mother."[1] The military arrived, scattered the crowd and cut down Franklin's body, but when the soldiers departed, the corpse was hoisted up again with cheers for Jefferson Davis. In a grisly climax, an Irish-American teenager named Patrick Butler dragged Franklin's body through the streets by the genitals as the crowd applauded—a final rite of desecration with a distorted and murderous attraction percolating through it. When black minister Henry Highland Garnet recalled another such riot-week lynching, it was the dialogue between one "demon in human form" who took "a sharp knife, cut out pieces of the quivering flesh, and offered it to the greedy blood-thirsty mob, saying 'Who wants some nigger meat?'" and the mob replying "'I' 'I' 'I,' as if they were scrambling for pieces of gold," that represented the riot's most indelible horror.[2]

Pennington had not witnessed these agonizing spectacles. Early in the summer he had taken a job as principal of a "colored school" in Poughkeepsie, and was only now, on July 18, with his students on vacation, returning to New York. But he knew enough of the riot to approach his house "quietly" that morning: "I found that the mob had attacked my residence; my own, with other colored families had been expelled, and I was at once set upon by a mob, with stones, brickbats, &c., with the shout, 'Kill the d——d black neager,' &c." Forced to flee, Pennington wandered the city for hours, searching unsuccessfully for his wife and children, "at the peril of my life at every step," before finally retreating to Poughkeepsie. Still marooned there days later, Pennington expressed his feelings of lament and defiance in a letter published in the *New York Times*: "I do not know where my wife is; I am debarred of access to my property; I claim the right as a citizen to visit my home."[3]

A former Maryland slave who escaped to the North and freedom in the late 1820s, Pennington had through strenuous effort not only learned to read and write but also attained international renown as an author and minister.[4] His

THE RIOTS IN NEW YORK : THE MOB LYNCHING A NEGRO IN CLARKSON-STREET.—SEE PAGE 141.

The Riots in New York: The Mob Lynching a Negro in Clarkson Street. Wood engraving. Published in *Illustrated London News.*

NEW-YORK
HISTORICAL
SOCIETY LIBRARY

plight in July 1863 was particularly keen. He had been, at least for a time, stripped of all of the material attributes of home and citizenship—indeed, all but shorn of his identity. He was later infuriated to learn that his wife had received a note saying, "The mob will come to this house, soon. You nigger wenches must leave here, and you must not carry away a bundle, or anything with you."[5] The mob had prevented Pennington from performing what was, in his mind, the defining role of a free man: protecting his household dependents. The situation was not so different from that of enslaved men who could not protect their wives and children from the violent advances of slave masters. Pennington must have felt his circumstances after the draft riots to be eerily familiar. Though he was not again enslaved in any legal sense, he was once more an outcast and a fugitive who had been reduced to a condition of impotence not unlike that of a slave.

Just days before this abortive homecoming, with the riots still ablaze in New York, Pennington served as president of a remarkable "Colored Convention" that met in Poughkeepsie to reaffirm black loyalty to the Northern government and take steps toward "enrolling and organizing colored troops." Black New Yorkers had lobbied for the government-sanctioned raising of "colored troops" from the outset of the war but had met concerted resistance from the state's Democratic governor, Horatio Seymour. The campaign still lacked the endorsement of the Lincoln administration (which had approved the creation of black regiments in other states). For all of this, the convention's eloquent "Manifesto," drafted by the minister P. B. Randolph, was full of hope. In the military outcome of the Civil War, the very future of Christian civilization was at stake. Blacks held "the balance of power" not only in the contest between North and South but also in a world-historical contest between barbarism and freedom, and for black New Yorkers the raising of black regiments was essential to that cosmic struggle. "Liberty is more than the golden vision of the past . . . more than the dream of the enthusiast; more than the plaything of tyrants and knaves . . . no man is fit for liberty who is unwilling or afraid to fight for it, if need be, to the bitter end." In advance of any government-sanctioned enrollment, the convention authorized the creation of a "Central Committee" to "enroll colored men all over the state . . . at once" and call upon "colored females" to "form themselves into colored soldier's aid societies all over the State."[6]

The words and actions of Pennington's convention had special poignancy amid the flames and lynch mobs of the riot week. Pennington sounded a ringing endorsement of the Northern nation as the guarantor of liberty at the very moment it could hardly guarantee him citizenship or even a home.

A consideration of black life in New York City during the Civil War must start with this stark contradiction between catastrophe and hope.[7] On the one hand, black New Yorkers were the victims of a sweeping political, social, and spiritual cataclysm during the riots of July 13 through 16, 1863. They witnessed white mobs burning their places of work; destroying their homes; lynching, burning, and mutilating their men; and terrorizing their women and children, wreaking a murderous and dehumanizing violence on the most

Colored Orphan Asylum, ca. 1861. Stereograph.

NEW-YORK HISTORICAL SOCIETY LIBRARY

defenseless, from the crippled and consumptive Franklin to the children of the Colored Orphan Asylum, whose place of refuge was burned to the ground on Monday, July 13, with the young inmates barely escaping out the back of the building while the mob cried "Kill the monkies."[8] The riot was nothing less than an effort, no less thorough for its being relatively unplanned and uncoordinated, to annihilate "black life" in New York City—to erase a black public presence on the streets, in the political halls, theaters, docks and factories; to enfeeble blacks' pursuit of political, economic, and cultural institution building; to undermine blacks' efforts, acting as their own agents, to expand their physical and material presence into the city and the nation and control the imaginative representations of themselves in urban and national politics and culture.

Henry Highland Garnet was correct when he announced at a memorial service for twelve of the slain black "martyrs" that slavery was at the heart of the riot.[9] But it is more precise to say that slavery and its new and potent political outgrowth, proslavery nationalism, were at the heart of the riot. The Confederate States of America had attempted to create a nation-state and a public life in which black people had no independent role to play. In this sense, it can be said that during the Civil War, Confederate proslavery nationalism and black nationalism were opposite sides of the same coin: the creation of each was based on the destruction of the other. While the often repeated charge that the rioters were being directed by Confederate operatives was unfounded, the mobs' zealous pursuit of the ultimate goal of proslavery nationalism—the dismantling of a black presence and erecting of a white political culture over its remains—was clear enough. This was the motive of the mobs that burned black homes and chased black families from Pennington's neighborhood, lynched Abraham Franklin, cursed "Black Republicans," and cheered for Jefferson Davis.

But—and it is a crucial "but"—on the other hand, during the Civil War, black New Yorkers emerged as some of the most imaginative, eloquent, and confident representatives of the new patriotic nationalism that swept the North. They played an especially important role in the reinvention of that nationalism as Northern war aims expanded from preserving the nation to ending slavery. Henry Highland Garnet's unprecedented speech before the House of Representatives in February 1865, to celebrate congressional passage of the Thirteenth Amendment abolishing slavery, was an example of black New Yorkers' contribution to the new Northern nationalistic ethos. No less impressive was the outpouring of black volunteers to enlist in the three United States Colored Troops regiments—the Twentieth, the Twenty-Sixth, and Thirty-First—that were raised in the months following the draft riots. These regiments were the result of the mobilizing efforts of black leaders such as Pennington and Garnet as well as their political collaboration with the white leaders of the city's Union League Club. With the war's promise of emancipation came a growing cultural and political confidence for New York's blacks that could be seen in the ambitious reportage and burgeoning advertisements of the city's leading black paper, the *Anglo-African*, as well as in the pluck of black women and men insisting on their right to promenade on Broadway or contesting whites for space on segregated streetcars.

THE CIVIL WAR years were the "worst of times" and the "best of times" for black New Yorkers. Indeed, there was a necessary relation between New York City blacks' situation as pariahs in the North's most proslavery city and their role as creators of the new Northern national consciousness. What made New York's black life so rich and productive of political eloquence and initiatives during the Civil War was the fact that New York's blacks (and, to a considerable extent, their white antislavery allies) were simultaneously both outsiders and insiders.

The situation was a familiar one in American history. In 1776, the American Revolution against British authority gained much of its political inventiveness from the fact that Americans were living on the margins of the British Empire and were at once insiders and outsiders: fully participant in British political culture and well-versed in "the rights of Englishmen" but alienated by their New World birth and geographic distance from the centers of power in England. New York City's blacks in the late-antebellum and Civil War years were similarly positioned. Indeed, they were doubly on the periphery. New York City was a proslavery outpost on the edges of the Confederate slave empire. But black New Yorkers knew the ways and means of a slave society intimately. Some, like Pennington, were former Southern slaves; others were illegal fugitives.[10] And because New York's own General Emancipation dated from 1827, some had grown up in New York's own slowly dying world of slavery or, more likely, had parents or grandparents who had done so. Moreover, black New Yorkers of the Civil War years were also living on the margins of Lincoln's new wartime Republican nation-state centered in Washington. As the draft riots revealed, they could hardly rely on that Republican government to protect them or guarantee their rights. But, of course, they were crucial members of the national antislavery movement that brought the Republican Party to national power.

In retrospect the support of black New Yorkers for the Republican wartime government may appear obvious and predictable, but at the time, there was nothing inevitable about it. From the point of view of the Republican administration in Washington, the winning of African American allegiance was a central triumph—perhaps *the* central triumph—of the war. Certainly the addition of 180,000 African American troops to the ranks of the Northern military played a crucial role in bringing about victory on the battlefield. But from the perspective of spring 1861, the Republican government's eventual endorsement of emancipation and black military service could barely be glimpsed. For roughly the first year and a half of the war, black New Yorkers' support for that government was hardly a given. Their distinctive status as outsiders and insiders encouraged creativity when it came to defining their relation to the emerging Northern nation-state. And even after the preliminary Emancipation Proclamation of September 1862 inspired in them much greater confidence in Lincoln's government, their loyalty to the Northern nation-state retained a highly strategic and instrumentalist quality.

Wondering whether black Americans were sufficiently a part of the ruling element of the United States to maintain their rights in that country, the Haitian newspaper *L'Opinion Nationale* observed on the eve of the Civil War: "They are scattered in isolated groups, of insignificant dimensions, without means, or influence . . . so that if they would, they could not act simultaneously in their own defense."[11] This shrewd insight into the plight of blacks in American political culture could also be applied to the circumstances of black New Yorkers: scattered geographically and politically, they faced large obstacles to effective action "in their own defense."[12] Both in the American polity and in New York City, blacks' geographic diffusion was one of the consequences of slavery; it was especially acute in New York, a city whose development had been so decisively shaped by slavery. In 1860, the city's 12,472 blacks were widely dispersed among eight different wards, in enclaves that, while often separate, were not sharply demarcated in the manner of the segregated ghettoes of twentieth-century Northern cities.

Black New Yorkers' choice of where to live was hardly a free one: they clustered in certain neighborhoods because few white landlords would rent to them.[13] But there were some compensating advantages to such clustering. It allowed a certain visibility in cultural and political terms—a modest claim both to urban space (if in the lowest rent districts) and neighborly support, at least an inchoate physical presence as a people, and perhaps the remote prospect of becoming part of the "ruling element."[14] On the eve of the Civil War, even this toehold was at risk, an ominous fact not lost on the enemies of black freedom. James Gordon Bennett's *Herald* intoned the results of the 1860 federal census like a proslavery sermon. The marked decrease in New York's black population since mid-century, the fact that only 85 of the city's 10,000-plus blacks owned real estate, and the almost complete absence of blacks among the ranks of the city's artisans, were, in Bennett's rendering, incontrovertible evidence that "the true position of the negro in the United States is one of servitude" and that "as a slave" the African American was "happy and contested, as a freeman despised and contemned."[15] Such diasporic conditions, and indeed, all of the trials of black life in New York, argued Bennett, were blacks' own fault, a necessary result of what he conceived of as blacks' innate inferiority and unfitness for freedom. It is no surprise that Bennett came to demand the reenslavement of all Northern blacks.[16]

Such arguments calculatedly ignored the extent to which black New Yorkers' plight stemmed from the vast power of white proslavery culture and the endless ridicule from arbiters of "respectable" opinion such as Bennett. In the proslavery campaign to demonize black culture, no weapon was more powerful than the increasingly fashionable "scientific racism" that maintained that African Americans were permanently and biologically inferior to whites—indeed, a separate species more akin to apes and monkeys than humans in the scale of creation. Proslavery culture and scientific racism gave prestige and sanction to recently arrived Irish immigrants' efforts to drive blacks into the most unskilled and repugnant jobs.[17] Ironically, before the draft riots, Democratic editors and orators raised the specter of brutalized black hordes flooding into New York City in the wake of emancipation to steal white jobs and violate white women when, in fact, the Irish had pushed blacks out of many trades, especially after the massive migration of the Great Irish Famine.[18] Black New Yorkers had to contend both with the fact of their fragmented and waning physical presence in the city and with a grossly distorting proslavery racism that insisted that blacks' predicament was an inevitable result of their own alleged deficiencies.

The decentralized and marginalized aspect of black life in New York City nonetheless produced a certain kind of creativity and opportunity when it came to creating political culture. It put a premium on the political alliances that New York's black activists were able to create with white abolitionists and helped make those relationships especially self-conscious and durable: the small minority of whites who sympathized with blacks were also culturally and politically marginalized, if protected by their ownership of a white skin against the daily harassment and threats of violence to which blacks were subject.[19] Living precariously on the edges of the city's public culture encouraged black activists to pursue simultaneously a wide range of plans to create a viable black community and nationality, some inside New York City and State, others in an array of international settings.

On the eve of the Civil War, James Pennington's problem of July 1863—how to create a strong and secure home, defined both in personal and political terms—was already a bedeviling issue for black New Yorkers. The years immediately following the Supreme Court's *Dred Scott* decision of 1857 were an especially grim time for Northern blacks, as the court's dictum that blacks had no rights that whites were bound to respect set the stage for the nationalization of slavery and new white campaigns against the modest civil and political rights that blacks still retained at the state level.

While a considerable number of New York's black activists supported the antislavery Republican Party in the election of 1860, for many this appears to have been a strategic decision. What stands out is the skepticism with which African Americans in the city regarded both of the major parties and their potent sense of their own cultural and political independence at a moment when the future of the United States and its government was in doubt.[20] The revolutionary attack on slavery by John Brown and his party of armed guerrillas at Harper's Ferry in October 1859 was supported by a wide range of New York's black leaders—Brown had sought out Henry Highland Garnet's participation

(Garnet thought it doomed and turned him down), and when Douglass declined to participate for similar reasons, he nonetheless relayed to Brown a $25 donation from James and Elizabeth Gloucester (Gloucester was a Brooklyn minister who would play a significant role in the city's black politics during the war) accompanied by a note encouraging Brown "to do battle to that *ugly foe* of slavery."[21] Black and white ministers including Garnet and Henry Ward Beecher held memorial services for the martyred Brown after the December 2, 1859, execution. Beecher, with his flair for the dramatic, produced the actual chains used to restrain Brown on the scaffold.[22]

Garnet's endorsement of a violent mass slave insurrection, which had so raised the hackles of white and black abolitionists when he issued it in 1843, was accordingly a political commonplace among the city's black activists by the time of Harper's Ferry. In April 1861, the *Anglo-African* epitomized the enthusiasm for revolutionary violence that had become de rigueur among black abolitionists: "We want Nat Turner—not speeches; Denmark Vesey—not resolutions; John Brown—not meetings."[23] Black New Yorkers were contemptuous of any compromise that would sustain the old Union with slavery intact. What would black martyrdom in a war to sustain Lincoln's Republican government mean, the *Anglo-African* wondered? Would blacks be called upon to fight and die for some new version of the Union that would once again brand them pariahs and outcasts? The "blood of Crispus Attucks" had been shamefully "paid for" in the "rendition of Sims and Burns." Blacks and white politicians alike knew "the long arrears of blood-bought rights this country owes us." Black New Yorkers would be witheringly skeptical of any attempt to "further use us as instruments to stir up this rotten sham, this hollow fraud, this charnel house of human rights,—the Federal Government."[24]

What loyalties would this edgy, militantly independent sensibility produce among black New Yorkers with the outbreak of civil war? The acute sense of frustration and threat in the years immediately following *Dred Scott* produced a growing interest among New York City blacks in schemes of emigration outside the United States. The African Civilization Society, created by Henry Highland Garnet in league with black and white allies in fall 1858, had as its goal the consolidation of a "grand center of negro nationality, from which shall flow the streams of commercial, intellectual and political power which shall make colored people respected everywhere."[25] But the African Civilization Society neither advocated a separation of blacks from American nationality nor did Garnet abandon any of his many forms of political agitation and institution building in his home city of New York. Most striking about the society was its political ambition and its geopolitical sweep: it would aid the emigration of black Americans to West Africa, at once creating a free-labor cotton economy there, supplanting the slave trade in that region with lawful commerce, and converting Africans to Christianity.[26] Not only would this expanded African supply of cotton undermine slavery in the American South, but the African Civilization Society project would mobilize the Christian and commercial energies of "educated men of color in the United States, thus aiding in the work of elevation HERE, which is so imperatively necessary."[27]

Garnet furiously denied accusations that he was capitulating to the racist premise of the white-led American Colonization Society that blacks were incapable of attaining equality in the United States. Rather he imagined an expanding black national presence in America complementing his initiative in Africa and a series of efforts in the Caribbean. He could, in the same breath, endorse plans to settle American blacks in Liberia and on Gerrit Smith's lands in upstate New York; around the time he helped found the African Civilization Society, he was deeply involved in the statewide campaign for equal suffrage that culminated in the failed referendum of 1860 (the state constitution's steep $250 property requirement for black voting allowed only about seventy black voters citywide).[28] In short, Garnet was building multiple beachheads of black nationality simultaneously.[29]

New York City was a center—perhaps *the* center—of such experimentation with ideas about black nationality in the United States on the eve of the war.[30] It was not just the substance of Garnet's programs that had gained an audience there, but also his charismatic style. To be sure, many of the city's black leaders refused to abide Garnet's emigrationist schemes: William P. Powell, the remarkable black waterfront boardinghouse keeper and labor contractor cum political activist whose "Colored Seamen's Home" had for years served as a kind of social service agency for black sailors and a rallying point for fugitive slaves, and James McCune Smith, the city's leading black physician, one of its wealthiest black residents, and spearhead of the statewide struggle for equal suffrage, prominent among them.[31] But on the eve of the events at Fort Sumter, Garnet's fraternity was expanding: William Wells Brown, William J. Watkins, and even Frederick Douglass flirted briefly with the possibility of black Americans' voluntary emigration abroad.[32]

In the end, few black New Yorkers migrated and even fewer settled permanently abroad, although the exact figures remain unknown. At the peak of the "Haitian fever" in 1861–1862, more than two thousand American blacks migrated to that island, but most black Americans (and black New Yorkers) were reluctant or skeptical.[33] But it was one thing to identify strongly with the nation of one's birth (in 1860 only about 3 percent of black New Yorkers were born outside the United States) and another to fight and die for the survival of Lincoln's new Republican government as the best hope for freedom.[34] "Our hope," the *Anglo-African* was certain after considering Lincoln's First Inaugural, "must be in ourselves."[35]

The outbreak of war on April 12, 1861, changed everything. Eight days later New Yorkers turned out en masse in Union Square for "the greatest popular demonstration ever known in America" and at once proclaimed the city's allegiance to the national government and buried the previous winter's talk of the city seceding from the North to create an independent republic friendly to slavery and free trade.[36]

The advent of war gave encouragement to all parties. Historically, declarations of war, calls for troops, and the movement of armies have always given hope of change to unfree peoples. New York's black men, like their counterparts in other Northern cities, immediately began to form regiments after the firing on Fort Sumter. Even with the patriotic upsurge, the prospect of black men toting guns in public was a radical one indeed in slavery-sympathizing New York. When "a number of Blacks quietly hired a public hall and commenced drilling therein, in view of the possibility of a call to active service,"

Henry Highland Garnet

Henry Highland Garnet took an idea—settlement of American black people outside the United States—that was long associated by Northern blacks with the disparagement of their potential for full incorporation into American society, and had the temerity to transform it into a sophisticated strategy for securing racial equality. Bold and visionary tactics were his trademark: his call for a violent mass slave insurrection, controversial among white and black abolitionists when he issued it in 1843, had become a political commonplace among the city's black activists by the time of John Brown's raid on Harper's Ferry in 1859. His audacity made him a symbol of independence to a black following that extended well beyond the walls of Brooklyn's Shiloh Presbyterian Church, where he served as minister.

Born a slave in Maryland in 1815, the young Garnet escaped bondage along with his parents and sister, the family ultimately making its way to New York City in 1825. He became a riveting public speaker, in part because he could evoke the experience of the slave with surpassing power and in part because of his commanding physical presence, made all the more arresting by a wooden leg (from a childhood injury that required amputation). With regard to Garnet's wide popularity, his boyhood friend Alexander Crummell would recall: "Amid the immense population of the Metropolis there never was a man of our race so well known and so popular as Dr. Garnet. The laboring classes of the whites . . . the great merchants of the city, the grand dames on the avenues knew him and respected him." The capstone of Garnet's career was achieved on February 12, 1865, when he spoke before the House of Representatives at President Lincoln's invitation, the first African American to address Congress.

—*Iver Bernstein*

REDRAFT
of
THE CASTELLO PLAN
NEW AMSTERDAM
1660

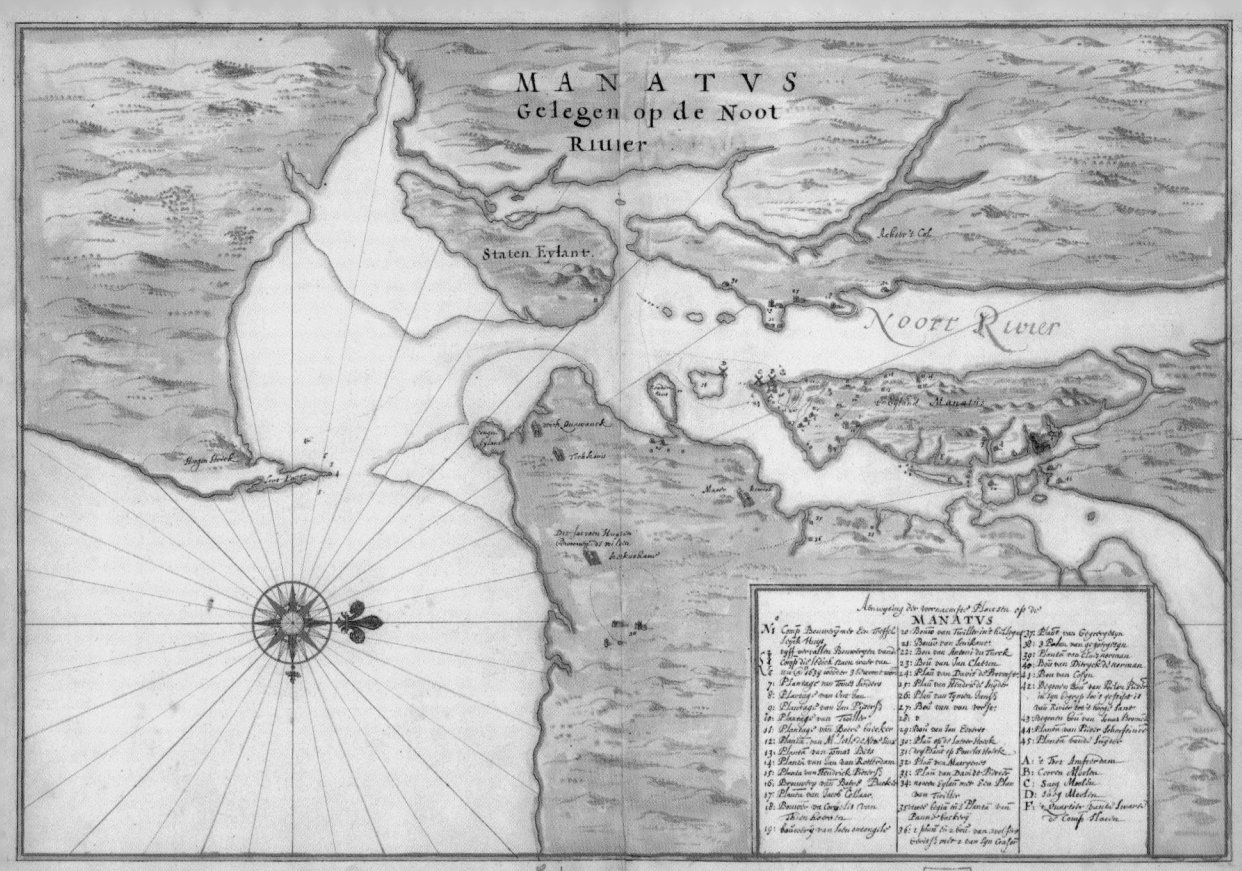

MANATVS
Gelegen op de Noot
Riuier

Staten Eylant.

Achter 't Col

Noort Riuier

't Eijlant Manathes

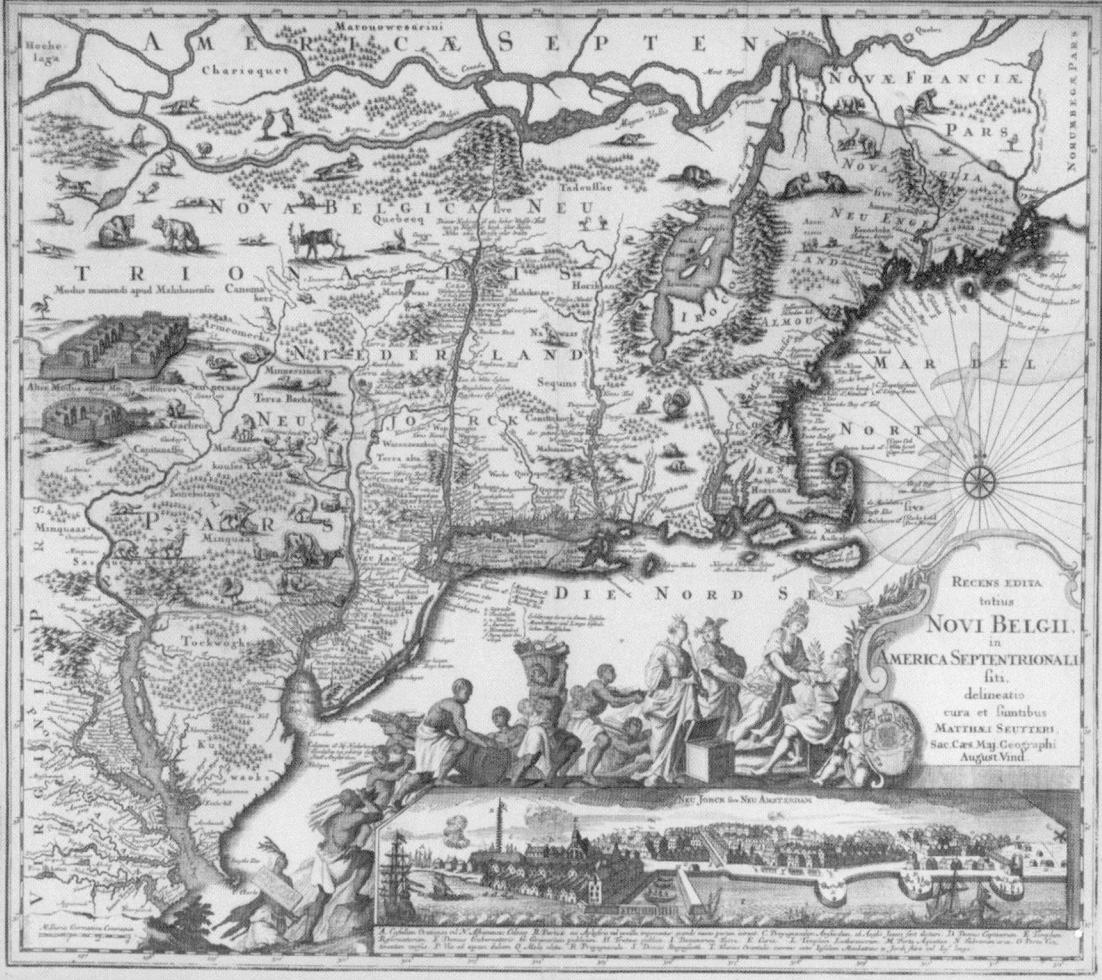

AMERICÆ SEPTEN

NOVÆ FRANCIÆ PARS

NORUMBEGA PARS

NOVA BELGICA sive NEU

TRIONALIS

NIDER LAND

NEU JORCK

PENSIL PAR

VIRGINIÆ PARS

MAR DEL NORT

Die Nord See

RECENS EDITA totius
NOVI BELGII
in
AMERICA SEPTENTRIONALI
siti,
delineatio
cura et sumptibus
MATTHÆI SEUTTERI
Sac. Cæs. Maj. Geographi
August. Vind.

NEU JORCK sive NEU AMSTERDAM

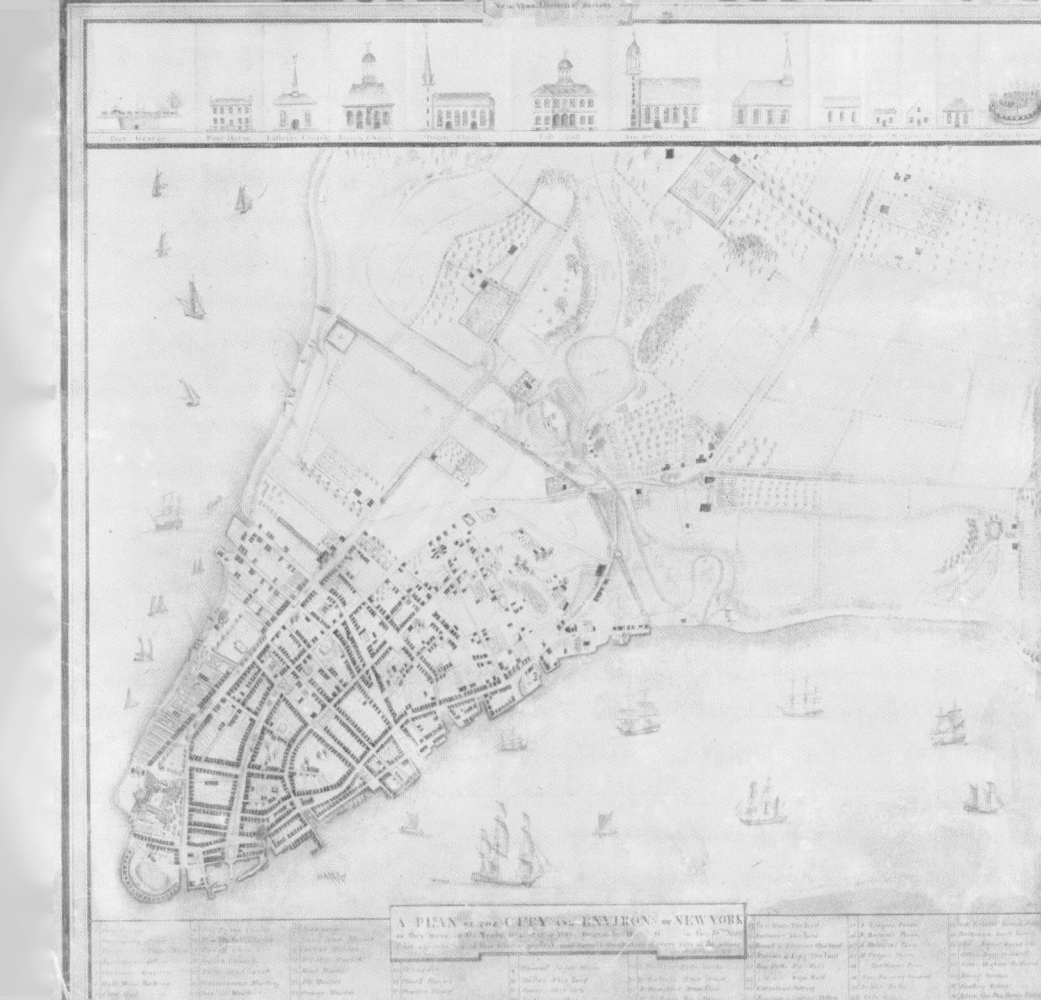

A PLAN of the CITY and ENVIRONS of NEW YORK

A Plan of the City of New York from an actual Survey

This 1754 map indicates the location of the "Negroes Burial Ground," known today as the African Burial Ground, just outside the Palisade (present-day Wall

The photograph and the map graphically depict the location in present-day Manhattan of some of the land owned by half-free blacks in Dutch New York. Although all half-free blacks were granted full freedom just before the start of British rule, they were unable to hold on to their land; by the mid-eighteenth century, free black landowners had virtually disappeared from New York City.

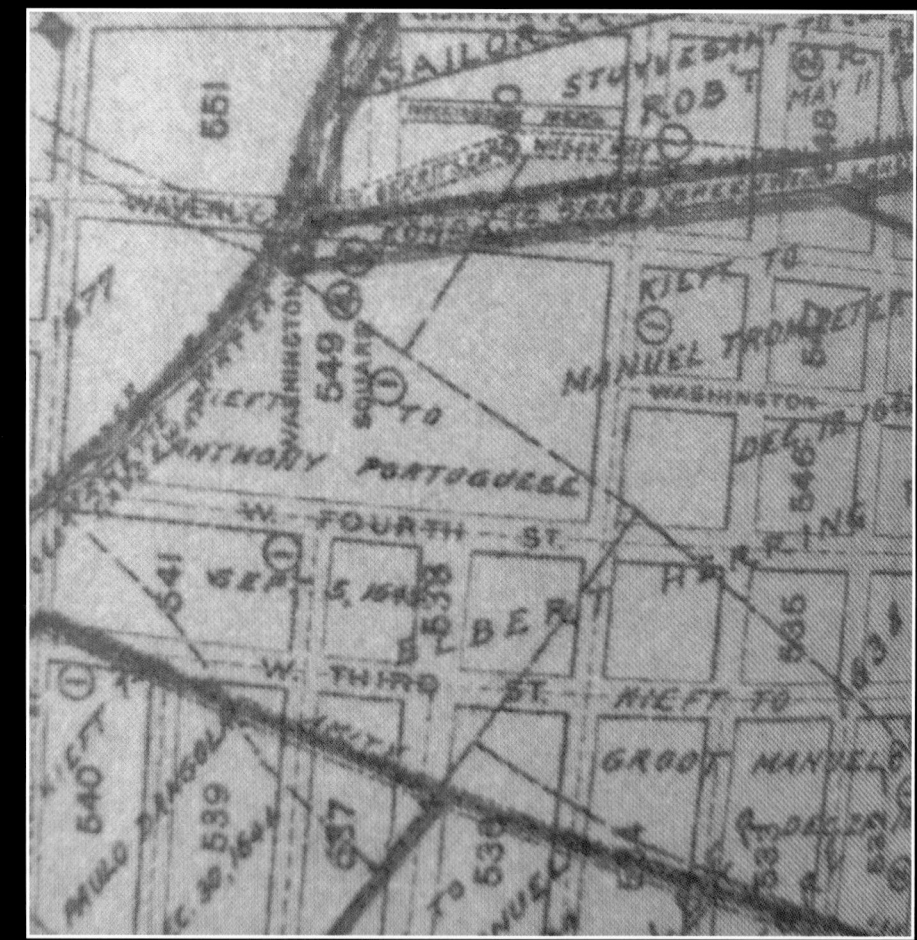

R.H. Dodd, "Plate 84Bb, Franklin Street to 23rd Street" from *Stokes' Iconography of Manhattan Island*, 1928.

Washington Square Park, Greenwich Village.

This drawing depicts the early settlement of New Amsterdam. The Africans at the bottom of the picture are stock representations of slavery in Dutch New World colonies and may bear little relationship to those actually present in New Amsterdam at the time of this drawing. Yet their presence in the illustration demonstrates the centrality of slavery to the colony. *Nieu Amsterdam. Cum Privilegio Ordinum Hollandiae et West-Frisae*, ca. 1640.

Police Superintendent John Kennedy promptly told them to desist as he could not guarantee their safety from white mob assault; there was no option but to obey. A delegation sought to discuss the matter of black enlistment with the governor, to no result.[37] Black men then convened to discuss alternative possibilities of serving as firemen (to replace those whites who enlisted) or a "Home Guard"; the prevailing sentiment opposed such measures since blacks' initial offers to fight had been rejected and it was undignified to "offer ourselves to be kicked and insulted, as others had been. . . . The whites *knew* that we were willing to fight."[38] The *Anglo-African* advised against forming volunteer companies that the federal government would surely reject. Better to "organize for military purposes . . . procure arms, and hold ourselves as Minute Men to *respond* when the *slave calls*."[39]

Accordingly, the starting point for all black considerations of political obligation during the first year of war was that lodestar, the death of slavery. James Pennington crafted a petition to the United States Congress that received wide attention among black Northerners in the last half of 1861. "African slavery as it now exists at the South," the document read, "is the prime cause of the present Crisis and . . . permanent peace cannot be restored until said cause be removed." A law immediately abolishing slavery was the only way to end hostilities.[40] All well and good, but what, then, were the implications of such a view for black New Yorkers' loyalties? In "A Word to Colored Politicians," a public letter published at about the same time, Pennington captured some of the complex calculations black New Yorkers were making at this moment *before* the conflict began to take on the attributes of a revolutionary struggle against slavery. Significantly, he assumed that his black audience was still deliberating whether "WE ARE BOUND BY PRINCIPLES, OR SWORN TO HELP FIGHT THE BATTLES OF THE PRESENT CIVIL PRO-SLAVERY WAR . . . some say yes, others say no." Pennington was convinced that with the South fighting for the perpetuation of slavery and the North for the restoration of "the Union as it was," it was "the duty of colored patriots to go for 'the Union without Slavery.'" For one thing, Pennington observed, in the same way free blacks in the North would be taxed by the federal government to support the Northern war effort, they would be swept up in the struggle, whether they liked it or not. But the treason which mattered most at this ambiguous moment was to the race: "To say we will sit back in the shade and take no part, is unpolitical, unphilosophical, unmanly, and I had almost said, traitorous to our own race." Pennington saw a providential momentum to the war even at this early stage, a confidence that would be shared by Garnet and many other black New Yorkers. "I believe," he put it, "that we are on the eve of the grand heroic age of the race." The practical reality of "an army of 25,000 black troops marching from the Northwest, upon the rear of Jeff. Davis, can recapture king cotton. And then the race will hold the position of the world."[41] The debate reverberated through fall 1861 as one "R.H.V." insisted that "the principle of neutrality is the only safe one to govern us at this time," and Alfred M. Green retorted that the mere physical fact of armed and trained black regiments at the ready could play a role in the outcome of the war. God, Green was sure, would help only those who helped themselves.[42]

Black New Yorkers could point to some encouraging signs as they looked around the city during the first year of war. The illegal African slave trade was one of New York's great open secrets, and with President James Buchanan's appointment of proslavery hoodlum Captain Isaiah Rynders as United States Marshal in 1857, the trade had all but taken on the aspect of a "secure and influential business interest."[43] When Republicans assumed national power in 1860, federal investigations were launched that resulted in the execution of slave-ship captain Nathaniel Gordon in New York in February 1862—an event which strongly signaled the drift of white opinion in the city from proslavery orthodoxy.[44] That same month, Frederick Douglass argued for emancipation and federal recruitment of black troops to a heavily white audience at Cooper Union, and four months later, newspaper editor William Cullen Bryant led the organization of a new "Emancipation League."[45] In countless encounters in the streets and on the streetcars, on the docks, and in the theaters, saloons, dance halls, and brothels, the outbreak of war doubtless brought little tremors in the dynamics of race relations— blacks more expansive in their occupation of urban space, whites less cock-sure in their accustomed patterns of dominance.

Observers noted a new aggressiveness in white behavior toward blacks. As early as spring 1862, James Pennington would later recall, a "riot spirit" was gathering force—as if the white lower class was sensing a weakening of the city's racial regime and needed to up the tempo of intimidation to compensate: "The police authorities were frequently applied to, by respectable colored persons, without being able to obtain any redress when assaulted and abused in the streets. . . . We have pointed to the street corners, and to the rowdies who stood at them, and in open day light assaulted colored persons, in passing."[46]

It was under the shadow of this mounting physical intimidation that Henry Highland Garnet decided to celebrate President Lincoln's preliminary Emancipation Proclamation at Shiloh Presbyterian Church on September 29, 1862. Garnet's friends had advised against creating such a target for mob anger and the black audience that turned out was displaying no small degree of courage. Black men, said Brooklyn minister George Levere, needed to "stand up against the outrages heaped upon them by the brutal portion of society."[47]

It would be hard, then, to underestimate the sense of world-historical breakthrough that black New Yorkers felt with the issuance of the Emancipation Proclamation on the first day of the new year. At a "Great Festival of Freedom" organized by New York's "Sons of Freedom" at the Cooper Institute on January 5 to commemorate the event, Garnet was elected president and asked to give the opening address, no small honor among a star-studded lineup that included Lewis Tappan and William Wells Brown.[48] The theme of Garnet's keynote was blacks' patriotic loyalty to the national government from the outbreak of rebellion, emphasizing that "the colored men of this city had gone to the Governor of this State, and offered their services as men—not as black men—to fight the battles of their native land to preserve the Union and Liberty." Then, Garnet recalled, black New Yorkers resolved to "wait till they were called for . . . much as they loved their land, much as their hearts burned for liberty." But now the call had come, and Garnet insisted, "They must go, and, if need be, be found in front, and so bequeath to future generations an heirloom in which their children and children's children would remember with pride their fathers were not cowards when their country called them to its defense." The minister closed with "a long list of heroes and martyrs of Liberty, finishing with John Brown, which brought the audience to their feet to give most rapturous shouts and applause."[49]

Garnet's exhortation to black New Yorkers to volunteer to fight for the survival of the national government in the wake of Lincoln's proclamation was a significant turning point. The former emigrationist's ethic of martyrdom and self-sacrifice to end slavery and create black nationality was securely wedded to a commitment to fight and die for the Northern nation-state. The federal government, Garnet was now sure, represented black New Yorkers' and black Americans' last, best hope of freedom.[50]

Yet through the first half of 1863, as Garnet, Douglass, Pennington, and others put their prestige behind black enlistment, they wrestled with a certain reluctance among city blacks. The fact that Lincoln's War Department had not yet sanctioned the recruitment of black men in New York State, that Governor Horatio Seymour remained adamantly opposed, and that blacks were not eligible for commissions were all disincentives for black men considering volunteering. Beginning in January, Garnet begun recruiting for the Fifty-Fourth Massachusetts regiment, formed with the endorsement of Massachusetts governor John Andrew. And at a series of war rallies in April 1863, Garnet lambasted the "tardy, back-door manner" in which blacks were being incorporated into the Union Army."[51] When only one recruit offered his services at the meeting at Shiloh on April 27, Frederick Douglass, who was in attendance, told the crowd he was ashamed of them. One Robert Johnson rose to the defense of black New Yorkers: they hesitated to enlist not from cowardice but out of "a proper respect for their own manhood." Let the government that "wanted their services . . . guarantee to them all the rights of citizens and soldiers, and, instead of one man, he would insure them 5,000 men in twenty days." Johnson's remarks were met "with tremendous and long-continued applause."[52] A resolution passed at a recruiting meeting three days later that black New Yorkers understood their military service, when proffered, to be a stand not only for the maintenance of a "good government, but against slavery, the parent and fosterer of the unjust prejudice we have been subjects of here in the North."[53]

By April, the winds of such prejudice were beginning to whip far more threateningly. The tone may have been set nearly nine months earlier, in August 1862, when white, mostly Irish, workers in Brooklyn assaulted the black women and children who were employed by a tobacco factory, driving them to the upper floors of the building and then attempting to burn them alive by setting fire to the first floor. The arrival on the scene of some African American men forestalled a catastrophe.[54] By spring 1863, the economic burdens of the war were being sorely felt by the city's vast working poor—taxes and inflation were taking their toll, and those white families who had sacrificed one or more male breadwinners to the Union Army were more often than not living on the edge.[55] Put otherwise, the situation of the white poor began to approximate that of the black poor, whose tenuous hold on regular employment kept them on the economic margins. Add to this a new federal conscription law passed in March 1863 that allowed the wealthy to buy their way out of the draft for $300—a real threat to the poor—and emancipation, which in the hands of Democratic politicos became a bugbear that would flood New York's labor markets with thousands of low-wage former slaves. The result was a mounting sense of panic among the white poor, particularly Irish Catholics, often recently arrived, in desperate straits and looking to the Democratic fearmongers for cues to becoming American.

As the planned enforcement of the draft in the second week of July approached, Bennett's *Herald* and still more inflammatory Democratic papers such as the Catholic *New York Freeman's Journal* and the *Weekly Caucasian* predicted an annihilation of white labor should slavery be abolished and conscription carried out.[56] Maria Daly captured the mood of hysteria among the poorest Irish laborers who had been convinced they stood on the verge of imminent dispossession of livelihood, of freedom, of self: "[They] say that they are sold for $300 whilst they pay $1000 for negroes."[57]

THE DRAFT RIOTS revealed the depth of the black community's vulnerability and suffering at the hands of the mobs. The riots, it must be emphasized, were nothing less than an effort to annihilate black life in New York City and its surrounding black enclaves. While black men and women here and there defended themselves collectively and with arms—in the "Arch" district of the Eighth Ward and in remote areas such as Flatbush and Weeksville—it was difficult for blacks to survive, let alone contest the mob onslaught, scattered as they were through the city.[58] By the third day of violence it was reported that "the negroes have entirely disappeared from the docks."[59] By the time the last mob had been vanquished, over 3,000 blacks were homeless; many had taken safe refuge on Blackwell's Island, in the woods north of the city, on Long Island, and in the hills and swamps of New Jersey.[60] For some blacks, the scattered pre-riot pattern of settlement was a death warrant, denying them allies at this vital moment. William P. Powell and his family, stranded among hostile Irish neighbors on the East Side waterfront, were no less isolated and vulnerable but more fortunate. On the first afternoon of the riot, Powell found himself and "four females," including an invalid daughter, "prisoners in my own house to king mob." Finally, the attackers broke in and drove the group to the roof of their five-story building. At that fateful moment, a Jewish man, himself deformed, providentially appeared, offered protection to Powell's "poor helpless daughter" and gave him a rope which he rigged into a bosun's chair and used to lower his family over a space of a hundred feet to the next roof and across a series of roofs until safely landed in a neighbor's yard. Late that night the family found refuge in a police stationhouse, and eventually made its way to Massachusetts.[61]

Accordingly, perhaps the most eloquent testimony to the riots' savage impact on black life in New York could be found in the further decline and dispersal of the black population. The Powells would ultimately make their way back but, one paper would report, "a large number of colored families have left the city with the intention of never returning to it again."[62] For months after the riots the public life of the city was a more noticeably white domain; by war's end, as many as 20 percent of New York's blacks had disappeared.[63]

Amazingly—and again, ironically, given the intentions of the rioters and their sympathizers—the catastrophe of the riots had the effect of opening up new political possibilities for black New Yorkers. How they began to turn disas-

BLACK AND GREEN

By 1861, at the time of the Civil War, tension between black and Irish New Yorkers was a familiar story. Indeed, even before the massive influx of Irish immigrants precipitated by the Great Famine of the mid-forties, Irish working-men often took the lead in driving African Americans from the artisanal trades that they had performed as slaves, and had also begun to crowd black workers from the ranks of menials. The advent of the war raised expectations on both sides, each group hoping that the military struggle would help them secure their tenuous claims to full incorporation into American society. But as the Lincoln administration expanded its war aims to include emancipation and black New Yorkers moved to solidify their precarious presence in the city, there was a quickening tempo of Irish intimidation and assault against black men, women, and children. With the encouragement of proslavery Democrats, the most desperate Irish Catholic poor came to see their interests pitted against the discriminatory draft, the war, and their more desperate black neighbors, who lacked what they believed was the only reliable marker of true American identity: a white skin.

Nevertheless, there was no small irony in the Irish American rioters' hysterical attempts to "purify" their neighborhoods and workplaces of black men through bonfires, lynch murders, and drownings. The lives of the city's poorest African American and Irish American families were intimately bound together. They lived in close proximity, and in many cases depended on each other for material and emotional sustenance. Both groups faced brutalizing racial slurs. The Irish mobs' riot-week campaigns to erase a black presence can only be understood, at the deepest levels of consciousness, as a kind of annihilation of self, intelligible only against the backdrop of panic in the face of the draft, emancipation, and the recent Confederate defeat at Gettysburg.

—Iver Bernstein

ter into opportunity forms the last chapter of the story of black life in Civil War New York City.

It became essential for black New Yorkers to highlight their well-established loyalty to the national government after the draft riots, in contrast to the treasonous Irish mobs and their Democratic sympathizers. After narrating his tale of miraculous rescue, William P. Powell said, "As a devoted loyal Unionist, I have done all I could to perpetuate and uphold the integrity of this free government." Indeed, he was willing to make the ultimate sacrifice—not only his own life, "which I am ready to yield in defense of my country," but also that of his eldest son, who "is now serving . . . as a surgeon in the U.S. army."[64] Indeed, "one reason why we were assailed," the *Anglo-African* observed, "was that we are the staunch friends of the government of the United States. This fact brought the rioters down on us, and hence it was that they who were continually cheering for Jeff. Davis." Blacks accordingly needed to "continue to deserve public sympathy" by upright behavior in "all walks of life" and by a continued exemplary patriotism—particularly through volunteering for the Union Army.[65] The contrast between black loyalty and the Irish rioters' treason was also noticed by no less an authority than President Lincoln, who alluded in a letter to the courage of the black Massachusetts Fifty-Fourth Regiment at Fort Wagner, South Carolina, on July 18: "There will be some black men who can remember that, with silent tongue, and clenched teeth, and steady eye, and well-poised bayonet, they have helped mankind on to this great consummation [of democratic government]; while, I fear, there will be some white ones, unable to forget that, with malignant heart, and deceitful speech, they have strove to hinder it."[66] Indeed, black observers were quick to compare the loyal bravery of the riot victims of New York with that of the black soldiers in the field: "What then shall we say for the negroes of New York?" asked the editors of the *Anglo-African*. "They faced with steady front a foe more terrible than any enemy in the field thundering with artillery."[67] Henry Highland Garnet held a solemn memorial service for the twelve known black "martyrs" of the draft riots at Shiloh Church on September 20, 1863. The honor roll of black martyrs in the struggle against slavery and for the survival of the national government was now expanded to include the men slain in uniform on the battlefields of the South *and* the defenseless men, women, and children who perished in pursuit of life and livelihood on the streets of New York.[68]

But it is crucial to emphasize that black New Yorkers continued to approach this new relationship with the federal government strategically, never forgetting that without guarantees of equal rights and equal protection by the government in the exercise of those rights, Northern victory and even the end of slavery in the South would mean little, and black Northerners would be vulnerable to future assault. In a remarkable speech delivered at Poughkeepsie in late August, James Pennington offered a host of remedies to prevent just such a recurrence: black New Yorkers needed, first, to "study the use of arms, for *self-defense*"; second, to "enter into a solemn free colored *protestant industrial or labor league*" that would claim the right to live, work, act as consumers and occupy public space in the city; third, to apprentice their daughters and sons in "industrial positions"; and fourth, to encourage black men to enter the United States armed forces rather "than have them among our loose population." Combining patriotic motives with those of an expansive black cultural nationalism, Pennington would urge his own sons into the military "for the sake of the strength it will give them, the education they will obtain, the pay they will get; and the good service they will do for God, the country, and the race." "We are performing all such service to the nation-state," Pennington stated emphatically, "with the distinct understanding that WE ARE TO HAVE ALL OUR RIGHTS AS MEN AND AS CITIZENS and, that there are to be no side issues, NO RESERVATIONS, either political, civil or religious."[69]

The enthusiastic enlistment of the city's black men by the hundreds into the ranks of the United States Colored Troops in fall and winter 1863–1864 can be understood only in the context of this strategic reaffirmation of the commitment of black people to the federal government after the draft riots. But the formation of three black New York regiments was also the outgrowth of a crucial political alliance between the black community and the city's Republican elite. Wealthy white Republicans may not have shared Pennington's insistence on full black civil and political rights as a condition of national service, but they did, in their

PRESENTATION OF COLORS TO THE 20TH U. S. COLORED INFANTRY, COL. BARTRAM, AT THE UNION LEAGUE CLUB HOUSE, N. Y., MARCH 5.—PAGE 7

Presentation of the Colors to the 20th Colored Infantry, Col. Bartram, at the Union League Club House, N.Y., March 5. Wood engraving. Published in *Frank Leslie's Illustrated Newspaper*, March 26, 1864.

own way, embrace the ethos of black martyrdom, depicting the city's pious and Protestant black working class as a kind of model loyal poor after the riots, in sharp contrast to a disorderly and treasonous Irish Catholic canaille.[70] Some Republican employers took special pains to hire black men and women now utterly bereft of job and home. Many more provided alms via the Merchants' Committee for the Relief of Colored People Suffering from the Riots in the City of New York, which raised over $40,000, and, through the agency of Henry

Highland Garnet, managed to distribute at least some money to most of the city's ravaged black families.[71] Garnet and other "colored ministers and laymen" presented "An Address" to that committee acknowledging the merchants' "Christian kindness" and especially that of the committee secretary and reform virtuoso Vincent Colyer, fresh from serving as the Army's "Superintendent of the Poor" in North Carolina, where he presided over the distribution of relief and jobs to black freedmen and white refugees.[72] The black ministers noted that in his New York role, Colyer had "on all occasions impressed even the humblest with the belief that he knew and felt that he was dealing with a crushed and heart-broken people."[73] It was no accident that Garnet invited Colyer to speak at the memorial service for martyred black riot victims in September or that Colyer was named by the Union League Club "general superintendent of recruiting."[74] It is impossible to imagine the white Union League Club's successful effort to raise three black regiments in late 1863 and 1864 going forward without mutual trust, part of a rich tradition of interracial alliances that had long characterized black politics in proslavery New York City. The post-riot commitment of white Republicans such as the Union Leaguers to raising black troops provided the political muscle to overcome Governor Seymour's opposition and finally gain Secretary of War Edwin Stanton's authorization for the Twentieth United States Colored Troops Regiment in December 1863. The rapid recruitment of the Twentieth was nothing short of remarkable: some 2,300 men enlisted in less than sixty days.[75]

One result of these efforts, from the perspectives of both the Union League Club and the black community, was the opportunity to collaborate in a grand urban spectacle: the presentation of regimental colors to the Twentieth and parading of the regiment down Broadway en route to debarkation for the front.[76] On the early afternoon of Saturday, March 5, 1864, the black soldiers, high spirited and resplendent in their blue uniforms, white gloves and leggings, ferried over from their camp on Riker's Island to the foot of East Twenty-sixth Street.[77] Almost immediately they were mobbed by white laborers on lunch break—but now police intervened quickly and decisively and order became the all-pervading theme of the day. Before twenty thousand cheering well-wishers in Union Square, Charles King, president of Columbia College (his house was nearly torched by the draft rioters) assured the men of the Twentieth that their families would be protected in their absence.[78] The highlight was the appearance of the "Mothers, Wives and Sisters of the members of the New York Union League Club" to present the black soldiers with a stand of colors, followed by a mammoth procession down Broadway that included the white Union Leaguers, the "Colored Clergymen of New York and Brooklyn," the "Sons of Freedom," and "Colored Citizens numbering about twelve hundred." The black community "made the event a sort of holiday"; the attendance of a "galaxy of black women" was considered especially significant. From the African American perspective, the symbolism of the spectacle was riveting: a massive turnout of blacks (well over a third of the city's black population) and sympathetic whites on New York's main thoroughfares to honor a black regiment went a long way toward redeeming the city from the draft rioters' anti-black purges. "A Partial Atonement for the Outrages of July" ran one headline.[79] For blacks, Superintendent of Police John Kennedy's appearance at the head of the parade—the very official who in 1861 had broken up a black recruitment meeting—was not the least of the day's vindications.[80]

"A pretty fair start for miscegenation" was the *Herald*'s contemptuous dismissal of the whole affair, taking an event the Union League Club and the black community understood in terms of elevated patriotism and interpreting it instead in sexual terms—as a "promiscuous" mixing of the black male soldiers and the white wives of the Union Leaguers.[81] The word "miscegenation" had gained currency in winter 1864 as a result of a pamphlet published the previous December under the title *Miscegenation: The Theory of the Blending of the Races, Applied to the American White Man and Negro* and later revealed to be the handiwork of proslavery Democratic journalists David Goodman Croly and George Wakeman.[82] The booklet, an elaborate production studded with references to science and history alongside quotations from Emerson and Shakespeare, appeared to have all the markings of a serious if half-baked abolitionist proposal to solve the American issue of race through the sexual union of whites and blacks. In fact it was a political trap set by anti-Lincoln forces, sent gratis to well-known black

Kimmel & Forster, *The Miscegenation Ball*, 1864.
Hand-colored lithograph.

Sex, Race, and Power in the City

In the era of slavery in the United States, prominent New York proslavery Democrats found much political advantage in publicly discussing black sexuality, and especially the matter of interracial sex. Though no explicit deal was ever struck between Southern planters and their New York City allies, it is not hard to see that slave owners would have had difficulty speaking about the matter of sex between whites and blacks without exposing the frequent sexual abuse of slave women. The New York press had no such difficulty, and it harped on the matter of black sexuality, particularly during moments of perceived political threat to the Southern slavery regime. In 1834, the year after the passage of the British Emancipation Act and the founding of the American Anti-Slavery Society (AASS), the New York press relentlessly associated abolition with racial amalgamation and set the stage for three days of rioting, wherein white New Yorkers assaulted blacks in what was the city's largest race riot prior to the Civil War. Sixteen years later, in May 1850, during the debates over the future of the Union, *New York Herald* editor James Gordon Bennett provoked a spasm of anxiety among the city's white Democratic masses when he portrayed the annual meeting of the AASS as an occasion for sex between whites and blacks. And, of course, the specter raised by the city's Democratic press on the eve of the draft riots—of hordes of brutalized black freedmen sweeping North to steal jobs and ravish white women—was another instance of white New Yorkers performing the work of sexual policing and rabble-rousing for the slavery regime at a moment after the Emancipation Proclamation when its political fortunes appeared to hang in the balance.

—*Iver Bernstein*

and white abolitionists with letters inviting endorsements. The hope was that once such leading Lincoln supporters had gone on record in favor of racial amalgamation, they could be tarred as "miscegenationists" in the coming presidential campaign, subverting Lincoln's re-election effort.[83]

Croly and Wakeman's *Miscegenation* scare fit a classic script: New York Democrats trumpeting the issue of interracial sex to bolster the political fortunes of the Southern slavery regime at a moment of perceived crisis. But now the story had a new twist. In 1864 the Confederacy was on the military defensive and slavery was a dying (though hardly dead) institution. Black and white New Yorkers alike were looking to the future. As one correspondent to the *Anglo-African* put it in February 1864, "The question of Race in the United States will come up for settlement at the close of the war."[84] White Democrats were jockeying to define racial caste in an America without slavery, and New York's blacks were right there contesting those definitions. For a generation, black New Yorkers had ceded public discussion of the matter of interracial sex to the Bennetts and the Rynders, but now black writers were debating *Miscegenation* in the pages of the *Anglo-African*. The shift spoke to a heightened black political confidence during the last year and a half of the war.[85]

Indeed, the miscegenation cry was an attempt to undermine a new repertoire of interracial initiatives in New York City during 1864–1865. "Somewhere a gear shifted in the universe," it could be said, when Mrs. Ellen Anderson decided to resist a conductor's order to leave the white car of the Eighth Avenue Railroad on Friday, June 17, 1864.[86] She had learned only days before that her thirty-nine-year-old husband, Sergeant William Anderson of the Twenty-Sixth Colored Regiment, had died in service to his country. "I said I was sick and wished to ride up home," she later testified. "I said I had lost my husband in the war." When the conductor summoned a policeman, Anderson insisted she "had a right to ride anywhere when I paid my fare," and repeated, "I . . . lost my husband in the war," to underscore that all-important fact. The officer was unmoved, she said, "He did not care for me, or my husband either," and then tried to drag her out. Anderson—ill, exhausted, still in her bereavement— grabbed hold of the straps and hung on for all she was worth. It took the strength of the two men to yank her out of the car, and not before a crowd of witnesses had gathered.[87]

Mrs. Anderson's case drew wide attention both in and outside the black community and revealed much about the inner workings of black politics and the alliances that made blacks' late-war political mobilization possible. The Andersons were pillars of black New York: William had been a member of the Union Church, a teacher in the Sabbath School, president of the Hannibal Benevolent and Literary Society ("amongst the first to send aid to the freedmen in South Carolina"), and a member of another aid society, the H.H. Garnet Tabernacle, No. 1, of Love and Charity. Ellen was "engaged in most of the benevolent and useful societies to which he belonged," but one of her most important connections was to Peter S. Porter, who had mentored her as a "Sabbath-school scholar of his and [one-time] member of his household." Porter was a legally and politically sophisticated black activist who had been instrumental in the desegregation of the streetcars before July 1863, but the Eighth Avenue and other railroad companies used the draft riots as a pretext for again excluding blacks. By spring 1864, a black boycott of the Eighth Avenue line had forced it to allow blacks to ride in every fourth car, and there the matter stood before Ellen Anderson took her stand.[88] From Peter Porter, Ellen Anderson "learned that she had rights that railroad employees and policemen were bound to respect and, consequently, [she] resisted their invasion."[89]

Ellen Anderson's legal and political savvy also extended to relationships with sympathetic whites. She immediately enlisted as counsel William Curtis Noyes, who agreed to represent her gratis, as he had the black draft riot victims.[90] Indeed, the whole post–draft riot phalanx swung into action—the Union League Club, Commissioner of Police Thomas C. Acton, and the Merchants' Relief Committee lobbied for the lifting of the whites-only rule on the Eighth Avenue line.[91] Mrs. Anderson won her lawsuit against the railroad company in late June and by July, all the streetcars in New York City were open to blacks. The *Anglo-African* printed instructions to all black riders in case of ejection—identify the offending conductor and any nearby police, offer no provocation so as to avoid a "disturbing the peace" charge, and then "report the case to the well-known philanthropist, Vincent Colyer, Esq., . . . fully substantiated."[92] The Anderson case brought together the sacrifice of blacks at home (and particularly the desperation of the many black women left to support themselves and families when male breadwinners departed for the front) *and* the martyrdom of black men on the battlefield in ways that were hugely compelling for black New Yorkers *and* their white Republican allies. The miscegenation charge that proslavery whites leveled in 1864 was an effort to thwart these new political marriages and the creative assertions of black citizenship that informed them, to undermine the political force of black-white collaboration by sexualizing and subsuming it into the always tantalizing and toxic fiction of black men invading the homes of white patriarchs to rape white women.

It is crucial to note that the war and the creation of the United States Colored Troops had attached special value to the patriotic sacrifice of black *men*. That Ellen Anderson, a poor African American widow, made her own sufferings on the home front the basis for a successful reclaiming of rights and city space suggested the opening of new possibilities for black New Yorkers in the wake of the devastating draft riots.[93]

Unfortunately, black New Yorkers' prospects remained all too tenuous. The slavery-era problems of population dispersal, rigid exclusion from all-white trades, and vulnerability to white intimidation and assault persisted even as Congress's passage of the Thirteenth Amendment and the now inexorable march of Grant's and Sherman's armies in winter 1865 spelled the death of chattel bondage in the South.[94]

That winter, the mood in the city's black precincts was nonetheless upbeat. A "Great National Demonstration" showcasing the full panoply of African American organizations in the city, benefiting wounded soldiers and the freed people, and celebrating the anniversary of the abolition of slavery in the District of Columbia was scheduled for mid-April. Wounded black soldiers and a galaxy of antislavery celebrities would be part of a festival of oratory at the Cooper Institute. A grand parade would circle through the city (including some of the draft riot districts) and end at City Hall. The *Anglo-African* took great pains to explain why the procession was so crucial: "Many years have elapsed since our people turned out in force, and the result has been that the Nation does not know our capacity to organize. They doubt that capacity because while other people *show themselves*, we are unseen, except in small numbers."[95]

This profound desire for visibility—for a display of black nationality in service to American nationality—was realized on Lincoln's Birthday, February 12, 1865, when Henry Highland Garnet spoke before the House of Representatives, the first black person to address Congress. The previous June, Garnet had moved to Washington to accept the ministry of the Fifteenth Street Presbyterian Church, live near his daughter, and work more directly on freedmen's relief. But he also wished to be close to the South, which, he sensed, would become the new "grand center of negro nationality" in the postwar era.[96] With floor and galleries overflowing with black and white dignitaries, Garnet did not disappoint. Anticipating the themes of Lincoln's Second Inaugural Address, he depicted the ferocious destruction of the war as part of a divine judgment: "We have paid some of the fearful installments, but there are other heavy obligations to be met." The "safety and perpetuity of our Republic," Garnet emphasized, would depend not only on the "total and complete destruction of this accursed sin" of slavery, but also on the finishing of God's work, which would include both equal citizenship and especially equal suffrage.[97] Voting rights were at the forefront of black New Yorkers' concerns in 1864 and 1865. The 144 blacks from eighteen states who convened a "National Convention of Colored Citizens of the United States" in Syracuse, New York, in October 1864 formed a "National Equal Rights League" that made equal suffrage its absolute priority. "Every colored man wants his voice at the polls," wrote a black reporter of the sentiment in New York City's black districts.[98]

Certainly the presence of Abraham Lincoln in the White House was one of Garnet's and other black New Yorkers' assurances that the liberation of African Americans and their full incorporation into the American nation-state was part of the divine plan at this moment in history. It was Lincoln who had asked Garnet to deliver the sermon before Congress to commemorate congressional passage of the amendment to abolish slavery. Black New Yorkers had come out strong for Lincoln in the election of 1864. "You and we may have thought that

Mr. Lincoln has not done what *we think* he could have done for the overthrow of oppression in our land; *but that is not the question now*," exhorted *Anglo-African* editor Robert Hamilton. "If you are a friend of liberty, you will give your influence and cast your vote for Abraham Lincoln, who, under God, is the only hope of the oppressed."[99] That respectable blacks were excluded from railway cars in New York, that black children were barred from ward schools, that some churches insisted on "negro pews," said William Howard Day, was not Lincoln's fault, but that of the white Northerners "whose agent he is."[100]

Like all Northerners, black New Yorkers were overwhelmed with shock and grief when they learned of Lincoln's assassination and death on April 14 and 15, 1865. The cataclysmic event swept away all before it; blacks' "Great National Demonstration" scheduled for April 18 was postponed indefinitely. Now the urgent concern was to be part of the funeral procession, as a train bearing the martyred president's bier wound its way through the major cities of the North en route to a final resting place in Springfield, Illinois, with elaborate ceremonies at each stop. This funeral journey became a ritual of the most profound political significance—it was not only a highly personal outpouring of grief for a leader who had assumed Christ-like proportions in the popular imagination but, indeed, also a symbolic constituting of the post–Civil War American nation for the estimated seven million who lined the tracks, solemnly marched with the cortege, filed by the body as it lay in state, or merely looked on.[101]

Three committees representing New York's black community petitioned to be included in the April 25 cortege that would usher Lincoln's body through their city: had not blacks been part of the pageant in Washington, Baltimore, and Philadelphia?[102] The response of the city's Democratic-led Common Council was firm: there were to be "positively no black people in our procession." A Chamber of Commerce committee supervising arrangements feared antagonizing the ruling powers on the council and similarly rejected all black requests.[103] The humiliation of these rebuffs can hardly be underestimated: it was as if the draft rioters' purges of blacks from the city's public spaces were being given official sanction. "Was Mr. Lincoln the President of the Irish only?" asked

James Pennington. "Of all other classes, was he not emphatically the President of the colored man? . . . The spirit that would exclude colored men from the President's funeral is the same that murdered him."[104] The Union Leaguers lobbied for inclusion, citing the insult to New York's proud black regiments, but to no avail.[105] It took a mandate from the War Department to force admittance of a black contingent at the rear, so far back that the coffin was on its way to Albany by the time the blacks fell in line.[106]

What was James Pennington thinking as he stood at the head of two hundred or so African American New Yorkers at the tail of that funeral procession?[107] We know that he believed it crucial that blacks march: "Colored men have a right in the funeral procession of a President of these United States," he wrote days later.[108] But he also conceded that he had at first opposed participating,[109] and it is not hard to imagine why—the Common Council's injustices, the undignified position at the rear, and the inevitable meager turnout—given all the controversy.[110] It was a bittersweet moment, mixing pride, rage, and an ineradicable sense of vulnerability that seemed the black New Yorker's lot.

An assessment of the prospects of black life in New York during the Civil War must end on a note of profound ambivalence. We can further wonder whether, standing in Lincoln's funeral procession, Pennington allowed his mind to wander back to the days of mid to late July 1863, when he sought so desperately to find his family and come home—to have a home. Did black New Yorkers, who on the eve of the war contemplated all kinds of plans for creating a home, in and outside of the United States, find one either in New York or in America? Clearly, against all odds, they had made a home for themselves in the victorious Northern nation and cemented it with their blood sacrifice on Southern battlefields and the streets of their city.[111] Whether their still-precarious life in New York City would become proud *and* powerful in the ways they so fervently sought was far from certain.

Chapter 11

RE-CREATING BLACK NEW YORK AT CENTURY'S END

———————◆———————

MARCY S. SACKS

Portrait of T. Thomas Fortune.

EARLY IN THE TWENTIETH CENTURY, Samuel R. Scottron, a longtime black Brooklynite, reflected nostalgically on an imagined community of black New Yorkers from an earlier era. In Scottron's mind, these entrepreneurs successfully forged economic opportunities for themselves and consequently enjoyed acceptance by whites. The "ancient colored New Yorker," lauded the elderly member of the Brooklyn Board of Education, "didn't wait for someone to hire him, he went at it alone and made a place for himself." His remarks came as race relations in the city were experiencing a precipitous decline. In the decades following the Civil War, as Northern whites sought reconciliation with their Southern counterparts, they renounced the project of black civic equality (to which they had never wholeheartedly committed), and created a new racism rooted in nascent myths of the Old South. In popular culture and intellectual circles, white New Yorkers enthusiastically embraced the "Lost Cause" and reinforced myriad visions of black inferiority.

Scottron and others of his generation sought explanations and a way to forestall this decline in race relations. Finding few plausible alternatives, they blamed the growing wave of Southern black migrants to New York City for the worsening racial climate. To combat the effects of white racism on their own social status, the old-time elite pursued a public strategy of high-

327

RE-CREATING
BLACK
NEW YORK AT
CENTURY'S
END

lighting their own similarity to middle-class whites and simultaneously distinguishing themselves from former slaves. By doing so, they hoped to divert white antipathy toward those black people who failed to conform to mainstream behavioral norms. Though privately many of the black elite continued their decades-old tradition of aiding in the uplift of the neediest among the race, the public celebration of the "old time aristocracy bearing Knickerbocker names" implicitly suggested that the Southern newcomers who had not achieved similar financial successes experienced failures of their own making. Worse still, in the perception of many Negroes of "the old Knickerbocker stamp," the black newcomers who brought with them the "taint of slavery" instigated the disturbing trend toward a marked increase of interracial tension in the city.[1]

Scottron's and other "Old Settlers'" denunciation of Southern black migrants exposed an emerging fissure within New York's black population, created by the impact of white racism. During the antebellum era, black New Yorkers had unstintingly and openly expressed their solidarity with Southern slaves, regularly employing a rhetoric of brotherhood and fighting relentlessly for abolition in no small part because they recognized an incontrovertible relationship between their own status and the existence of racial slavery. This continued to hold true in the immediate aftermath of the Civil War. Northern black men and women struggled to better the lives of the freed people, both out of a feeling of fraternity with them and because they believed that the elevation of the former slaves would provide a corresponding improvement in their own civic condition. Abolition marked only one step on the path toward their ultimate goal of full equality. They had long believed that the major impediment to that objective had been slavery. But the institution's destruction quickly revealed the fallacy of that assumption. White racism proved more intractable than previously imagined. Whites' intransigence on issues of race and the eventual retrenchment of blacks' civic progress bred tensions between black Knickerbockers and Southern migrants. Some black New Yorkers came to view the end of slavery and even the former slaves themselves as obstacles to their own progress toward full acceptance as citizens.

SLAVERY IN

NEW YORK

The years immediately following the Civil War marked a period of genuine optimism for black people nationwide, not least in New York City. New York's black population rejoiced in President Abraham Lincoln's issuance of the Emancipation Proclamation, the triumphal and feted return of the Twentieth United States Colored Regiment to New York City in 1864, and the ratification of the Thirteenth Amendment finally ending slavery.[2] But even as they celebrated political advancements, harbingers of new conflicts became apparent. White Northerners, even latter-day allies in the abolitionist cause, grew tired of the "Negro problem" almost as soon as the Civil War ended. E. L. Godkin expressed as much in the first issue of his magazine, *Nation*, published on July 6, 1865. "[E]verybody is heartily tired of discussing [the Negro's] condition, and his rights," Godkin wrote.[3] During the antebellum era, white opponents of slavery fought to destroy chattel bondage primarily because they believed in its inherent immorality. Few expressed a genuine commitment to racial equality. With slavery's destruction, many abolitionists declared victory and moved on to tackle other social concerns. And while Republicans initially hailed the freed people as paragons of industriousness and productivity, that perception soured over the Reconstruction years with Southern blacks' persistent pleas for governmental protection. As the age of Social Darwinism dawned, the demand for perceived "special favors" suggested that black people had failed to absorb the American value of individualism. Worse still, it implied that black people were indolent, marking them, collectively, as poor candidates for the privileges of citizenship.[4]

By the last days of Reconstruction in 1877, white New Yorkers had lost any feelings of munificence they might have once exhibited toward the black residents of the city. Although legal barriers to equality had collapsed, racial antipathy was visibly mounting. The flurry of civil rights legislation passed in the late 1860s and 1870s gave way to efforts at social and political rapprochement with white Southerners by the late 1870s and 1880s. Eager to reunite with their former enemies, Yankees began imbibing in—and indeed fostering—a popular culture that elevated the Old South to mythical status. New Yorkers who not long since had scorned plantation life as languid, violent, and incom-

Thomas Nast cartoon from *Harper's Weekly*, September 5, 1868. NEW-YORK HISTORICAL SOCIETY LIBRARY

patible with the industrializing economy emerging in the North suddenly began to lament its passing.[5] On Broadway and Tin Pan Alley, in the workplace, saloons, and tenements, and in the city's police stations and courtrooms, white New Yorkers followed the lead of their Southern compatriots in disparaging the viability of black freedom and equality.

New Yorkers' empathy for Southerners could be measured against the growth of the city's black population. The 1863 draft riots precipitated a sharp decline in the number of black residents in the city. But a reversal of this trend became apparent by the 1870s, realizing whites' fears of a black "invasion" expressed even before the war's end.[6] In that decade, the black population increased at double the rate of the white population.[7] The collapse of Reconstruction helped to trigger a further escalation in the number of Southern black people seeking friendlier environs in the North. "One who looks Southward can almost see the army of Negroes gathering from out of the cities, villages, and farms," wrote the journalist Ray Stannard Baker, "bringing nothing with them but a buoyant hope in a distant freedom, but tramping always Northward." The *New York Times* hyperbolically warned its readers in 1892 that the "great exodus" would have a profound impact on race relations. "The result will be that the South will have solved what the Yankees call its negro problem in a very simple though unexpected way . . . by sending enough of its negroes to the North so that both halves of the country will be in the same boat."[8] In 1865 the black population of Manhattan and Brooklyn totaled fewer than fifteen thousand. By the turn of the twentieth century it had soared to over sixty thousand, more than half of whom hailed from the old Confederacy.[9]

Mounting white concern about the "wholesale exodus of the Negro from the South" became increasingly virulent as the numbers swelled. Yankees' "prevailing dread of an overwhelming influx" propelled them to the forefront of a philanthropic effort to aid black people—*Southern* black people. In 1868, Samuel Chapman Armstrong founded Hampton Institute in Virginia, the first markedly successful industrial education program for former slaves. Like other white Northern missionaries in the South, Armstrong brought a conservative racial bias to his reform efforts, emphasizing the value of industrial education to combat the "shiftlessness, extravagance, and immorality" of "dependent" black people. He held a deep conviction that freedmen and women were "slothful, backward, lascivious, and inferior" and needed skills and training in order to become productive members of an industrial society. Armstrong's call for black people to remain in the rural South with their "best friends," Southern whites, held special attraction for Yankees.[10] In the same year that Armstrong founded Hampton, New York's African Mission School Association publicized its "repeated disappointments" in raising the necessary funds to purchase a building in the city and hoped to "enlist the sympathies" of "Christian minds" toward that end. Black social activist William Pickens contemptuously noted the hypocrisy, reproaching "the good white inhabitants of our Northern cities" for having "so much sympathy for the handicapped Negro that they cannot bear to live near him. They think he is all right at a great distance; and if he will only remain in the South they will strenuously advocate his freedom and equality through their magazines and missionary publications."[11]

At home, the migration resulted in a hardening of racial divisions between white and black. White churches that had previously welcomed black members began urging them to seek religious ministrations elsewhere. Hotels, restaurants, theaters, and bars refused to serve black patrons. Service organizations such as the YMCA organized segregated branches rather than permit white and black patrons to share facilities. Hoping to prevent other humiliating defeats like the one that occurred when the boxer Jack Johnson became heavyweight champion in 1908, the New York State Boxing Association prohibited matches between whites and blacks. And though it was unsuccessful, the New York legislature in 1910 attempted to ban interracial marriages and void any already in existence in the state.[12]

The evolution of white New Yorkers' attitudes toward their black neighbors and the reassertion of white unity on Southern terms became apparent in New York City's diverse cultural venues. Theatrical productions and songs promoted white New Yorkers' reinterpretation of the "race problem," largely through a revisionist reconsideration of the Old South. The images on stage and in song led to a new respect for a place and culture formerly excoriated. By the 1880s, Civil War plays had become the rage in New York's theaters. This new genre of drama helped to soften sectional divisions by evoking sympathy and admiration for the Confederacy and those who had laid down their lives to preserve it. The productions invariably presented an idyllic image of the Old South that romanticized the genteel manners, chivalry, and charm of the planter class. The turmoil and calamity of war were compounded by the often-doomed romance between a dashing Union officer and a beautiful Southern belle, unable to consummate their true love while their societies violently collided around them. Northern white audiences discovered to their dismay that the war had been a mistake after all, a tragedy that had created an artificial rift between people who had no reason to be divided. Productions such as Bronson Howard's *Shenandoah* and David Belasco's *The Heart of Maryland*, both performed on Broadway and taken on national tour after long and successful runs in New York City, helped erase Northerners' already dim recollection of the insidious slave power and fiendish slaveholders like Simon Legree. Yankees embraced the glorious memories of a fictive Old South. As one theater critic observed, at the close of each show "there was as much love, and more tears, for the Gray as for the Blue." By the final decades of the nineteenth century, the Myth of the Lost Cause had gained wholesale credence in the white Yankee heart.[13]

The fictive "old darkey" became an integral part of white New Yorkers' new sympathy for the Old South. Minstrel shows of antebellum origins continued to portray subordinate slaves on large Southern plantations. Blacks were represented in rural scenes as tattered but simple and untroubled, often playing the banjo and eating watermelon. They were vulnerable to mistreatment and needed protection against their natural indolence. The plantation legend reflected many whites' sentimental desire that blacks continue to behave as the good-natured, humble creatures that they supposedly had been during slavery days. But minstrel shows also adapted to the events of the post–Civil War era. With characteristic hyperbole, they portrayed hapless black people devastated by the responsibilities foisted upon them with the procurement of freedom. Aged ex-slaves, searching desperately for their former masters, returned home only to find that the plantation had been destroyed during the war. The "loyal darkey" yearned for a return to the carefree, secure, and contented days of slavery.[14]

Although slavery had existed in New York City into the first quarter of the nineteenth century, the "passing breed" of ideal servants came to be explicitly associated with the Southern slave institution. "All this genuine old time southern atmosphere seems to have disappeared from the colored race as we now know it in New York," a student of New York's social scene noted regretfully at the turn of the century. The tendency to associate the South with the cultivation of "proper" black behavior contributed to the growing popularity of plantation melodies among white Northern audiences. Traveling troupes of singers from the Hampton Institute, entertaining Yankees with spirituals and nostalgic visits to antebellum America, found themselves in increasing demand with the passing years. Troupes from Hampton and elsewhere in the South helped solidify Yankees' appreciation of the Old South and confirmed the audience's perceptions that Southern black people were more docile, tractable, and safe than their urban brethren.[15]

White New Yorkers argued that the city itself, where black men and women could live free of whites' oversight, destroyed the desirable qualities of a black servant. Absent the civilizing influence of white masters, blacks reverted to their "natural" savagery. New York City's police commissioner, William McAdoo, warned of the havoc wrought by this transformation. Though he characterized Southern black migrants to the city as "decent colored people," their behavior inevitably changed soon after arrival, influenced by the urban "coons" who "never work, and . . . go heavily armed, generally carrying, in addition to the indispensable revolver, a razor." McAdoo explained that "one of these

333

RE-CREATING
BLACK
NEW YORK AT
CENTURY'S
END

[coons] will get hold" of the newcomer, "and not only will he rob him, but before he is through with him he will probably make him as bad as himself." In the liberal urban environment, free from white control or rigid discipline, even honest members of the race would soon succumb to their basest natural instincts.[16]

The categorization of black New Yorkers as dangerous, violent, and menacing represented a dramatic shift from earlier views. Though they had long been convinced of blacks' inferiority, Yankees had not previously seen black people as a physical threat to whites' welfare. Indeed, shortly after the Civil War, the *New York Times* ridiculed Southern whites for their abrupt revision of black stereotypes in order to justify the implementation of restrictive new laws. In a contemptuous editorial, the newspaper remarked sarcastically on the "sudden and astonishing ethnological change" that had transformed the emancipated Negro from the "meek sufferer under slavery, the Uncle Tom of the plantation, the mild and uncomplaining victim of oppression," into "a ferocious and bloodthirsty ruffian."[17] But by the waning years of the nineteenth century, white New Yorkers had come to accept Southerners' claims that black people posed both a physical and moral threat to whites.

The acquiescence to Southern assertions represented a devastating unification of white racial attitudes. Northern whites had at last joined their Southern brethren in their views of black Americans. The coherence of black stereotypes, embodied in the literature, art, music, and theater of the time, encompassed a range of racist perceptions that laid both the intellectual and emotional foundation for the conviction that blacks were biologically inferior, disorderly, emotional rather than rational, and most importantly, unassimilable. The evolution of the attitudes of New York Presbyterian minister and anti-vice crusader Charles H. Parkhurst was representative of the transformation occurring throughout white New York. Though he had once supported antilynching campaigns, by the early twentieth century Parkhurst expressed a change of heart. "[N]iggers . . . (because that is what they call themselves)" were unqualified for citizenship, he declared, and "they never, never, never will contribute, in any part, toward forming the national type of the Americans of the future." Physical and biological differences proved that blacks could not be integrated into American society. Worse, the racial distinctions suggested something sinister and dangerous. "They grow blacker and blacker every day," Parkhurst avowed. "Their color forms a physical barrier, which even time, the great leveler, cannot sweep away."[18]

As a herald of this trend, renowned lithographers Currier and Ives—remembered today for their romanticized depictions of rural, bucolic America—published a collection of prints during the last two decades of the nineteenth century entitled the *Darktown Comics*. Boasting nearly two hundred lithographs drawn in the minstrel tradition, this series portrayed a fictive community in which "indescribably funny" black men and women, free from all white influence, grappled farcically with the challenges of everyday life. Characteristic scenes of "our colored friends" included images of their ludicrous attempts to engage in fashionable activities such as fox hunts and horse racing, only to blunder at every turn. Hapless jockeys fell from scrawny horses (or even mules!) and ever-present liquor undermined blacks' pretensions to sobriety.[19] The most exten-

Darktown Fire Brigade: The Chief on Duty, 1885. Lithograph. Published by Currier & Ives, New York.

sive subset of the *Darktown Comics* drew on themes long celebrated by Currier and Ives. "To my mind," recalled Henry Collins Brown, a longtime New York socialite, "the series entitled 'The Darktown Fire Brigade' were the most laughable things I had ever seen." These lithographs were a barbed counterpoint to the heroic images of white fire laddies that Currier and Ives produced earlier in the century. The comics achieved wild popularity among contemporary white audiences.[20]

The evolution of white Northerners' opinions and their dehumanization of black people allowed Yankees to support Southern racial policies of terrorism, brutality, and subjugation, and to commit their own acts of violence against their black neighbors with increasing impunity. Interracial conflicts became increasingly frequent in New York City's neighborhoods in the latter decades of the nineteenth century. Journalist Jacob Riis chronicled the "hostile camps" of blacks and European immigrants fighting each other on crowded streets. Rosanna Weston experienced some of the tough times. "They used to go out . . . with bats and things," she recalled. "The Irish would call 'em bad names, niggers and everything like that, and they'd be out there fightin'."[21] San Juan Hill in midtown Manhattan became one of the most contested neighborhoods in the city. According to New York lore, San Juan Hill received its name not to honor the famous battle of the Spanish-American War but to satirize the constant clashes that erupted there between black and white residents.[22] The New York Central Railroad's open tracks, "which maimed black and white impartially," offered neutral ground between blacks in San Juan Hill and "white enemies" to the west. Anna Murphy, a black woman, described the uneasy game played out on the Hill's streets. "The Irish kids wouldn't let the black kids cross St. Nicholas to go into the park and sleigh-ride," Murphy recalled. The conflicts became part of neighborhood culture. "One Saturday the Irish would run, and the next Saturday the blacks would run across that street. It was almost a ritual." Rosanna Weston's parents warned her away from the Irish side of the street. "That was forbidden territory. You weren't supposed to go over there. They used to come over on this side and they would fight."[23]

Major race riots erupted in New York City in 1900 and 1905, the first since the horrific violence of 1863. A stunned and repulsed white elite responded to the 1863 violence by raising tens of thousands of dollars "for the Relief of Colored Sufferers," and by supporting the black community against the "outrages of the mob." Their responses to subsequent upheavals, however, differed dramatically.[24] Although the *New York Times* provided extensive coverage of the three days of fighting in the summer of 1900, in the riot's aftermath no black person received official redress for flagrant police brutality and no committees were formed by white elites to mitigate any long-term suffering resulting from the violence.[25] Five years later, widespread violence against the city's black residents generated an even more tepid reaction from white elites. When a riot ensued after a street scuffle between a white and a black man, policemen quickly joined the fracas, clubbing any black person they could find.[26]

Police Commissioner McAdoo immediately responded to the 1905 outbreak by ordering the black population to disarm. White New Yorkers received no equivalent injunction. While the city's black residents clamored for an investigation, Commissioner McAdoo left for his vacation home after admonishing all black people to "deposit their revolvers, blackjacks, and razors" with the police. He also issued a statement assuring "the lawless colored element of the Twenty-Sixth Precinct" that he would make no "change of policy . . . with regard to dealing with them." The precinct captain received official permission to enforce the law "fearlessly" and to "suppress promptly any disorder in that section." And the *New York Times*, which had aggressively covered the 1900 riot, buried its few articles on the 1905 disturbance deep within the paper. White New Yorkers had become desensitized to and more accepting of violence against black people.[27]

New York's "old time [black] aristocracy" witnessed the deterioration of race relations with horror as they felt their own tenuous social position in the city slipping away. Decades of casting their lot with the slaves and freed people had yielded little success in enhancing the condition of black people as a whole. Indeed, what progress had been achieved seemed to be disappearing. As a result, the black elite in New York now shifted strategies, hoping to at least garner whites' forbearance for themselves by publicly distinguishing black Knickerbockers from the newcomers to the city. They openly blamed the "epidemic of negrophobia" on Southern migrants. Longtime black residents rained epithets upon the recent migrants, referring to them as "scum," "illiterate," "criminals," "loafers," "thoughtless," "lazy," "overdemonstrative," "undesirable," and "riff-raff." When a black man shot "promiscuously" into a crowd of people disembarking from a ferry boat at New York's dock, the city's black newspaper, the *New York Age*, pointedly noted that the man was a recent migrant from South Carolina, not a native New Yorker.[28] Southern migrants "make it hard for us wherever they light," complained a black Northerner. "The well-meaning, industrious, progressive Negroes, as a rule, remain in the South to fight out the question there. The lazy, shiftless, worthless class come [sic] to northern cities to reduce our opportunities and privileges to a minimum."[29] Like the most ardent social Darwinists of his day, Samuel Scottron proclaimed that the city would either civilize the crass and unsophisticated behavior of the black migrants from the South or, he cautioned, they would die out.[30]

Blaming the transplanted Southerners for the "spread of race antipathy in the North," the black elite hoped to forestall the "stream of young negro life" from coming to New York. "Oh, is there no way to keep these people from rushing away from the small villages and country districts of the South up to the cities, where they cannot battle with the terrible force of a strange and unusual environment?" lamented Paul Laurence Dunbar in his cautionary novel about the migration experience, *Sport of the Gods*. "Is there no way to prove to them that woolen-shirted, brown-jeaned simplicity is infinitely better than broadclothed degradation?"[31] Like whites who preferred that blacks remain in the South, black elites also disingenuously advocated the "free, independent, clean and wholesome life . . . which is possible anywhere in the South" over the "huge dilapidated tenements" in Northern cities. The *New York Age* made a special appeal to blacks looking for better economic opportunities in the North. It is "a sad mistake," the editor, T. Thomas Fortune—ironically himself a migrant—admonished in 1891, to think that New York "is simply a paradise where employment of all kinds can be had for the asking." He assured the dubious that only menial jobs could be acquired, and not easily at that. Many found themselves living in abject poverty. "New York is a good place to shun," the editorial warned, "unless you have plenty of money or a position secured before coming here."[32]

T. Thomas Fortune

Born in 1856 in Marianna, Florida, a slave of mixed African American, Irish, and Native American ancestry, Timothy Thomas Fortune grew to become one of the nation's most influential black newspaper editors and political thinkers of the late nineteenth century. After Southern emancipation, his family relocated to Jacksonville where Fortune gained his first experience in the newspaper industry, working as a typesetter for a local publication. At age eighteen, he enrolled at Howard University, though financial troubles forced him to abandon his studies after just one year.

After marrying and spending a handful of years working at various newspapers back home in Jacksonville, Fortune migrated to New York City in 1880. He spent the next quarter of a century as the editor of the city's black weekly newspaper, the *New York Globe* (which subsequently changed its name to the *Freeman* and later the *New York Age*). In that capacity, he began to espouse publicly his political views. Disaffected with the Republican Party, Fortune broke with mainstream black political thought and counseled political independence. He charged Republicans with hypocrisy and ingratitude toward black voters who had been loyal to the party, and announced the motto, "Race first, then party."

Fortune's views became increasingly radical as race relations in the country deteriorated. In 1890, he founded the Afro-American League, which promoted racial self-help and solidarity. Under Fortune's leadership, for two decades the Afro-American League stridently defended agitation, and even revolution if necessary, in the fight for racial equality and economic opportunity. In 1923, Fortune became the editor of Marcus Garvey's *Negro World*, the official organ of the Universal Negro Improvement Association. He served in that capacity until his death in 1928.

—*Marcy S. Sacks*

The caveats issued by longtime black New Yorkers were not intended to protect prospective migrants from hardship. To the contrary, they were grounded in concern about how the newcomers' behavior cast aspersions upon their own character. Black Knickerbockers, therefore, simultaneously warned Southerners away and dissociated themselves from those who came regardless. "There has been of late a remarkable increase of crimes against person and property by Afro-Americans," complained T. Thomas Fortune, due primarily to "the large increase in the Afro-American population, among which there necessarily would be some bad characters[.]" While Fortune laid some blame at the feet of white employers unwilling to hire black workers, he saved the harshest rebuke for the migrants "who come into greater New York with the hope to better their condition only to find that they have jumped out of the frying pan into the fire." Their behavior upon arrival "is to be deplored, as sentiment toward the entire Afro-American population is being affected for the worse," Fortune reproved.[33]

The denunciations made by New York's black elite echoed whites' escalating conviction that the former slaves had failed to make an effective transition to freedom, relying on government largesse rather than absorbing middle-class values of hard work and independence. Hoping to salvage their own upward mobility, many black New Yorkers, especially the elites who felt their position most acutely threatened, chose to distinguish themselves publicly from the Southern blacks whom they had long supported. Black elites deliberately highlighted their history of accomplishment—achieved, they stressed, without gratuitous handouts. They emphasized their desire for continued "fair treatment" in order to take advantage of the city's economic opportunities. In contrast with the Southern freed people, who faced increasing criticism for appearing to expect the government to provide for them, New Yorkers "ask[ed] no more" than the elimination of barriers, after which they intended to "demonstrate our right to proper recognition."[34] By articulating their aspirations in this way, longtime black New Yorkers offered a subtle, but critically important, alternative paradigm to race as a marker of group behavior. In opposition to those who "typed" people by race, black New Yorkers proposed a substitute for measuring a group's civic acceptability, suggesting that a heritage of slavery or freedom dictated values and character. It was slavery that ruined black Southerners, they implied, not race. In this way, black Knickerbockers could simultaneously privilege their own position while avoiding consigning former slaves to permanent degradation. If race itself did not indicate civic capacity, then even those "tainted" with slavery could presumably elevate their status with proper effort.

In this way, the criticism of Southern migrants became interwoven with a more generalized argument about class being cultivated by the black elite. As they stressed their distinction from Southern freed people, black Knickerbockers also differentiated themselves from "the lowest grades . . . of blacks," whom "no respectable negro would want to associate with." Using language as rancorous as that employed by white racists, the elites maligned those who might embody stereotypes of degradation or inferiority. "We are not to be judged by the street loungers and drunkards of our race," one woman insisted in 1895. By casting aspersions on the black lower class, she sought to undermine the "humiliating" presumption of racial solidarity foisted upon her by whites. Other black elites followed suit. "Respectability is too frequently victimized by men and women who compose the 'flashy,' 'impudent' element of our people," warned Dr. William Howard Griffiths, the minister at the Tenderloin's Bethel African Methodist Church. "This element, unfortunately, is a large one," Griffiths continued, "and does us more solid injury than any other agency of evil. It is 'loud' to dress and 'loud' in speech. On the cars, in the streets, or in the drawing-room, their vulgarity mortifies quiet colored people and scandalizes the race."[35] In marked contrast to the camaraderie they expressed for slaves during the antebellum era, New York's black elite turned away from their long-standing public empathy for black southerners as the racial climate within the city and the nation grew increasingly hostile in the final decades of the nineteenth century. They instead sought to dissociate themselves from slavery and the former slaves themselves in an ill-fated effort to gain full entrée into American society.[36]

But despite their public denunciations, the black elite still felt compelled to assist in the elevation of freed people. The black elites' model of civic accept-

341

RE-CREATING
BLACK
NEW YORK AT
CENTURY'S
END

VICTORIA EARLE MATTHEWS

In 1873, Victoria Earle Matthews, born a slave in rural Georgia at the outbreak of the Civil War, moved with her mother and eight siblings to New York City. She attended public school but ended her formal education in order to support her family as a domestic servant. She married at age eighteen and settled in Brooklyn, where she began writing for the *Brooklyn Eagle* and *Waverly Magazine*. Matthews read extensively and exhibited a deep interest in issues affecting black women. She became an active member of the local women's club.

The death of Matthews's sixteen-year-old son in 1895 marked a turning point in Matthews's life. Her profound bereavement triggered a devotion to social reform and racial uplift with a particular focus on young women. In 1897, Matthews, along with a handful of other women, organized the White Rose Mission on East Ninety-seventh Street in Manhattan. The following year, she incorporated the mission as the White Rose Industrial Association, with the purpose of maintaining "a Christian, non-sectarian Home for Colored Working Girls and Women, where they may be trained in the principles of practical self-help and right living." The White Rose aided young emigrant women, meeting them at the train stations and docks, directing them to temporary lodgings, and helping them

Portrait of Victoria Earle Matthews.

MANUSCRIPTS, ARCHIVES AND RARE BOOKS DIVISION, SCHOMBURG CENTER FOR RESEARCH IN BLACK CULTURE, NEW YORK PUBLIC LIBRARY, ASTOR, LENOX AND TILDEN FOUNDATIONS

gain reputable employment. In addition, the association offered training in a variety of skills. Matthews devoted the remainder of her life to saving "unprotected young colored women" from the potential dangers of the city. She died of tuberculosis in 1907.   —*Marcy S. Sacks*

ability opened the door to reform efforts designed to mitigate the perceived ill effects of slavery: moral degradation. Anti-vice reform organizations allowed the black elite to publicly distinguish themselves from the black lower class while still providing assistance. Black Knickerbockers' promotion of moral behavior and industriousness among the black lower class highlighted the black elites' conformity to pervasive middle-class values and social norms. The black elite's efforts to eliminate vice conceded the veracity of whites' claims that black people exhibited moral weaknesses. This concession further indicated their commitment to the nation. Elites chose to target black people themselves for reform, not a racist system that hampered black people's efforts at civic advancement. At the same time, success in the fight against vice in the black population would benefit all black people by proving that slavery, whose legacy could be surmounted, had caused moral weakness, not race.

As early as 1890, a number of New York's most influential black residents, among them T. Thomas Fortune and the Reverend Alexander Walters, called for the "organizing of societies, or the establishment of homes reclaiming fallen women." This goal was realized in 1897 when Victoria E. Matthews opened the White Rose Mission on East Ninety-seventh Street. The following year, she incorporated the organization as the White Rose Industrial Association, the first of a number of organizations formed specifically to deal with the particular needs confronting black women in New York City. Like later organizations, White Rose identified a connection between the migration experience, working conditions, and the home life of the young women coming to New York. Consequently, it offered traveler's aid, temporary lodgings to black women arriving in the city with no place to stay, and a job placement service with the organizing philosophy of training young black women in the "principles of practical self-help and right living."[37]

Through her work, Matthews also hoped to mitigate the widespread belief in black female immorality caused by the visibility of "these women haunting these certain portions of the city in such an unfailing stream." She complained that whites "take it for granted that all black people—all Afro-Americans—are naturally low." By diminishing the presence of black prostitutes in the city and

343

RE-CREATING
BLACK
NEW YORK AT
CENTURY'S
END

by simultaneously demonstrating that a cadre of black women held middle-class values, Matthews intended to show "that there is another class than is represented by the depraved class commonly met with on the streets and in certain localities." The mission tempered the "dangerous" influences of the tenements by securing only live-in positions for female domestic workers. In its first ten years of existence, the home provided temporary room and board to over 5,000 women and met countless boats at Norfolk, Virginia, and at New York City's docks to steer single women to reputable homes and employment.[38]

The National League for the Protection of Colored Women (NLPCW) also sought to "start the [female] traveler aright" in New York City. In tones evocative of the criticisms made by whites, members of the NLPCW cautioned that the urban environment placed naive black women at particular risk. "Degrading influences" such as dance halls, lodging houses, and the streets themselves threatened the moral fiber of the "untrained Southern woman" and indicated a need to persuade black women not to come to the city. When they did arrive, organization workers met them at the docks, providing the addresses of reputable homes and information on an amusement club for girls that offered lectures and wholesome entertainment.[39]

While they interacted with the black masses through the reform organizations, the black elite held to rigid social demarcations of difference. By the turn of the twentieth century, however, the impact of black Knickerbockers' diminished proportional importance in the overall population became conspicuous in the social and cultural institutions that served black people in the city. This was most marked in the city's black religious institutions. The last decades of the nineteenth century marked a rise in the number of churches serving New York's black population. By 1900, large and small congregations together numbered nearly forty spread among seven or eight primary denominations. The city's principal black Episcopal Church, the venerable St. Philip's, with its roots dating back to the eighteenth century, catered to a privileged membership. St. Philip's boasted a congregation of bluebloods—descendants of elite free blacks from New York's slave era who sought to distinguish themselves from those with less estimable heritages. But as the population grew, Knickerbockers found their religious preeminence challenged by outsiders. Caribbean-born immigrants to New York City overwhelmingly preserved their affiliation with the Episcopal Church, having a strong heritage of this denomination in the British islands. In the early twentieth century, they established the Episcopal St. Cyprian's Chapel to serve an almost exclusively Caribbean congregation and established their own definitions of elite religiosity. The "predominance of mulatto" members considered themselves among the "aristocracy of the negro." They attended "formal" services during which the pastor delivered sermons "without the emotional strain." Consistent with their desire to demonstrate an elite status, the congregants arrived "excellently dressed" each Sunday. "Display, pride, and intellect" characterized St. Cyprian's.[40]

Like Caribbean immigrants, Southern black migrants resisted conformity to the black Knickerbockers' behavioral expectations and instead formed religious institutions of their own that catered to their customs and traditions from home. The Union Baptist Church, for example, located in a storefront and led by the Reverend Dr. George H. Sims of Virginia, gathered the "very recent residents of this new, disturbing city" and made Christianity come "alive Sunday morning." Ministering to a mostly Virginian congregation, the Reverend Sims ensured that the worshippers felt comfortable in their new church. In addition to offering a "Southern style" of services, Union Baptist also provided special events such as fairs, suppers, and lectures that resembled the church activities back home. Union Baptist held annual revival meetings that attracted as many as one hundred new converts and performed baptisms every second week. It became known within the black population as a "shouting church."[41] The increasing commitment demonstrated by the various churches to serving the specific needs of newcomers revealed the growing importance of that portion of the population. Not only were newcomers numerically significant (comprising a majority of the black population by the turn of the twentieth century), they were gaining power as culture brokers, forcing the creation of new institutions that served their interests.[42]

Southerners brought their particular style of preaching and music to New York City and introduced gospel to the North. It made its way into Protestant

345

RE-CREATING
BLACK
NEW YORK AT
CENTURY'S
END

congregations founded largely by the migrants. The gospel churches stressed vocal expressions of spirituality; when the Reverend Martin R. Franklin, A. M. E. Zion ("Mother Zion") Church's leader in the late nineteenth century, ministered from the pulpit, he expected to hear a traditional "call and response" from his flock. Silence from the congregation would precipitate action from the minister, asking them if they loved their Jesus and prompting a resounding "Yes, Lord!" or "Amen!" Ejaculations of "Hallelujah," "Praise Be," and "Glory to God" might follow. The exchanges continued until many parishioners collapsed, exhausted, with tears streaming down their cheeks.

Many longtime black New Yorkers rejected the new sound as sensual and overly expressive, making the church one more site of contestation between newcomers and established residents of black New York. The Reverend T. H. Gilbert, pastor of the Mount Olivet Baptist Church, became one victim of the conflict when he introduced an "intellectual manner" to the services. Gilbert's congregation found his method of preaching "distasteful," preferring the previous pastor's "emotional" style. His tenure at the church lasted only briefly. After just a short appointment, Gilbert resigned under pressure and left New York City, much to the dismay of T. Thomas Fortune, who had welcomed Gilbert's imposition of a more orderly and reserved mien to Sunday services.[43]

Informal churches also began proliferating, responding to the growth and diversity of the black migrant population. Unable to purchase permanent buildings, these storefront churches met the spiritual needs of those uncomfortable with the formality of New York's established black churches. According to one observer, every block in the heart of Harlem housed between two and five of these organizations, allowing the "Danish West Indian [to have] his chapel, as has also the West Indian from Barbadoes [sic]," and so forth. To attract the wayward back into the fold, some churches offered "open air" preaching. Naomi Washington remembered her parents "testifying" on street corners. "There were quite a few people doing that. If there was one on 135th Street and Lenox Avenue, there might be another one on 134th and Seventh. They were called street meetings. They would sing. . . . Large crowds would come around and listen, and they would take up a collection."[44]

Just as Southern migrants made their mark on New York's black churches, their growing presence influenced broader social experiences. They fled from the South's repression and sought out the expanded opportunities and excitement of city life. "Every person, I don't care who he is nor where he is, wants to see New York some day," affirmed a South Carolinian migrant. The tales spreading through the South of the Northern "promised land" were often exaggerated and at times outright lies. Still, they enticed black Southerners who dreamt about a better life. "Don't blame us for leaving," begged one migrant. "We hear 'bout people in the North. Some have automobile. Some have victrola." Though few black people in New York could afford such luxuries, the city nevertheless enticed Southern blacks who sought refuge from the worst of Jim Crow's atrocities and the chance to "better my condition."[45]

Once in New York, migrants took full advantage of the numerous and diverse recreational activities open to them and added some of their own, often within the comfortable and safe presence of their compatriots. In that way, they maintained a vital connection to the life they left behind. In dances held especially for former Southerners, migrants used music to "invoke tradition." The pianist James P. Johnson recalled that at these gatherings the participants would sometimes call out, "Let's go home." Johnson understood that they were asking for a more Southern style of music. For those few hours, homesick migrants "recreated the South right in the middle of Manhattan." Similarly, Caribbean immigrants organized cricket teams and tennis clubs while southerners participated actively in baseball. The Hotel Maceo profited from regional distinctions by sponsoring an "old-fashioned Southern dinner." The menu included "roast possum, pigstails and cabbage, Virginia ham, cutlings, conepone, sweet potato pie and other delicacies."[46] In the company of others with similar backgrounds, black New Yorkers reproduced entertainments reminiscent of home; in so doing, they perpetuated the geographic and ethnic distinctions that were gradually redefining the black population of the city and undermining the efforts of black Knickerbockers to preserve a privileged status.

Perhaps most important to the preservation of distinct identities was the formation of mutual aid societies and social organizations based on geography and

347

RE-CREATING
BLACK
NEW YORK AT
CENTURY'S
END

nationality. In 1884, partly as a response to the growing Southern population in the city and to guard against the encroachment on their standing as elites, the "cream" of the black population formed the Society of the Sons of New York. Two years later they established a women's auxiliary. Though they periodically admitted members of impeccable character not born in New York, such as T. Thomas Fortune of Florida, Adam Clayton Powell of Virginia, and Alexander Walters from Kentucky, these "honorary" New Yorkers could not participate in the deliberations of the group. This society, the first to specify geographic origin as the basis for creating status and community, represented Knickerbockers' effort to cling to their privileged status. More recent black New Yorkers, however, rejected the notion that having long roots in the city conferred a mark of distinction. Instead, newcomers used the society's model to promote the formation of a variety of organizations representing Southern states and Caribbean islands.[47]

In quick succession, migrants established the Sons and Daughters of South Carolina, Sons of North Carolina, Sons of Virginia, Sons of the South, and the Southern Beneficial League. Forty individuals hailing from Bermuda organized the Bermuda Benevolent Association in 1897, while Cuban immigrants created the Cubans' Society of Thirty and the Cuban Fraternity. The Montserrat Progressive Society formed in 1914 to "assist in uplifting [the members] socially, morally and intellectually, to care for its sick, and those in distress, and to bury its dead."[48] The following year a group of Virgin Island women created the Danish West Indian Ladies Aid Society to address the specific needs of immigrant women. All of these organizations, designed to provide mutual assistance in times of sickness and death, served also the important function of creating distinctions among a people seen by white outsiders as a homogeneous group. Each society restricted membership to those born—or who could claim a minimum residence—in a specific geographic locale. This requirement helped to bring together people of similar cultural and ethnic backgrounds, "keeping alive the feeling of love for the native land and of respect for the homely virtues they learned there." When a native of North Carolina was appointed in 1910 as assistant district attorney of New York County, his compatriots responded "in the fullness of North Carolinian pride" by throwing a celebration. This expression of geographic unity reflected many migrants' continued sense of identity with their place of birth as they confronted the many challenges of life in New York City, including the disdain foisted upon them by the old-time black elite. At the same time, these organizations exaggerated the differences between Northerners, Southerners, and Caribbean-born blacks, exacerbating tensions between the groups and undermining attempts to present a unified front in the struggle against white racism.[49]

In the end, black Knickerbockers' attempt to use the Society of the Sons of New York to bolster their social status failed. The influx of newcomers overwhelmed the native-born population and forced them into a numerical—and ultimately cultural—minority among the city's black residents. Old-time black New Yorkers could not stanch the migration of black people into the city. Nor could they command uncontested authority within the black population. Southern emancipation, with the attendant migration of freed people northward, had not yielded the racial egalitarianism so long anticipated. To the contrary, it exacerbated and expedited the deterioration of race relations in the city and weakened the former elites' social standing. But the emergent black population, marked by diversity and even divisiveness, forged a new culture that drew on Southern, Northern, and immigrant traditions. The confrontation of identities created dynamic tension. In ensuing decades, this ethnic blending would establish the foundation for the cultural and artistic awakening that came to be known worldwide as the Harlem Renaissance.

RE-CREATING
BLACK
NEW YORK AT
CENTURY'S
END

NOTES

---

1. A WORLD OF POSSIBILITIES: SLAVERY AND FREEDOM IN DUTCH NEW AMSTERDAM by Christopher Moore

1. Edmund Bailey O'Callaghan's 1867 *Voyages of the Slavers* is the commonly quoted source of an unverifiable account of the first three female slaves arriving in 1628. O'Callaghan's presumption may have come from the 1857 discovery of an 11 August 1628 letter, written by New Amsterdam's first clergyman, Jonas Michaelius. His correspondence to a friend back home in Holland made the pioneer minister best known for his inability to find good female slaves in New Amsterdam. Michaelius's presence in the colony was unknown to scholars until the letter surfaced.

2. "Holland Documents III," in E.B. O'Callaghan, ed., *Documents Relative to the Colonial History of the State of New York*, 15 vols. (Albany: Weed, Parsons, 1856–1887); I.N.P. Stokes, ed., *Iconography of Manhattan Island, 1498–1909* (New York: R.H. Dodd, 1915–1928), 4:41–60.

3. Ira Berlin, *Many Thousands Gone: The First Two Centuries of Slavery in North America* (Cambridge, MA: Belknap Press of Harvard University Press, 1998).

4. Gerald F. De Jong, *The Dutch Reformed Church in the American Colonies* (Grand Rapids: Eerdmans, 1978), 17–19. Michaelius was the first Dutch clergyman to arrive in New Netherland.

5. A. Leon Higgenbotham, *In the Matter of Color: Race and the American Legal Process* (New York: Oxford University Press, 1978), 110. Legal historian Higgenbotham considered the proviso "that they shall not be bound to do it for a longer time than they shall think proper" as evidence that the legal status of blacks in the colony was to be decided on an ad hoc basis.

6. Samuel G. Nissenson, *The Patroon's Domain* (New York, 1937); A.J.F. Van Laer, ed., *Van Rensselaer Bowier Manuscripts, Letters of Kiliaen Van Rensselaer, 1630–1643* (Albany: University of the State of New York, 1908), 136–53.

7. The church, where the bulk of the black baptisms and marriages took place, was used by the Dutch and later English for more than a century until it was destroyed in 1741, in a fire allegedly set by slaves.

8. Edgar J. McManus, *A History of Negro Slavery in New York* (Syracuse, NY: Syracuse University Press,

1996); Leslie M. Harris, *In the Shadow of Slavery: African Americans in New York City, 1626–1863* (Chicago: University of Chicago Press, 2003).

9. In the Netherlands, England, and Scotland, the term *dominie* was used as a title for learned men, especially clergymen.

10. *Records of the Reformed Dutch Church in New Amsterdam and New York: Marriages from 11 December, 1639, to 26 August, 1801* (New York: Printed for the Society, 1890); *Records of the Reformed Dutch Church in New Amsterdam and New York: Baptisms, 1639–1739* (New York: Printed for the Society, 1901); DeJong, *The Dutch Reformed Church in the American Colonies*, 161–69.

11. Leo Herskowitz, "The Troublesome Turk: An Illustration of Judicial Process in New Amsterdam," *New-York Historical Society* 46 (1965): 300–306. Anthony Jansen Van Salee held property on Manhattan Island prior to 1643.

12. Thomas Osborne, ed., *A Collection of Voyages and Travels, Containing "Voyages and Travels into Brazil" by Capt. Johannes Nieuhof* (London, 1752), 757, in Manuscripts Archives and Rare Books, Schomburg Center for Research in Black Culture, New York Public Library.

13. Charles T. Gehring, *New York Historical Manuscripts: Dutch Land Papers* (Baltimore: Genealogical Publishing Co., 1980); E.B. O'Callaghan, ed., *Calendar of New York Colonial Manuscripts: Endorsed Land Papers, 1643–1803* (New York: Weed, Parsons, 1864; reprint, Harrison, NY: Harbor Hill Books, 1987).

14. Other free black communities existed in Spanish colonies in Florida and Mexico in the seventeenth century and earlier. New Amsterdam's group manumissions are distinguished by their local legislative dynamic. Ward Barrett, *The Sugar Hacienda of the Marqueses del Valle* [Mexico] (Minneapolis: University of Minnesota Press, 1970); Colin Palmer, *Slaves of the White God: Blacks in Mexico, 1570–1650* (Cambridge, MA: Harvard University Press, 1976); Robert LaDon Brady, "The Emergence of a Negro Class in Mexico, 1524–1640" (PhD diss., University of Iowa, 1965).

15. Edward T. Corwin, ed., *Ecclesiastical Records of the State of New York* (Albany: J.B. Lyon, 1901–1916), 1:548.

16. Adriaen Van der Donck, "Remonstrance of New Netherland to the States General of the United Netherlands, on the 28th July 1649; with Secretary van Tienhoven's Answer," in O'Callaghan, ed., *Documents Relative to the Colonial History of the State of New York*, 41.

17. E.B. O'Callaghan, ed. and trans., *Laws and Ordinances of New Netherland, 1638–1674* (Albany: Weed, Parsons, 1868). For an extensive accounting of laws affecting enslaved and free blacks in colonial New York City, see Higgenbotham, *In the Matter of Color*, 101–14.

18. McManus, *A History of Negro Slavery in New York*, 21–22.

19. O'Callaghan, ed., *Laws and Ordinances of New Netherland*, 32

20. On March 17, 1681, a group of eleven men from Manhattan, including DeVries and Manuel, purchased a tract of land from the Tappan Indians in the upper Hackensack River Valley. Because the land was located on the disputed boundary between New York and New Jersey, the patent was not recognized until March 17, 1686, by Governor Thomas Dongan of New York.

21. Charles T. Gehring, ed. and trans., *Curaçao Papers, 1640–1665* (Interlaken, NY: Heart of the Lakes, 1987). All other references to Captain Jan DeVries, see Arnold J.F. Van Laer's *New York Historical Manuscripts: Dutch Council Minutes 1638–1649* (Baltimore: Genealogical Publishing Co., 1974), and O'Callaghan's *Records of New Netherland*, vol. 3.

22. The 1647 baptismal entry for Jan DeVries II records the names of Captain Jan DeVries and Swartinne as the boy's parents. Though there is no known record of their marriage, had the couple not been wed, Jan II customarily would have been listed as illegitimate.

23. There are no records of DeVries owning slaves, but this may have been an effort by the Dutch to make DeVries appear to fit into their views of what Europeans should do.

24. Van Laer, ed., *New York Historical Manuscripts: Dutch Council Minutes 1638–1649*, 4:331–33.

25. Sandra W. Meditz and Dennis M. Hanratty, eds., *Islands of the Commonwealth Caribbean: A Regional Study* (Washington, DC: Government Printing Office, 1989); Richard S. Dunn, *Sugar and Slaves: The Rise of the Planter Class in the English West Indies, 1624–1713* (Chapel Hill: University of North Carolina Press, 1972); Richard B. Sheridan, *Sugar and Slavery: An Economic History of the British West Indies, 1623–1775* (Baltimore: Johns Hopkins University Press, 1973); E.B. O'Callaghan, ed., *Voyages of the Slavers St. John and Arms of Amsterdam* (Albany: J. Munsell, 1867). The development of a sugar plantation society based on slave labor, provided by the Dutch West India Company, was a watershed in Caribbean history.

26. In February 1660, Stuyvesant sent a lengthy letter to Vice Director Beck in Curaçao, urgently requesting horses and slaves to help battle the Indians at Esopus (Kingston). O'Callaghan, ed., *Documents Relative to the Colonial History of the State of New York*, 13:142.

27. For a discussion of Dutch folk culture among Afro-Dutch populations, see David Steven Cohen, *The Ramapo Mountain People* (New Brunswick, NJ: Rutgers University Press, 1974), 142–45. Regarding Sinterklaas and Piet de Moor, *Santa and Pete: A Novel of Christmas Present and Past* by Christopher Moore and Pamela Johnson (New York: Simon & Schuster, 1998) is based on an Afro-Dutch Christmas custom. Allison Blakely's *Blacks in the Dutch World: The Evolution of Racial Imagery in Modern Society* (Bloomington: Indiana University Press, 1993) notes the historically diminished status of blacks in general, and blacks in Dutch folklore during and after the slavery era.

28. In his 1682 will, Cornelius Van Borsum left his real property to Sara, his widow (New York City Wills, 1665–1707). The Van Borsum land covered nearly the precise boundaries of the five-acre "Negroes Burial Ground" as detailed on an unsigned Manhattan map drawn in 1739 and the 1755 Maershalk map. See also the map of the cemetery, "Diagram 8," in Murray Hoffman, ed., *Treatise Upon the Estate and Rights of the Corporation of the City of New York* (New York: E. Jones & Co., 1862).

29. Michael Kammen, *Colonial New York: A History* (New York: Scribner, 1975), 71–80; Thomas J. Davis, "Slavery in Colonial New York City" (PhD diss., Columbia University, 1975), 55–56.

2. The Tightening Vise: Slavery and Freedom in British New York
by Jill Lepore

Most subjects raised in this essay are discussed at greater length in Jill Lepore, *New York Burning: Liberty, Slavery, and Conspiracy in Eighteenth-Century Manhattan* (New York: Knopf, 2005).

1. David Grim, "Notes on the City of New York," New-York Historical Society.

2. The 1737 census can be found in E.B. O'Callaghan, *The Documentary History of the State of New-York* (Albany: Weed, Parsons, 1851), 4:186. For corrections to mathematical errors in the original, see Gary Nash, "The New York Census of 1737: A Critical Note on the Integration of Statistical and Literary Sources," *William and Mary Quarterly* 36 (July 1979): 428–35. For a full discussion of the population of New York ca. 1741, see Lepore, *New York Burning*, Appendix A; Patrick M'Robert, *A Tour through Part of the North Provinces of America* (Edinburgh, 1776; reprint, New York: New York Times, 1968), 5.

3. The population of New Netherland in 1664 was 8,000, "of whom approximately 700 to 850 were black": Vivienne L. Kruger, "Born to Run: The Slave Family in Early New York, 1626 to 1827" (PhD diss., Columbia University, 1985), 1:68. Stuyvesant quoted in Elizabeth Donnan, *Documents Illustrative of the History of the Slave Trade to America* (Washington, DC: Carnegie Institute of Washington, 1932; reprint, New York: Octagon Books, 1969), 3:411, 420–21. On slavery under the Dutch, see Joyce D. Goodfriend, "Burghers and Blacks: The Evolution of a Slave Society at New Amsterdam," *New York History* 59 (1978): 124–44, as well as Christopher Moore's essay in this volume. See also Ira Berlin, *Many Thousands Gone:*

The First Two Centuries of Slavery in North America (Cambridge, MA: Belknap Press of Harvard University Press, 1998), 17–28. On Central Africans, see Joseph C. Miller, "Central Africa During the Era of the Slave Trade, c. 1490s–1850s," in Linda Heywood, ed., *Central Africans and Cultural Transformations in the American Diaspora* (Cambridge: Cambridge University Press, 2002), 21–69. On the slave trade, see Edgar J. McManus, *A History of Negro Slavery in New York* (Syracuse, NY: Syracuse University Press, 1966), 23–24 and, more importantly, James G. Lydon, "New York and the Slave Trade, 1700 to 1774," *William and Mary Quarterly* 35 (April 1978): 375–94. Lydon has offered a "minimum estimate" that at least 6,800 Africans were imported into the colony of New York between 1700 and 1774, 2,800 directly from Africa and 4,000 from the West Indies and other parts of North America, although "a maximum figure of 7,400 might be justified" (383, 387). See Cadwallader Colden, *The Interest of the Country in Laying Duties* (New York: John Peter Zenger, 1726).

4. Thelma Foote, "Black Life in Colonial Manhattan, 1664–1785" (PhD diss., Harvard University, 1991), 30–41. Charles Z. Lincoln, William H. Johnson, and A. Judd Northrup, *Colonial Laws of New York from the Year 1664 to the Revolution* (Albany: J.B. Lyon, 1894*)*, 2:768–74 [hereafter *Col. Laws of N.Y.*].

5. John Thornton, "The Coromantees: An African Cultural Group in Colonial North America and the Caribbean," *Journal of Caribbean Studies* 32 (1998): 161–78. On naming practices, see John Thornton, "Central African Names and African-American Naming Patterns," *William and Mary Quarterly* 50 (October 1993): 727–42; and Jerome S. Handler and JoAnn Jacoby, "Slave Names and Naming in Barbados, 1650–1830," *William and Mary Quarterly* 53 (July 1996): 685–728.

6. Donnan, *Documents*, 3:440; Rip Van Dam to the Lords of Trade, 2 November 1731, in E.B. O'Callaghan, ed., *Documents Relative to the Colonial and Revolutionary History of New York* (Albany: Weed, Parsons, 1855–1861), 6:32–33 [hereafter *Docs. Col. N.Y.*]; *New-York Weekly Journal*, 15 April 1734. On death rates, see Joseph C. Miller, *The Way of Death: Merchant Capitalism and the Angolan Slave Trade, 1730–1830* (Madison: University of Wisconsin Press, 1988), 440–41.

7. Census figures are taken from Evarts B. Greene and Virginia D. Harrington, *American Population Before the Federal Census of 1790* (New York: Columbia University Press, 1932), 97–98. See also Ira Rosenwaike, *Population History of New York City* (Syracuse, NY: Syracuse University Press, 1972).

8. *New-York Gazette*, 17 April 1727; Michael Blakey, et al., "Biocultural Approaches to the Health and Demography of Africans in Colonial New York" (paper, World Archaeological Congress 4, University of Cape Town, 1999). The scholarship on the African-descended population of colonial New York is scattered. Early essays are principally concerned with slave codes. See Edwin Vernon Morgan, "Slavery in New York with Special Reference to New York City," in Maud Wilder Goodwin et al., eds., *Historic New York* (New York: G.P. Putnam's Sons, 1897; reprint, Port Washington, NY: I.J. Friedman, 1969), 1:3–29; William Renwick Riddell, "The Slave in Early New York," *Journal of Negro History* 13 (January 1928): 53–86; A. Judd Northrup, "Slavery in New York, a Historical Sketch," State Library *Bulletin* 4 (Albany, 1900); Edwin Olson, "Social Aspects of Slave Life in New York," *Journal of Negro History* 26 (January 1941): 66–77; Edwin Olson, "The Slave Code in Colonial New York," *Journal of Negro History* 29 (April 1944): 147–65; and Roi Ottley and William J. Weatherby, eds., *The Negro in New York: An Informal Social History* (New York: New York Public Library, 1967), 1–30. A book-length study was published in 1966: Edgar J. McManus, *A History of Negro Slavery in New York* (Syracuse, NY: Syracuse University Press, 1966). See also Joyce Goodfriend, *Before the Melting Pot: Society and Culture in Colonial New York City, 1664–1730* (Princeton, NJ: Princeton University Press, 1992), chapter 6. Two dissertations provide some of the fullest accounting: Foote, "Black Life," and Kruger, "Born to Run." See also *New-York Weekly Journal*, 25 September 1749.

9. Blakey, "Biocultural Approaches," 5–7. See also Foote, "Black Life," chapter 2. *New York Post-Boy*, 19 December 1748; *New York Post-Boy*, 27 May 1751; *New York Weekly Post-Boy*, 17 May 1756; and *New-York Weekly Journal*, 10 May 1736.

10. Cadwallader Colden to Dr. Home, 7 December 1721, *Letters and Papers of Cadwallader Colden*, in *New-York Historical Society Collections*, 1:51.

11. *New-York Gazette*, 12 September 1737. See also *New-York Weekly Journal*, 20 September 1737, which at least mentioned a kind of remorse: "Since it is well known that Children will mimic, I think it very imprudent to leave such dangerous Instruments in their Reach."

12. Cadwallader Colden to Mrs. Cadwallader Colden, 29 August 1744, *Letters and Papers of Cadwallader Colden*, 8:307.

13. Cadwallader Colden to Mr. Jordan, 26 March 1717, *Letters and Papers of Cadwallader Colden*, 1:39; *New York Mercury*, 16 June 1760. The best discussion of slave childhood in New York is Kruger, "Born to Run," chapter 6.

14. Kruger, "Born to Run," 93, 128–64. See also Olson, "Social Aspects of Slave Life," 66–67; James Alexander to Cadwallader Colden, 25 July 1730, *Letters and Papers of Cadwallader Colden*, 2:16; and Cadwallader Colden to Captain Van Pelt, in North Carolina, 17 December 1726, *Letters and Papers of Cadwallader Colden*, 1:59.

15. Kruger identified family as the motivation in forty-five of sixty-nine runs in which the motivation was known."Born to Run," 234–35.

16. Daniel Horsmanden, *A Journal of the Proceedings in the Detection of the Conspiracy* (New York: J. Parker, 1744), 104.

17. *New-York Gazette*, 13 November 1732; *New-York Evening Post*, 17 December 1744; *New-York Gazette*, 28 August 1727. On languages spoken among New York's blacks, see Edna Greene Medford et al., "The Transatlantic Slave Trade to New York City: Sources of Routing of Captives" (unpublished paper, World Archaeological Congress 4, University of Cape Town, 1999). On languages spoken by runaways, see Kruger, who, using a sample of 194 runaway slave ads from 1726 to 1814, finds forty which specify linguistic abilities: fourteen spoke English well, five spoke it poorly, six spoke no English at all, and fifteen were bilingual ("Born to Run," 86). On Gã, and on Akan as a lingua franca, see Thornton, "The Coromantees," 165.

18. Alexander Hamilton, *Gentleman's Progress: The Itinerarium of Dr. Alexander Hamilton, 1744*, ed. Carl Bridenbaugh (Pittsburgh: University of Pittsburgh Press, 1948), 40–41.

19. *New-York Evening Post*, 4 May 1747. On runaway literacy rates, see Foote, "Black Life," 246.

20. Foote, "Black Life," 91–127.

21. The Assembly did vote to levy a tax on slaves in 1737 and it was first collected in 1738, at one shilling per slave. Records of this tax collection survive only for the single year of 1738, and only for the Outward. "Head or Title of the Tax Role," Vanderwater Manuscripts, "New York, 1700–1760," New-York Historical Society.

22. Bruce Wilkenfeld, "New York City Neighborhoods, 1730," *New York History* 57 (1976): 165–182. Wilkenfeld argues that neighborhoods, by ward, clustered whites by occupation, religion, and wealth; the East River wards were the richest. As for occupations: "Thus, over two-thirds of the shipwrights and half the tailors were to be found in the East Ward; silversmiths and coopers clustered in the North Ward; blacksmiths were concentrated in the nearby regions of the Outward" (173).

23. Horsmanden, *Journal of the Proceedings*, 33.

24. See Lisa C. Tolbert, *Constructing Townscapes: Space and Society in Antebellum Tennessee* (Chapel Hill: University of North Carolina Press, 1999), 205–7. On slave mobility in antebellum cities, see Richard C. Wade, *Slavery in the Cities: The South, 1820–1860* (New York: Oxford University Press, 1964).

25. Horsmanden, *Journal of the Proceedings*, 113.

26. "An Act for the more effectual preventing and punishing the Conspiracy of Negro and other slaves, for the better regulating them and for repealing the Acts herein mentioned relating hereto," *Col. Laws of N.Y.*,

2:679–88; "A Law for Regulating Negro's & Slaves in the Night Time," *Minutes of the Common Council of the City of New York, 1675–1776* (New York: Dodd, Mead, 1905), 4:51–52 [hereafter *MCC*]; "A Law for the Observation of the Lords Day Called Sunday," *MCC*, 4:79; "A Law for Punishing Slaves who Shall Ride Disorderly through the Streets," *MCC*, 4:89–90; "A Law to Prohibit Negroes and Other Slaves Vending Indian Corn Peaches or any other Fruit with this City," *MCC*, 4:497–98.

27. New York's major provincial slave codes include laws passed in 1682 (*Proc. Gen. Court of Assizes*, 37–38), 1702 ("An Act for Regulateing of slaves," *Col. Laws of N.Y.*, 1:519–21), 1712 ("An Act for preventing Suppressing and punishing the Conspiracy and Insurrection of Negroes and other Slaves," *Col. Laws of N.Y.*, 1:761–67), 1730 ("An Act for the more effectual preventing and punishing the Conspiracy of Negro and other slaves, for the better regulating them and for repealing the Acts herein mentioned relating hereto," *Col. Laws of N.Y.*, 2:679–88). By 1731, a host of slave codes were in effect in the City of New York, including "A Law Appointing a Place for the More Convenient Hiring of Slaves," "A Law Restraining Slaves, Negroes, & Indians from Gaming with Moneys or For Moneys," "A Law Giving a Reward to Any Person or Persons who shall Apprehend any Negro, Mulatto or Indian Slaves Offending Against any of the Acts of General Assembly of this Colony," "A Law for Punishing Slaves who Shall Ride Disorderly through the Streets," "A Law for Regulating the Burial of Slaves," and "A Law for Regulating Negro's & Slaves in the Night Time," in *MCC*, 4:85–90, 51–52. "A Law to Prohibit Negroes and Other Slaves Vending Indian Corn Peaches or any other Fruit with this City" was passed in 1740 (*MCC*, 4:497–98). On city slave codes, see also Oscar R. Williams, "The Regimentation of Blacks on the Urban Frontier in Colonial Albany, New York City and Philadelphia," *Journal of Negro History* 63 (October 1978): 329–38; and Bernard Bush, comp., *Laws of the Royal Colony of New Jersey* (Trenton, NJ: New Jersey State Library, Archives and History Bureau, 1977–1986), 2:28–30.

28. On the 1712 revolt, see Governor Robert Hunter to the Lords of Trade, 23 June 1712, *Docs. Col. N.Y.*, 5:341–32; Kenneth Scott, "The Slave Insurrection in New York in 1712," *New-York Historical Society Quarterly* 45 (1961): 43–74; Thelma Wills Foote, "'Some Hard Usage': The New York City Slave Revolt of 1712," *New York Folklore* 18 (1992): 147–59; and, on the connections between 1712 and 1741, Eric W. Plaag, "'Greater Guilt than Theirs': New York's 1741 Slave Conspiracy in a Climate of Fear and Anxiety," *New York History* 84 (2003): 275–99. On the role of Coromantees in the revolt, see Thornton, "The Coromantees."

29. Robert Hunter to the Lords of Trade, 23 June 1712, *Docs. Col. N.Y.*, 5:342. "An Act for preventing Suppressing and punishing the Conspiracy and Insurrection of Negroes and other Slaves," 1712.

30. On manumission, see McManus, *A History of Negro Slavery*, chapter 8.

31. Governor Robert Hunter to the Lords of Trade, 14 March 1713, *Docs. Col. N.Y.*, 5:356; King's Instructions to Governor Thomas Donaghan, 29 May 1686, *Docs. Col. N.Y.*, 3:374; Lords of Trade to Governor Robert Hunter, 23 December 1709, *Docs. Col. N.Y.*, 5:157.

32. Quoted in Scott, "The Slave Insurrection," 67.

33. Jon Butler, *The Huguenots in America: A Refugee People in a New World Society* (Cambridge, MA: Harvard University Press 1983), 161–69.

34. Thornton, "Central African Names," 729–30. "Lawes . . . 1664," *New-York Historical Society Collections* 1 (1809): 322–23; *Laws of New-York, from the year 1691 to 1751, inclusive* (New York, 1757), 69; Earl of Bellomont to the Lords of Trade, April 27, 1699, *Docs. Col. N.Y.*, 4:510–11; "An Act to Incourage the Baptizing of Negro, Indian and Mulatto Slaves," *Col. Laws of N.Y.*, 1:597–98.

35. "A List of Slaves taught by Mr. Neau since the year 1704, Enclosed in his Letter of the 10 November 1714," Society of the Propagation of the Gospel in Foreign Parts Letterbooks, series A, 10:220–23, Library of Congress Manuscripts Division. "A List of Negroes Taught by Mr Neau December the 23 1719," ibid., 14:141–43.

36. David Humphreys, *An Historical Account of the Incorporated Society for the Propagation of the Gospel in Foreign Parts* (London: Joseph Downing, 1730), 232–44; Graham Russell Hodges, *Root and Branch: African Americans in New York and East Jersey, 1613–1863* (Chapel Hill: University of North Carolina Press, 1999), 55–63; William Taylor to Elias Neau, 6 November 1712 and Elias Neau to William Taylor, 15 October 1712, in Letters and Reports of Missionaries and Other Correspondents, Papers of the Society of the Propagation of the Gospel in Foreign Parts [hereafter SPG Papers], Library of Congress [hereafter LOC], series A, vol. 7 (1711–1712), box 5450, 276–77 and 226–27.

37. See Stokes, *Iconography of Manhattan Island*, 4:563.

38. George Whitefield, *Three Letters from the Reverend Mr. G. Whitefield* (Philadelphia: B. Franklin, 1740), 13–16. See also Alan Gallay, "The Great Sellout: George Whitefield on Slavery," in Winfred B. Moore Jr. and Joseph F. Tripp, eds., *Looking South: Chapters in the Story of an American Region* (New York: Greenwood Press, 1989). See also Whitefield's sermons discussed in *New-York Weekly Journal*, 10 March 1740 and *New-York Gazette*, 12 February 1740.

39. James Mascoparran to Philip Bearcroft, 4 May 1741, SPG Papers, LOC, vol. 9, box 5473; Richard Charlton to Philip Bearcroft, 30 October 1741, SPG Papers, LOC, vol. 9, box 5473.

40. "Anonymous Letter from a New Englander," *Letters and Papers of Cadwallader Colden*, 8:270–71.

41. Horsmanden, *Journal of the Proceedings*, 47.

42. Ibid., 66. Early interpretations of the 1741 conspiracy, most of which labeled it a "delusion," include Walter Franklin Prince, "The Great Slave Conspiracy Delusion: A Sketch of the Crowning Judicial Atrocity of American History," *New Haven Saturday Chronicle*, 28 June–23 August 1902; T. Wood Clarke, "The Negro Plot of 1741," *New York History* 25 (1944): 167–81; Henry H. Ingersoll, "The New York Plot of 1741," *The Green Bag* 20 (1908); Winthrop Jordan, *White Over Black: American Attitudes Toward the Negro, 1550–1812* (Chapel Hill: University of North Carolina Press, 1968; reprint, New York: W.W. Norton, 1977), 117–18; Herbert Aptheker, *A Documentary History of the Negro People in the United States* (New York: Citadel Press, 1951), 4; and Ferenc M. Szasz, "The New York Slave Revolt of 1741: A Re-Examination," *New York History* 48 (1967). A modern reprint of Horsmanden's *Journal*, edited by Thomas J. Davis, appeared in 1971 as *The New York Conspiracy* (Boston: Beacon Press, 1971) and occasioned the publication of a number of journal articles which found the existence of an extensive conspiracy somewhat more plausible: see, for example, Thomas Davis's essay, "The New York Slave Conspiracy of 1741 as Black Protest," *Journal of Negro History* (January 1971): 17–30; and Leopold S. Launitz-Schurer, "Slave Resistance in Colonial New York: An Interpretation of Daniel Horsmanden's New York Conspiracy," *Phylon* 41 (1980): 137–151. Davis published the first book-length study of the conspiracy in 1985, *A Rumor of Revolt: The "Great Negro Plot" in Colonial New York* (New York: Free Press, 1985; paperback ed., Amherst: University of Massachusetts Press, 1990). This work, more narrative than analytical, dismissed the was-there-a-conspiracy-or-not question as simplistic and distorting and instead attempted to demonstrate "beyond question that blacks in New York City during 1741 clearly talked of doing damage to the society enslaving them, expressed hopes of gaining freedom and the material benefits being denied them, and acted against the laws restraining their liberty" (xii). More recent interpretations include Peter Linebaugh and Marcus Rediker's Marxist reading asserting that New York's slaves and poor whites were involved in a plot "Atlantic in scope . . . by a motley proletariat to incite an urban insurrection." See *The Many-Headed Hydra: Sailors, Slaves, Commoners, and the Hidden History of the Revolutionary Atlantic* (Boston: Beacon Press, 2001), 174–210. In their invaluable history of New York, Edwin G. Burrows and Mike Wallace draw heavily from Szasz and Launitz-Schurer to argue that although "the actual evidence" for a conspiracy "is less than convincing . . . it's quite likely" that "some less widespread or well-organized coup" or arson "to cover up multiple burglaries" lay behind it all. See Edwin G. Burrows and Mike Wallace, *Gotham: A History of New York City to 1898* (New York: Oxford University Press, 1999), 159–66. Most

recently, legal historian Peter Hoffer has argued that the slaves "conspired," in the narrow legal sense of the term, but were innocent of the vast plot described by the prosecution. See *The Great New York Conspiracy of 1741: Slavery, Crime, and Colonial Law* (Lawrence: University Press of Kansas, 2003). Serena Zabin used Horsmanden's *Journal* as a chief source in her attempt to reconstruct life in eighteenth-century New York while, at the same time, dismissing any genuine understanding of the conspiracy as impossible. See "Places of Exchange: New York City, 1700–1763" (PhD diss., Rutgers University, 2000), an interpretation she also offers in the introduction to her greatly abridged edition of Horsmanden's *Journal*. See Serena R. Zabin, ed., *The New York Conspiracy Trials of 1741* (New York: Bedford/St. Martin's, 2004).

43. On untangling the plots Horsmanden describes, see Lepore, *New York Burning*, especially chapters 5 and 6.

44. Neville, *Acts of the General Assembly*, 443–44. *New York Weekly Post-Boy*, 16 February 1756.

45. Thomas E. Drake, *Quakers and Slavery in America* (New Haven: Yale University Press, 1950; reprint, Gloucester, MA: P. Smith, 1965); J. William Frost, ed., *The Quaker Origins of Antislavery* (Norwood, PA: Norwood Editions, 1980); John Woolman, *The Journal and Major Essays of John Woolman*, ed. Phillips P. Moulton (New York; Oxford University Press, 1971; reprint, Richmond, IN: Friends United Press, 1971), 200, 93.

46. *New York Weekly Post-Boy*, 24 March 1760.

3. LIBERTY AND CONSTRAINT: THE LIMITS OF REVOLUTION by Graham Russell Gao Hodges

1. Murphy Stiel letter, 16 August 1781. In Henry Clinton Papers, vol. 170, item 97, Clements Library, University of Michigan. For Stiel quote, see Graham Russell Hodges, *Root and Branch: African Americans in New York and East Jersey, 1613–1863* (Chapel Hill: University of North Carolina Press, 1999), 160; and Judith Van Buskirk, *Generous Enemies: Patriots and Loyalists in Revolutionary New York* (Philadelphia: University of Pennsylvania Press, 2002), 152–53. Stiel is identified as Murphy Steele in Graham Russell Hodges, ed., *Black Loyalist Directory: African Americans in Exile After the American Revolution* (New York: Garland Publishers, 1996), 177. On dreams as identity, see Mechal Sobel, *Teach Me Dreams: The Search for Self in the Revolutionary Era* (Princeton, NJ: Princeton University Press, 2000).

2. For use of the term cockpit, see Leonard Lundin, *Cockpit of the Revolution: The War for Independence in New Jersey* (Princeton, NJ: Princeton University Press, 1940); and Hodges, *Root and Branch*, 140. For numbers, see *Root and Branch*, 274–75.

3. Paul Gilje, *Road to Mobocracy: Popular Disorder in New York City, 1763–1834* (Chapel Hill: University of North Carolina Press, 1987), 32; Paul Gilje, *Liberty on the Waterfront: American Maritime Culture in the Age of Revolution* (Philadelphia: University of Pennsylvania Press, 1994), 25; Edward Countryman, *A People in Revolution: The American Revolution and Political Society in New York, 1760–1790* (Baltimore: Johns Hopkins University Press, 1981), 41–42; Joseph Tiedemann, *Reluctant Revolutionaries: New York City and the Road to Independence* (Ithaca: Cornell University Press, 1997), 47, 62–101. For blacks in riots in other cities, see Gary Nash, *Forging Freedom: The Formation of Philadelphia's Black Community, 1720–1840* (Cambridge, MA: Harvard University Press, 1988), 38–39; and James Horton and Lois Horton, *In Hope of Liberty: Culture, Community and Protest Among Northern Free Blacks, 1700–1860* (New York: Oxford University Press, 1997), 59.

4. For Livingston quote, see William Livingston to Unknown, 21 November 1774, Pierpont Morgan Library, in Hodges, *Root and Branch*, 137.

5. Hodges, *Root and Branch*, 130–31, 140; Graham Russell Hodges, *Slavery, Freedom and Culture Among*

Early American Workers (Armonk, NY: M.E. Sharpe, 1998), 72–74; Van Buskirk, *Generous Enemies*, 136–37; Shane White, *Somewhat More Independent: The End of Slavery in New York City, 1770–1810* (Athens: University of Georgia Press, 1991), 131–43. For Pennsylvania and Virginia, see Gary Nash and Jean Soderlund, *Freedom by Degrees: Emancipation in Pennsylvania and Its Aftermath* (New York: Oxford University Press, 1991), 76–77; Woody Holton, *Forced Founders: Indians, Debtors, Slaves, and the Making of the American Revolution in Virginia* (Chapel Hill: University of North Carolina Press, 1999), 139–40; and Sylvia Frey, *Water from the Rock: Black Resistance in a Revolutionary Age* (Princeton, NJ: Princeton University Press, 1991), 62.

6. For Dunmore quotes, see Francis L. Berkeley, ed., *Dunmore's Proclamation of Emancipation* (Charlottesville: Tracy W. McGregor Library, University of Virginia, 1941). For discussion of Dunmore, see Hodges, *Root and Branch*, 139–40.

7. Hodges, *Root and Branch*, 141–44.

8. Ibid., 141–42.

9. For discussion of black organizations, see Hodges, *Root and Branch*, 146–48; and for Peters, see Gary Nash, "Thomas Peters: Millwright, Soldier and Deliverer," in Gary Nash, ed., *Race, Class and Politics: Essays on American Colonial and Revolutionary Society* (Urbana: University of Illinois Press, 1986), 269–83.

10. Van Buskirk, *Generous Enemies*, 141–43.

11. Ibid., 138–39; Hodges, *Root and Branch*, 154.

12. Hodges, *Root and Branch*, 149.

13. Ibid., 149–50. For James and other employees at the brewery, see William D. Faulkner, brewer, ledger book D (1773–1790), Manuscripts, New-York Historical Society.

14. Van Buskirk, *Generous Enemies*, 150–51. For other cities, see Nash, *Forging Freedom*, 79–88; and Ira Berlin, *Many Thousands Gone: The First Two Centuries of Slavery in North America* (Cambridge, MA: Belknap Press of Harvard University Press, 1998), 239–40.

15. Hodges, *Root and Branch*, 146.

16. James Walker, *Black Loyalists: The Search for a Promised Land in Nova Scotia and Sierra Leone, 1783–1870* (New York: Africana Publishing Co., 1976), 4; Hodges, ed., *Black Loyalist Directory*.

17. Van Buskirk, *Generous Enemies*, 150–51.

18. For colonial injunctions against black expressive clothing, see Graham White and Shane White, *Stylin': African American Expressive Culture from Its Beginnings to the Zoot Suit* (Ithaca: Cornell University Press, 1998), 14–18; for Black Pioneers, see Hodges, *Root and Branch*, 153.

19. Ibid., 150–51; Van Buskirk, *Generous Enemies*, 151–52.

20. William E. Dornemann, trans., "A Diary Kept by Captain Walldeck During the Last War," *Journal of the Johannes Schwalm Association* 2 (1983–1984): 35, in Van Buskirk, *Generous Enemies*, 152.

21. "Memoirs of Mr. Boston King," *Methodist Magazine*, March 1798, 155.

22. Hodges, *Root and Branch*, 155–57.

23. Ibid., 155–56.

24. "Memoirs of Mr. Boston King," 155.

25. Hodges, *Root and Branch*, 158.

26. Fred Lewis Pattee, ed., *The Poems of Philip Freneau: Poet of the American Revolution*, 3 vols. (Princeton: University Library, 1903–1907), 1:139–40; for quote cursing blacks, see *New York Packett*, 4 April 1785.

4. THE LONG DEATH OF SLAVERY by Patrick Rael

1. All population statistics are derived from Inter-University Consortium for Political and Social Research, *Historical, Demographic, Economic, and Social Data: The United States, 1790–1970* (computer file, Ann Arbor, MI, 1992).

2. Shane White, *Somewhat More Independent: The End of Slavery in New York City, 1770–1810* (Athens: University of Georgia Press, 1991), 3.

3. Samuel Johnson, "Taxation Not Tryanny," in *The Yale Edition of the Works of Samuel Johnson* (New Haven: Yale University Press, 1977), 10:454.

4. John Jay, "Address to the People of Great Britain" (1774), in *The Correspondence and Public Papers of John Jay*, ed. Henry P. Johnston (New York: G.P. Putnam's Sons, 1890–1893), 1:18, 27, 30.

5. John Jay to Robert Livingston and Gouverneur Morris, 29 April 1777, in *The Correspondence and Public Papers of John Jay*, I:136.

6. John Jay to Egbert Benson, 17 September 1780, in *The Correspondence and Public Papers of John Jay*, 1:407.

7. William Jay, *The Life of John Jay: With Selections from His Correspondence and Miscellaneous Papers* (New York: J. & J. Harper, 1833), 1:231.

8. *New Jersey Gazette*, 20 September 1780, quoted in Arthur Zilversmit, *The First Emancipation: The Abolition of Slavery in the North* (Chicago: University of Chicago Press, 1967), 142.

9. *Journals of the Provincial Congress, Provincial Convention, Committee of Safety and Council of Safety of the State of New York* (Albany: T. Weed, 1842), 1:887.

10. *New Jersey Gazette*, 11 April 1781, quoted in Zilversmit, *First Emancipation*, 146.

11. *Journals of the Provincial Congress*, 1:887.

12. Quoted in Leo H. Hirsch Jr., "The Slave in New York," *Journal of Negro History* 16 (October 1931): 387.

13. "A Son of Liberty" [Silas Downer], "A Discourse Delivered . . . at the Dedication of the Tree of Liberty" (1768), in Bruce Frohnen, ed., *The American Republic: Primary Sources* (Indianapolis: Liberty Fund, 2002), 143.

14. Noah Webster, "An Examination into the Leading Principles of the Federal Constitution" (1787), in Philip B. Kurland and Ralph Lerner, eds., *The Founders' Constitution* (Chicago: University of Chicago Press, 1987), 1:596.

15. "Massachusetts" [Sidney Edwards Morse], *The New States, or a Comparison of the Wealth, Strength and Population of the Northern and Southern States* (Boston, 1813), 32–33, quoted in Matthew Mason, "'Nothing Is Better Calculated to Excite Divisions': Federalist Agitation against Slave Representation during the War of 1812," *New England Quarterly* 75 (December 2002): 543.

16. *New Jersey Journal*, 29 November and 27 December 1780, quoted in Zilversmit, *First Emancipation*, 143.

17. The society's full and complete name was "The New York Society for promoting the Manumission of Slaves and protecting such of them as have been or may be liberated."

18. White, *Somewhat More Independent*, 81.

19. M.J. Heale, "From City Fathers to Social Critics: Humanitarianism and Government in New York, 1790–1860," *Journal of American History* 63 (June 1976): 28.

20. Ibid.

21. *Journal of the Assembly of the State of New-York* 8 (New York, 1785), 119–20, reprinted in David N. Gellman and David Quigley, eds., *Jim Crow New York: A Documentary History of Race and Citizenship, 1777–1877* (New York: New York University Press, 2003), 31–32.

22. *New-York Packet*, 4 April 1785, reprinted in Gellman and Quigley, eds., *Jim Crow New York*, 34–35.

23. J.C. Dongan to John Jay, John Jay to J.C. Dongan, 27 February 1792, in Jay, *The Correspondence and Public Papers of John Jay*, 3:413–15.

24. "Report of the Committee on Ambiguities in the Confiscation Act and to Consider a Petition for Gradual Abolition," New York Manumission Society, "Committee Reports," 19 February 1793, as quoted in Zilversmit, *First Emancipation*, 176.

25. Everett S. Lee and Michael Lalli, "Population," in David T. Gilchrist, ed., *The Growth of the Seaport Cities, 1790–1825* (Charlottesville: University Press of Virginia, 1967), 33.

26. Robert A. Davison, "Comment on New York Foreign Trade," in Gilchrist, *Growth of the Seaport Cities*, 70.

27. George Rogers Taylor, "Comment on Population," in Gilchrist, *Growth of the Seaport Cities*, 44.

28. White, *Somewhat More Independent*, 35, 41–43, 46.

29. Ibid., 33–36, 48–49.

30. Ibid., 127–43.

31. Harry B. Yoshpe, "Record of Slave Manumissions in New York During the Colonial and Early National Periods," *Journal of Negro History* 26 (January 1941), 78–107.

32. Ibid., 111–12.

33. White, *Somewhat More Independent*, chapter 7.

34. Joseph Sidney, "An Oration, Commemorative of the Abolition of the Slave Trade in the United States" (New York, 1809), in Dorothy Porter, ed., *Early Negro Writing, 1760–1837* (Baltimore, MD: Black Classic Press, 1995), 361.

35. Ibid., 362.

36. William Hamilton, "An Address to the New York African Society, for Mutual Relief" (New York, 1809), in Porter, *Early Negro Writing*, 37, 40.

37. Henry Highland Garnet, *A Memorial Discourse by Reverend Henry Highland Garnet with an Introduction by James McCune Smith, M.D.* (Philadelphia: Joseph M. Wilson, 1865), 20–21.

38. Quoted in Graham Russell Hodges, *Root and Branch: African Americans in New York and East Jersey, 1613–1863* (Chapel Hill: University of North Carolina Press, 1999), 216.

39. *National Advocate*, 24 September 1821, quoted in Gellman and Quigley, *Jim Crow New York*, 88.

40. Gellman and Quigley, *Jim Crow New York*, 125, 136.

41. Ibid., 117, 121, 122, 128.

42. Ibid., 116, 123.

43. Ibid., 129.

44. Rhoda Golden Freeman, *The Free Negro in New York City in the Era Before the Civil War* (New York: Garland Publishing, 1994), 92–93.

45. Quoted in Shane White, *Stories of Freedom in Black New York* (Cambridge, MA: Harvard University Press, 2002), 45.

5. BLACK LIFE IN FREEDOM: CREATING A POPULAR CULTURE by Shane White

I would like to thank the Australian Research Council for funding the research trips to New York that provided the material on which this article is based, and Graham White (no relation), as ever, for his editorial skills. I would also like to thank Ira Berlin for his help with this piece and, while I am at it, his extraordinarily generous critical reading of virtually all I have written in the last decade and a half.

1. *Journal of Commerce*, 24 January 1838.

2. *National Advocate*, 3 March 1826.

3. Chloe Russell, *The Complete Fortune Teller, and Dream Book, By Which Every Person May Acquaint Themselves with the Most Important Events That Shall Attend Them Through Life* (Exeter, 1824). I am indebted to Phil Lapsansky for directing me to this publication.

4. *New York Spectator*, 6 January 1826.

5. For more on the importance of stories for the recovery of African New Yorker history in the early decades of the nineteenth century, see Shane White, *Stories of Freedom in Black New York* (Cambridge, MA: Harvard University Press, 2002), 7–12.

6. Statement of James Arden, *People v. James Arden*, filed 11 April 1811, District Attorney Indictment Papers, Municipal Archives of the City of New York.

7. *New York Spectator*, 6 January 1826.

8. The point about audibility is developed at length in Shane White and Graham White, *The Sounds of Slavery: Discovering African American History Through Songs, Sermons and Speech* (Boston: Beacon Press, 2005).

9. White, *Stories of Freedom in Black New York*, 46–48.

10. *The American*, 2 October 1820; *Commercial Advertiser*, 17 April 1832; *New York American*, 23 July 1830.

11. *The Cries of New York* (New York, 1809). For a fascinating account of the larger tradition of which this was a part, see Sean Shesgreen, *Images of the Outcast: The Urban Poor in the Cries of London* (New Brunswick, NJ: Rutgers University Press, 2002).

12. Bayard Still, "New York City in 1824: A Newly Discovered Description," *New-York Historical Society Quarterly* 46 (1962): 137–70, quotation from 149.

13. Petition to the Corporation of the City of New York, 12 August 1817, reprinted in Paul A. Gilje and Howard B. Rock, eds., *Keepers of the Revolution: New Yorkers at Work in the Early Republic* (Ithaca: Cornell University Press, 1992), 218–21.

14. *National Advocate*, 3 August 1821; *New-York Columbian*, 23 August 1820; Henry Bradshaw Fearon, *Sketches of America: A Journey of Five Thousand Miles through the Eastern and Western States of America* (London: Longman, Hurst, Rees, Orme, and Brown, 1818), 9; Stephen Davis, *Notes of a Tour in America in 1832 and 1833* (Edinburgh: Waugh & Iness, 1833), 75.

15. E.T. Coke, *A Subaltern's Furlough: Descriptive of Scenes in Various Parts of the United States* (New York: J. & J. Harper, 1833), 139.

16. *National Advocate*, 18 May 1815; *New York Evening Post*, 22 September 1826.

17. *New-York Enquirer*, 28 March 1827. On black parades, see also Shane White, "'It was a Proud Day': African Americans, Festivals, and Parades in the North, 1741–1834," *Journal of American History* 81 (June 1994): 13–51.

18. *New York American*, 6 July 1827.

19. *National Advocate*, 21 June 1823.

20. Alfred Frankenstein, *William Sidney Mount* (New York: Abrams, 1975), 91–93.

21. Ibid., 164.

22. Frederick C. Moffatt, "Barnburning and Hunkerism: William Sidney Mount's *Power of Music*," *Winterthur Portfolio* 29 (1994): 19–42, esp. 42.

23. On Mount's interest in music, see Frankenstein, *William Sidney Mount*, 79–94.

24. The working sketches are reproduced in Frankenstein, *William Sidney Mount*, 157.

25. Elizabeth Johns, *American Genre Painting: The Politics of Everyday Life* (New Haven: Yale University Press, 1991), 120.

26. Moffatt, "Barnburning and Hunkerism," 41.

27. George S. Schuyler, *Black and Conservative: The Autobiography of George S. Schuyler* (New Rochelle,

NY: Arlington House, 1966), 21.

28. Gertrude Lefferts Vanderbilt, *The Social History of Flatbush and Manners and Customs of the Dutch Settlers in Kings County* (Brooklyn, NY, 1909), 386–87.

29. C.W. Larison, *Silvia Dubois, a Biografy of the Slav Who Whipt Her Mistres and Gand Her Fredom*, ed. Jared C. Lobdell (Ringos, NJ: C.W. Larison, 1883; reprint, New York: Oxford University Press, 1988), 59–60.

30. Thomas F. DeVoe, *The Market Book: A History of the Public Markets of the City of New York* (New York, 1862; reprint, New York: A.M. Kelley, 1970), 344–45.

31. For a brilliant riff on the dancing at Catharine Market and its importance down to the twentieth century, see W.T. Lhamon Jr., *Raising Cain: Blackface Performance from Jim Crow to Hip Hop* (Cambridge, MA: Harvard University Press, 1998), 1–55.

32. Shane White, *Somewhat More Independent: The End of Slavery in New York City, 1770–1810* (Athens: University of Georgia Press, 1991), 17–18, 93–95.

33. DeVoe, *The Market Book*, 344–45.

34. *Daily Advertiser*, 15 February 1799.

35. The details of the dance at Johnson's place have been gleaned from *Murders: Report of the Trial of James Johnson, a Black Man* (New York: Southwick and Pelsue, 1811). For a fuller exposition of this case, see Shane White, "The Death of James Johnson," *American Quarterly* 51 (December 1999): 753–95.

36. *National Advocate*, 11 August 1824.

37. *The Sun*, 18 December 1834.

38. Charles Dickens, *American Notes and Pictures from Italy* (1842; reprint, New York, 1966), 90–91.

39. Stuart M. Blumin, ed., *New York by Gas-Light and Other Urban Sketches by George G. Foster* (Berkeley: University of California Press, 1990), 142–43.

40. See, for example, *Morning Courier and New-York Enquirer*, 2 August 1833.

41. *New-York Enquirer*, 13 March 1827; *New-York National Advocate*, 18 March 1825.

42. *New-York Enquirer*, 9 December 1828.

43. "The African Fancy Ball," *Philadelphia Monthly Magazine* 2 (1828): 53–57.

44. *National Advocate*, 21 September 1821.

45. *New York Times*, 3 June 1999.

6. Black Life in Freedom: Creating an Elite Culture by Carla L. Peterson

1. Rhoda Golden Freeman Research Collection, Manuscript Division, Schomburg Research Center in Black Culture, New York Public Library.

2. "Crummell, Alexander," in Rayford Logan and Michael R. Winston, eds., *Dictionary of American Negro Biography* (New York: W.W. Norton, 1982), 145; Alexander Crummell, *Africa and America: Addresses and Discourses*, 1891 (New York: Negro Universities Press, 1969), 272–74; Thomas M. Morgan, "The Education and Medical Practice of Dr. James McCune Smith (1813–1865), First Black American to Hold a Medical Degree," *Journal of the National Medical Association* 95 (July 2003): 605; Anne M. Boylan, *The Origins of Women's Activism: New York and Boston, 1797–1840* (Chapel Hill: University of North Carolina Press, 2002), 64.

3. I did not pick these two men out of the archives at random; they are my great-great-grandfather and great-grandfather and are at the heart of a book-length project on the social and cultural history of nineteenth-century black New Yorkers.

4. Craig Wilder, *In the Company of Black Men: The African Influence on African American Culture in New York City* (New York: New York University Press, 2001), 36–47.

5. John Zuille, *Historical Sketch of the New York African Society for Mutual Relief* (New York, 1892), 26.

6. Carleton Mabee, *Black Education in New York State from Colonial to Modern Times* (Syracuse, NY: Syracuse University Press 1979), 4–6, 17–21.

7. Charles C. Andrews, *The History of the New-York African Free School* (New York: M. Day, 1830), 121.

8. Walter R. Johnson, *The Scientific Class-Book* (Philadelphia: Key & Biddle, 1836), 1:5; Rev. J. Joyce, *Scientific Dialogues, Intended for the Instruction and Entertainment of Young People* (Philadelphia: M. Carey & Son, 1815), 1:x; J.L. Comstock, *Natural History of Birds* (Hartford: Robinson, 1830).

9. James McCune Smith, *A Memorial Discourse by Rev. Henry Highland Garnet* (Philadelphia: J.M. Wilson, 1865), 22.

10. *Records of the New-York African Free Schools: Regulations, By-Laws, and Reports, 1817–1832*, vol. 2, Manuscript Collection, New-York Historical Society.

11. Andrews, *History of the New-York African Free School*, 26, 47.

12. Ibid., 135–36.

13. Ibid., 62.

14. Enid Vivian Barnett, *Education for African Americans in New York State, 1800–1860* (Kingston, ON: Harbor House Press, 2003), 10–11.

15. Andrews, *History of the New-York African Free School*, 121-122, 127.

16. Ibid., 132; *Records of the New-York African Free Schools*, vol. 3.

17. *Colored American*, 8 December 1838, 3.

18. Pierre Toussaint Papers, microfilm reel 3, New York Public Library.

19. *Frederick Douglass' Paper*, 27 July 1855.

20. George C. Foster, *New York Naked* (New York: De Witt & Davenport, 1850), 63.

21. "Crummell, Alexander," 145; *Colored American*, 2 February 1839, 4; "Charles Lewis Reason" in Jessie Carney Smith, ed., *Notable Black American Men* (Detroit: Gale Research, 1999), 999.

22. "Crummell, Alexander," 145; Thomas M. Morgan, "The Education and Medical Practice of Dr. James McCune Smith (1813–1865)," *Journal of the National Medical Association* 95 (July 2003): 606–8.

23. Curt Wimmer, *The College of Pharmacy of the City of New York* (Baltimore: Read-Taylor, 1929), 20–21.

24. *Frederick Douglass' Paper*, 18 May 1855 and 27 May 1852.

25. *New York Times*, 19 February 1891.

26. *North Star*, 11 February 1848, 3; *New York Tribune*, 18 November 1851; *Frederick Douglass' Paper*, 8 June 1855.

27. *Colored American*, 10 July 1841, 2.

28. Kenneth A. Scherzer, *The Unbounded Community: Neighborhood Life and Social Structure in New York City, 1830–1875* (Durham: Duke University Press, 1992), 51.

29. Leslie M. Harris, *In the Shadow of Slavery: African Americans in New York City, 1626–1863* (Chicago: University of Chicago Press, 2003), 74.

30. Edwin G. Burrows and Mike Wallace, *Gotham: A History of New York City to 1898* (New York: Oxford University Press, 1999), 475.

31. William M. Bobo, *Glimpses of New York City. By a South Carolinian (who had nothing else to do)* (Charleston: J.J. McCarter, 1852), 126.

32. Joseph Alfred Scoville, *The Old Merchants of New York City*, 5 vols. (New York: Carleton, 1864), 1:251–58; Ann L. Buttenwieser, "Exalted Spaces: Recapturing the Glorious Underpinnings of the Brooklyn Bridge," *South Street Seaport Museum Magazine* (Fall 1983): 25–26.

33. Scherzer, *The Unbounded Community*, 31, 66.

34. Harris, *In the Shadow of Slavery*, 194–98.

35. *Frederick Douglass' Paper*, 22 April 1852.

36. Maritcha Remond Lyons, "Memories of Yesterdays, All of Which I Saw and Part of Which I Was—An Autobiography," Harry Albro Williamson Papers, Schomburg Center for Research in Black Culture, New York Public Library, n.d., 46.

37. Lyons, "Memories of Yesterday," 32–33, 38. The Anglican communion descends from the Church of England and has established itself worldwide. All its churches continue to express loyalty to the Archbishop of Canterbury. Anglicanism follows the doctrines and practices of the Book of Common Prayer. It holds to the Catholic faith as expounded by the Scriptures and early church fathers. Its public worship is liturgical and formal style.

38. Craig Townsend, *An Inexpedient Time: Race and Religion Among New York City Episcopalians* (Ann Arbor: UMI Dissertation Services, 1998), 22.

39. St. Philip's Vestry Minutes, 4 August 1853, Manuscript Division, Schomburg Center for Research in Black Culture, New York Public Library.

40. *Colored American*, 9 December 1837, 4.

41. Smith, *Memorial Discourse*, 23.

42. Rhoda Golden Freeman, *The Free Negro in New York City in the Era Before the Civil War* (New York: Garland Publishing, 1994), 245–46.

43. *Colored American*, 9 November 1839, 3.

44. Freeman, *The Free Negro in New York City in the Era Before the Civil War*, 253–55.

45. *North Star*, 19 May 1848, 2.

46. Freeman, *The Free Negro in New York City in the Era Before the Civil War*, 250.

47. *New York Tribune*, 17 July 1855, 1.

48. *Colored American*, 2 May 1840, 2.

49. *Colored American*, 13 July 1839, 2.

50. Dorothy Porter, "The Organized Educational Activities of Negro Literary Societies, 1828–1846," *Journal of Negro Education* 5 (1936): 569; Dorothy Sterling, *We Are Your Sisters: Black Women in the Nineteenth Century* (New York: W.W. Norton, 1984), 112; Harris, *In the Shadow of Slavery*, 180.

51. *Colored American*, 9 May 1840, 2.

52. *Colored American*, 19 August 1837, 3.

53. *Colored American*, 2 September 1837, 1.

54. Charles L. Reason, "The Spirit Voice Or, Liberty Call to the Disfranchised (State of New York)," in Benjamin Brawley, ed., *Early Negro American Writers* (New York: Dover Publications, 1970), 257–60.

55. *Frederick Douglass' Paper*, 18 December 1851.

56. *Frederick Douglass' Paper*, 5 August 1853.

57. *Frederick Douglass' Paper*, 26 February 1852 and 16 March 1853.

7. BLACK LIFE IN FREEDOM: CREATING A CIVIC CULTURE by Craig Steven Wilder

1. Maria W. Stewart, "An Address, Delivered at the African Masonic Hall in Boston, Feb. 27, 1833," *The Liberator*, 27 April 1833; Marilyn Richardson, ed., *Maria W. Stewart: America's First Black Woman Political Writer* (Bloomington: Indiana University Press, 1987), 93–95.

2. Jupiter Hammon, "An Address to the Negroes of the State of New-York," in Carter G. Woodson, ed., *The Mind of the Negro as Reflected in Letters Written During the Crisis, 1800–1860* (Washington, DC: Association for the Study of Negro Life and History, 1926). See also Rayford W. Logan and Michael R. Winston, *Dictionary of American Negro Biography* (New York: W.W. Norton, 1982), 281–82.

3. Arthur A. Schomburg, "Jupiter Hammon Before the New York African Society," *New York Amsterdam*

News, 22 January 1930; Leslie M. Harris, *In the Shadow of Slavery: African Americans in New York City, 1626–1863* (Chicago: University of Chicago Press, 2003), 72–77; Craig Steven Wilder, *In the Company of Black Men: The African Influence on African American Culture in New York City* (New York: New York University Press, 2001), 35–53.

4. Harry B. Yoshpe, "Record of Slave Manumissions in New York During the Colonial Era and Early National Periods," *Journal of Negro History* 1 (January 1941): 81–85.

5. Wilder, *In the Company of Black Men*, 45–53; Christopher Rush with George Collins, *A Short Account of the Rise and Progress of the African Methodist Episcopal Church in America* (New York, 1843), 9–10; William J. Walls, *The African Methodist Episcopal Zion Church: Reality of the Black Church* (Charlotte: A.M.E. Zion Publishing House, 1974), 40–48.

6. Abyssinian Baptist Church, *The Articles of Faith, Church Discipline, and By-Laws of the Abyssinian Baptist Church in the City of New York, April 3, 1833* (New York, 1833), 11–14; George H. Hansell, *Reminiscences of Baptist Churches and Baptist Leaders in New York City and Vicinity, from 1835–1898* (Philadelphia: American Baptist Publication Society, 1899), 24–26; Anne M. Boylan, *The Origins of Women's Activism: New York and Boston, 1797–1840* (Chapel Hill: University of North Carolina Press, 2002), 129.

7. Harris, *In the Shadow of Slavery*, 171; A Member [Peter Vogelsang], *An Address Delivered Before the New York African Society for Mutual Relief, in the African Zion Church, 23d March 1815, Being the Fifth Anniversary of Their Incorporation* (New York, 1815), 3–4, New-York Historical Society.

8. The case is reprinted in Howard B. Rock, ed., *The New York City Artisan, 1789–1825: A Documentary History* (Albany: State University of New York Press, 1989), 172–73; *The Liberator*, 20 December 1850.

9. Shane White, *Somewhat More Independent: The End of Slavery in New York City, 1770–1810* (Athens: University of Georgia Press, 1991), 156–58, 164–65; Graham Russell Hodges, *New York City Cartmen, 1667–1850* (New York: New York University Press, 1986), 64.

10. *The Constitution of the New York African Society for Mutual Relief, Passed June 6th, 1808. Amended February 8th, 1869*, New York African Society for Mutual Relief (NYASMR) Papers, Long Island University, Brooklyn; Vogelsang, *Address Delivered Before the New York African Society for Mutual Relief*, 3–4.

11. Vogelsang, *Address Delivered Before the New York African Society for Mutual Relief*, 6–11; John Teasman, *An Address Delivered in the African Episcopal Church, On the 25th March, 1811. Before the New York African Society, for Mutual Relief; Being the First Anniversary of Its Incorporation* (New York, 1811), 7.

12. On the sociopolitical impact of black parading, see Susan G. Davis, *Parades and Power: Street Theatre in Nineteenth Century Philadelphia* (Philadelphia: Temple University Press, 1986), 46–47.

13. *Minutes of the Common Council of the City of New York, 1784–1831*, (New York: M.B. Brown, 1917), 4:663, 682; Wilder, *In the Company of Black Men*, 105; James McCune Smith, "Introduction" to Rev. Henry Highland Garnet, *A Memorial Discourse Delivered in the Hall of the House of Representatives, Washington, D.C., on Sabbath, February 12, 1865* (Philadelphia: J.M. Wilson, 1865), 24–25.

14. "An Act to Incorporate the Wilberforce Philanthropic Association, Passed June 8, 1812," *Laws of the State of New-York, Passed at the Thirty-Fifth Session of the Legislature* (Albany, 1812), 189–90; *Constitution of the African Marine Fund, for the Relief of Distressed Orphans, and Poor Members of This Fund* (New York, 1810), Collection of the New-York Historical Society.

15. Robert J. Swan, "John Teasman: African-American Educator and the Emergence of Community in Early Black New York City, 1787–1815," *Journal of the Early Republic* 12 (Fall 1992): 334–37; Wilder, *In the Company of Black Men*, 125–26.

16. Charles C. Andrews, *The History of the New-York African Free Schools, from Their Establishment in 1787, to the Present Time; Embracing a Period of More Than Forty Years: Also a Brief Account of the*

Successful Labors, of the New-York Manumission Society: With an Appendix (New York: M. Day, 1830; reprint, New York: Negro Universities Press, 1969), 57–58; Boylan, *Origins of Women's Activism*, 129–30; *The Liberator*, 29 June 1833.

17. Maritcha Remond Lyons, "Memories of Yesterday: All of Which I Saw and Part of Which I Was: An Autobiography" (unpublished manuscript), 6, Collection of the Schomburg Center for Research in Black Culture, New York Public Library; Charles A. Reason's Obituary, *New York Times*, 17 August 1893. See also Logan and Winston, *Dictionary of American Negro Biography*, 516–19.

18. Boylan, *Origins of Women's Activism*, 130.

19. *Constitution and By-Laws of the Abyssinian Benevolent Daughters of Esther Association of the City of New-York* (New York, 1853), Collection of the Society for the Preservation of Weeksville and Bedford-Stuyvesant History, Brooklyn, New York.

20. *The Liberator*, 10 December 1831 and 9 April 1836.

21. *The Liberator*, 19 April 1834.

22. "Order of Admission to the Dorcas Society," misc. mss., Dorcas Society, Collection of the New-York Historical Society; St. Mark's Church, Ladies Benevolent (Dorcas) Society, *Minute Book, 1861–1864*, passim, Collection of the New-York Historical Society.

23. *Constitution and By-Laws of the Abyssinian Benevolent Daughters of Esther Association*; *The Liberator*, 10 December 1831.

24. Charles B. Wilson, *The Official Manual and History of the Grand United Order of Odd Fellows in America. Authorized by the Third B.M.C., and Approved and Published by the Sub-Committee of Management* (Philadelphia: G.F. Lasher, 1894), 11–19, 65–67; Wilder, *In the Company of Black Men*, 117–18.

25. Harry A. Williamson, "A History of Freemasonry among the American Negroes" (unpublished manuscript, 1929), 19–30, Collection of the Schomburg Center for Research in Black Culture, New York Public Library; *The Liberator*, 12 February 1831.

26. Smith, "Introduction," 41–43.

27. *Colored American*, 2 October 1841 and 30 October 1841; *Weekly Advocate*, 22 February 1827.

28. *Freedom's Journal*, 16 March 1827.

29. Carter Godwin Woodson, *The Negro Professional Man and the Community, with Special Emphasis on the Physician and the Lawyer* (Washington, DC: Association for the Study of Negro Life and History, 1934; reprint, New York: Negro Universities Press, 1969), 17; W[illiam] Wells Brown, *The Rising Son; or, The Antecedents and Advancement of the Colored Race* (Boston: A.G. Brown & Co., 1874), 473; Charles H. Wesley, "The Negroes of New York in the Emancipation Movement," *Journal of Negro History* 24 (January 1939): 70–71, passim; *Weekly Advocate*, 7 January 1837.

30. Wilder, *In the Company of Black Men*, 148, 165; *The Liberator*, 6 August 1836; Lyons, "Memories of Yesterday," 26; "The First Annual Report of the New York Committee of Vigilance, for the Year 1837," in Herbert Aptheker, ed., *A Documentary History of the Negro People in the United States* (New York: Citadel Press, 1951; reprint, 1969), 161–63.

31. Phillip Foner, *Essays in Afro-American History* (Philadelphia: Temple University Press, 1978), 88–97; Harriet A. Jacobs, *Incidents in the Life of a Slave Girl, Written by Herself* (Boston, 1861; reprint, Cambridge, MA: Harvard University Press, 1987), 190–91; Wilder, *In the Company of Black Men*, 171–72; *The Liberator*, 4 April 1851.

32. Minutes of the First and Fourth Annual Conventions, in Howard Holman Bell, ed., *Minutes of the Proceedings of the National Negro Conventions, 1830–1864* (New York: Arno Press, 1969); Harris, *In the Shadow of Slavery*, 170–75.

33. R.J.M. Blackett, *Building an Antislavery Wall: Black Americans in the Atlantic Abolitionist Movement,*

1830–1860 (Baton Rouge: Louisiana State University Press, 1983), 196, passim; Smith, "Introduction," 42; *The Liberator*, 6 August 1836.

8. BLACK ABOLITIONISM: THE ASSAULT ON SOUTHERN SLAVERY AND THE STRUGGLE FOR RACIAL EQUALITY by Manisha Sinha

1. Edgar J. McManus, *A History of Negro Slavery in New York* (Syracuse, NY: Syracuse University Press, 1966); Graham Russell Hodges, *Root and Branch: African Americans in New York and East Jersey, 1613–1863* (Chapel Hill: University of North Carolina Press, 1999); Shane White, *Somewhat More Independent: The End of Slavery in New York City, 1770–1810* (Athens: University of Georgia Press, 1991); Leslie M. Harris, *In the Shadow of Slavery: African Americans in New York City, 1626–1863* (Chicago: University of Chicago Press, 2003).

2. *First Report of the New York Colonization Society Read at the Annual Meeting, October 29, 1823* (New York, 1823), 18; *African Colonization: Proceedings on the Formation of the New-York State Colonization Society; Together with an Address to the Public, from the Managers thereof* (Albany: Websters and Skinners, 1829). On colonization, see P.J. Staudenraus, *The African Colonization Movement, 1816–1865* (New York: Columbia University Press, 1961); George M. Frederickson, *The Black Image in the White Mind: The Debate on Afro-American Character and Destiny, 1817–1914* (New York: Harper & Row, 1971), chapter 1.

3. C. Peter Ripley, ed., *Witness for Freedom: African American Voices on Race, Slavery, and Emancipation* (Chapel Hill: University of North Carolina Press, 1993), 2–4; *Freedom's Journal*, 16 March 1827.

4. "A Discourse delivered by Peter Williams at St. Philip's Church, July 4, 1830," in Carter G. Woodson, ed., *Negro Orators and Their Orations* (Washington, DC: Associated Publishers, 1925; reprint, New York: Russell & Russell, 1969), 78–80; Samuel E. Cornish and Theodore S. Wright, *The Colonization Scheme Considered, in its Rejection by the Colored People—In its tendency to uphold Caste—In its Unfitness for Christianizing and Civilizing the Aborigines of Africa, and for putting a stop to the African Slave Trade: In a letter to the Hon. Theodore Frelinghuysen and the Hon. Benjamin Butler* (Newark: A. Guest, 1840), 3–12.

5. William Hamilton, "An Oration Delivered in the African Zion Church, on the Fourth of July, 1827, In Commemoration of the Abolition of Domestic Slavery in this State" (New York, 1827), in Dorothy Porter, ed., *Early Negro Writing, 1760–1837* (Boston: Beacon Press, 1971), 101.

6. The phrase "appeal to the heart" comes from Richard Newman, *The Transformation of American Abolitionism*; *Walker's Appeal and Garnet's Address to the Slaves of the United States of America* (New York, 1969; reprint, Chapel Hill: University of North Carolina Press, 2002). On Walker, see Peter P. Hinks, *To Awaken My Afflicted Brethren: David Walker and the Problem of Antebellum Slave Resistance* (University Park: Pennsylvania State University Press, 1997); Robert Alexander Young, "Ethiopian Manifesto" (1829), in Richard Newman, Patrick Rael, and Phillip Lapansky, eds., *Pamphlets of Protest: An Anthology of Early African-American Protest Literature* (New York: Routledge, 2001), 84–89.

7. Newman, *The Transformation of American Abolitionism*; Benjamin Quarles, *Black Abolitionists* (New York: Oxford University Press, 1969); Donald Jacobs, ed., *Courage and Conscience: Black and White Abolitionists in Boston* (Bloomington: Indiana University Press, 1993); Paul Goodman, *Of One Blood: Abolitionism and the Origins of Racial Equality* (Berkeley: University of California Press, 1998); David Brion Davis, "The Emergence of Immediatism in British and American Antislavery Thought," *Mississippi Valley Historical Review* 44 (September 1962): 209–30. On Garrisonian abolitionism, see Aileen Kraditor, *Means and Ends in American Abolition: Garrison and His Critics on Strategy and Tactics, 1834–1850* (New York: Pantheon Books, 1969).

8. Bertram Wyatt-Brown, *Lewis Tappan and the Evangelical War Against Slavery* (Cleveland: Press of Case

Western Reserve University, 1969); Arthur Tappan is quoted on p. 91. For snapshot portraits of New York abolitionists, see Gerald Sorin, *The New York Abolitionists: A Case Study of Political Radicalism* (Westport, CT: Greenwood Publishing, 1971).

9. On the riot, see Linda Kerber, "Abolitionists and Amalgamators: The New York City race Riots of 1834," *New York History* 48 (January 1967): 28–39; and Harris, *In the Shadow of Slavery*, 194–202. Williams is quoted in John H. Hewitt, "Peter Williams, Jr. : New York's First African-American Episcopal Priest," *New York History* 79 (April 1998): 123.

10. Dorothy Porter, "David Ruggles: An Apostle of Liberty," *Journal of Negro History* 28 (January 1943): 23–50.

11. "Founding the New York Committee of Vigilance" and "Speech by Peter Paul Simons" in C. Peter Ripley, ed., *The Black Abolitionist Papers*, vol. 3, *The United States, 1830–1846* (Chapel Hill: University of North Carolina Press, 1991), 168–75, 292; Harris, *In the Shadow of Slavery*, 210–15.

12. *Address of the Rev. Theodore S. Wright before the Convention of the New York State Antislavery Society, on the Acceptance of the Annual Report, held at Utica, Sept. 20, 1837* and Theodore S. Wright, *Prejudice Against the Colored Man* (1837) in Woodson ed., *Negro Orators and Their Orations*, 86–95; Harris, *In the Shadow of Slavery*, 270–71.

13. Philip S. Foner and George E. Walker, eds., *Proceedings of the Black State Conventions, 1840–1865* (Philadelphia: Temple University Press, 1979), 1:8–9, 17–23, 32–33, 39–41; David N. Gellman and David Quigley, eds., *Jim Crow New York: A Documentary History of Race and Citizenship, 1777–1877* (New York: New York University Press, 2003), 249–59.

14. *An Address to the Three Thousand Colored Citizens of New York, Who are the Owners of one Hundred and Twenty Thousand Acres of Land, in the State of New York, Given to them by Gerrit Smith Esq., of Peterboro September 1, 1846* (New York, 1846); Benjamin Quarles, ed., "Letters from Negro Leaders to Gerrit Smith," *Journal of Negro History* 27 (October 1942): 432–53; "James McCune Smith to Gerrit Smith, 28 December 1846," in Ripley, ed., *The Black Abolitionist Papers*, 3:479–81. On Smith and his relationship with black abolitionists, see John Stauffer, *The Black Hearts of Men: Radical Abolitionists and the Transformation of Race* (Cambridge, MA: Harvard University Press, 2002). On McCune Smith, see also David W. Blight, "In Search of Learning, Liberty, and Self-Definition: James McCune Smith and the Ordeal of the Antebellum Black Intellectual," *Afro-Americans in New York Life and History* 9 (July 1985): 7–25.

15. Foner and Walker, eds., *Proceedings of the Black State Conventions*, 1:100; Gellman and Quigley, eds., *Jim Crow New York*, 271–77.

16. On the schism in the abolition movement, see Kraditor, *Means and Ends in American Abolition*; "Charles B. Ray to James G. Birney and Henry B. Stanton, 20 May 1840," in Ripley, ed., *The Black Abolitionist Papers*, 3:334.

17. The quote is from Vincent Harding, *There Is a River: The Black Struggle for Freedom in America* (New York: Harcourt Brace Jovanovich, 1981).

18. *Walker's Appeal and Garnet's Address*, 90–96; "Debate over Garnet's 'Address to the Slaves of the United States of America'" (1843) and "Proceedings of the National Convention of the Colored People" (1847), in Newman, Rael and Lapansky eds., *Pamphlets of Protest*, 157–59, 176; *The North Star*, 6 July 1849. On Garnet, see Joel Schor, *Henry Highland Garnet: A Voice of Black Radicalism in the Nineteenth Century* (Westport, CT: Greenwood Press, 1977); Martin B. Pasternak, *Rise Now and Fly to Arms: The Life of Henry Highland Garnet* (New York: Garland Publishing, 1995).

19. Craig Wilder, *In the Company of Black Men: The African Influence on African American Culture in New York City* (New York: New York University Press, 2001), 171–72.

20. *The North Star*, 5 September and 3 October 1850; *Frederick Douglass' Paper*, 9 June 1854; John W. Blassingame, ed., *The Frederick Douglass Papers, Series One: Speeches, Debates, and Interviews*, vol. 2,

1847–54 (New Haven: Yale University Press, 1982), 130–32, 148–58, 272–77; "Speech by Samuel Ringgold Ward Delivered at Faneuil Hall Boston, Massachusetts, 25 March, 1850," in C. Peter Ripley, ed., *The Black Abolitionist Papers*, vol. 4, *The United States, 1847–1858* (Chapel Hill: University of North Carolina Press, 1991), 51; *Weekly Anglo-African* (New York), 27 April 1861, in C. Peter Ripley, ed., *The Black Abolitionist Papers*, vol. 5, *The United States, 1859–1865* (Chapel Hill: University of North Carolina Press, 1992), 112. On Delany and Douglass, see Robert S. Levine, *Martin Delany, Frederick Douglass, and the Politics of Representative Identity* (Chapel Hill: University of North Carolina Press, 1997).

21. Benjamin Quarles, ed., *Blacks on John Brown* (Urbana: University of Illinois Press, 1972), 6, 9, 17–18, 27, 37–39; John W. Blassingame, ed., *The Frederick Douglass Papers, Series One: Speeches, Debates and Interviews*, vol. 3, *1855–63* (New Haven: Yale University Press, 1985), 312–22, 412–20.

22. *Minutes of the National Convention of Colored Citizens: Held at Buffalo, On the 15th, 16th, 17th, 18th, and 19th of August, 1843. For the Purpose of Considering their Moral and Political Condition as American Citizens* (New York, 1843), 5; *Proceedings of the National Convention of Colored People, and Their Friends, Held in Troy, N.Y., on the 6th, 7th, 8th and 9th October, 1847* (Troy, NY, 1847), 31; *Proceedings of the Colored National Convention, Held in Rochester, July 6th, 7th and 8th, 1853* (Rochester, 1853), 16; *Proceedings of the Colored National Convention, Held in Franklin Hall, Sixth Street, Below Arch, Philadelphia, October 16th, 17th and 18th, 1855* (Salem, NJ, 1856), 30; all in Howard Holman Bell, ed., *Minutes of the Proceedings of the National Negro Conventions, 1830–1864* (New York: Arno Press, 1969); Harris, *In the Shadow of Slavery*, 274.

23. *Freedom's Journal*, 16 March, 20 April, 27 April, 4 May, 11 May, 18 May, 15 June, 29 June, 12 October 1827, and 18 January, 28 January, 8 February, 15 February 1828. All quotations are from 6 April 1828; *Colored American*, 4 June, 7 August, 28 August, 2 October, 9 October 1841.

24. Harris, *In the Shadow of Slavery*, 272–75; Alexander Crummell, *Destiny and Race: Selected Writings, 1840–1898*, ed. Wilson Jeremiah Moses (Amherst: University of Massachusetts Press, 1992), 174. On Crummell, see Wilson Jeremiah Moses, *Alexander Crummell: A Study of Civilization and Discontent* (New York: Oxford University Press, 1989).

25. *African Civilization Society. Constitution of the African Civilization Society; Together with the Testimony of Forty Distinguished Citizens of New York and Brooklyn, to the Importance of the Objects Contemplated By its Friends. Also, the Anniversary Address Delivered by Rev. Joseph P. Thompson, D.D at the Annual Meeting of the Society, May 19th, 1861* (New Haven, 1861), 1–4; Wilder, *In the Company of Black Men*, 173–76; "James McCune Smith to Henry Highland Garnet," in Ripley, ed., *The Black Abolitionist Papers*, vol. 5, *The United States, 1859–1865* (Chapel Hill: University of North Carolina Press, 1992), 100–105.

26. David W. Blight, *Frederick Douglass' Civil War: Keeping Faith in Jubilee* (Baton Rouge: Louisiana State University Press, 1989).

370

NOTES

9. Southern Slavery in a Free City: Economy, Politics and Culture by David Quigley

1. William Hamilton, *Oration Delivered in the African Zion Church, on the Fourth of July 1827, in Commemoration of the Abolition of Domestic Slavery in This State* (New York: Gray & Bunce, 1827).

2. Philip S. Foner's *Business and Slavery: The New York Merchants and the Irrepressible Conflict* (Chapel Hill: University of North Carolina Press, 1941), the classic work on the late antebellum relationship between New York City business interests and the slave South, is now over sixty years old. Other sources dealing with dimensions of the history of slavery in New York City after 1827 include Iver Bernstein, *The New York City Draft Riots: Their Significance for American Society and Politics in the Age of the Civil War*

(New York: Oxford University Press, 1990); Edwin G. Burrows and Mike Wallace, *Gotham: A History of New York City to 1898* (New York: Oxford University Press, 1999); John Hope Franklin, *A Southern Odyssey: Travelers in the Antebellum North* (Baton Rouge: Louisiana State University Press, 1976); David N. Gellman and David Quigley, eds., *Jim Crow New York: A Documentary History of Race and Citizenship, 1777–1877* (New York: New York University Press, 2003); Leslie M. Harris, *In the Shadow of Slavery: African Americans in New York City, 1626–1863* (Chicago: University of Chicago Press, 2003); Graham Russell Hodges, *Root and Branch: African Americans in New York and East Jersey, 1613–1863* (Chapel Hill: University of North Carolina Press, 1999); and Craig Steven Wilder, *A Covenant with Color: Race and Social Power in Brooklyn* (New York: Columbia University Press, 2000).

3. Eric Lampard, "The New York Metropolis in Transformation: History and Prospect. A Study in Historic Particularity," in Hans-Jurgen Ewers, John B. Goddard, and Horst Mazerath, eds., *The Future of the Metropolis: Berlin, London, Paris, New York, Economic Aspects* (Berlin: W. de Gruyter, 1986), 44.

4. Robert Albion, *Square-Riggers on Schedule: The New York Sailing Packets to England, France, and the Cotton Ports* (Princeton: Princeton University Press, 1938), 40; Lampard, "The New York Metropolis in Transformation," 44.

5. In 1822 the city exported $9,228,000 worth of domestic products, $3,925,000 in cotton. Flour was a distant second at $794,000, while the upper South crop of tobacco was third at $754,000. Albion, *Square-Riggers on Schedule*, 52; Lampard, "The New York Metropolis in Transformation," 44.

6. Of the 47,952 bales of cotton shipped to New York by packet ship in 1835, 15,429 came from New Orleans, 11,534 from Mobile, 10,882 from Savannah, and 10,107 from Charleston. Albion, *Square-Riggers on Schedule*, 72.

7. Foner, *Business and Slavery*, 164–65.

8. Robert Albion, *The Rise of New York Port, 1850–1860* (New York: C. Scribner's Sons, 1939), 211.

9. Burrows and Wallace, *Gotham*, 861.

10. Foner, *Business and Slavery*, 164–65.

11. Albion, *The Rise of New York Port*, 212.

12. Albion, *Square-Riggers on Schedule*, 41.

13. Davy Crockett, *An Account of Col. Crockett's Tour to the North and Down East, Written by Himself* (Philadelphia: E.L. Carey and A. Hart, 1836), 44, quoted in Franklin, *A Southern Odyssey*, 92.

14. Albion, *The Rise of New York Port*, 120.

15. Albion, *Square-Riggers on Schedule*, 76.

16. Lampard, "The New York Metropolis in Transformation," 44.

17. "Hinge of Union," in Lampard, "The New York Metropolis in Transformation," 40.

18. Albion, *The Rise of New York Port*, 112.

19. Albion, *Square-Riggers on Schedule*, 73.

20. J.C. Myers, *Sketches on a Tour through the Northern and Eastern States, the Canadas and Nova Scotia* (Harrisonburg, VA: J.H. Wartmann and Bros., 1849), quoted in Franklin, *A Southern Odyssey*, 21–22.

21. Franklin, *A Southern Odyssey*, 83.

22. Ibid., 163.

23. J.A. Turner, "What Are We To Do," *DeBow's Review* 29 (July 1860), quoted in Franklin, *A Southern Odyssey*, 42.

24. Franklin, *A Southern Odyssey*, 69.

25. Ibid., 25.

26. James P. Thomas, *From Tennessee Slave to St. Louis Entrepreneur: The Autobiography of James P. Thomas*, ed. Loren Schweninger (Columbia: University of Missouri Press, 1984), quoted in John Hope

Franklin and Loren Schweninger, *In Search of the Promised Land: A Black Family and the Old South* (New York: Oxford University Press, 2005).

27. Franklin, *A Southern Odyssey*, 139–47; Franklin and Schweninger, *In Search of the Promised Land*.

28. See Gellman and Quigley, *Jim Crow New York*, for an extended discussion of the 1821 state constitutional convention.

29. Wood would later claim "no northern man could go further than myself in behalf of Southern rights." Jerome Mushkat, *Fernando Wood: A Political Biography* (Kent, OH: Kent State University Press, 1990), 20, 94.

30. Irving Katz, *August Belmont: A Political Biography* (New York: Columbia University Press, 1968).

31. Burrows and Wallace, *Gotham*, 861.

32. Edward Widmer, *Young America: The Flowering of Democracy in New York City* (New York: Oxford University Press, 1999), 206.

33. Ottis C. Skipper, *J.D.B. DeBow, Magazinist of the Old South* (Athens: University of Georgia Press, 1958), 24–25, 125, in Franklin, *A Southern Odyssey*, 99–100.

34. William G. Simms to Alfred Billings Street, 15 September 1853, in *The Letters of William Gilmore Simms*, ed. Mary Simms Oliphant and T.C. Duncan Eaves (Columbia: University of South Carolina Press, 1954), 3:249, quoted in Franklin, *A Southern Odyssey*, 103.

35. Franklin, *A Southern Odyssey*, 242.

36. Rhoda Freeman, *The Free Negro in New York City in the Era Before the Civil War* (New York: Garland Publishing, 1994), 55.

37. *The Liberator*, 5 April 1834, quoted in Wilder, *A Covenant with Color*, 74.

38. Wilder, *A Covenant with Color*, 63.

39. Hodges, *Root and Branch*, 245–48.

40. Ibid.

41. Freeman, *The Free Negro in New York City*, 54.

42. Benjamin Quarles, *Black Abolitionists* (New York: Oxford University Press, 1969), 163.

43. Ibid., 154.

44. Wilder, *A Covenant with Color*, 75–77.

45. Freeman, *The Free Negro in New York City*, 67.

46. Foner, *Business and Slavery*, chapter 4.

47. Franklin, *A Southern Odyssey*, 98.

48. Bernstein, *The New York City Draft Riots*, chapter 4.

49. J.D.B. DeBow, *Interest in Slavery of the Southern Non-Slaveholder* (Charleston: Evans & Cogswell, 1860), quoted in Foner, *Business and Slavery*, 4.

50. Turner, "What Are We To Do."

51. Stephen Colwell, *The Five Cotton States and New York; or, Remarks upon the Social and Economic Aspects of the Southern Political Crisis* (n.p., 1861), 22.

52. Ibid., 12.

53. Thomas Prentice Kettell, *Southern Wealth and Northern Profits, as Exhibited in Statistical Facts and Official Figures: Showing the Necessity of Union to the Future Prosperity and Welfare of the Republic* (New York: G.W. & J.A. Wood, 1860), 172–73.

54. *Richmond Dispatch*, April 1861, reprinted in *New York Herald*, 30 April 1861, quoted in Foner, *Business and Slavery*, 317.

55. Thomas Kessner, *Capital City: New York City and the Men Behind America's Rise to Economic Dominance, 1860–1900* (New York: Simon & Schuster, 2003), 47.

56. See David Quigley, *Second Founding: New York City, Reconstruction and the Making of American*

Democracy (New York: Hill and Wang, 2004), for an extended discussion of the New York–South axis of Democratic politics during Reconstruction.

10. Securing Freedom: The Challenges of Black Life in Civil War New York by Iver Bernstein

I thank Ira Berlin and Leslie Harris for their expert editorial advice; Steven Jaffe, Phillip Lapsansky, and William Seraile for sharing their deep knowledge of sources; and Henry Berger, Wayne Fields, and John Stauffer for their thoughtful comments. I am grateful to Katherine Stevens for her research assistance. This essay could not have been written without the indefatigable efforts of librarians at the New-York Historical Society, the New York Public Library's Schomburg Center for Research in Black Culture, and the Union League Club of New York.

1. *Anglo-African*, 1 August 1863. On the murders of James Costello and Abraham Franklin, see Iver Bernstein, *The New York City Draft Riots: Their Significance for American Society and Politics in the Age of the Civil War* (New York: Oxford University Press, 1990), 28–30. For an account of the draft riots, see Bernstein, especially chapters 1 and 2, and Adrian Cook, *The Armies of the Streets: The New York City Draft Riots of 1863* (Lexington: University Press of Kentucky, 1974).

2. *Anglo-African*, 22 October 1864.

3. Letter from J.W.C. Pennington to Hon. W.C. Noyes, reprinted in the *New York Times*, 25 July 1863.

4. See R.J.M. Blackett, *Beating Against the Barriers: Biographical Essays in Nineteenth-Century Afro-American History* (Baton Rouge: Louisiana State University Press, 1986), 1–84, for a full treatment of Pennington's life and career; also, Herman Edward Thomas, *James W.C. Pennington: African American Churchman and Abolitionist* (New York: Garland Publishing, 1995). In 1851 the University of Heidelberg had recognized Pennington's achievements with an honorary Doctor of Divinity degree. One of those achievements was the publication of the autobiographical narrative *The Fugitive Blacksmith; or, Events in the History of James W. C. Pennington, Pastor of a Presbyterian Church, New York, Formerly a Slave in the State of Maryland, United States* (London: C. Gilpin, 1849).

5. *Principia*, 14 January 1864.

6. *New-York Daily Tribune*, 22 July 1863.

7. Such contradictions between catastrophe and hope existed, with varying degrees of intensity, throughout the antebellum period (certainly from the mid-1840s on), as blacks imagined new forms of selfhood and political community amidst an expanding slave republic that was denying rights to blacks.

8. See "A Week of Horror," *Anglo-African*, 25 July 1863.

9. "Services at the Shiloh Church," *New-York Daily Tribune*, 21 September 1863.

10. Roughly 14 percent of New York City blacks were born in slave states, according to the Census of 1860. *New York Herald*, 25 January 1861.

11. *L'Opinion Nationale* [n.d.], quoted in "Timely Words," *Anglo-African*, 6 April 1861.

12. Ira Berlin's discussion of Northern free blacks as "maroons" is most relevant here. See Ira Berlin, *Generations of Captivity: A History of African-American Slaves* (Cambridge, MA: Belknap Press of Harvard University Press, 2003), 236.

13. See Leonard P. Curry, *The Free Black in Urban America, 1800–1850: The Shadow of the Dream* (Chicago: University of Chicago Press, 1981), chapter 4, for an excellent discussion of antebellum black residential patterns. In an era in which the walk to work was an important aspect of residential choice for the laboring poor both black and white, black New Yorkers also were constrained in that choice by the location of the few white employers who would hire them.

14. Certainly proslavery New York Democrats and their Southern slaveholding allies worried about the power that the very few black voters in New York City might exercise. See F[itz] W[illiam] Byrdsall to John C. Calhoun, New York [City], 12 November 1849, in Clyde N. Wilson, ed., *The Papers of John C. Calhoun* (Columbia: University of South Carolina Press, 1959, 2001), 26:272–76 (although Byrdsall vastly exaggerated the number of black voters in New York County).

15. "The Negro in the Metropolis," *New York Herald*, 25 January 1861.

16. See Edwin G. Burrows and Mike Wallace, *Gotham: A History of New York City to 1898* (New York: Oxford University Press, 1999), 858, on Bennett's 1859 call for the re-enslavement of Northern blacks.

17. For an example of this New York–style fusion of scientific racism, proslavery ideology, and Democratic politics, see John H. Van Evrie, *Negroes and Negro "Slavery": The First an Inferior Race, the Latter Its Normal Condition* (New York: Van Evrie, Horton & Co., 1853); on Van Evrie's significance, see George M. Fredrickson, *The Black Image in the White Mind: The Debate on Afro-American Character and Destiny, 1817–1914* (New York: Harper & Row, 1971), 62–63, 69–70; Forrest G. Wood, *Black Scare: The Racist Response to Emancipation and Reconstruction* (Berkeley: University of California Press, 1970), 35–36, 166–67.

18. Wood, *Black Scare*, 27.

19. I am obliged to John Stauffer for deepening my appreciation of this point.

20. See, for instance, *Anglo-African*, 17 March 1860.

21. Burrows and Wallace, *Gotham*, 863.

22. Ibid.

23. *Anglo-African*, 27 April 1861. See Manisha Sinha, "An Alternative Tradition of Radicalism: Black Abolitionist Ideology, 1775–1865," (paper delivered at Organization of American Historians annual meeting, Boston, 2004), for a discussion of the long antecedents of this perspective dating back to the era of the American Revolution.

24. *Anglo-African*, 23 March 1861. The editor of the *Anglo-African* was referring to Thomas Sims and Anthony Burns, two enslaved men who fled bondage only to be recaptured in Massachusetts under the provisions of the Fugitive Slave Law of 1850. Both were remanded back into slavery in highly celebrated cases of 1851 and 1854, respectively.

25. *Anglo-African*, 10 September 1859; Earl Ofari, *"Let Your Motto Be Resistance": The Life and Thought of Henry Highland Garnet* (Boston: Beacon Press, 1972), 86; Martin B. Pasternak, *Rise Now and Fly to Arms: The Life of Henry Highland Garnet* (New York: Garland Publishing, 1995), 90.

26. "Circular by the African Civilization Society," 16 February 1859, in C. Peter Ripley, ed., *The Black Abolitionist Papers* (Chapel Hill: University of North Carolina Press, 1992), 5:3–6.

27. Ibid., 5.

28. *New York Herald*, 25 January 1861 (on number of black voters in New York City in 1860).

29. See Ofari, *"Let Your Motto Be Resistance,"* 86–87, quoting Garnet ("If we do not establish a nationality in the South [especially with the added black population provided by the revival of the African slave trade], I am mistaken in the spirit of my people" and "In Jamaica there are forty colored men to one white; Haiti is ours; Cuba will be ours soon, and we shall have every island in the Caribbean Sea"). On Garnet's simultaneous support for colonization in Liberia and on the Smith lands of upstate New York, see John Stauffer, *The Black Hearts of Men: Radical Abolitionists and the Transformation of Race* (Cambridge, MA: Harvard University Press, 2002), 141–42.

On the defeat of the 1860 statewide black suffrage campaign in New York, see Burrows and Wallace, *Gotham*, 858; Phyllis F. Field, *The Politics of Race in New York: The Struggle for Black Suffrage in the Civil War Era* (Ithaca: Cornell University Press, 1982), 114. The referendum was defeated statewide, 337,984 to 197,503; in New York County, the referendum was rejected 65,082 to 10,483. See Howard Dodson,

Christopher Moore, and Roberta Yancy, *The Black New Yorkers: The Schomburg Illustrated Chronology* (New York: John Wiley, 2000), 83.

30. See Floyd J. Miller's observation that the African Civilization Society had by 1859–60 managed to "build a substantial following—principally in New York City, where interest in Yoruba emigration had first developed to visible proportions." Floyd J. Miller, *The Search for a Black Nationality: Black Emigration and Colonization, 1787–1863* (Urbana: University of Illinois Press, 1975), 228–29.

31. On William P. Powell, see Phillip Foner, "William P. Powell: Militant Champion of Black Seamen," in Phillip Foner, *Essays in Afro-American History* (Philadelphia: Temple University Press, 1978), 88–111; on James McCune Smith, see Stauffer, *Black Hearts of Men*. Powell, it should be noted, did spend a decade, 1851–1861, in England.

For all of their influence, Garnet and the African Civilization Society's emigrationist schemes always provoked concerted opposition. An April 12, 1860, meeting called at Zion Church in New York to discredit the African Civilization Society and disparage its motives as those of white colonization and proslavery erupted in a fistfight; when the dust cleared, the effort to associate black New York with an anti–African Civilization Society position had failed. A few days later Garnet presided over a tightly orchestrated meeting more sympathetic to the African Civilization Society, but the debate rumbled on in the pages of the *Anglo-African*. See Ofari, 90–91; Howard Holman Bell, *A Survey of the Negro Convention Movement, 1830–1861* (New York: Arno Press, 1969), 232–35; Joel Schor, *Henry Highland Garnet: A Voice of Black Radicalism in the Nineteenth Century* (Westport, CT: Greenwood Press, 1977), 167–69.

32. Bell, *Survey of the Negro Convention Movement*, 221–24; on Douglass's brief flirtation with emigrationist schemes, see David W. Blight, *Frederick Douglass' Civil War: Keeping Faith in Jubilee* (Baton Rouge: Louisiana State University Prses, 1989). I use the word "fraternity" advisedly. See Bruce Dorsey, "A Gendered History of African Colonization in the Antebellum United States," *Journal of Social History* 34 (Fall 2000), on the masculinist dimension of black colonization projects in the antebellum period.

33. James M. McPherson, "Abolitionist and Negro Opposition to Colonization during the Civil War," *Phylon* 26 (1965): 392.

34. See *New York Herald*, 25 January 1861, on "Birthplaces of Colored Population" in 1860.

35. *Anglo-African*, 16 March 1861.

36. Bernstein, *The New York City Draft Riots*, 144.

37. Horace Greeley, *The American Conflict: A History of the Great Rebellion in the United States of America, 1860–'65* (Hartford: O.D. Case & Co., 1866), 2:514–15; Benjamin Quarles, *The Negro in the Civil War* (Boston: Little, Brown, 1953), 27, 29; James M. McPherson, *The Negro's Civil War: How American Negroes Felt and Acted During the War for the Union* (New York: Pantheon Books, 1965), 22.

38. McPherson, *The Negro's Civil War*, 30.

39. Quoted in William Seraile, *New York's Black Regiments During the Civil War* (New York: Routledge, 2001), 17.

40. *Anglo-African*, 17 August 1861; McPherson, *The Negro's Civil War*, 40–41.

41. *Anglo-African*, 10 August 1861.

42. *Anglo-African*, 12 October 1861; Ripley, ed., *Black Abolitionist Papers*, 5:117–27, esp. 119.

43. *New York Times*, 18 March 1861; see also Edward K. Spann, *Gotham at War: New York City, 1860–1865* (Wilmington, DE: Scholarly Resources, 2002), 125. On Rynders's appointment by President James Buchanan, see Jerome Mushkat, *Tammany: The Evolution of a Political Machine, 1789–1865* (Syracuse, NY: Syracuse University Press, 1971), 303.

44. Ernest A. McKay, *The Civil War and New York City* (Syracuse, NY: Syracuse University Press, 1990), 143.

45. Spann, *Gotham at War*, 125.

46. *Principia*, 14 January 1864.

47. Quarles, *The Negro in the Civil War*, 163–64.

48. *Anglo-African*, 3 January 1863.

49. *Anglo-African*, 10 January 1863.

50. It should be emphasized that the distance Garnet traveled from 1861 to 1863 was shorter than it might appear—he had never abandoned his efforts to expand blacks' cultural and political power in the United States even at the height of his Africa campaign. What had changed was Garnet's now heightened confidence that divine providence had appointed America, through the instrumentality of the war, as the main theater for the development of black freedom and nationality. That Garnet was asked to preside at the January 5 grand demonstration suggests that black New Yorkers understood this and at no time thought of his early war activities as treasonous. Black New Yorkers' sense of the unfolding war and of their relation to the national government was at all times strategic, even after Lincoln proclaimed emancipation as government policy.

51. Schor, *Henry Highland Garnet*, 188; *Anglo-African*, 9 May 1863.

52. *Liberator*, 22 May 1863; McPherson, *The Negro's Civil War*, 177.

53. *Liberator*, 29 May 1863.

54. Williston H. Lofton, "Northern Labor and the Negro During the Civil War," *Journal of Negro History* 34 (July 1949): 261.

55. See David Montgomery, *Beyond Equality: Labor and the Radical Republicans, 1862–1872* (New York: Knopf, 1967), 96.

56. Albon P. Man Jr., "Labor Competition and the New York Draft Riots of 1863," *Journal of Negro History* 36 (October 1951): 381; Wood, *Black Scare*, 23; Bernstein, *New York City Draft Riots*, especially 113.

57. Maria L. Daly, "Diary of Maria L. Daly," I, 14 July 1863, Charles Patrick Daly Papers, New York Public Library.

58. *Christian Recorder*, 25 July 1863 (blacks arm in self-defense in Flatbush and Weeksville); *Anglo-African*, 25 July 1863 (blacks organize against rioters in Eighth Ward).

59. Lofton, "Northern Labor and the Negro," 267.

60. Ibid.

61. *Anglo-African*, 1 August 1863; McPherson, *The Negro's Civil War*, 73–74.

62. *New-York Daily Tribune*, 3 August 1863.

63. Bernstein, *The New York City Draft Riots*, 66. The city's black population declined from 12,472 in 1860 to 9,943 in 1865. On the disappearance of blacks from specific districts of the post-riot city, see Citizens' Association of New York, *Report of the Council of Hygiene and Public Health of the Citizens' Association of New York Upon the Sanitary Condition of the City* (New York: D. Appleton & Co., 1865), 24–25, 279.

64. *Anglo-African*, 1 August 1863; McPherson, *The Negro's Civil War*, 62. Powell himself had just received a commission in the United States Navy.

65. *Anglo-African*, 15 August 1863.

66. Roy P. Basler, ed., *The Collected Works of Abraham Lincoln* (New Brunswick, NJ: Rutgers University Press, 1953), 6:410.

67. *Anglo-African*, 1 August 1863.

68. *New-York Daily Tribune*, 21 September 1863. The pamphlet by Vincent Colyer, *To the Memory of the Martyrs* (New York, 1863), was distributed at the end of the Shiloh service on September 20.

69. *Principia*, 7 January 1864.

70. See Bernstein, *The New York City Draft Riots*, esp. chapters 2, 4, and 5.

71. See *Report of the Merchants' Committee for the Relief of Colored People Suffering from the Riots in the City of New York. July, 1863* (New York, 1863).

72. See Vincent Colyer, *Report of the Services Rendered by the Freed People to the United States Army, in North Carolina, in the Spring of 1862, after the Battle of Newbern* (New York: V. Colyer, 1864).

73. "An Address to the Executive Committee of Merchants for the Relief of Colored People . . . Presented by Colored Ministers and Layman. New York, Aug. 22, 1863" in ibid., 33–34.

74. Seraile, *New York's Black Regiments During the Civil War*, 25.

75. Ibid. I am also grateful for the opportunity to have read Thomas L. Jones's unpublished paper, "The Union League Club and New York's First Black Regiments in the Civil War" (Collection of the Union League Club Library).

76. See Bernstein, *New York City Draft Riots*, 66–68, on the Union League Club's campaign to raise black regiments and the presentation of the colors on March 5, 1864.

77. *Anglo-African*, 12 March 1864.

78. Ibid.

79. Ibid.

80. *Anglo-African*, 12 March 1864.

81. *New York Herald*, 9 March 1864.

82. [David Goodman Croly and George Wakeman], *Miscegenation: The Theory of the Blending of the Races, Applied to the American White Man and Negro* (New York: H. Dexter, Hamilton, & Co., 1864); see also Sidney Kaplan, "The Miscegenation Issue in the Election of 1864," *Journal of Negro History* 34 (July 1949): 274–343.

83. See esp. William Edward Farrison, *William Wells Brown: Author & Reformer* (Chicago: University of Chicago Press, 1969), 384–87.

84. *Anglo-African*, 13 February 1864.

85. See Leslie M. Harris, *In the Shadow of Slavery: African Americans in New York City, 1626–1863* (Chicago: University of Chicago Press, 2003), esp. 247–48, on antebellum blacks' ceding of public discourse on interracial sex to the white Democratic press.

86. The phrase is William Manchester's, with regard to Rosa Parks's decision not to yield her seat to whites on a Montgomery, Alabama, bus in December 1955. William Manchester, *The Glory and the Dream* (New York: Bantam Books, 1988), 740.

87. Ibid.

88. See "Colorphobia," *Anglo-African*, 27 February 1864.

89. *Anglo-African*, 16 July 1864.

90. *Anglo-African*, 2 July 1864.

91. Seraile, *New York's Black Regiments During the Civil War*, 100.

92. *Anglo-African*, 2 July 1864.

93. On the dilemmas that the emphasis on male patriotism on the battlefield posed for Northern women during the Civil War, see Nina Silber, *Daughters of the Union: Northern Women Fight the Civil War* (Cambridge, MA: Harvard University Press, 2005).

94. The Thirteenth Amendment was enacted by Congress on January 31, 1865; it was not ratified by the states until December 6 of that year.

95. *Anglo-African*, 18 February 1865. On black New Yorkers' confident mood in winter 1865, see James Pennington's and others' proposal of the creation of an "Anglo-African Historical and Statistical Bureau," *Anglo-African*, 1 April and 22 April 1865. ("We have no right to trust to the whites to write our history," wrote Pennington. "Hitherto, our enemies have done it.") On the makings of a religious revival reported at Zion Church, see *Anglo-African*, 18 March 1865.

96. James McCune Smith, ed., *A Memorial Discourse; By Rev. Henry Highland Garnet, Delivered in the Hall of the House of Representatives, Washington City, D.C., on Sabbath, February 12, 1865* (Philadelphia:

Joseph M. Wilson, 1865), 65; Schor, *Henry Highland Garnet*, 201.

97. Smith, ed., *A Memorial Discourse*, 88–91. On Garnet's speech to Congress, also see Craig Steven Wilder, *In the Company of Black Men: The African Influence on African American Culture in New York City* (New York: New York University Press, 2001), 176–78.

98. McPherson, *The Negro's Civil War*, 286–88. "The question of universal suffrage is now prominently discussed in the district of Africa," wrote a black reporter who surveyed "the colored folks of New York." See "The Colored Folks of New York: How They Live and What They Need. Sketches of the Rich and Influential Africans of the Metropolis and the Country. A Colored Man's Picture of Colored Men. An Unwritten Leaf in Our Municipal History Restored," *New York Citizen*, 5 August 1865.

99. McPherson, *The Negro's Civil War*, 306–7.

100. Ibid., 304.

101. Scott D. Trostel, *The Lincoln Funeral Train: The Final Journey and National Funeral for Abraham Lincoln* (Fletcher, OH: Cam-Tech Publishing, 2002).

102. "Caste Hate at the Great Funeral," *Anglo-African*, 29 April 1865.

103. Ripley, ed., *The Black Abolitionist Papers*, 5:317–20, and especially the excellent footnotes on 319–20 are a valuable source on this episode.

104. *The Liberator*, 5 May 1865; *Anglo-African*, 28 April and 6 May 1865. *New-York Daily Tribune*, 24 April 1865. For the April 27 letter of J.W.C. Pennington, see *Anglo-African*, 13 May 1865. Also see the comments of J. Sella Martin, in Ripley, ed., *The Black Abolitionist Papers*, 5:319.

105. See especially speeches of John Jay and Vincent Colyer, at Shiloh Church meeting, *Anglo-African*, 6 May 1865. The Union League Club was able to elicit from Superintendent of Police Kennedy "an expression of willingness to guard the colored people, should they accept the position assigned them (the rear end)." Ibid.

106. "The Colored Delegation" in *New-York Daily Tribune*, 26 April 1865.

107. Ibid., on Pennington at the head of the black contingent.

108. *Anglo-African*, 13 May 1865.

109. Ibid.

110. Indeed, Pennington all but says this in his letter of April 27. Ibid.

111. The Twentieth and Twenty-sixth USCT Regiments performed garrison duty through the end of the war; the Thirty-first did see battlefield action, notably at the Crater. See Seraile, *New York's Black Regiments During the Civil War*.

11. RE-CREATING BLACK NEW YORK AT CENTURY'S END by Marcy S. Sacks

1. "Knickerbocker" was the term used for original Dutch settlers in New York and their descendants. S.R. Scottron, "The Industrial and Professional Pursuits of the Colored People of Old New York," *Colored American Magazine* 13 (October 1907): 266; Mary White Ovington, *Half a Man: The Status of the Negro in New York* (New York: Longmans, Green, and Co., 1911; reprint, New York: Hill and Wang, 1969), 96; *New York Age*, 27 July 1905; Gilbert Osofsky, *Harlem: The Making of a Ghetto*, 2nd ed. (Chicago: Ivan R. Dee, 1996), 5, 43.

2. See, for example, "Ovation to Black Troops," *New York Times*, 6 March 1864, 8; "The Ovation to the Black Regiment," *New York Times*, 7 March 1864, 4; "Amusements, Scenes, Incidents," *Brooklyn Eagle*, 2 August 1865, 2; "The Colored Celebration Yesterday," *Brooklyn Eagle*, 23 September 1865, 2.

3. Quoted in David Quigley, *Second Founding: New York City, Reconstruction, and the Making of American Democracy* (New York: Hill and Wang, 2004), 29–30.

4. Heather Cox Richardson, *The Death of Reconstruction: Race, Labor, and Politics in the Post–Civil War North, 1865–1901* (Cambridge, MA: Harvard University Press, 2001), 32, 195, 205.

5. James Weldon Johnson, *Along This Way: The Autobiography of James Weldon Johnson* (New York: Penguin Books, 1990), 158.

6. See, for example, "An Experiment and Its Result," *New York Times*, 22 March 1864, 4.

7. Quigley, *Second Founding*, 81–82.

8. Ray Stannard Baker, *Following the Color Line: American Negro Citizenship in the Progressive Era* (New York: Doubleday, Page & Co., 1908), 130; "Negroes Leaving the South," *New York Times*, 18 March 1901, 2; "Negroes Leave the South," *New York Times*, 24 November 1892, 1.

9. *United States Tenth Census, 1880, Population* (Washington, DC, 1883), 1: 417–22, in Seth M. Scheiner, *Negro Mecca: A History of the Negro in New York City, 1865–1920* (New York: New York University Press, 1965), 221; Thomas Jesse Jones, "The Negroes of the Southern States and the U.S. Census of 1910," *Southern Workman* 41, no. 8 (August 1912); Richard R. Wright Jr., "The Migration of Negroes to the North," *Annals of the American Academy of Political and Social Science* 27 (May 1906): 98–99.

10. August Meier, *Negro Thought in America, 1880–1915* (Ann Arbor: University of Michigan Press, 1969), 88–89.

11. African Mission School Association, *A Mission School Among the Colored People of New York* (New York, 1868), Schomburg Center for Research in Black Culture, New York Public Library; William Pickens, "The Educational Condition of the Negro in Cities," *The Voice* 3 (October 1906): 427–28.

12. Osofsky, *Harlem*, 41–43.

13. Rayford W. Logan, *The Betrayal of the Negro: From Rutherford B. Hayes to Woodrow Wilson* (London, 1969), 169; Rollin G. Osterweis, *The Myth of the Lost Cause, 1865–1900* (Hamden, CT: Archon Books, 1973), 102, 105.

14. Alexander Saxton, *The Rise and Fall of the White Republic: Class Politics and Mass Culture in Nineteenth-Century America* (London: Verso, 1990), 176; Robert Toll, *Blacking Up: The Minstrel Show in Nineteenth-Century America* (New York: Oxford University Press, 1975), 88.

15. *Valentine's Manual* 6 (1922): 30; "Hampton Entertainments in the North," *Southern Workman* 30 (April 1901): 188.

16. William McAdoo, *Guarding a Great City* (New York: Harper & Bros., 1906), 93–94, 96–97.

17. Nina Silber, *The Romance of Reunion: Northerners and the South, 1865–1900* (Chapel Hill: University of North Carolina Press, 1993), 124. For antebellum stereotypes see, for example, David R. Roediger, *The Wages of Whiteness* (London: Verso, 1991), especially chapters 5 and 6; and Jean H. Baker, *Affairs of Party: The Political Culture of Northern Democrats in the Mid-Nineteenth Century* (Ithaca: Cornell University Press, 1983), chapter 6; "That Dreadful Negro," *New York Times*, 17 October 1872, 4.

18. Kevin Gaines, *Uplifting the Race: Black Leadership, Politics, and Culture in the Twentieth Century* (Chapel Hill: University of North Carolina Press, 1996), 70.

19. Henry Collins Brown, *In the Golden Nineties* (Hastings-on-Hudson: Valentine's Manual, 1928), 294; Currier & Ives's *Darktown Comics* Collection, Albion College Archives; Logan, *The Betrayal of the Negro*; Henry Collins Brown, *Brownstone Fronts and Saratoga Trunks* (New York: E.P. Dutton & Co., 1935), 269–70.

20. Brown, *In the Golden Nineties*, 294; Brown, *Brownstone Fronts and Saratoga Trunks*, 269–70.

21. Jacob Riis, *The Battle with the Slum* (New York: Macmillan, 1902), 110–11; Jeff Kisseloff, ed., *You Must Remember This: An Oral History of Manhattan from the 1890s to World War II* (Baltimore, MD: Johns Hopkins University Press, 1999), 190.

22. Thomas Jesse Jones, *The Sociology of a New York City Block* (New York, 1904), 35, 103; Lloyd Morris, *Incredible New York: High Life and Low Life of the Last Hundred Years* (New York: Random House, 1951), 275.

23. Mary White Ovington, *The Walls Came Tumbling Down* (New York: Harcourt, Brace, 1947), 35; Kisseloff, ed., *You Must Remember This*, 190, 268.

24. See, for example, Association for Improving the Condition of the Poor, *Twentieth Annual Report, 1863* (New York, 1863), 35–36, Butler Library, Columbia University; "Report of the Committee of Merchants for the Relief of Colored People, Suffering from the Late Riots in the City of New York," Daniel A.P. Murray Collection, Library of Congress; "The Lessons of the Riot," *New York Times*, 27 July 1863, 3.

25. See, for example, Citizens Protective League, *Persecution of Negroes* (New York, 1900), 3; *New York Times*, 25 August 1900, 1; *New York Times*, 20 September 1900, 12.

26. *New York Times*, 20 July 1905, 12; *New York Age*, 27 July 1905, 1.

27. *New York Times*, 20 July 1905, 12; *New York Times*, 25 July 1905, 12.

28. Paul Laurence Dunbar, *The Sport of the Gods* (New York: Dodd, Mead, and Co., 1902; reprint, Salem, NH, 1990), 213; Osofsky, *Harlem*, 43; W.E.B. Du Bois, *The Black North in 1901: A Social Study* (New York: Arno Press, 1969), 45; "Shoots into Ferry Crowd," *New York Age*, 13 June 1907, 6.

29. Quoted in David A. Gerber, *Black Ohio and the Color Line, 1860–1915* (Urbana: University of Illinois Press, 1970), 419.

30. Craig Steven Wilder, *A Covenant with Color: Race and Social Power in Brooklyn* (New York: Columbia University Press, 2000), 114; *New York Age*, 31 August 1905.

31. Dunbar, *Sport of the Gods*, 212–13.

32. "Movement of the Afro-American Population," *New York Age*, 10 January 1907, 4–5; "The Problem of Living in the North and the South," *New York Age*, 25 April 1907, 4; Kelly Miller, "The City Negro: The Inter-Relation of the Country and City Negro," *Southern Workman* 32 (April 1903): 238; "The Negro in New York," *Southern Workman* 31 (June 1902): 308; "West Indians in New York," *New York Age*, 5 September 1891, 2; "Thinks New York the Negro's Hope," *New York Times*, 1 October 1911, 16.

33. *New York Age*, 4 July 1907, 4.

34. Quigley, *Second Founding*, 32; Richardson, *The Death of Reconstruction*, chapter 6, passim; "Wealthy Negro Citizens," *New York Times*, 14 July 1895, 17; Wilder, *A Covenant with Color*, 114–15.

35. "Wealthy Negro Citizens," *New York Times*, 14 July 1895, 17; "Men and Women," *New York Globe*, 20 January 1883, 2.

36. W.E.B. Du Bois, "The Black North," *New York Times*, 1 December 1901; Wilder, *A Covenant with Color*, 114–15.

37. *New York Age*, 22 November 1890, 2; "The White Rose Mission," *New York Age*, 22 March 1906, 1; "Victoria Earle Matthews," *New York Age*, 14 March 1907, 6; Lassalle Best, "History of the White Rose Mission and Industrial Association," Writer's Program Research Paper (New York, n.d.), 2–3; Mary L. Lewis, "The White Rose Industrial Association," *The Messenger* 7 (April 1925): 158.

38. Mrs. V.E. Matthews, "Some of the Dangers Confronting Southern Girls in the North," *Hampton Negro Conference* 2 (July 1898): 67; White Rose Industrial Association, *Annual Report for the Year Ending December 31, 1912* (n.p., n.d.), 4–6, White Rose Home Papers, Schomburg Center for Research in Black Culture, New York Public Library; *The Crisis* 3 (December 1911): 51.

39. National League for the Protection of Colored Women, *Report, 1910* (New York, 1911), 3–7; National Urban League, *Report, 1910–1911* (New York, 1912), 23; Cheryl Hicks, "Confined to Womanhood: Women, Prisons, and Race in the State of New York, 1890–1935" (PhD diss., Princeton University, 1999), 66–68.

40. William Fielding Ogburn, "The Richmond Negro in New York City: His Social Mind as Seen in His Pleasures" (master's thesis, Columbia University, 1909); Carrie Ward Moore, "A Study of a Group of West

Indian Negroes in New York City" (master's thesis, Columbia University, 1913), 68–70.

41. Du Bois, *The Black North in 1901*, 16–17; Osofsky, *Harlem*, 13–14; Ogburn, "Richmond Negro," 48–49, 68–70; National League on Urban Conditions Among Negroes, *A Study of Negro Employees of Apartment Houses in New York City* (New York, 1916); for a description of a Union Baptist revival, see, for example, *New York Age*, 5 April 1890, 3.

42. See, for example, *New York Age*, 10 May 1906, 1; and *New York Age*, 30 May 1907, 6.

43. Du Bois, *The Black North in 1901*, 17; Gerald W. McFarland, *Inside Greenwich Village: A New York City Neighborhood, 1898–1918* (Amherst: University of Massachusetts Press, 2001), 22–23; Farah Griffin, *"Who Set You Flowin'?": The African-American Migration Narrative* (New York: Oxford University Press, 1995), 61; *New York Age*, 14 November 1907, 1.

44. Scheiner, *Negro Mecca*, 90; Frances Blascoer, *Colored School Children in New York* (New York: Public Education Association of the City of New York, 1915), 61; Robert Van Wyck Papers, VWRA-12, folder 9, New York Municipal Archives; Kisseloff, ed., *You Must Remember This*, 272–73.

45. Clyde Vernon Kiser, *Sea Island to City: A Study of St. Helena Islanders in Harlem and Other Urban Centers* (New York: Columbia University Press, 1932; reprint, New York, Atheneum, 1969) 122, 132.

46. Griffin, *"Who Set You Flowin'?,"* 55; Benjamin H. Locke, "The Community Life of a Harlem Group of Negroes" (master's thesis, Columbia University, 1913); R.B. Moore Papers, box 1, folder 1, Schomburg Center for Research in Black Culture, New York Public Library; *New York Age*, 28 February 1907, 7.

47. Scheiner, *Negro Mecca*, 94; Irma Watkins-Owens, *Blood Relations: Caribbean Immigrants and the Harlem Community, 1900–1930* (Bloomington: Indiana University Press, 1996), 65.

48. Watkins-Owens, *Blood Relations*, 69.

49. Osofsky, *Harlem*, 32; *New York Age*, 10 December 1887, 3; Watkins-Owens, *Blood Relations*, 26, 66, 67, 69; Samuel B. Jones, "The British West Indian Negro. Fifth Paper: The West Indian Immigrant," *Southern Workman* 41, no. 3 (March 1912).

NOTES

ACKNOWLEDGMENTS

HISTORY, CHARLES BEARD WROTE, is an act of faith. Presenting the history of slavery in New York is something closer to an act of audacity, for few New Yorkers, black or white, believe slavery had a significant existence in the Empire City. More than a few actively deny slavery's historic presence. Hopefully, *Slavery and the Making of New York*—both this book and the exhibit it represents—will convert the skeptics and enlarge the general understanding of a subject long cloaked by the stifling combination of ignorance and conceit. If it does, it is because we have had a lot of help.

Kenneth Jackson and Rick Beard, respectively the former president and chief operating officer of the New-York Historical Society, understood the importance of the subject to a full appreciation of New York's history and had faith that we could make a convincing case. Their successor, Louise Mirrer, was if anything more adamant that the Society present a full history of New York's past, even that part of its past some would rather forget. Her insistence that our book be both a comprehensive history of slavery in New York and the catalog of record for the exhibit complicated our task, but made it more fun as well. For providing the resources to do the job as we wished, we thank her, along with the Society's Board and especially Richard Gilder, who took a special interest in this project.

Once work began, the Society's staff rummaged through the vast archives of the building on Central Park West to create an extraordinary inventory of the material and intellectual remnants of slavery's long history in New Amsterdam and New York. They then canvassed other repositories, going far beyond the call of duty to draw together the evidence of New York's slave past. We are most appreciative of the work of Steven Jaffe,

Cynthia Copeland, and Kathleen Hulser. When Steve left the Society, Lilly Tuttle picked up some of his duties. Her extraordinary register of every known image related to New York slavery will be a resource for scholars for decades to come. Through it all, David Mandel—part gatekeeper, part watchman, part banker—kept the trains on time.

Ultimately this volume and the exhibit that it represents rest upon the work of a cadre of scholars—historians, anthropologists, and folklorists, along with students of the arts, architecture, and literature—all of whom, at short notice, put aside their own important work to explain precisely how slavery helped make New York. Through what may have seemed like endless drafts, they kept good cheer as we collectively fulfilled the Society's mandate. Aiding this process were David Blight of Yale University, Eric Foner of Columbia Unversity, James O. Horton of George Washington University, and Steven Mintz of the University of Houston, who served as an informal board of advisers. When we neared completion, Eric Foner, Marc Favreau, Edna Medford of Howard University, and Richard Rabinowitz of the American History Workshop reviewed the introductory essay. Along the way, Trisha Posey of the Department of History at the University of Maryland and Anna Swenson of the W.E.B. Du Bois Institute for African and African American Research checked footnotes, read proofs, and did much of the dirty work that assured *Slavery in New York* met the highest standards of scholarship.

The role of Richard Rabinowitz extended far beyond that of informal adviser. As curator of the exhibit, he, along with Lynda Kaplan and the staff of the American History Workshop, created a lively partnership between "our" book and "his" exhibit, so that personal pronouns eventually became irrelevant. He supervised the preparation of the maps, vetted nearly every image in the volume, authored the color inserts, and made *Slavery in New York* a truly collaborative work. His deep knowledge of museums and public presentation of history made us better.

Finally, Marc Favreau of The New Press guided *Slavery in New York* from idea to manuscript to print, seamlessly connecting the various disparate elements of a complicated volume. His willingness to wait until the last moment for just the right image, map, or table gave new meaning to the word patience. He and his colleagues delivered every author's hope, a volume whose beauty respects their efforts. One can ask for nothing more.

Ira Berlin
Leslie M. Harris

ACKNOWLEDGMENTS

CONTRIBUTORS

LESLIE M. ALEXANDER is assistant professor of history at the Ohio State University, where she teaches early African American history. She is currently completing a book-length study of the black community in antebellum New York. She has a special interest in Seneca Village.

IRA BERLIN is Distinguished University Professor at the University of Maryland and a Fellow at the W.E.B. Du Bois Institute for African and African American Research at Harvard University. He is the author of *Many Thousands Gone: The First Two Centuries of Slavery in North America* (Harvard University Press, 1998) and *Generations of Captivity: A History of American-American Slaves* (Harvard University Press, 2003).

IVER BERNSTEIN is Professor of History at Washington University in St. Louis and author of *The New York City Draft Riots: Their Significance for American Society and Politics in the Age of the Civil War* (Oxford University Press, 1990). He is a leading expert and commentator on nineteenth-century American political culture and has published widely on subjects ranging from the rhetoric of Abraham Lincoln to how and why Americans came to sacrifice themselves for the nation-state in the Civil War.

LESLIE M. HARRIS is Associate Professor of History and African American Studies at Emory University. She is the author of *In the Shadow of Slavery: African Americans in New York City, 1626–1863* (University of Chicago Press, 2003).

GRAHAM RUSSELL GAO HODGES is George Dorland Langdon Jr. Professor of History at Colgate University. He is the author of numerous studies of African American history in New York City, including *Root and Branch: African Americans in New York and East Jersey, 1613–1863* (University of North Carolina Press, 1999).

JILL LEPORE is Professor of History at Harvard University and the author of *New York Burning: Liberty, Slavery, and Conspiracy in Eighteenth-Century Manhattan* (Alfred A. Knopf, 2005); *A Is for American: Letters and Other Characters in the Newly United States* (Alfred A. Knopf, 2002); and *The Name of War: King Philip's War and the Origins of American Identity* (Alfred A. Knopf, 1998), which was awarded the Bancroft Prize.

CHRISTOPHER MOORE is curator and research coordinator for the New York Public Library's Schomburg Center for Research in Black Culture. He is author of *Fighting for America: Black Soldiers, the Unsung Heroes of World War II* (Ballantine Books, 2004), and co-author of *The Black New Yorkers: 400 Years of African American History* (John Wiley & Sons, 2000) and *Standing in the Need of Prayer: A Celebration of Black Prayer* (The Free Press, 1994). Moore helped write and produce the History Channel's award-winning 1994 documentary *The African Burial Ground: An American Discovery*. He is a member of the New York City Archival Review Board and the New York City Landmarks Preservation Commission.

CARLA L. PETERSON is Professor in the Department of English at the University of Maryland, and affiliate faculty of the departments of Women's Studies, American Studies, and African American Studies. She is the author of *"Doers of the Word": African-American Women Speakers and Writers in the North (1830–1880)* (Oxford University Press, 1998). She has published numerous essays on nineteenth-century African American literature and culture. Her current project is a social and cultural history of African Americans in nineteenth-century New York City as seen through the lens of family history.

DAVID QUIGLEY is Associate Professor of History at Boston College. He is the author of *Second Founding: New York City, Reconstruction, and the Making of American Democracy* (Hill and Wang, 2003); and co-editor, with David N. Gellman, of *Jim Crow New York: A Documentary History of Race and Citizenship, 1777–1877* (New York University Press, 2003).

———

CONTRIBUTORS

PATRICK RAEL is Associate Professor of History at Bowdoin College. He is author of *Black Identity and Black Protest in the Antebellum North* (University of North Carolina Press, 2001), and co-editor, with Richard Newman and Philip Lapsansky, of *Pamphlets of Protest: An Anthology of Early African-American Protest Literature, 1790–1860* (Routledge, 2000).

MARCY S. SACKS is Assistant Professor of History at Albion College. Her book, *Making the Negro Metropolis: The Black Experience Before World War I in New York City*, is forthcoming from the University of Pennsylvania Press. She is currently at work on a biography of the heavyweight boxing champion Joe Louis.

SEAN SAWYER is an architectural historian who has taught at Columbia University, Harvard's Graduate School of Design, and Fordham University. He is presently Executive Director of the Wyckoff House and Association, which operates New York's oldest structure, the Pieter Claesen Wyckoff House in Brooklyn.

MANISHA SINHA is Associate Professor of Afro-American Studies and History at the University of Massachusetts, Amherst. She is the author of *The Counterrevolution of Slavery* (University of North Carolina Press, 2000) and co-editor of the two-volume *African American Mosaic: A Documentary History of African Americans from the Slave Trade to the Twenty-First Century* (Prentice Hall, 2003). She is presently completing a study of black abolitionist thought.

JOHN MICHAEL VLACH is Professor of American Studies and Anthropology at the George Washington University. Specializing in the study of traditional material culture for more than three decades, he has focused especially on the domestic architecture and folk arts and crafts of African Americans in the Caribbean and the American South. His books include *The Afro-American Tradition in Decorative Arts* (University of Georgia Press, 1978, 1990); *Back of the Big House: The Architecture of Plantation Slavery* (University of North Carolina Press, 1993); and *The Planter's Prospect: Privilege and Slavery in Plantation Paintings* (University of North Carolina Press, 2002).

JUDITH WELLMAN is Director of Historical New York Research Associates, a consulting firm that specializes in the history of the Underground Railroad, women's history, local history, and historic preservation. She is professor emerita from the State University of New York at Oswego. Her most recent book is *The Road to Seneca Falls:*

Elizabeth Cady Stanton and the First Woman's Rights Convention (University of Illinois Press, 2004).

SHANE WHITE is Chair of the History Department at the University of Sydney. He is the author of several books about African American history, including *Stories of Freedom in Black New York* (Harvard University Press, 2003), and co-author, with the unrelated Graham White, of *The Sounds of Slavery* (Beacon Press, 2005).

CRAIG STEVEN WILDER is Professor of History at Dartmouth College. He is the author of *A Covenant with Color: Race and Social Power in Brooklyn* (Columbia University Press, 2000) and *In the Company of Black Men: The African Influence on African American Culture in New York City* (New York University Press, 2001).

SHERRILL D. WILSON holds a doctorate in urban anthropology and is presently Director of the Office of Public Education and Interpretation for the New York African Burial Ground. She has been recognized by the Office of the Mayor of New York as one of the city's centennial historians.

INDEX

INDEX